THE MONSTER
IN THE MIRROR

UNIVERSITY OF HULL PUBLICATIONS

The Monster in the Mirror

Studies in Nineteenth-Century Realism

Edited by
D. A. WILLIAMS

Published for the UNIVERSITY OF HULL *by*
OXFORD UNIVERSITY PRESS

Oxford University Press, Walton Street, Oxford OX2 6DP

OXFORD LONDON GLASGOW
NEW YORK TORONTO MELBOURNE WELLINGTON
NAIROBI DAR ES SALAAM CAPE TOWN
KUALA LUMPUR SINGAPORE JAKARTA HONG KONG TOKYO
DELHI BOMBAY CALCUTTA MADRAS KARACHI

© *University of Hull 1978*

First published 1978
Reprinted 1980

British Library Cataloguing in Publication Data

The monster in the mirror.
1. Fiction – 19th century – History and criticism
2. Realism in literature
I. Williams, David Anthony   II. University of Hull
809.3'9'12   PN3499   78–40261

ISBN 0 19 713433 5

*Set, printed and bound in Great Britain by
Fakenham Press Limited, Fakenham, Norfolk*

Foreword

THE MAIN aim of this book, which originated in a series of lectures
given in the University of Hull in 1974, is to throw light on the
phenomenon of Realism by providing a close analysis of a wide
range of novels drawn from different national literatures. Realism
has often been presented as a philosophical or aesthetic problem;
perhaps because the word itself creates a kind of semantic vacuum,
critics have often felt the need to launch into prolonged and tortured
attempts at definition or, disturbed by the more extravagant claims
found in Realist propaganda, have sought to correct simplistic views
of the relationship between literature and life. Some of the theoretical problems associated with Realism—the conflict between objectivity and subjectivity, the relation between realism as a perennial
mode and Realism as a self-conscious movement—are dealt with by
Cecil Jenkins in his introductory chapter but the main emphasis of
subsequent chapters has been on the practice rather than the theory
of Realism. Remembering Oscar Wilde's observation in *The Picture
of Dorian Gray* that 'the nineteenth-century dislike of Realism is the
rage of Caliban who sees his own face in a glass', we have sought a
close critical encounter with the monster in the mirror. Proceeding
in this way has the negative advantage of not ruling the Realist
out of court on the grounds of his 'bad aesthetics' and the positive
advantage of rooting the whole process of defining what is meant by
Realism in the appreciation of Realist works themselves. Some of the
most striking similarities of theme, character, and method are
discussed in the chapters on individual novels but a concluding
chapter attempts an analysis of all that, beneath their manifest differences, the various works have in common, by virtue of the
profound mimetic urge shared by all the novelists considered.

University of Hull
July 1977   D. A. WILLIAMS

Contents

I

Realism and the Novel Form

CECIL JENKINS

REALISM NOWADAYS—with or without the capital *R* with which it was endowed by aggressive artistic movements in the nineteenth century—may not be a word to bring blood to the cheeks or to inflame the critical imagination. It calls to mind all too readily the neat tabulations of the literary histories which have piled up on library shelves over so many years, it suggests the innocent categories from which our more recent critics have already weaned us: it sounds somewhat dull and unfashionable. And yet this impression is doubtless due to a faulty perspective. For it is not simply that, as the range of this volume itself indicates, the term relates to a highly important area of world literature. The subject of realism is in fact a difficult, highly paradoxical and even exciting one which leads directly to the larger problems concerning the novel: its nature as representation, its function within the culture, its life-cycle as an influential literary form, and its 'death' in our time.

However, the subject is also a vast one and any attempt to treat it in a short space must begin by indicating an approach. For a large literary problem of this kind—what is the nature of realism, or what is tragedy?—may be viewed broadly in one of two ways: either as a philosophical or as a formal problem. In so far as both aspects are necessarily involved, this is obviously a matter of emphasis, of deciding at which end of the problem to begin. Nevertheless, the emphasis can in practice be decisive, and it may provide a useful parallel if this is very rapidly illustrated with reference to the equally heavily debated question of tragedy.

If, like some standard works on this subject, one starts by considering tragedy as an idea given dramatic expression, one may readily identify the idea with fate or destiny and, going back to the Greeks, define it in terms of the gods. Whereupon, one may have to devise sub-divisions to account for the particularity of fate in Shakespeare or Racine, and be led to multiply fresh categories thereafter—until one may run out of these and be led to tell people who lived through Auschwitz or the Stalinist purges that the twentieth century, being an agnostic age bereft of any transcendent god or gods, is incapable of tragedy. All of which tends to put paid to the relevance and the fundamentality of the idea, without accounting adequately for the continuity of the form.

Alternatively, and perhaps more profitably, one may see tragedy initially not as an idea but as a dramatic form, and examine it as a structure of persuasion. One may then find the defining constant to be a pattern of inevitability—an inevitability correlating in practice with quite different and even opposed determinants or 'fates' in different cultures. In the *Oedipus*, for example, it might seem to correspond to a monolithic order underlying the diversity of the gods; in Racine's *Phèdre* to an internalized fate in the form of the background Christian view of a vitiated human nature; in Arthur Miller's *Death of a Salesman* to a change in the marketing pattern of the capitalist economy. The essential philosophical meaning of tragedy, in a word, is what is implicit in the form itself rather than in the diverse and conflicting ideas of destiny with which dramatists and their audiences may at different times invest it.

The comparison may be instructive when it comes to that 'vague, elastic word' realism, as Baudelaire called it over a century ago—before he could have envisioned 'socialist realism', 'fantastic realism' and all the many types and gradations of realism now to be found in critical writing. For there has been a similar tendency to treat realism as though it were *given* as a philosophical rather than a literary problem, to emphasize theory and intention rather than actual practice and, indeed, to subsume realism as an artistic mode used in different arts at different periods under the more or less scientific determinist philosophy broadly underlying the aesthetic theories of nineteenth-century Realist movements. Yet there is an elementary distinction to be drawn between realism *as an artistic convention or technique*—to be found also in mediaeval sculpture or in Dutch painting, for example, as in eighteenth-century fiction or bourgeois drama—and the intellectually self-conscious Realism of the nineteenth century. And even if it were possible to equate aesthetic assumptions with artistic effect, the fact would remain that such major nineteenth-century figures as Balzac, Flaubert, Tolstoy, and Dostoevsky did not share the same world-view, let alone that of Vermeer or the makers of mediaeval Christian statuary. To proceed as though significant imaginative literature were simply the illustration of a pre-existing philosophical position generally leads to curious results, and it has in this case tended to produce an anti-realist argument which might seem everywhere to add up to a kind of optical illusion.

In essence, this argument depends upon the view that realism, as René Wellek puts it, is ultimately bad aesthetics.[1] That great creative artists tend to be poor philosophers or aestheticians is not something one might wish to contest, but are we to accept the implication that the major nineteenth-century novelists were great despite the fact that they were Realists? Can one really believe that writers with the temperament of a Balzac, a Flaubert, or a Zola would have produced better novels if the romantic strain in each of them had not been contained by the disciplines of Realism—whatever the intellectual terms in which they conceived it? It is critically rather embarrassing that Realism should be seen as a misguided direction which happens to connote one of the great areas of world literature.

Again, it is suggested in one form or another by a whole line of critics and writers that Realism was the somewhat innocent expression of a now bankrupt nineteenth-century deterministic humanism; that the growing subjectivism of modern art is due to this having been superseded; and that the development of fiction from Proust or Joyce to the New Novel demonstrates that the postulates underlying realism no longer carry force within our culture. Here again, the perspective is so narrow as to lead to misconception with regard not only to realism, but to the situation of the novel form and the nature of modern culture.

While it is clear that the very mechanistic kind of scientific determinism of the nineteenth century has indeed been superseded, it is equally clear that it has been superseded only by a more open and sophisticated form of the same world-view: our own preoccupation with the environment, socio-economic structures, and innate or learned behaviour patterns is not different in kind from the concerns of the age of Marx and Darwin. It is precisely for this reason that the growing subjectivism of Western art is hardly to be seen as the product of some new, unifying philosophical idealism, as discerned by Erich Heller;[2] it is more obviously a function of the individualism which goes with our increasingly agnostic and relativistic culture. Again, no one familiar with the cinema, with the programmes produced in vast quantities by multi-channel television,

or indeed with the unending paperback series in which our problematic age expresses itself, is likely to conclude that realism as an
artistic or intellectual mode is dying out of our culture. It may well,
of course, be dying out of the high novel, but this might mean that it
is not so much realism which is dying as the novel.

In attempting in this chapter to sketch an alternative perspective
within which literary theory may be more closely aligned to artistic
achievement, I shall first comment on realism as a literary technique
or convention. It may then emerge that the great nineteenth-century
Realists, if they were often unable to resolve intellectually certain
contradictions in their theoretical position, contrived triumphantly
to resolve these artistically in such a way as not only to establish
realism as the dominant mode of the genre, but to establish the novel
itself as a high art form. If it is obvious that such a demonstration
has to be conducted in adequately specific terms, it is equally
obvious that it is not possible within a short span to do so with
reference to the whole Western phenomenon of realist literature—
ranging as this does from Russia to North America. Given the need
for a coherent field of reference, I shall therefore concentrate to a
large extent on the situation in France.

There are in fact various reasons why France may be taken as a
suitable test case. In the first place, it provides the example of a fairly
representative nineteenth-century Western society as regards the
social, intellectual, and political background. Again, realism reached
a high degree of self-conscious organization in France—in the two
distinct stages of Realism and Naturalism—and it was here indeed
that some of the decisive engagements in the great theoretical and
political battle over realism were fought. The 'triumph' of Realism
may be situated in the mid-1850s, with the exhibition of Courbet's
paintings, the scandal surrounding Flaubert's *Madame Bovary*,
Duranty's review *Réalisme* and Champfleury's collection of essays
entitled *Le Réalisme*. The more applied and more explicitly determinist Naturalism, firmly tied by Zola to the new scientific interest
in heredity and milieu-conditioning, was already emerging with the
'clinical' novels of the Goncourts and Zola himself in the 1860s, and
it continued controversially as a movement into the 1880s.

Finally, and equally important for the purposes of this argument,
it is also from France that the most deliberate challenge to the traditional realist novel has come, not only with Proust or Beckett but in
the form of the New Novel. And it is piquant that this New Novel

should have emerged more or less exactly one hundred years after the new novel of the mid-1850s, in a climate marked by a not dissimilar scientism and against the background of a further stage in essentially the same debate about objectivism *versus* subjectivism, freedom *versus* necessity. As indeed it is piquant that the iconoclast Alain Robbe-Grillet should have begun his career with a sustained attempt over four novels to realize an old dream of 'the father of Realism', Gustave Flaubert.

Realism, like tragedy, is not simply an idea. It is an artistic mode or convention which, as has already been indicated, was employed in various arts long before the emergence of self-conscious Realism in the nineteenth century. Indeed, it has been the distinctive mode of the novel as a form, and remains its dominant stylization up to the present time. How then does this technique work, and what does its use imply?

Suppose I enter a train at Victoria Station and open a novel in which a man enters a train at Victoria Station. I shall not be surprised if the writer gets him 'realistically' to Brighton or Belgrade before I myself get to East Croydon. I know that this realist novelist is not offering me 'reality'—how many hundreds of pages of description would be required to render the complex reality of Victoria Station?—but that he is selecting, concentrating, and re-ordering in relation to a game of make-believe conducted through the signs on these processed sheets of vegetable matter. I may sense that I am in fact less interested in 'reality' than in the alternative order which the artificiality of art provides, that the story itself is a symbolical structure which is compelling in so far as it corresponds not to the immediate surface of life—if it did, I should hardly be reading on my way to East Croydon—but to the finality of life. At all events, I know that I am at best being offered an illusion of reality—which will at once evaporate if some disconcertingly real and furry thing starts crawling along the third line on page eleven.

Why then should the reader pretend to believe in the illusion of reality, fragile as it is, which realism provides? The reason is obviously that he accepts it as an implicit and necessary frame of reference, that he tends naturally to share with the writer—or has been conditioned to share with the writer—the tacit assumption that a human life is most truthfully presented in terms of the individual's milieu, of the particularity of social situation and historical circumstance. What is implicit in the stylization itself, therefore, and independently of any views about reality or realism held formally by writer or reader, is an idea which is at once quite simple and very powerful. For although realism, being an artistic convention, is not of itself truer or more real than other 'isms' or conventions, it has dominated the novel form to the extent almost of defining it. So much is this the case that it has been the mode of writers with an idealist or anti-historical world-view, such as Tolstoy, Dostoyevsky or the twentieth-century Catholic novelists. If the curious debate surrounding the work of Mauriac or Bernanos raised the question as to whether or not it was possible to achieve an expression of Divine Grace in the novel, or whether the novelist had to fall back on a negative picture of the desolation of a world without God, it seems clear that this problem had less to do with theology than with the technical difficulty of fitting God into the realist conventions.

For the reason why the idea implicit in the stylization is a powerful one is obviously that it coheres directly with the relativistic, agnostic, man-centered culture which has grown up in the West over the past few centuries: a development, as it happens, which is particularly clear in the French context. Underlying the analysis of seventeenth-century moralists such as La Bruyère and La Rochefoucauld, and underlying the very stylization of the theatre of a Racine—writing his a-historical plays about the ancient world—there is the background Christian idea of a 'human nature', seen as static, God-given and therefore immutable. This idea is milled through the growing cultural relativism of the eighteenth century and through certain intermediates in literature—such as a still essentialist view of 'character'—until it is quite transformed in the nineteenth century under the impact of the industrial revolution, the development of the natural sciences, and the rise of the social sciences. The Darwinian theory being of itself sufficient to destroy the idea of a fixed human nature, what now emerges is rather the very different conception of a 'human situation' open to a progressive biological and cultural conditioning. And it is not by accident that the development of the novel form itself is coextensive with the history of modern literary realism as it reflects this radical transformation of Western culture.

Self-conscious Realism of the nineteenth-century is no more than an advanced stage in this development. What comes to be said explicitly by the Realists in their theoretical statements is already said implicitly in the novel of the eighteenth century; picaresque novels, pseudo-memoirs, and novels of adventure are already eroding the old view of human nature by bringing out the variety of humanity, the geographical and cultural relativity of experience. So that when Balzac says at the beginning of *Old Goriot* of 1834 that the reader may not understand the novel if he does not know Paris—and says most tellingly that Madame Vauquer implies her boarding-house as the boarding-house implies Madame Vauquer—he is as much marking the culmination of one phase as anticipating another, intellectually more self-conscious one.

As regards what is implicit in the stylization itself, therefore, there might seem to be no great theoretical problem. Realism—which in a broad historical sense could be seen as the meaning of the novel form—implies something simple but culturally quite central. And of course it is largely because of this centrality that the term has proved to be elastic to the point that critics may speak of the 'psychological realism' of Nathalie Sarraute, say, or the 'neo-realism' of Robbe-Grillet. Realism, understandably, has tended quite naturally to follow a changing sense of reality, and has long since escaped identification with narrow nineteenth-century social or biological determinism—as tragedy has long since escaped its dependence upon the gods.

If there is a 'problem of realism', it resides essentially in the theory rather than in the practice of the major nineteenth-century novelists: in their failure to resolve at the intellectual level an apparent contradiction in their approach which is best seen in the context of their views as a whole.

Given that the French Realists and Naturalists—and the terms were confusedly and often interchangeably employed—were formulating their views over some fifty years, that they belonged to different generations, and that they varied greatly in temperament as in their political attitudes, it is perhaps surprising that they should have agreed about so much. However, there was a broad consensus as to the more obvious features of Realism: the need for observation and documentation, for fictional characters to be constituted as typical or representative, and for the writer to regard as his rightful territory the whole range of society and experience, not excluding the working classes or sexual relations. Nevertheless, a significant division of opinion emerges over the question of style, with

Champfleury at one end of the spectrum arguing for a 'transparent style' or non-style, and Flaubert and the Goncourts arguing at the other for what the latter called *le style artiste*. And this disagreement points at once to the obvious and central contradiction in the theoretical approach of these writers, which lies in an unresolved conflict between objectivity and subjectivity.

The presentation of reality clearly implies objectivity—that is to say the world itself rather than the writer's personal view of it—and of course Zola and others laid claim to an objectivity of a scientific order. And yet, as has been seen, the novel is in practice a kind of sustained lie which the reader provisionally accepts while remaining aware that the writer is necessarily selecting and re-ordering in the service of a controlled illusion. Add that the writer is obviously limited to his own experience, knowledge, perception, or capacity for empathy and it is clear that the novel cannot finally be other than the expression in projection of an individual subjectivity. How then did the Realists cope with this problem at the theoretical level?

It is fair to say that with the possible exception of Maupassant, who arrived late on the scene, they could make neither head nor tail of it. Flaubert, although he in fact raised realism and the novel itself to a high art form in *Madame Bovary*, is a striking example of this. If he detested any display of subjectivity or emotion in the novel, he also denied that it should serve any social or moral function. If on the one hand he aspired to the semi-platonic perfection which he called 'the Beautiful', he aspired on the other to what he called 'the precision of science'. He appears to have thought that by abstracting from a great volume of secondary historical materials, as for *Salammbô*, he could provide a scientifically precise picture—and that this would somehow, thereby, also constitute 'the Beautiful'. In fact, it was only by equating such majuscularized entities as 'the Beautiful', 'the True', 'the Real' and 'the Ideal' at a high level of symbolical abstraction that he contrived to stabilize the conflict between them. Zola, to take the other obvious example, was perhaps more aware of the problem—which serves only to emphasize his failure to solve it. On the one hand, armed with Claude Bernard's treatise on scientific method and Lucas's treatise on heredity, he proceeded to set up his Rougon-Macquart cycle as a vast, controlled, 'scientific' experiment plotting the combined effect of heredity and environment. On the other hand, he knew that what he called the writer's 'temperament' was decisive and he even argued, as against

Flaubert, that the novelist must express his own individuality and philosophical views. The contradiction becomes the more starkly obvious.

It may perhaps serve usefully to reinforce the necessary distinction between aesthetic theory and artistic practice if we ask why it was that these writers, gifted and intelligent men as they were, failed to solve this problem. It should be said at once that as working writers they did not in fact have to solve it at the theoretical level (that is rather the task of literary critics, who have perhaps not done significantly better), and that men like Flaubert, Champfleury. Edmond de Goncourt, or Courbet shared the practitioner's characteristic dislike of labels, schools, and journalistic inflation. It may be added that the problem involved is in any event not specific to realism: ideality is hardly more readily rendered through black symbols on the page than is reality. Nevertheless, against the confused background of the rapid historical, social, political, and intellectual change through which these writers lived, several answers suggest themselves.

One is that their aesthetic views, in an age when Flaubert or Baudelaire could come under direct attack from the law, tended in practice to be *a posteriori* rationalizations or self-justifications propounded under the pressure of polemics with moral and political overtones. In a society increasingly divided by 1848, the Commune of 1871 and attendant class conflict, they were in a situation in which the real itself was symbolical—and threatening. Not only was the introduction of everyday realities into literature or painting felt obscurely to attack the old romanticized ideality which art was expected to sustain and protect—there were cries of outrage when Renoir put a folded newspaper into one of his paintings—but the depiction of 'low life' was felt to be morally and politically subversive. In the light of this situation one might be tempted to think that the Realists used the new prestige of science as a cudgel with which to defend themselves against their adversaries.

However, such a view would doubtless be too simple—or perhaps not simple enough. The fact is that the Realists tended, as innocently as we ourselves might do today on a similar basis of second-hand scientific knowledge, to justify their activity, to themselves as well as to others, in the intellectual terms which had come to dominate their culture. And this was an age so enthused by science that even many of the Impressionists, ushering in the most sharply stylized art that Europe had seen for centuries, tended to conceive of their enterprise in the intellectual terms of optics or scientific theories of colour. Nor did the Realists possess the formal framework of ideas—in that they were unaware of our projective or gestalt psychology, as of our remarkably recent 'intentional fallacy'—which might have enabled them at the theoretical level to resolve the apparent contradiction between objectivity and subjectivity.

They resolved it as best they could. They resolved it at the artistic level—the level at which it mattered—in their work.

The artistic achievement of the Realists is best perceived not in terms of the unattainable objectivity—as Maupassant pointed out, we each have our own version of reality—but in terms of the technique of impersonality to which the forces making for an objective rendering of the world almost inevitably led them. While a formal impersonality was of course not uniformly practised across the international reaches of Realist literature, it is basically through the use of this technique that the major writers of the time—to a large extent unknowingly—not only resolved the apparent contradiction between objectivity and subjectivity, but brought about a decisive enrichment and sophistication of the novel form.

This sophistication of the genre was in any event necessary at a time when the novel was becoming perhaps the most important art form in the West, the representative literary expression of post-revolutionary industrial society. More accessible than the theatre in an age of extended literacy, and obviously better equipped to describe the increasing variety of life-styles and locales, it was poised to undertake an exhaustive stocktaking of societies changing under great new historical and social pressures: from Balzac, who saw himself as the 'amanuensis of History', to Zola, who said 'we are doing practical sociology', the intention is clear. Yet the form which the Realists inherited was as yet insufficiently developed to present in adequate depth and with proper artistic control a correspondingly new image of man. And it is against this background that one may measure the achievement of Flaubert, who with his *Madame Bovary* alone might be said to have brought about a kind of mutation in the genre which raised it to the level of high art.

Imagine a production of a realist play by Ibsen, say, but in which the author himself is present on the stage among his own characters: supplying background information, analysing motives, philosophising about heredity or drawing moral conclusions. This, not too strongly caricatured, is broadly what the novel was up to and including Balzac: a kind of illustrated argument, rather than a properly autonomous action. Until Flaubert got the novelist as far as possible off his stage and off the page—an effect perfectly expressed by Taine when he said 'your perpetual absence is all-powerful'— the novel was in fact something of a bastard genre. Except in special circumstances where a self-contained quality was achieved almost by accident—through first-person narration, or the use of the epistolary form—the novel lacked the apparent separate existence, the autonomy of stylization which tends to characterize high art.

It is the size of the technical task facing the Realists in this situation which lends depth and complexity to their enterprise, as it everywhere surrounds it with irony and paradox. For the Realist novelist wishes to render the real, and to do so objectively, but can in practice achieve only an illusion of reality and an appearance of objectivity. If the illusion is to be convincing and to have objective force, it must impinge as something separate from himself—as Zola put it economically enough, 'as soon as the author shows his hand the illusion stops'. And the achievement of this apparently impersonal illusion of reality, in so far as the author is now obliged to manipulate his situation and his characters invisibly from backstage, called for a whole new set of fictional techniques. Realism, ironically, is bringing the novel to terms with the artificiality of art.

For if the emphasis begins insensibly to shift from external reality to internal structure, it is because realistic descriptions and other surface effects are clearly not enough. What the novelist must now ideally do is to contrive a coherent and apparently autonomous structure of persuasion which will of itself, through eloquent juxtaposition or other indirect means, say what the writer wants to say without his actually having to intervene directly to say it. The illusion of reality must in effect be a kind of alternative, fictive world which will suggest the depth and the order which the reader—as much influenced by new ideas of conditioning as the writer, and needing more than a realistic surface—postulates for the world itself. And it is ironically logical that under the burden of this task Flaubert himself should have come at one stage to dream about a pure, totally autonomous work which might stand up by the perfection of its structure and style alone, without having to depend upon correlation with anything external to it—the 'father of

Realism' aspiring to the separate reality of the illusion: to the 'book about Nothing'!

The impersonal mode, which was to become the standard stylization of the novel, generally deepened the fictional world and greatly increased the expressive possibilities of the genre. In *Madame Bovary*, Flaubert himself lays down the basic techniques of the high art form that will be exploited so successfully by such as Henry James, Proust, or Thomas Mann. He sets up a very elaborate orchestral or suggestive structure whereby meaning *emerges*—as a function of structure itself, of what he called 'the harmony of the whole', rather than of direct statement. And so we have the symphonic organization of themes, the controlled parallelism and opposition of characters and events, subtle shifts of narrative tense, a clever modulation of point of view, ironical juxtaposition—a whole range of new techniques which were to become part and parcel of the novel. While the desire to be faithful to the real may itself have added to the form, it was the technique of impersonality which in effect transformed the genre.

And it is in the heat of this artistic achievement that the central theoretical conflict between objectivity and subjectivity melts in practice into a non-problem. There is an ultimate irony here— measured most fully once again by Flaubert himself, when he grimly put on his hair shirt to write about a mediocre provincial romantic and ended up by discovering that 'Madame Bovary, c'est moi.' For now that the novelist has adopted the impersonal mode, he is in a new relation to his own writing. The explicit world-view which had previously mediated not only between himself and the reader, but between himself and his own fiction, has gone from the work. His task is correspondingly greater and more complex, so much so that he can no longer maintain the intellectual control which he could exercise over the novel as illustrated argument. It is organically or artistically now that he is giving shape and coherence to this alternative or 'autonomous' world of his impersonal fiction. And consequently it is in depth now, beyond the defence mechanisms of the self, that he is confronting and realizing himself, often to the point of going beyond or against his own intentions and world-view.

In a word, the irony is that the more impersonal he is, the deeper the writer himself is involved. The more he realizes his fiction in terms of the objective world the more also, paradoxically but logically, he is structuring and increasing his own subjective awareness;

the more he distances his world artistically, the more he achieves himself in projection in relation to the world. So that in practice, whether we call realism the concretizing of a private vision in terms of the real or a rectification of reality in the service of a private vision, objectivity and subjectivity are from the point of view of the writer not in contradiction. On the contrary, they are necessarily interdependent and interfused.

The point may perhaps be restated in terms of Shakespeare's image of art as the mirror held up to nature. Stendhal saw the novel in the early nineteenth century as the mirror of life, but was perhaps somewhat innocent in his view of reflection and in seeing art as the simple servant of nature. Proust, in attacking what had become the established Realist tradition, saw more profoundly that genius lay rather in the quality and refractive capacity of the mirror itself, but then the subtlety of Proust's refraction cannot operate without something to refract—and his achievement is in practice consubstantial with the presentation of a whole dimension of French society. From subjectivity at one end of the process and the world at the other there can be no escape, and the achievement of realism is that it deepened the relationship between them which the novel, simply, is all about. It thereby produced what is at once, probably, the fullest picture of the modern world and one of the highest expressions of subjectivity in Western literature.

What, then, of realism in relation to the novel today? Is realism dead? Or is the novel dead?

Almost a century after *Madame Bovary*, Alain Robbe-Grillet proclaimed that Flaubert's old dream of a pure and completely autonomous 'book about Nothing' had now become 'the ambition of the novel as a whole'. And his own first four novels constitute precisely an impressively rigorous, phased attempt to escape chronology, story, and psychology in such a manner as to write this novel about 'Nothing'. In the last of these, *In the Labyrinth* of 1959, he does indeed achieve an extraordinary sense of freedom in that the novel—coextensive with pages piling upon a table—seems to build itself up through the interplay of random fragments before our eyes. Yet there are everywhere ironical hints that Robbe-Grillet realizes that autonomy is finally impossible, and that the more he tries to abolish psychological interest the more he is simply displacing it back towards the writer. In the sense that Madame Bovary is Flaubert, the novel about Nothing is about the imagination of Robbe-Grillet confronting the possibility of the novel about Nothing. Flaubert and Robbe-Grillet, meeting in the middle of the perfidious hall of mirrors of 'impersonal' fiction, might have had much to say to each other.

Yet the difference between their situations as writers—between Flaubert's *littérature* and Robbe-Grillet's *écriture*—is a fundamental one in that the equation of subjectivity and objectivity is not in each case equally reversible. Flaubert's mirror still reflected outwards, and Madame Bovary was not just Flaubert—she was also and pre-eminently Madame Bovary: a provincial woman so firmly and so impersonally established in terms of concrete historical and social correlatives as to have become a prototype. Flaubert was at least as concerned with form and structure as Robbe-Grillet, but he was writing at a time when the novel was still about the world rather than about the novel and, in addition to perfecting his cadences and balancing his volumes, he still had to dress his shop-window for the customers passing by. The difference, obviously, is not that by the 1950s the imagination is dead, any more than the language is dead—Robbe-Grillet's own work is impressive evidence, if any were needed, to the contrary. It is rather that the goods in the shop-window have become available elsewhere, that the customers have begun to disperse towards other attractions and that the high novel, under the same pressures that impelled the plastic arts towards abstraction, is tempted increasingly to become its own subject—an understandable but implausible ambition for what has essentially been a behavioural form.

If the novel has lost its place in the culture it is because it has lost its appropriateness in relation to a whole range of functions. The centrally important and unifying role which it played in the heyday of the Realists was such that one might almost say that it was at once the entertainment, the history, the sociology and the psychology of the West. Yet so many functions once specific or most appropriate to it—the description of locale, the social placing of behaviour, story-telling, entertainment—have gradually been taken over to a large extent by a succession of newer forms of expression: photography, colour reportage, radio, cinema, and then the all-engulfing television. Just as important is the fact that history, sociology, and psychology have over the past hundred years constituted themselves as separate intellectual disciplines—which, in our problem-centred and paperback culture, are at once popularized. If the equivalent of

Zola's *Germinal* today might be a television documentary about mining, or more probably North Sea oil, the equivalent of *Madame Bovary*—if not a cinematographic poem in filtered semi-tones—might well be a case-study of the incidence of extra-marital involvement as a function of secondary goal-confusion in a controlled sample of forty-five social-grade-three French provincial housewives. Madame Bovary, in fact, is alive and well, but living elsewhere than in the old house of fiction.

Realism also, whether as stylization or as connoting a way of looking at the world, is also alive and well. If it is going from the high novel, this is less because it has been superseded than because the world itself has in some sense gone from the novel, which—as a working writer like Gore Vidal complains, and as Céline complained forty years ago—is becoming increasingly marginal. Indeed it may well be that the novel was 'morally' superseded a long time ago, and that it was the historical and social tensions of the inter-war years which helped writers like Céline or Hemingway or Malraux to keep it healthily alive—the birth of the New Novel in the mid-1950s coincides with the end of the Cold War as well as with the extension in France of television. At all events, there is surely an ironical innocence about the narrowly nineteenth-century progressivist view of those who, like Nathalie Sarraute in her *Age of Suspicion*, tend to see the novel as evolving by some natural process of growth into the New Novel. While the form may survive in the longer term as a new kind of high poetry, it is barely conceivable that it would ever again occupy the controlling place in our culture which it enjoyed in the days of Balzac, Dickens, or Tolstoy.

If this is indeed the case, it at once sets realism in the novel much more sharply in perspective. I have already suggested that realism—far from being a period piece based on false ideas and bad aesthetics, and now superseded by some internal evolutionary progress of the genre—might in a broad historical sense be seen as the very meaning of the novel form. It may well be that, in the perspective opened up by the present situation of the novel, one should venture to say more than this.

It may well be, in a word, that realism *was* the novel.

NOTES

1. 'The Concept of Realism in Literary Scholarship' in *Concepts of Criticism*, Yale University Press, New Haven and London, 1963, pp. 222–55.
2. 'The Realistic Fallacy' in G. J. Becker (ed.), *Documents of Modern Literary Realism*, Princeton University Press, Princeton, 1963, pp. 591–8.

2

H. de Balzac: *Lost Illusions* (1837-43)

A. J. MOUNT

ALTHOUGH BALZAC is frequently referred to as a Realist, the term is really an anachronism in his case, since the literary debate concerning Realism in France did not get under way until after his death in the middle of the nineteenth century. It is important to realize therefore that Balzac himself did not think in terms of Realism as a doctrine or a formal mode of writing. Nevertheless he does insist, at the beginning of *Old Goriot* in 1834, that 'all is true'—as clear an indication as any of a 'Realist' intent—and he does show a concern for social problems and historical accuracy which anticipates the famous 'documentation' of the later Realists and Naturalists. Again, where characterization is concerned, his aim is often to create characters who are not only credible individuals in their own right but also 'types', representing a whole category of mankind (misers, criminals, or careerists, for example), and this extra dimension, a further link between literature and life, is another prime characteristic of Realism. This idea of the 'type' seems to be borrowed from an author who was extremely popular in France and had a considerable influence upon Balzac—Sir Walter Scott. This novelist, rather surprisingly at first sight, was an important figure in the development of Realism, for he creates major characters with universal human attributes who come not from the ranks of the aristocracy, as is generally the convention in earlier literature, but from the lower strata of society. Balzac continues this development and makes two distinctive contributions of his own: he emphasizes the importance of passion in all its various forms as a motivating force in human behaviour, including that of women, who in Scott tend to be rather lifeless, passive creatures; and secondly he builds on Scott's concept of 'second sight' or 'inner vision' to develop a technique of observation plus intuition as the basis of his creative method. This is well illustrated by Baudelaire, who tells the story of Balzac looking at a painting of a winter scene which included some peasants and their huts; he contemplated the picture for a while and then exclaimed, 'How b eautiful it is! But what are they doing in that hut? What are they thin king about? What are their worries? Did they have a good harvest? They must have bills to pay.'[1] Balzac himself describes his brand of observation as 'intuitive', explaining that it can 'penetrate to the soul without disregarding the body', and 'grasp the significance of external details so effectively that it immediately goes beyond them.'[2]

The first novel that Balzac signed with his own name was a kind of historical novel, *The Chouans*, published in 1829. Although the events described, in a Royalist uprising in Brittany, took place only thirty years earlier, the debt to Scott is immediately apparent in the striking descriptions of the Breton countryside and in the narrative techniques employed, such as plunging the reader into the middle of a complex situation and then carefully explaining away the apparent mysteries as the narrative develops. It is in this field of literary method that Balzac's chief debt to Scott lies: its application to the area of contemporary society and everyday existence—the subject-matter now associated with Realism—is Balzac's contribution to the development of the movement.

Another respect in which Balzac may be seen as a precursor of Realism is his adherence to the 'determinist' theories associated with the school: he believes that man is fashioned by heredity and environment, and for this reason he places great emphasis upon the importance of the physical settings in which his characters live—he sees the same intimate relationship between a man and his house as between an oyster and its shell, to use his own famous image. Indeed it was the long, detailed descriptions of physical background which led contemporary critics to believe that Balzac was trying to reproduce reality on the printed page, and it is here that we find the beginnings of the controversy surrounding nineteenth-century Realism.

It is interesting that early critics such as Fontaney and Janin[3] draw a comparison between Balzac's descriptions and the background to paintings, for it was in painting that the term 'Realism' first became established, and it was Courbet's 'art réaliste' which after 1848 had such an influence upon Champfleury's thinking. Less charitable critics write disparagingly of lists and inventories drawn up by an auctioneer, and accuse Balzac of 'externality', of being pre-occupied with inanimate objects at the expense of human beings. They are reluctant to accept the depiction of the physical world as a valid part of the novel, probably because it had previously played little part in French literature—the vaguely palatial or classical settings of the seventeenth-century stage for example represent a complete disregard for environmental forces, whereas Balzac believed that it was impossible to isolate man from his milieu in this manner. Once his readers became accustomed to this basic idea, the descriptions were in fact criticized less often than other aspects of his work such as plot, style, and historical accuracy, and when Balzac's popularity was at its height in the years 1846–56 he was acclaimed as a great painter of reality, George Sand going so far as to say that it would be his use of detailed description which would constitute his main interest for posterity. At this point entered a new and important element in the discussion of Balzac's work and this has influenced the critical reaction to his writing ever since—the self-styled 'Réalistes' appeared. With their avowed aim of reproducing reality on paper as faithfully as possible Murger and Monnier, and a little later Champfleury and Duranty, adopted Balzac's technique of long material descriptions to give their work an air of authenticity and truth. Such a superficial similarity with Balzac's work was enough for some critics and, disregarding the ideas and theories which lay behind the authors' descriptions, they dubbed Balzac posthumously as 'leader of the Realist school'. From this moment on Balzac's reputation was caught up in the literary battle over Realism and his work was subjected to the same charges that the 'Réalistes' brought upon their heads: of being obsessed with the sordid and ugly sides of life and of having immoral intentions. Yet some good came from this confusion: by comparing the *Human Comedy* (the generic title Balzac gave to his novels in 1842) with the products of the new school it became clear that Balzac's work was infinitely superior: when placed beside an attempted transcription of reality by a 'Réaliste' the 'visionary' aspect of his work became apparent. Even his descriptions were now seen to be part of a distinctively 'Balzacian' world, having strong links with the real world and yet possessing a separate and distinctive existence. As Baudelaire perspicaciously explains, 'his prodigious taste for detail, which stems from an immoderate desire to see everything, and to make us see everything, to divine the meaning of everything and to

make us divine the meaning of everything, obliged him to draw the
main outlines more boldly in order to preserve our view of the whole
picture.'⁴ Later critics have tended to accept and develop this concept: Brunetière believes that Balzac cannot be regarded as a Realist
because of the strong element of imagination in his work,⁵ and
Maurice Blanchot goes so far as to deny any but the most superficial
relationship between Balzac's creation and the real world:

> [Balzac's world] is neither a carbon-copy nor a caricature of reality. It is
> intended to exist on its own. His aim was to draw the reader into his
> world and to hold him there by making the real world uninhabitable for
> him.⁶

As for the detailed descriptions which others have taken as proof of
Balzac's allegiance to realism, Blanchot has a quite different interpretation: 'This mass of minute detail is not there to transcribe and
imitate external reality. It has a quite different purpose. . . . These
details are to prepare our sensibilities so that at the appropriate
moment the drama may be understood and appreciated to the full.'⁷
This conviction that there is more to Balzac's descriptions than the
faithful reproduction of material reality is now the general view:
Albert Béguin perceives two dimensions in Balzac—reality and
mystery, 'la réalité du mystère',⁸ as he calls it, and Maurice Levaillant finds in Balzac's details all the elements of real life but magnified
into a distortion of everyday forms; he regards Balzac as 'a visionary
of reality'.⁹ This belief that behind the façade of solid detail lies the
essence of reality is shared by Lukács, who links Balzac with
Stendhal as a writer who can at the same time describe and transcend
the trivial and average.¹⁰ The summing-up on this aspect of
Balzac's 'Realism' may be left to Georges Pradalié:

> It is because observation and intuition are so closely inter-related in
> Balzac's work that it is difficult for us to decide between those who
> consider Balzac to be an observer and those who see him as a pure
> visionary. He was most certainly both.¹¹

It is clear then that we must be wary of the term 'Realist' in its
application to Balzac. What we can say is that he undoubtedly fits
into the category of writers who believe that the tangible, everyday
world about us is of importance in our understanding of ourselves
and other people. He conforms perfectly well to Erich Auerbach's
definition of 'modern realism',¹² for he depicts lower-class characters,

portraying universal, tragic themes against a fluid historical back-ground, usually of contemporary society, in physical settings which have a deterministic influence upon the characters. On the other hand his personal interventions into the text, his impressionistic descriptions, his tendency to exaggerate or over-emphasize are elements associated with the 'visionary' aspect of his work and are at variance with the Realist mode of writing. It is against this general background that we are to consider our particular text, *Lost Illusions*,[13] to see how our appreciation of the work may be heightened by placing it in the context of the Realist movement.

There are in *Lost Illusions* several elements which are clearly drawn directly from Balzac's own experience: the sharp contrast between provincial and Parisian life in the novel reflects the author's own attitude, which probably derives from his moving from Tours to Paris at the impressionable age of fifteen—he never lost the sense of fascinated horror which the wicked, exciting capital inspired in him, a reaction which is shared by Lucien in our novel. Like Lucien's too was Balzac's struggle to make a career for himself in Parisian society (which included adopting the aristocratic parti-cule 'de' in his name, just as Lucien tries to shed the common 'Chardon' in favour of the noble 'de Rubempré'); he also met social snobbery and financial difficulties before his force of character and literary genius gained him a place in the Parisian scene. The picture of Lucien as a struggling beginner trying desperately to interest pub-lishers in his *The Archer of Charles the Ninth*, probably reflects Balzac's similar experiences with his historical novel *The Chouans* in 1829. Nor is Lucien the only character who owes much to his creator's real-life experiences: D'Arthez, the talented, honourable novelist of integrity obviously represents Balzac's ideal—this was how he strove to be after 1829; previously he had written under pseudonyms (Lord R'hoone and Horace de Saint-Aubin) churning out 'literary muck' ('cochonneries littéraires', his own term) in an attempt to make a quick fortune before settling down to a serious literary career. He is certainly thinking in terms of the conflict between serious art, as represented by D'Arthez, and a prostitution of talent, as represented by Lousteau, in *Lost Illusions*. It seems likely that in Lousteau Balzac is showing us some of the temptations the serious writer is subjected to, for he himself had dabbled in the *petits journaux* and even had a hand in running one, *La Caricature*, at the beginning of his career. There is also an autobiographical element in the character of Finot, for Balzac himself bought a journal, *La Chronique de Paris*, in 1836 and founded *La Revue Parisienne* in 1840. In none of these ventures did he have any success, and his portrayal of the treacherous journalists in *Lost Illusions* may well be a form of revenge rather than a dispassionate review of the newspaper scene. Nor is it difficult to see personal animosity in Balzac's description of publishers in the novel: Fendant and Cavalier, 'these semi-scoundrels' (p. 417), unscrupulously exploit struggling young authors for a quick profit—and are described as being perfectly typical of their kind; the decrepit, grasping Doguereau is clearly the real-life figure of Pigoreau, whom Balzac approached as humbly as Lucien does his fictional counterpart; and the scheming Barbet is patently the historical Barba, with whom Balzac did business in 1822. Similarly Dauriat has all the attributes of the famous bookseller, Ladvocat.

The journalists in *Lost Illusions* may also be modelled to some extent on people whom Balzac knew in real life: the prototype for Lousteau seems to have been a certain Auguste de Viellerglé, an opportunist of variable opinions, who in 1822 worked with Balzac on a 'literary paper', *le Feuilleton littéraire*, which devoted a few lines of review to such figures as Victor Hugo and Alfred de Vigny, whereas pages of discussion were devoted to works by Horace de Saint-Aubin, which just happened to be Balzac's pseudonym at the time. An interesting feature of this episode is that some of these reviews were highly critical, presumably intended to stir up an artificial controversy, a technique employed by Blondet and Lucien in *Lost Illusions* (see pp. 375 and 376). It seems likely also that there is some degree of self-confession as well as revenge in Balzac's vehement denunciation of journalists and their methods. In the same way Balzac's own ideal of artistic integrity is embodied in the person of D'Arthez and in the Cénacle. No real-life source for this group has been recorded, and it seems doubtful if any such group actually existed or, indeed, could have existed. Balzac here appears to be thinking in terms of black and white—the journalists are shown, for reasons suggested above, to be very black, and the writers must, for the sake of contrast, appear dazzlingly white. Their self-sacrifice, their loyalty, their moral integrity, their generosity and above all their devotion to Art make them into saintly creatures rather than ordinary human beings. With them Balzac seems to have stepped outside the bounds of Realism in order to show us his vision of artistic purity in the midst of moral corruption and commercial temptation—they symbolize the standards by which the journalists and Lucien are ultimately to be judged.

This use of characters to represent ideas or ideals bring us again to a similar aspect of Balzac's characterization briefly mentioned above, his concept of the 'type'. As he explains in his *Introduction* to the *Human Comedy* of 1842, he divides human society into categories —'social species' analogous to zoological species. His characters therefore exist at two levels, that of the individual and that of the type—Old Grandet in *Eugénie Grandet* is both a wily merchant living in Saumur and a representative of the Miser; Old Goriot is an impoverished old man lodging in the 'maison Vauquer' in Paris and 'the Christ of Fatherhood'. And so in addition to their roles as individuals the main characters in *Lost Illusions* also fulfil a representative function: Lucien represents the 'type' of the ambitious young provincial; Carlos Herrera/Vautrin the unscrupulous criminal; David Séchard the unworldly genius, and so on.

There is clearly a danger that in creating a 'type' the author may imbue a character with too many of the attributes of his 'species', and certainly in the case of Balzac some of his characters, notably Carlos Herrera/Vautrin, come close to being larger-than-life, even melodramatic, creations. Old Séchard is an example of another category of characters in Balzac's work—the 'monomaniac' who is obsessed with a single idea which dominates his whole existence. Séchard, like Gobseck and Old Grandet elsewhere in the *Human Comedy*, is a miser whose love of money warps his personality and blights the lives of those around him, 'killing all other emotions, even fatherly affection, in him' (p. 7), and so distorting his emotions that he can say to Eve, when Lucien returns, a broken man, from Paris, 'You're making as much fuss of him as if he were bringing you loads of money' (p. 586). The moral of such a story as his is made quite clear by Balzac—on his death he leaves a fortune to David but the money comes too late. If he had helped his son financially earlier in his career things might have turned out very differently. Old Séchard demonstrates the utter futility of avarice and the distress it can bring to a family. He clearly has a representative function and is at the same time a distinctive individual in his own right, with his wily tipsiness, which is as convenient for getting his own selfish way as is Old Grandet's stammer in *Eugénie Grandet*. The main victim of Séchard's avarice is his son David, but the inventor himself must bear some of the blame for the 'tribulations' which beset him. He lacks energy and ambition, and as the theorist with no practical experience or ability he is insensitive to changing circumstances and fails to adapt to their needs: 'his indifference to the religious reaction which set in under the Restoration government [was] equalled by his unconcern about the Liberal movement. He maintained in political and religious matters a neutrality which was most injurious to his interests' (p. 18). Rather than modernize the business he prefers to pursue his own researches: he may be 'predestined to arduous effort' (p. 25), but in practical matters he is 'lacking in self-confidence' (p. 27). He is characteristically anxious about Lucien's ambitions, 'ideas above his station' (p. 102), as he calls them, revealing his own cautious attitude. Part I of the novel concludes with David climbing back into his symbolically 'shabby' trap, his heart heavy with 'horrible presentiments of the fate in store for Lucien in Paris' (p. 148). Even when he is successful in his researches, he allows himself to be cheated out of his due reward because of lack of practical sense: in the crucial negotiations with the Cointets, 'what was worrying him was neither the discussion of his [financial] interests nor the debate about the deed to be drawn up, but the opinion the paper-manufacturers were likely to form about the work he had done' (p. 667). He is quite simply ignorant of the difficulties of mass-production and so is an easy prey for the unscrupulous Cointets: 'David was flattered. It was a case of Practice talking in positive terms to Theory, which only uses the future tense' (p. 669). So in the end it is only the inheritance from his father which saves David from poverty— ironically one man's obsessive concern for money comes to the rescue of one who has a total disregard for it.

In marked contrast to the unworldly David is Lucien, in whom we see the representative of ambition and 'arrivisme', a prominent type in the literature of Realism. He undoubtedly has ability—he was an outstanding pupil at school and later in his career his reviews are witty and informed, his sonnets and novel genuinely admired by respectable critics. The main obstacles to his success are that he is a provincial and of lowly birth, both of which disadvantages he tries hard to overcome or disguise; but if fate has been harsh to him in these two respects it has been kind in giving him a handsome appearance and 'the grace of bearing with which sculptors have endowed the Indian Bacchus' (p. 26), attributes which are mentioned frequently in the text and undoubtedly help to further his career;

but his great motivating force is ambition, ambition for 'glory' or for wealth, or both. Although it was Parisian society which really stimulated Lucien, the seeds of his desire to improve his lot can be seen in Angoulême, for his desire to escape from the petty restrictions of this small-town community is strong—and understandably so. Throughout his work Balzac always draws a clear distinction between life in the provinces—dull, limited, and frugal—and life in Paris—exciting, sophisticated, and extravagant. The shock and amazement Lucien feels when he arrives in the capital are hardly surprising when we consider his upbringing in Angoulême: Balzac stresses the rigidity of the social structure in this provincial town by addressing himself directly to the unfortunates who live in such places: 'You alone, poor provincial helots for whom social gaps yawn wider than in Paris, where they are narrowing from day to day, you, whom inexorable barriers exclude from that fine world within which each social group anathematizes and cries *Raca* to the rest, you alone will understand what a turmoil seethed in Lucien Chardon's head and heart when his headmaster portentously announced that the doors of the Bargeton mansion were about to be opened to him!' (p. 48).

To have the misfortune to be born in L'Houmeau, the commercial quarter of Angoulême, the son of a chemist and bearing a laughably 'common' name are not only severe obstacles for Lucien to overcome but even jeopardize the status of Madame de Bargeton as queen of the social élite simply because she accepts him into her salon; indeed had she received David Séchard, an out-and-out commoner, she would almost certainly have been disgraced and 'forced to leave the town where her own caste would shun her as a leper was shunned in the Middle Ages' (p. 62). Although Lucien's aristocratic connection on his mother's side of the family saves him from such absolute pariahdom, he still meets a great deal of prejudice from the local dignitaries, particularly the women, who are outraged at the sight of 'an apothecary's son strutting about as if he were master in Madame de Bargeton's house!' (p. 122). Not that they themselves, Balzac makes clear, are in any sense worthy or admirable people; only in a small provincial town could such an unprepossessing group pass for a social élite: 'All the people who gathered there had the most pitiable mental qualities, the meanest intelligence, and were the sorriest specimens of humanity within a radius of fifty miles. . . . The women were mostly stupid, devoid of grace and badly dressed; every one of them was marred by some imperfection; everything fell short of the mark, conversation, clothes, mind and body alike' (p. 46). In this claustrophobic community the main occupation is gossip, and malicious gossip at that, for 'provincial people are by nature malicious and love to balk nascent passion' (p. 127). The whole town is just waiting for Madame de Bargeton to commit an indiscretion with Lucien: servants, callers, and scandal-mongers all conspire to ensure that 'Madame de Bargeton's life was open to the public' (p. 127). With no cultural awareness of any sort, as the ignorant, insensitive reception of Lucien's poetry shows, the upper class of Angoulême has nothing to occupy its attention except the personal lives of its members; small wonder that Louise, like Lucien, becomes 'sick to death of provincial life' (p. 133) and her thoughts turn to Paris, 'the capital of the intellectual world' (p. 141); or that Lucien, in the face of so much social prejudice and cultural philistinism should feel stifled and misunderstood: 'he saw himself while living in Angoulême as a frog under a stone at the bottom of a swamp. He had a vision of Paris in all its splendour: Paris, an Eldorado to the imagination of every provincial; clad in gold, wearing a diadem of precious stones, holding its arms out to talent' (p. 142).

Although the initial experiences of Lucien and Louise in the capital are a disappointment this simply serves to emphasize the gap between provincial and Parisian life—it is so wide that a period of transition and adjustment is required before Paris can be appreciated by people brought up in the stultifying atmosphere of Angoulême.

Once Lucien arrives in Paris he quickly realizes that ability is of little use without money: 'Certainly a voice was crying within him: "Intelligence is the lever which moves the world". But another voice insisted that money is the fulcrum of intelligence' (p. 167). Yet he feels sure that he will be able to reap a rich reward in this new field, and in a letter to his sister he shows how hopeful he is of success now that he has broken free from the fetters of provincial existence: 'If the present is cold, bare and mean, the future is un-clouded, rich and splendid' (p. 191). Brimming over with self-confidence he declares, 'I shall be rich', and after his first promising encounter with the publisher Doguereau it seems that his optimism may be justified, and that it really is true that 'talent easily makes good in Paris' (p. 204.)

Yet the disillusionment indicated in the title of the novel is not long delayed, represented by the reduction of Doguereau's offer from one thousand francs to eight hundred, to six hundred, to four hundred, as he slowly becomes aware of the extent of Lucien's penury and vulnerability. Balzac is here showing us a society where money is the great mainspring, deciding fates and moulding characters. It is all too easy to see why the impoverished Lucien tries to take the short cut of making money in journalism, especially as he does not at first realize that such a step means that he must abandon his literary ideals, for he believes quite wrongly that the two goals, making money and achieving 'glory', are compatible: 'He did not know he had to choose between two different paths, two systems for which the Cénacle and journalism respectively stood: the one being long, honourable and certain, the other beset with reefs, dangerous, full of miry runnels in which his conscience was bound to get bedraggled' (p. 252). The absolute necessity for money soon comes to dominate his existence and forces him to sacrifice his ideals: 'These insistent tickings of the great Money pendulum throbbed through his head and heart' (p. 285), and as he remembers his discussions of Art with David Séchard and the evenings spent with the Cénacle, 'A tear glistened in the poet's eye'. He has at last become aware of the necessity for shedding the principles which David and the Cénacle represent—but he does not shed them willingly. He realizes that if he retains them in the society in which he is now moving, he will be held back, and this is something he will not contemplate. In a vivid image Balzac shows Lucien being overwhelmed by the tidal wave of fashionable society's attractions: 'Two sorts of corruption [easy money and easy women] were advancing towards him in parallel motion like twin sheets of water uniting to form a flood. They swirled over the poet' (p. 293). Balzac here seems to come close to absolving Lucien from moral blame—the environment is too strong for him to resist: 'Could a man whose every instinct was for enjoyment and sensation, bored with the monotony of provincial life, drawn into the vortex of Parisian society, weary of poverty, tormented by enforced continence, tired of his monastic seclusion in the rue de Cluny and his unfruitful labours, could such a man have held aloof from this glittering banquet?' (p. 311); and so he succumbs to the twin charms of Coralie and journalism, both akin to prostitution in their different spheres. Yet the metamorphosis from idealistic provincial to cynical Parisian is neither instantaneous nor painless: he still has illusions to lose, the most tenacious being the belief that he can combine a literary career with his new life: 'But what about my reputation as a writer', he can still exclaim, only to hear Lousteau's jeering reply, 'God save us! The man still has his illusions' (p. 354).

Yet Lucien takes to his new life all too readily: personal animosity and petty spite come easily to him, and in his first public quarrel we see that, 'the desire for vengeance on Dauriat stood in lieu of conscience and inspiration', and he revels in his new-found power over the publisher: 'The sultan among publishers had become a slave' (p. 365). His is no unwitting acceptance of new standards—he knows what he is doing and what is happening to him, as he accepts the standards of his new colleagues: 'They are right!' exclaimed Lucien, once he was alone with Coralie. 'Men must serve as tools in the hands of competent people. Four hundred francs for three articles! Doguereau scarcely offered as much for a book which cost me two years' labour.' No statement could show more clearly the criteria he is now using to judge the worth of his writing, or demonstrate more graphically his transformation from poet to journalist: 'His heart, mind and soul had undergone a like metamorphosis: he no longer thought of quibbling about the means in view of the great ends achieved' (p. 388). The 'great ends' are defined for us: 'a well-furnished house, a mistress whom the whole of Paris envied him, carriage and horses, and finally, incalculable sums to be drawn from his pen' (p. 388). In abandoning himself to material success his moral nature disintegrates: he changes political and literary allegiance for reasons of opportunism and spends money he does not possess, adopting 'the ridiculous sophistry of rakes in the matter of debts' (p. 412). When we consider how Lucien has lost all ideals and moral probity in the course of his Parisian adventure, it is no great surprise to us when he commits the unpardonable act which is to have such disastrous consequences, the forging of David Séchard's signature on the promissory notes. At a time of crisis, with his world collapsing about him, he grasps inevitably at the only thing in which he still has faith—money: 'Money! Money! a voice cried out within him' (p. 469). These are the depths to which he has been driven by a pernicious environment. This, the interaction of a given individual with a given society, is one of the main themes of this novel and of Realist literature, and it is one to which we shall return shortly. For the moment we should note that our detailed knowledge of Lucien, the way Balzac follows his emotional and intellectual development, makes him an intensely credible character—we see enough of him, his vices and his virtues, to feel that we actually know him. There may well be a degree of self-identification with him in our recognition of the difficulties he has to overcome and the temptations which seduce him from the path of strict principle. He is an eminent example of the Realist character who is both a convincing individual in his own right and a representative of a universal social, or simply human, type.

The question of the exact historical location of *Lost Illusions* is a complex one: while it is true that certain general features of the 1821–1822 period are faithfully described, more precise details are ignored. Jean Gaulmier illustrates this point[14] by looking at the royalist periodical, the *Drapeau blanc* (the editor of which was Martainville, who appears quite prominently in *Lost Illusions* as the only journalist to show any sort of loyalty towards Lucien) for the precise period in which our novel is set, between September 1821 and October 1822: on 9th October 1821 the *Drapeau blanc* carried a report of the papal bull condemning the *carbonari*, a secret society of anti-monarchists and anti-Catholics whose membership was growing rapidly at this time and gaining great notoriety. They are not mentioned in Balzac's novel. On 3 December 1821 a bill was passed strengthening the laws against the Press and extending censorship, but not a single journalist, of any political persuasion, comments upon this controversial measure in *Lost Illusions;* and even more surprisingly there is no mention of the influential article by Martainville himself in the *Drapeau blanc* of 27 October which led to the notorious trial and imprisonment of Béranger for writing his second collection of *Chansons* satirizing the abuses of the Restoration regime. In January and February 1822, when Lucien was at his most active in journalism, there was a lively public debate in France concerning the freedom of the Press which culminated on 7 February in the infamous law imposing severe censorship on all newspapers, and it was at this time that Martignac declared that papers served no useful purpose and should be regarded simply as industrial enterprises. Not one journalist, editor or newspaper-owner raises the subject in *Lost Illusions*!

These few examples make the point that Balzac did not consult detailed historical sources in order to create the social background to his novel—his 'documentation' is nothing like as thorough as that of Flaubert or Zola later in the century. What he does try to do is to create the atmosphere of the historical period and to imbue his own imaginary world with that same atmosphere. It is sufficient for this purpose to show the political and literary scene in broad, even simplistic, outline:

Literature is primarily divided into several zones; but our great men are split into two camps. The royalists are romantics, the liberals are classicists [p. 240].

In just the same way the predicament of the writer at this time, having to choose between lucrative journalism and serious literature, is described in absolutely black and white terms, as we have seen in the case of Lucien.

The reader needs no more information than a broad outline to appreciate that Lucien is playing a very dangerous game when he changes his literary/political allegiance:

And so Lucien, now an out-and-out Royalist and Romantic, after having begun as a rabid Liberal and Voltairian, found himself under the same weight of enmity as hung over the man most abhorred by the Liberals at that period: Martainville [p. 442].

The use of historical figures in the narrative is an effective device: a glimpse of Benjamin Constant, a mention of 'the joy of seeing Talma in his famous roles' (p. 197), mockery of Louis XVIII's failing sexual powers: 'he was passing, it [Lousteau's article] said, from deeds to ideas' (p. 459), all this serves to stimulate the memories of those readers who were alive at this period or to create an impression of the time for those who were not. There are similar allusions to contemporary affairs: the vogue for the Gothic novel 'in the manner of Mrs Radcliffe' (p. 204) and 'the famous discussion between Cuvier and Saint-Hilaire over a momentous question which was to divide the world of scientists into two camps behind these men of equal genius' (p. 218). Nor is the physical face of Paris overlooked: Balzac is scathing in his criticism of the capital's hotels with their 'squalid rooms which are the disgrace of Paris where despite all its pretensions to elegance there is not yet a single hotel in which any wealthy traveller can feel at home' (p. 152); and above all there is the description of the Wooden Galleries, the 'disreputable bazaar' (p. 260) which Balzac reconstructs with his pen in a wave of nostalgia now that 'all this inglorious poetry has gone'. Like the destruction of *Les Halles* in our own time, 'the demolition of these ignoble wooden erections aroused wide-spread and unanimous regret' (p. 265). As the self-styled 'annalist of his time'[15] Balzac is enthusiastic about his 'archaeological' role, asking rhetorically: 'Why should not the historian of French society preserve these curious manifestations of the past?'[16]

This aim is shown most clearly in *Lost Illusions* in the extensive descriptions of the printing and paper-making trades. The description of David Séchard's printing-press in Angoulême is thought to be based on the actual press which Balzac bought in Paris in 1827 and sold to his partner Barbier a year later. With the detailed knowledge he had acquired he was able to give full details of the antiquated equipment in the Séchard workshop, with such technicalities as, 'The old "bear" lowered the frisket on to the tympan and the tympan on to the imposing-stone and rolled it under the press' (p. 11). The ensuing bargaining between father and son confirms what we have suspected from the beginning—that this cumbersome apparatus is 'just old lumber, not worth three hundred francs' (p. 11), and that Old Séchard is callously swindling his son with the pretext that 'old tools are always best' (p. 13). The accurate description of the printing machinery adds an air of reality to the psychological conflict in the scene which might otherwise seem a little improbable—Old Séchard being somewhat 'larger than life' in his tipsy avarice. In the same way the clearly defined historical and social context of paper-making is used to give David an individuality and particularity which he might otherwise lack, cast as he is in the role of the archetypal inventor, impractical and exploited. Balzac feels quite justified in digressing from the action in order to give us various discourses on the importance of paper in the nineteenth century. After all, he says, 'information about paper-making . . . will not be out of place in a work which owes its very existence as much to paper as to the printing-press' (pp. 107–8). He then proceeds to give us a history of paper-making: its origins in China and Asia Minor, the development of cotton paper and rag paper, the various sizes and uses of paper after the advent of printing, the invention of vellum paper in the eighteenth century, and the technicalities of contemporary paper-making, with special emphasis on the inferiority of paper made from cotton compared with that made from linen, which was in increasingly short supply. This is the background to David's invention, for, realizing that, 'Holland paper, that is to say paper made of linen rags, will be altogether unobtainable' (p. 112), he

has hit upon the idea of making paper from 'certain fibrous plants'.
Once again by embedding the fictional character in a recognizable
cultural setting Balzac forges links between the real world and his
novel, which he goes on to strengthen in the third part of the work,
An Inventor's Tribulations. Here he stresses the supreme importance
of paper in society, as if to increase the stature of the protagonists in
the struggle to come: this is no petty squabble over a minor technical
invention but rather a battle over one of the most influential instru-
ments in society:

Newspapers and politics, the tremendous strides made in the production
and marketing of books, the advance of science, the prevalent tendency
to make every national interest a matter for public discussion, in fact the
entire social movement which got under way once the Restoration
regime seemed settled, was sure to demand almost a ten-fold increase in
the supply of paper [p. 489].

Only if we realize how essential paper is to a developing society
can we appreciate Balzac's brief epilogue when his tale is told:

David Séchard's invention was assimilated into French manufacture as
food is assimilated into the body of a giant. Thanks to the introduction
of other materials than rag-stuff, France is able to manufacture paper at a
cheaper rate than any other European country [p. 681].

However, the historical setting of the novel is a rather more complicated subject than may at first appear; it is best regarded as an
amalgam of political atmosphere appropriate to the period in which
the action is set and a somewhat anachronistic account of later
developments in the commercial world, for it is clear that much of
the description of paper-making, publishing, journalism, and the
theatre owes a great deal to Balzac's experience of these spheres after
the July Revolution. For example, it was not until after the change
of regime in 1830 that the press became a powerful political force,
and it was at this time that papers were bought up by industrialists,
bankers, and even the government itself: in 1840 the latter was said
to have control of nine journals, the editors of which were briefed
daily by Thiers on 'how to butter the bread the public is made to
swallow'.

Balzac's own experiences of publishing and journalism at this
later period also seem to be reflected in the novel. *Lost Illusions* was
written over a period of ten years, the first mention of the project

occurring at the end of 1833, the first section being published in February 1837, the second in June 1839 and the complete work in June 1843. During this time Balzac was engaged in various activities so closely connected with the subject-matter of this novel that it was inevitable that his experiences should be reflected in the book, even though it is set more than a decade earlier. In 1830, for example, Balzac wrote a study of 'The Present State of the Book Trade', in which he analysed the decline of publishing as a profession, claiming that it attracted the ignorant and greedy who readily fell into bankruptcy. He points out the growth in the numbers of 'middle-men' plying a dubious trade between publishers and writers and these are called 'real parasites'. In 1833 Balzac's ambition was to launch a publishing and book-selling business which would succeed by under-cutting rivals; for this enterprise he required a paper of high quality and low cost—exactly David Séchard's aim in the novel. To this end he consulted his friends the Carrauds in Angoulême, and in September 1833 sent them a sample of the required paper, asking them to find a paper-maker who could meet his specification. Alas, no David Séchard was to be found in real life!

The years 1834 to 1836 saw Balzac at his most active in social life: he set out to conquer high society with the splendour and extravagance of his way of life. It was consequently a financial disaster of the first order when his publisher, Werdet, went bankrupt just as he was anticipating the receipts from *The Two Poets*, and he himself was harrassed by William Duckett in just the same way as the bankruptcy of Fendant and Cavalier allows Camusot to tighten the screw on Lucien in *Lost Illusions*.

It seems clear that the unscrupulous exploitation of writers for financial gain is a feature of both the decade in which the novel is set and that in which it was written; the view of society we get transcends reality in order to highlight the basic underlying cause of this social phenomenon, of which precise historical facts are no more than effects. As Georg Lukács sees it, from a Marxist standpoint, 'the writers and journalists are exploited, their talent has become a commodity, an object of profiteering by the capitalist speculators who deal in literature. They are exploited but they are also prostitutes; their ambition is to become exploiters themselves, or at least overseers over other exploited colleagues.'[17] The tripartite structure of *Lost Illusions* makes the point that 'this complete "capitalization" of every sphere of intellectual, literary and artistic activity'[18] runs throughout the whole of society at all levels. Balzac's concern is to show the essential self-interest and financial greed at the heart of the society in which he found himself.

Given this aim Balzac cannot be expected to confine himself to the precise historical confines of any particular period, and certainly in one obvious respect he does not make any pretence of doing so, and that is in his treatment of the passage of time. By any standards the pace of the action in *Lost Illusions* is improbably rapid, particularly in *A Great Man in Embryo*, where the whole career of Lucien in Paris seems to be compressed into an incredibly short period: he leaves Angoulême in September 1821 and by the end of the month he has been befriended by D'Arthez and gained acceptance into the exclusive Cénacle. By the end of October he has become involved with Lousteau and the world of journalism and acquired the desirable Coralie as a mistress, together with the wealth provided for her by her protector, Camusot, and has had his sonnets accepted for publication. During the winter of 1821/1822 Lucien enjoys prestige and success until in March 1822 things start to go wrong: he gets into debt, gambles, fails to get his novel published, and changes political allegiance. In April he forges David Séchard's signature on the promissory notes. On 27 August Coralie dies and in October he returns to Angoulême. The whole adventure takes only slightly more than a year—a whirlwind career indeed. And yet the average reader is probably unaware of the accelerated pace of these events— dates are mentioned only infrequently, and Balzac's errors concerning the dates of the promissory notes and Lucien's arrival back in Angoulême in September, after leaving Paris in October, indicate how little importance the author attached to them. The impression we have is of a much longer career, for we subconsciously accept the literary convention that there are periods of blank time in Lucien's life which are not worth recording in detail—we automatically impose our own standards of what is a likely pace for the events described, and the lack of reference to dates or to specific historical events gives us the freedom to do this.

Balzac shows considerable skill in setting his novel ostensibly at a precise period in French history while allowing himself sufficient flexibility in his narrative to choose which scenes to emphasize and develop without reference to the constraints of chronology. In fact, despite the length of the novel, it could be described as 'dramatic' in construction—the division into three sections immediately suggests

three Acts, and the 'big scenes' in each Act spring readily to mind—
the Séchards' haggling over the printing-press and Lucien's poetry-
reading in Madame de Bargeton's salon in the first; the scene in
Madame d'Espard's box at the Opera-house and Lucien's introduction to Parisian orgies in the second; and the arrest of David
Séchard in the third. This episodic construction ignores periods of
relatively uninteresting time and stresses the incidents which contribute to our understanding of the characters; it is clearly no part of
Balzac's plan to describe the whole of Lucien's life—he is content to
show us the high spots. This problem of selectivity is one of the
greatest difficulties for the Realist writer—since he is unable to
reproduce life in its entirety his selection of material must inevitably
distort the picture of reality he presents. In the case of *Lost Illusions*
the distortion takes the form of a 'foreshortening' of Lucien's career,
the events in it following in swift succession instead of being spaced
out as in real life, but nevertheless as these events seem convincing
and recognizable scenes from life as we know it, we come to feel that
Lucien might well exist in real life, and we attach little importance
to the chronological inconsistencies or improbabilities which undoubtedly occur in the story.

The attempt to make a character seem 'real' to the reader obviously lies at the heart of the realist attitude: in Balzac this is largely
achieved by showing characters reacting to changing environments
and circumstances—they develop or deteriorate under the influence
of events and are shown to be the protean creatures which we recognize as human beings. In the case of Lucien and Louise we have
extreme examples of people who are uprooted from their native
surroundings, both physical and cultural, and transplanted into
another world. When they first arrive in Paris from Angoulême,
Lucien 'found his Louise scarcely recognizable', the reason being
that 'certain persons neither look nor are the same once they are
detached from the faces, places and objects which constitute their
normal environment' (p. 152). The mental disorientation he feels is
reflected in his physical appearance: while the Baron du Châtelet is
'dressed with all the elegance of Parisian fashion', Lucien appears
before Louise 'in his last-year's nankeen trousers and his shabby
little frock-coat'. He cannot fail to notice her reaction and realizes
'that for her he was no longer the Lucien of Angoulême' (p. 155).
The same sort of comparison also operates to Louise's disadvantage:
seeing her next to the fashionable Marquise d'Espard, Lucien notices

that 'both the dress and the woman in it lacked grace and bloom: the mottled velvet went with a mottled complexion'. Lucien is ashamed at having loved this 'cuttle-bone' (p. 169). But Lucien fails to realize that in Paris a complete physical transformation is possible—only a little later he sees her in Madame d'Espard's carriage on the Champs-Élysées: 'She was unrecognizable: the colour-scheme of her clothes had been chosen to match her complexion; she was wearing a most attractive dress; the graceful arrangement of her hair became her well, and her hat, in exquisite taste, was conspicuous even beside that of Madame d'Espard, the leader of fashion' (pp. 183–4).

Such physical changes reflect the spiritual ones experienced by the two provincials: Louise discards Lucien and ignores his presence, and he is consumed with envy and rage. In order to avenge himself he must have money—and the acquisition of money is in direct opposition to his 'provincial' reason for coming to Paris: 'Great God! Gold at all cost!' Lucien was saying to himself. 'Gold is the only power which this society worships on bended knees.' But his conscience cried out: 'No! Not Gold, but glory. And glory means hard work! Hard work! That's what David said. My God, why am I here? But I will win through! I will drive along this avenue in a barouche with a flunkey behind me!' (p. 185). Parisian society has introduced a completely new motivating force into Lucien's life— the need for money and the things money can buy—a force which simply did not exist for him in Angoulême, and once Lucien has been changed by his Parisian experience, he can never revert to his former self: as he writes to his sister after Coralie's death, 'Paris is at once the glory and all the infamy of France. I have lost many illusions here' (p. 549). And when he returns to Angoulême and re-visits Madame de Bargeton's salon, he can hardly believe that it once inspired him with awe: 'When I saw the little grey salon again in which I had trembled like a child two years ago, when I examined the furniture, the painting and people's faces, the scales fell from my eyes! How one's ideas change in Paris!' (p. 625). It needs only the sinister encouragement of Carlos Herrera/Vautrin to revive those Parisian ideas which are lying dormant beneath a façade of provincial remorse: 'The Spanish priest's latest words had set many chords in his heart vibrating. . . . Lucien could see himself in Paris once more, snatching again at the reins of domination which his un-skilled hands had let fall, and taking his revenge!' (p. 652). The seeds of vengeful ambition which were sown by the rebuffs and humiliations he had met in Paris have grown and become the dominant features of his personality; he has been so radically changed that he cannot regain the simple ideals of his early provincial life.

When we come to the question of Balzac's style and presentation of subject-matter, we find the biggest objection to the designation of 'Realist' for his work. Whereas the later Realists and Naturalists adopt an impersonal, 'objective' manner of presentation, 'keeping off the stage' as Flaubert puts it, Balzac not only appears on stage but comes down among the members of his audience to make sure they are reacting correctly and drawing the right conclusions from what they have seen. So, just in case we are not familiar with misers and avarice, for example, Balzac offers us the following general observations:

Avarice begins where poverty ends [p. 4].

Generous souls make poor business men [p. 14].

Avarice, like love, is endowed with second sight as regards future contingencies; it sniffs them out and worries them [pp. 17–18].

Avarice and scandal-mongering poison life in the provinces [p. 39].

Or Balzac may feel that we need instruction in the effects of various forms of social behaviour:

Drunkenness, like addiction to study, makes a fat man fatter and a thin man thinner [p. 7].

Theft always leads to murder [p. 20].

Ridicule is most often incurred by the carrying of fine sentiment, good points and special ability to extremes [p. 39].

And he may feel a word of explanation from him, as omniscient narrator, is necessary for a proper understanding of the action:

Here perhaps a word about Séchard's establishment is needed [p. 8].

Ninety per cent of our readers will find the following details as appetizing as the spiciest news-item [p. 523].

The more succinct our account of Petit-Claud's feats, the better this page of exclusively judicial information will be for the understanding of the story [p. 543].

To put debtors under arrest in the provinces is as exceptional and abnormal an occurrence as could be imagined [p. 557].

Or Balzac may give his own interpretation of a moral problem, such as suicide:

> Suicide results from a feeling which if you like we will call self-esteem in order not to confuse it with sense of honour. The day when a man despises himself, the day when he sees that others despise him, the moment when the realities of life are at variance with his hopes, he kills himself and thus pays homage to society, refusing to stand before it stripped of his virtues or his splendour. Whatever one may say, amongst atheists (exception must be made for the Christian view of suicide) cowards alone accept a life of dishonour [p. 633].

All these digressions, truisms, and personal interventions which are such a conspicuous part of Balzac's writing are at variance with the impersonality of the later Realist writers. In the same category must fall certain aspects of his work which are more typical of Romantic literature than Realist writing: such details as, 'Thereupon Lucien explained Coralie's situation, in a low voice and whispering in the silk-merchant's ear, so close that the latter could hear the humiliated poet's heart-beats' (p. 450); or 'Petit-Claud looked at Lucien with his gimlet-shaped nose screwed up to resemble a question-mark' (p. 604) can hardly be considered to owe much to observation of real life. Similarly, literary conventions such as a character thinking aloud and being conveniently overheard, as when Petit-Claud says to himself, 'Oh! If only Cérizet were here!' and from behind a partition comes the response, ' "I *am* here", said Cérizet,' cannot be regarded as characteristic of Realism. Nor can such sentimental descriptions as Lucien's final departure from his sister—the incident itself may be true to life but Balzac's presentation makes it into pure Romanticism: 'After writing this letter Lucien went noiselessly downstairs, laid it on his nephew's cradle, imprinted a last kiss, moist with tears, on the brow of his sleeping sister and left the room' (p. 632).

Yet there is very little point in picking out such non-Realist elements in Balzac's work—we have seen above that he was too early to subscribe to Realist doctrine and there is no cause for surprise in the fact that he does not follow to the letter theories formulated after his death. What we can say is that by his choice of characters, his treatment of contemporary society and his use of physical settings he conforms to the main tenets of modern Realism. His 'circumstantial view of life' has come to be accepted as the 'formal realism' of the novel, as Ian Watt puts it,[19] that literary attitude which is most typical of the novel form. Although, as we have seen, the events in Lucien's life are not always convincing in themselves, when viewed as a whole they create a world with enough resemblances to the real world to persuade us that Lucien might have existed and that the society in which he lived was very much as Balzac describes it. The illusion of reality is such that it is almost impossible for us not to bridge the gap between literature and life and to draw conclusions from the novel which are applicable to our own existence: to be on our guard against people such as Lucien and against societies which embrace the values shown in *Lost Illusions*. It is perhaps in this fundamental respect that the novel has most claim to be called a realist work.

NOTES

1. C. Baudelaire, *Curiosités esthétiques*, Conard, Paris, 1923, pp. 225–6.
2. H. de Balzac, *La Comédie humaine*, Bibliothèque de la Pléiade, Paris, 1951, vi. 66.
3. Details of the contemporary critical reaction to Balzac may be found in the compilation by B. Weinberg, *French Realism: the critical reaction, 1830–1870*, O.U.P., 1937, pp. 39–71.
4. C. Baudelaire, *L'Art romantique*, Conard, Paris, 1925, p. 168.
5. F. Brunetière, *Le Roman naturaliste*, Calmann-Lévy, Paris, 1896, p. 7.
6. M. Blanchot, *Faux Pas*, Gallimard, Paris, 1943, p. 213.
7. M. Blanchot, op. cit., p. 216.
8. A. Béguin, *Balzac visionnaire*, Skira, Geneva, 1946, p. 118.
9. M. Levaillant, 'Balzac visionnaire de la réalité' in *Le Livre du Centenaire*, Flammarion, Paris, 1952, p. 35.
10. G. Lukács, *Studies in European Realism*, Hillway, London, 1950, p. 33.
11. G. Pradalié, *Balzac historien. La Société de la Restauration*, Presses universitaires de France, Paris, 1955, p. 296.
12. E. Auerbach, *Mimesis*, Princeton U.P., 1953, p. 6.
13. References to the text are to the translation by H. J. Hunt in the Penguin Classics series, published by Penguin Books in 1971. (The original French text was first published in three parts between 1837 and 1843.)
14. J. Gaulmier, 'Monde balzacien et monde réel: notes sur *Illusions perdues*' in *Balzac and the Nineteenth Century*, ed. D. G. Charlton and others, Leicester U.P., 1972, p. 79.
15. H. de. Balzac, op. cit., iv. 335.
16. H. de. Balzac, op. cit., iv. 69.
17. G. Lukács, op. cit., p. 50.
18. G. Lukács, op. cit., p. 49.
19. I. Watt, *The Rise of the Novel*, Chatto and Windus, London, 1960, p. 32.

3

I. S. Turgenev: *Fathers and Sons* (1862)

Peter Henry

CHOOSING TURGENEV, by common consent the smallest of the three Russian literary giants, to represent the Russian contribution to nineteenth-century Realism requires explanation. Tolstoy and Dostoyevsky tower above the scene of literary controversy, schools and movements and cannot be encompassed—as Turgenev can—within a study of Realism as envisaged here. Moreover, Turgenev was the first Russian writer to become known in the West, his works being the first to be translated into Western languages. His novels—*Rudin* (1856), *A Nest of the Gentry* (1859), *On the Eve* (1860), *Fathers and Sons* (1862), *Smoke* (1867) and *Virgin Soil* (1877)—appeared within the period of Realism and established his fame as one of the world's great writers. His personality and his work made a major impact. A wealthy land-owning aristocrat of great erudition and enlightened outlook, he spent a considerable part of his life in the West, notably in France, where this 'gentilhomme russe et citoyen du monde' was hailed as arbiter on artistic, moral, and social issues on whom the status of near-oracular wisdom was conferred; above all as the interpreter and incarnation of Russia, revealing to an incredulous West the vastness, complexity, and the cultural riches of his enigmatic country.

In France he was instantly revered as one of the masters and innovators of prose fiction—some of the praise lavished on him strikes the modern reader as excessive. Flaubert and Turgenev became intimate friends during the last decade of their lives—Flaubert died in 1880 and Turgenev three years later—and maintained an active correspondence of major importance to the student of prose fiction. Another personal friend and admirer of his art was the American novelist and critic Henry James, then at the beginning of his career; and it is symptomatic of Turgenev's standing in the French literary world that James included his essay on Turgenev in a volume entitled *French Poets and Novelists*.[1] What Turgenev had done for Russian literature was well stated by Maurice Baring, who said that it was chiefly through his work that 'Europe became aware that novels were being written [in Russia] in which dramatic issues, as poignant and terrible as those of Greek tragedy, arose simply out of the clash of certain characters in everyday life.'[2]

On these grounds, Turgenev's most important novel occupies a rightful place in a volume on nineteenth-century Realism. A further justification lies in his importance, and that of *Fathers and Sons*, for several of the other writers in this volume. When writing *The Red Room*, Strindberg was well aware of Turgenev's work, and Bazarov is of self-evident importance within that novel. There is a striking similarity in the attitudes to the common folk of Flaubert's Sénécal and Bazarov. George Eliot, in *Middlemarch*, deals with artistic, social, and ethical issues arising from the cult of Science and these are echoed in Turgenev's novel. There are also striking similarities between him and Fontane, in their cautious scepticism and their approach to writing. Turgenev was Dean Howells's hero as practitioner of the Realist craft.

Turgenev's work may pale alongside the range, depth, and power of Tolstoy and Dostoyevsky. His restrained tone, the leisurely pace of his narrative, the restricted scale in time, space, and characters, and his preference for ideological compromise inevitably cause him to suffer in comparison. Yet this, combined with a certain 'Victorian' quality about his outlook and work, made him all the more acceptable as a 'European'.

From its inception, Russian Realism stressed the importance of the environment as conditioning human character and behaviour. Hence the prominence of descriptions of the hero's social background and his reaction to it. A general feature of Russian Realists is that they produced biographical novels, containing character studies rather than elaborate action-filled plots. They probed deeper into the human mind than most of their Western contemporaries, and their Realism, notably that of Dostoyevsky and Tolstoy, contains a major psychological dimension, including investigations of the irrational, the pathological and the mystical experience.

The works of Realist writers, the Russians in particular, pose fundamental issues—the meaning of life, the nature of Man, human relationships, the structure of Society. The Realist seeks to understand reality at a deep level: as Turgenev said 'to try not only to capture life in all its manifestations, but to understand it, understand the laws according to which it moves, which are not always revealed; and through and beyond the play of the fortuitous he must attain to types—and for all that remain faithful to the truth, not be content with a superficial study, and avoid cheap effects and falsity'.[3] This is the writer speaking as artist-philosopher, and less as recorder or social reformer.

Among the characteristics of the Russian novelists one must include: an enlightened if not always narrowly 'progressive' philosophy and the presence in their works of a valid 'general idea'; a probing into the complexity and deeper causal links of life; a broad range of vision and a closeness to contemporary life; a concern for 'the Truth' that subsumes and transcends factual accuracy and credibility. The 'expository' factor, a high degree of 'civic' commitment, is important in their works, though attempts to reduce their art to the level of statements of social indignation—'It is wrong to live like this!'—take the sociological approach to absurd lengths. On the other hand, owing to the deep and explicit social involvement of the Russian novelists, it is difficult and misleading to judge Russian Realist literature along narrowly aesthetic lines. Protests against the 'prostitution of the arts for utilitarian ends' and the condemnation of applying 'extra-literary criteria' are therefore both unhelpful and often irrelevant.

Turgenev's novel is a good example of the 'technique of impersonality' described by Jenkins.[4] It is as much a 'convincing lie' as any other work of fiction: the fact that his picture of life lacks the reliable accuracy of a historical document is not a defect; we believe in this fictional and fictitious record, fully aware how 'untrue' it is. Turgenev has said, comparing Russian and French prose fiction: 'Our imagination is poor . . . yet we are not as far from the truth of life as the French.'[5] He may have been unfair to the French and can hardly have been thinking of Dostoyevsky, but his point is clear.

It is probable that in Russia the term 'Realism' was first used to describe an artistic method (as opposed to a philosophical outlook) in 1849 in a discussion of the early work of Turgenev and Goncharov,[6] but came to be widely used only in the 1860s. It is symptomatic of the interaction of art and politics in Russia that within a few years of being introduced as a literary concept, 'Realism' had acquired a political meaning and replaced 'Nihilism', when the radical critic D. I. Pisarev wrote a long article, 'Realists' (1864), in

which he discussed Turgenev's Bazarov as the representative of
'Our Realism'—that of the Russian revolutionaries.

According to the nineteenth-century democratic critics—
Belinsky, Chernyshevsky, and Dobrolyubov[7]—the pioneers of
Russian Realism were Gogol and other men of the 'Natural School'
of the 1840s and 50s—the early work of Turgenev (especially *A
Sportsman's Sketches*) and Dostoyevsky (*Poor Folk*), Herzen and
others. These early 'Realists' produced accurate pictures of the
'physiology' of contemporary life, with emphasis on the seamy
side. They recorded this external reality in great detail and their
works abound in meticulous, ethnographical descriptions of local
customs, the speech, mannerisms, and modes of dress of artisans
and peasants, and provided photographically detailed pictures of
streets, shops, and offices and the interiors of seedy apartments and
peasant huts. Traces of such descriptive realism can be seen in
Fathers and Sons.

Committed to providing accurate pictures of contemporary life,
Russian writers often selected little-known parts of the country or
neglected social groups. This is particularly true of Turgenev, whose
first major work, *A Sportsman's Sketches* (1847–52), abounds in
ethnographical and sociological information about the Russian
peasant. It was also his contribution to the cause of Emancipation.
He expected his works to be judged on their factual accuracy and the
typicality and life-like qualities of his characters, aware that the
purely aesthetic aspect often came a poor second in the critics'
minds. In an assessment of his Realism this factor must therefore be
taken into account.

In his novels and stories Turgenev describes ordinary people who
are typical of their times and social class. This stress on normalcy and
the subsequent absence of the heroic, the melodramatic, and the
exceptional—well described by Williams as the Realist wager[8]—is,
of course, a characteristic of all Realist fiction. It is not invalidated
by the fact that Turgenev focuses on 'new' men like Rudin, Insarov,
and Bazarov, who as representatives of new social types are perfectly credible in the context of their times; they are 'exceptional' in
a relative sense only.

Prosper Mérimée said aptly that Turgenev 'excludes from his
works the themes of great crimes, you will find no tragic scenes in
them. There are few events in his novels. Their plots are very

simple, there is nothing in them that diverges from normal life and this is a consequence of his love of Truth.'⁹ As regards *Fathers and Sons* the only point here that has to be refuted is the 'absence of tragic scenes'. The death of Bazarov, described in terms of controlled intensity, is not only deeply moving, but tragic in the precise, Greek sense of the word.

Stated in crude, skeletal form, the typical Turgenevian novel is a short, compact work of some 200 pages, it covers a short time span, involves a small number of characters, and operates within a restricted location. Basically, it is 'a month in the country', where the main action takes place, followed by some sort of epilogue. The narrative is in strict chronological order, with some explanatory biographical digressions. The setting is a Russian country estate, 'a nest of the gentry', and into this static aristocratic microcosm movement is injected by the intrusion of an Outsider—Rudin, Insarov, Bazarov. The Outsider exerts a powerful impact on what is an uncongenial and even hostile social environment, like some bacillus suspended in an alien culture, with the author standing by to observe and record the reactions it sets off. The conflicts and tensions that arise normally include a love relationship between the Outsider and the young heroine, the daughter of the aristocratic household, e.g. Rudin and Natalya. The hero arouses in her a resolve to escape from her idle, claustrophobic world and involve herself in some worthwhile Cause in the outside world, and she sees him as her saviour. The crisis occurs in a confrontation between them, when his inspiring words have to be transformed into decisive action. He fails the test and is exposed as her moral inferior, a fraud and a weakling, and disappears from the scene to wander through life to a futile death. The heroine is left with a legacy of disillusionment and shattered hopes, while for the others life goes on along its pre-ordained course.

Fathers and Sons is a more complex and at the same time more refined variant on this formula. Bazarov is a strong man—perhaps the only successful one in all of Turgenev's novels—who is exposed to the destructive power of love, or rather, the unexpected and unwelcome confrontation with his own sexuality, which disrupts his inner balance and threatens to transform him into a creature of self-doubt. And he comes close to losing control of his life and to losing faith in his mission. It is true that the disturbance of his self-assuredness was set off by an encounter with an intriguing woman, but

Odintsova at twenty-eight and widowed is no young Turgenevian virgin on the threshold of life. That role, in diluted form, is shared by secondary characters—Fenichka, Nikolai Petrovich's mistress, and Odintsova's younger sister Katya, whose aspirations are significantly more prosaic and attainable than those of Natalya, Elena, and Liza in the earlier novels. Nonetheless, those who insist that all of Turgenev's novels are love stories are entitled to include *Fathers and Sons* in their list. The love theme is undeniably there, in triplicate even: Ivan Petrovich and Fenichka, Arkady and Katya, Bazarov and Odintsova—one could even add Pavel Petrovich with his nostalgic memories of 'Countess R.' and his ambiguous relationship with Fenichka. Thus, at one level, this, too, is a love story. The Russian critic Yu. Aikhenval'd had a point when he described Turgenev's novels as 'parthenocentric'.[10]

But *Fathers and Sons* is more than that. It is an important political novel recording a crucial stage in Russian social history, the emergence of the militant, revolutionary wing of the Russian Intelligentsia. What fascinated the social historian in Turgenev was the appearance of new men and new attitudes in contemporary Russian Society. He had a unique gift for observing and recording these subtle shifts at the very beginning of their occurrence. As a Realist he therefore asks and deserves to be judged on the historical validity, as well as the aesthetic merits, of his portrayal of the succeeding waves of 'new' men: Rudin, the compulsive and eloquent idealist of the 1840s who died on the barricades of Paris of 1848; Lavretzky, the Westerner disillusioned by the failure of that Year of Revolution and returning to the native soil of Russia and the nostalgic dreams of the Slavophile; Insarov, a first attempt at portraying a revolutionary, whom Turgenev felt compelled to make a Bulgarian patriot, precisely because he could not yet detect a Russian prototype and would not rely on imagination alone; and Bazarov, the Russian Nihilist, drawn from contemporary life in the most real sense, about whose veracity Turgenev had doubts, because 'no one else had yet portrayed this type, and I was afraid I was chasing a phantom'.[11] Yet he went ahead, because his intuition convinced him of the crucial importance of the Nihilists and because he had met at least one real-life Nihilist himself. He admitted that he saw Bazarov 'powerfully but not very clearly.' Later, in *Virgin Soil*, he portrayed, less successfully, the Russian Populists of the 1870s. One reason for the relative failure of this novel was that at the time of writing Turgenev had been living abroad for many years and was out of touch with Russian life. This contributed both to the lack of credibility of his Populists as fictional characters and to their rejection by his Russian readers as representatives of the movement. For Turgenev, historical veracity seemed to be a pre-condition for achieving artistic truth.

Turgenev's Realism consists in a picture of reality severely subordinated to his own artistic principles. Real life was not given free rein, there is no rambling documentary narrative, that *bytovaya literatura* that was being poured out in quantity about this time, whether in long descriptive chronicles in the manner of the Natural School, or the factual sketch (*ocherk*) by Gleb Uspensky or other Populists.[12] With him, the principle of selection had a high priority. There is no round-the-clock diary, no indiscriminate camera technique. While his novel has the air of simple and straightforward narrative, he manipulates his material in a number of significant ways that will be discussed below.

The overriding priority in Turgenev's artistic credo was loyalty to his personal vision of reality. Out of his raw material he created a subtly balanced and aesthetically satisfying work of art, subordinated to exacting standards of artistic design and control. This fitted him more closely into the European literary tradition than his greater contemporaries, Tolstoy and Dostoyevsky. A penetrating observer of the human dilemma, he describes his characters with sympathy, understanding, and benevolent irony. But with regard to form, it has been objected that in his hands the novel became too elegantly shaped, too well controlled, too well rounded, that he imposed an impossibly well ordered patterning on the amorphous chaos of real life, his raw material. But his enduring achievement is that, at least in his best works, his conscious artistry has not resulted in artificiality. The illusion of life as conjured up in his novels generally succeeds; when it does, it has an uncontrived, three-dimensional quality and his characters are alive and psychologically convincing within the studied elegance of his artistic form.

Turgenev first mentioned the idea of writing *Fathers and Sons* in August 1860, while staying at Ventnor on the Isle of Wight. He began writing it there, then moved to Paris where he continued working on it, until in November he wrote to Leo Tolstoy that 'the tale had got stuck half-way'. He returned to Russia and completed the first version of the novel at his estate in Spasskoye in August

1861, almost exactly a year after starting it. It appeared in the conservative literary journal *The Russian Messenger* early in 1862 and was published in book form later that year. There are a number of discrepancies—some of them of major importance—between the manuscript, the first version as published in the journal, and the final text.

It is typical of Turgenev's art that what drove him to writing the novel was not an insistent idea he wanted to expound, nor did he start from any major event or controversy. His novels are primarily character studies and he always started from a 'living person', who was the basis for his central character. 'I have never attempted to "create a character" unless as my point of departure I had, not an idea, but a living person, to whom appropriate elements were gradually added.'[13] He disclaimed any great powers of inventiveness and therefore needed 'firm ground under his feet'. This 'living person' was a young Russian provincial doctor whom he had met on a train journey and who had impressed him profoundly. In Turgenev's view, 'this remarkable young man embodied an element that had only recently come into being and had not yet crystallised, which was subsequently given the name of Nihilism.'[14] Much speculation as to the identity of this 'Dr. D.', who, Turgenev states, had died just before he started on the novel, has yielded no conclusive answers; nor is this ultimately very important. Though the dividing line between real-life prototypes, literary portraits, and fictional characters is necessarily a very fine one, Turgenev angrily rejected suggestions that he ever 'copied' scenes and persons from life, denied that he drew portraits of real persons or even consciously used prototypes; all that he would acknowledge was that he needed some real person or persons as his 'point of departure', that is, he used reality as his spring-board, to use Flaubert's expression. While he created the character of Bazarov persons other than 'Dr. D.' must have entered his mind—he states that he looked around for other representatives of this type and studied them closely. Belinsky—to whose memory the novel is dedicated—and Dobrolyubov have been suggested as being among these, as well as the 'men of *The Russian Word*,' the radical critic Pisarev and his associates. These, and doubtless others, provided some of 'the elements that were gradually added'. But beyond 'Dr. D.' Turgenev named no other prototypes for Bazarov, though after the hostile reception his novel had had, he felt driven to 'identify' some of the other characters: 'Nikolai

Petrovich—that's me, Ogaryov and thousands others.'[15] Arkady's father therefore represents a Russian social type of the times, but it is not implied that the author himself or any other specific person was his prototype. He said similarly vague things about Pavel Petrovich and Odintsova, and it seems that Turgenev wanted the best of both worlds: while denying that he 'copied from life', he insisted on the typicality and life-like qualities of his characters. This is perhaps what makes them both 'realistic' and truly fictional.

Bazarov is therefore not 'Dr. D.' lifted from life and placed in the novel any more than Nikolai Petrovich is a self-portrait by the author. Even Leo Tolstoy, though he openly admitted that he 'drew from life' and introduced friends and relatives, and himself, into his novels, did not leave his prototypes as untransformed 'things of fact'. To this extent, the very notion of 'reproduction of reality' in terms of character portraits is a virtual impossibility. Tolstoy's Napoleon or Tsar Alexander are no more 'real' than his 'fictional' characters.

It was Turgenev's method to focus on a particular character, sometimes, arguably, on two—Rudin, Liza—Lavretzky, Elena—Insarov, Bazarov. *Fathers and Sons* is not so much a novel about Nihilism, but about a Nihilist, and Bazarov is no mere mouthpiece for an ideology, but a person of flesh and blood, capable of self-contradiction and error. Turgenev's concept of man caused him to endow the 'strong' Bazarov, his 'favourite child', with weaknesses that were seriously to affect his capacity for decisive action and for fulfilling his life purpose.

As in most of his novels, the action grew out of the personalities and interplay of his characters. Turgenev's method was first to develop his main character, then add others, writing out their biographies on separate sheets of paper. Only then did he write a brief summary of the action. In order to get 'inside' his main character, he made up Bazarov's diary and notebook, containing his probable experiences and views. It is therefore very much a planned novel and his characters did not take on an independent existence during the writing—which is important when considering the view that the 'break' in Bazarov in the middle of the novel, as well as his death, are both unexpected and inappropriate, that, as Hertsen had suggested, Turgenev killed off his hero because he did not know what to do with him. Richard Freeborn persuasively argues that he may well have started from the death of Bazarov.[16] Turgenev was satisfied that his portrayal of Bazarov was psychologically valid; that the contemporary Radicals refused to see themselves mirrored in him is another matter.

Turgenev once said of his novels that they lacked 'architecture'. The structural pattern of *Fathers and Sons* would cause one to disagree with him. The story is told in strict chronological sequence, with the addition of several biographical digressions. It opens with the arrival of two young men, Arkady and his friend Bazarov, at Maryino, the estate of Arkady's father, Nikolai Petrovich Kirsanov. They have newly graduated from St. Petersburg University and now stay at Maryino for about a fortnight. During this time a personal and ideological antagonism develops between the 'Fathers', represented primarily by Pavel Petrovich, Arkady's uncle who is also living on the estate, and the 'Sons', represented by the radical Bazarov and, to a sharply decreasing extent, by Arkady. Another important member of the Kirsanov household is Fenichka, a former peasant girl who is Nikolai Petrovich's mistress and mother of his baby son. The two young friends pay a visit to the provincial town, where, at the Governor's ball, they meet Anna Sergeyevna Odintsova, the young widow of a rich landowner, who is the heroine of the novel. From here, Arkady and Bazarov visit Odintsova at her estate at Nikolskoye, where they spend another fortnight and Bazarov to his own astonishment and dismay falls in love with Odintsova, while Arkady is attracted to her younger sister Katya. Next they visit the small estate of Bazarov's parents, where they stay only three days and abruptly return to Maryino, calling briefly at Nikolskoye on the way. At Maryino, during Arkady's absence—he has gone to woo his Katya—the conflict between Bazarov and Pavel Petrovich culminates in a duel, in which the latter is slightly injured. Bazarov departs, calls again at Nikolskoye, takes his leave of Odintsova, and returns to his parents. Here he helps his father, a retired army surgeon, in his medical practice. While working in a typhus epidemic among the peasants, Bazarov performs an autopsy, is himself infected and dies.

In all, the action extends over no more than two months.[17] There is an Epilogue, set six months after Bazarov's death, which contains a description of a double wedding (Nikolai Petrovich and Fenichka, Arkady and Katya). The further lives of the other surviving characters are briefly filled in—Pavel Petrovich has emigrated and lives the life of an aristocratic exile in Dresden. Odintsova has married again, this time an able lawyer, 'kind-hearted and as cold as ice', thereby putting the seal on her emotional and social adventures. The final paragraph shows Bazarov's aged parents visiting their son's grave.

Thus the events are confined to four places, each with its own unmistakable identity. The action is broken up into more or less self-contained sections by the travels of Bazarov and Arkady between these places. These provide a simple and convenient device for achieving movement and change in the narrative, while preserving unity and continuity. What further emerges is that the action is not a steady flow of events, but rather a skilfully linked series of episodic 'scenes'.

One is immediately struck by the wonderfully visual quality of Turgenev's work. He describes carefully the natural surroundings of his action, though there are few nature descriptions for their own sakes, few set pieces, such as occur frequently in his other works. The physical setting is done with a fine selective eye for the telling detail, which sometimes distracts attention from the fact that a total picture has in fact not been provided. Such descriptions are regularly broken up and placed strategically in the action at the psychologically right moment, rather than being delivered *in toto* at the first available opportunity. The drive to Maryino in Chapter 3 is a good example of how such a description is built up gradually in small appropriate amounts, without unduly holding up the narrative. Similarly, the description of Nikolskoye is given in several stages, and that of Arkady's and Katya's 'special' place—'the Grecian portico made in Russian brick'—is delayed until Chapter 26, when it has become emotionally relevant.

The same is true of the characters. One sees them clearly and fully described—their clothing, their facial expression, their stance, their gesturing and the way they move about. Here Turgenev reveals his great powers of observation, or rather his skill in conveying visually the fiction he is creating. He had the ability, so vital for the Realist with his concern with the commonplace, to make the most ordinary and ephemeral character fascinating. This is the possibly overelaborate description of the steward of Bazarov's parents: 'This Timofeich, a seasoned and astute old man with faded yellow hair, a red weather-beaten face and tiny teardrops in his shrunken eyes had unexpectedly confronted Bazarov, wearing a short coat of greyish-blue cloth belted with a leather thong, and tarred boots' (p. 97). This person has a temporary importance in that his arrival at Nikolskoye caused a forward movement in the action and he is a visual reminder to Bazarov that he had forgotten about his purpose of going straight to his parents. Timofeich is engaged in conversation long enough for the reader to take in his appearance. At the end of the scene he is seen pulling his cap over his eyes with both hands and getting into his rickety *drozhky*. Timofeich is a minor character, but his image is fixed in the reader's mind and he will recognize him at his next appearance.

Henry James was the first to draw attention to the visual and dramatic qualities of Turgenev's novels.

Turgenev might often be a vain demonstrator and a very dull novelist if he were not so constantly careful to be a dramatist. Everything, with him, takes the dramatic form; he is apparently unable to conceive anything independently of it, he has no recognition of unembodied ideas; an idea, with him, is such and such an individual, with such and such a nose and chin, such and such a hat and waistcoat . . . In this way, as we read, we are always looking and listening.[18]

Fathers and Sons is an excellent example of this. It has a basically dramatic, i.e. scenic, structure, consisting, as stated, of a series of visually effective episodes. It has to be admitted that, in making such extensive use of dramatic devices, Turgenev reaches the outer limits of Realist technique. This aspect of Turgenev's art is convincingly discussed in Richard Freeborn's classic study of Turgenev.[19] The novel's restricted number of 'foci', as Freeborn puts it, are Maryino, struggling to retain its standing and economic viability, the provincial town, the neat and prosperous Nikolskoye, and the modest, homely, and old-Russian estate of Bazarov's parents. The characters are psychologically and practically related to their location, from which they do not move; if they do, there is an artistic reason for making them appear out of place, like Sitnikov's unwarranted and unwelcome visit to Nikolskoye in Chapter 19.

Frequently Turgenev places his characters in specific settings where their encounters are enacted, occasionally in a group situation, as in the vital discussion over dinner in Chapter 10, the Governor's ball in Chapter 14, or the double wedding in the Epilogue; more commonly in a one-to-one situation, as in the several duologues between Arkady and Bazarov, the conversations between the brothers Kirsanov, Bazarov and Odintsova, Arkady and Katya, etc.

Hence the structural importance of dialogue in the novel, in particular duologues, which mark vital stages in the narrative. In them important ideological and social attitudes are expounded, often in the manner of the Socratic dialogue. Several chapters consist entirely of conversation. But such conversations are not allowed to develop into extended and independent elements divorced from their proper place in the novel. Their content is never allowed to break the overall artistic form. They are generally kept down to manageable proportions and tend not to exceed the confines of a brief chapter. If they do become too long, they are broken off and resumed at a later stage.

Turgenev was at pains to integrate much of his material into such dialogues, even when this created new structural problems. Thus in Chapter 6 Arkady, while talking to Bazarov, prepares to give his uncle's biography, 'which the reader will find in the following chapter'. The action is stopped and the author takes over from Arkady, with an attempt at the end of the chapter to reintegrate this information into the conversation of the two characters: 'So you see, Eugene,' said Arkady, *ending his account* [my italics; the words are omitted in the Signet translation], 'how unfair you were in judging my uncle!' (p. 39). Similarly, the biography of Nikolai Petrovich, already referred to, is inserted into the opening scene of the novel.

Conversations, like most episodes in the novel, do not take place in some visual vacuum. However significant, they never lose their concrete setting and one hears the characters speak—each has his own distinctive vocabulary and intonation—even more, one *sees* them speak. For example, on hearing the word Nihilism for the first time, Pavel Petrovich has a typically melodramatic response: 'he poised his knife in the air with a piece of butter on the tip of the blade and froze into immobility', and only resumed his buttering later, when he had commented that a Nihilist must be 'somebody who respects nothing' (p. 29). His slightly comical frozen gesture is more eloquent of his distaste for Bazarov and his Nihilism than the actual words he uttered.

Monologues, as distinct from thoughts and emotions briefly summarized by the author, are almost totally absent, although on occasion they are used in the nature of humorous 'asides'. When during his visit to Fenichka in Chapter 8 Pavel Petrovich makes the inevitable comparison between his young nephew and his brother, ' "Whom else should he be like?" Fenichka thought.' Such 'asides' are used to brilliant effect during the duel between Bazarov and

Pavel Petrovich. The entire action is seen through Bazarov's eyes and his amused, down-to-earth remarks to himself enhance the ludicrous effect of the confrontation of the two socially very disparate adversaries. Previously, after being detected kissing Fenichka, he had congratulated himself on 'joining the ranks of the gay Lotharios'. Similarly, in a simultaneous aside both Arkady and Katya try to dismiss Odintsova from their minds: 'The thought flashed through his mind: "What's she got to do with it?"—"What's she got to do with it?" [was the thought that] also flashed through her mind' (p. 171).

The absence of other literary devices like letters and diary entries, beloved of most novelists and dramatists, enhances the illusion that events occur entirely in the present and in the presence of author-narrator and reader. Dispensing with such devices gives the work a compact and severely controlled form.

Yet the analogy with the theatre may be taken further. Turgenev the novelist provides stage directions in the manner of playwright and producer. Not only every 'speaking' character, but even some of the 'walk-on' characters are accorded full visual description, though the method varies according to the standing of the character in the hierarchy of the cast. In addition to the description of Timofeich (above), the beginning of Chapter 4 provides a good example of the description of minor characters. As Nikolai Petrovich, his son and Bazarov arrive at the estate, they are greeted only by a girl of about twelve, followed by a 'lad, very like Peter [who has already been described], wearing a grey livery jacket with white crested buttons' (p. 21). If the girl is nameless and does not exist visually, the young boy, also nameless, is described entirely in terms of his clothes, emphasizing perhaps that he is not an independent individual, but is the property of Pavel Petrovich.

Essential information about a major character like Pavel Petrovich is provided in a more complex way, being distributed within the narrative in a seemingly random manner. He was mentioned twice in the biography of his brother; Arkady's first question is about his uncle; he is referred to when his servant appears on the porch. He makes a suitably delayed appearance, unnamed at first, and described in terms of his elegant clothes—his dark English suit, fashionable low cravat and patent leather shoes, which emphasize his incongruity on an estate deep in the Russian countryside. His good looks and aristocratic bearing are stressed throughout and even visually he makes a striking contrast with Bazarov, illustrating this latent anti-pathy between the two ideological and social antagonists that is present from the start. Later, an entire chapter is devoted to his biography (Chapter 8).

These descriptions are remarkable for the amount of detail they provide—there is nothing here resembling a visual cliché. Tur-genev is at pains to convey the uniqueness of his character, described in an almost Dickensian manner of emphasizing the odd and the unusual; a few degrees further in this direction would give us a caricature, a danger from which Turgenev's sense of moderation usually saves him. A minor character is given the full visual treat-ment in one go, as he comes on stage. The staggered method of releasing information, reserved for his important characters, achieves a full portrait without unduly retarding the action. In a similar, apparently casual manner, we are provided with essential socio-economic information during the drive to Maryino.

That nothing whatever is said about Bazarov's past makes him unique in Turgenev's novels, and this is another method of stress-ing his 'strangeness'. He exists entirely in the present, his personality being gradually revealed in his impact on virtually all other charac-ters, not only his aristocratic opponents, but Fenichka, his parents, peasants, village boys, his briefly loyal acolyte Arkady, and Sitnikov and Kukshina, his spurious sympathizers.

A typically Turgenevan device for heightening the dramatic ten-sion is to create a mood of expectancy, where a character, expected to occupy the centre of the stage, fails to appear or does not have attention focused on him; instead, the 'wrong' person arrives and takes his place. *Fathers and Sons* opens with the father waiting for his son, while it is his unexpected and unknown plebeian companion who is to dominate and disrupt life at Maryino. A further echo of this device occurs in Chapter 11. Nikolai Petrovich sits late at night absorbed in loving memories of his dead wife, when he hears the voice of Fenichka, her substitute in the present. The result is an emotional turmoil, the elegaic mood is broken and the normally liberal and gentle Nikolai Petrovich curtly dismisses his mistress, aware of the traces of the feudal lord welling up in him. A similar deception is worked in that initially it had been Arkady and not Bazarov who felt drawn towards Odintsova.

Another dramatic device that Turgenev used in this novel was later to be made famous by Chekhov, that of 'strophe' and 'anti-

strophe'. Two separate groups of characters are on stage simultaneously and among one of these a lyrical mood of hopefulness,
make-believe, or intimacy builds up. This mood is then rudely,
though, it seems, inadvertently, shattered by the other group, their
intrusion being timed to occur as the mood reaches its high point.
The obvious but by no means only example in *Fathers and Sons* of
this device occurs during the drive home in Chapter 3. Arkady and
his father are in an intimate, sentimental mood, and as the latter is
reciting Pushkin—' "Arkady!", Bazarov shouted from the tarantass.
"Will you send some matches over? I've none left to light my pipe
with." Nikolai Petrovich fell silent.' Arkady, in imitation of his friend
and mentor, also starts smoking a pipe and the acrid smell of cheap
tobacco obliterates the mood of intimacy between father and son.

The pairing of characters forms an important element in the
structure of *Fathers and Sons*—Arkady and Bazarov, Ivan and Pavel
Petrovich, Odintsova and Katya, Bazarov's parents, Sitnikov and
Kukshina. In this way he is able to make the characters reveal themselves and render their attitudes and actions comprehensible without having to resort to authorial statements or to use the inner
monologue or other literary conventions. By this method he is also
able to fix their position within the hierarchy of his characters. The
consequent increase in the use of dialogue maintains the dramatic
movement of the narrative.

Turgenev develops the simple scheme of pairing by making a
number of permutations, as persons basically paired with their
'proper' partner are brought into temporary one-to-one relationships with members of other pairs. An obvious example is Fenichka.
Most typically she is shown with her baby son and Dunyasha. But
a number of emotional currents emanate from her, and at some stage
she attracts all the males in turn and thus is 'paired' with Arkady,
Bazarov, and Pavel Petrovich. Each of these encounters is important
for the novel: for Arkady the legalization of her status is of primary
concern; the antagonism between Bazarov and the Kirsanovs is
brought into relief by the trust Fenichka instinctively feels for him,
while his amorous impulse towards her provokes the duel between
him and Pavel Petrovich; Pavel Petrovich's visits embarrass her,
while for him she is a surrogate for his beloved 'Countess R.'—after
the duel he says that Fenichka has something in common with her,
'especially the upper part of her face. *C'est de la même famille*'
(p. 163).

It is a brilliant stroke of irony on Turgenev's part that Bazarov and Pavel Petrovich, so sharply contrasted in every way, are endowed with an essential identity as unsuccessful lovers as they face each other in the duel, consumed by emotions of hopeless love, each aware that he is fighting over a substitute for his real love. In the night before the duel, Bazarov had dreamt of Odintsova, who suggestively enough assumed 'the likeness of his mother and was followed by a kitten with black whiskers; the kitten turned out to be Fenichka' (p. 157). When Bazarov had injured his opponent, they both felt embarrassed and 'both were aware that they understood each other' (p. 171).

Here the parallelism is taken further, with the scales weighted in favour of Bazarov. His opponent is described as increasingly absurd, hypocritical, and irrelevant, and this is conveyed partly by the author and more importantly by Fenichka's response to the two men. Both had kissed her—Bazarov on a happy sunny morning in an idyllic setting, and Pavel Petrovich as he lay recovering from his trivial wound. Bazarov had implanted a protracted kiss on her lips, the latter pressed her hand to his lips without kissing it, only sighing feverishly. She had not resented Bazarov's kiss beyond the required display of outraged modesty; Pavel Petrovich's action is feebly disguised as growing out of concern that she love and never leave his brother. She cannot accept his attempt as anything but incredible and abnormal ('Good God, is he having a fit or something?'). Though her role is not as important as Odintsova's, she is both a focal character around whom much of the action revolves and an authority who in a feminine way passes judgement on the three dominant males of the novel—Bazarov, Nikolai Petrovich, and Pavel Petrovich.

If Turgenev wrote his novels in dramatic form—he was, after all, a dramatist, too[20]—it has to be conceded that on occasion he abused the rights of the producer, as when he has sets of characters overhearing each other so that crucial or embarrassing information is passed on 'by accident'. An example of this occurs in Chapter 26 where Arkady is telling Katya of his love for her and they overhear Bazarov and Odintsova discussing them; they also learn that Bazarov and Odintsova agree to terminate their relationship— emotional climax and anti-climax coinciding in too contrived a manner. Several other episodes have a 'stagey' quality, as for example the scene between Bazarov and Fenichka in Chapter 23, with Pavel

Petrovich as it were appearing at the back of the stage the very moment Bazarov implants the fatal kiss upon her lips. He appears almost in the manner of the Victorian villain and less as the instrument of retribution.

Other devices that contribute to the structural patterning of the novel include the foreshadowing of events and characters, and the repetition of situations with new meaning and emotional content. Thus Nihilism is expounded on two major occasions, once by Arkady and once by Bazarov. The duel between Pavel Petrovich and Bazarov is preceded by a narrowly avoided duel between Arkady and Bazarov, which is meaningful at both the personal and the ideological levels. It is stressed that Bazarov takes leave of Odintsova in the very room in which he had declared his love for her. There are numerous other examples of this technique.

One can also detect a number of symbols in the novel, generally too well concealed to obtrude unduly. One is the symbol of the crossroads, illustrating the agonizing problem of choice as in Chapter 22, where one road leads to Maryino, and the other to Nikolskoye—Bazarov makes the mistake of choosing the latter; and the parting of the ways of the two friends in Chapter 26. Another, conceivably, is that of the caged bird in Fenichka's room; and, explicitly, that of Pavel Petrovich on his bed after the duel. 'He moistened his brow with eau-de-Cologne and closed his eyes. ... His handsome, emaciated head lay on the white pillow, like the head of a corpse. ... Indeed, he was a corpse' (p. 169). His 'death' represents the dying of his class and his fake agony contrasts with the poignant death of his adversary.

Turgenev employs a sleight-of-hand technique to achieve an easy transition from authorial narrative to dramatic action, changing both tone and direction at the same time. Thus, during his unsuccessful card game with the priest in Chapter 21, Bazarov feels particularly frustrated and when his doting mother offers him yet another drink of wholesome blackcurrant juice, 'Bazarov merely shrugged his shoulders. "No," he said;' but this 'No', while appearing to be addressed to his mother, is addressed to Arkady on the following day. This transition terminates a stagnant emotional situation and replaces it by a vigorous and energetic mood, a prelude to action.[21]

On occasion, he conveys the illusion that the author is a mere observer, as on p. 183: ' "Of course you are free", Bazarov was heard to say after a while. But the rest was lost, the steps faded away . . . and silence supervened.' He denies himself any authorial omniscience and only rarely gives us definitive statements on his characters' inner motivations. In emotionally crucial situations, his sense of discretion causes him to tread delicately, as when Bazarov and Odintsova take leave of each other. 'Thus spoke Bazarov, and thus spoke Anna Sergeyevna; they both believed they were speaking the truth. Was there truth, the whole truth, in their words? They themselves didn't know, still less does the author' (p. 204).

Turgenev provides a picture of the prevailing intellectual and ideological ferment in terms of the preoccupations of his principal characters. He does this both in direct statements from the author, and more typically in dramatic form, in dialogue and full-scale debate, where opposing points of view are expounded.

This was the age of early 'vulgar' Materialism and Positivism, with Science as the new panacea for all those social ills that earlier generations of idealistic philosophisers had failed to cope with. Darwin's epoch-making *The Origins of Species* had been published in 1858, a year before the action of Turgenev's novel. If the 'fathers' were still concerned to define the essence of truth, the Good, and the Sublime, the 'sons' were engaged in scientific investigation along strictly empirical lines. They rejected not only all moral, philosophical, and aesthetic concepts, but all absolutes, overall 'truths', theories, and principles.

That this cult of Science was not confined to Russia is shown, for example, by George Eliot's *Middlemarch*, if it can be assumed that it deals essentially with mid-Victorian life and issues, where scientific inquiry is similarly regarded not merely as academically valid, but of relevance for social progress. The Tsarist Establishment was quick to sense this new threat to the *status quo* and the Natural Sciences came under strong official attack. It was not only that the Darwinian concept of Man contravened Christian teaching, but Science faculties were with every justification regarded as the breeding ground for social critics and revolutionaries.

The positive emphasis of the new men was on social utility and they were scornful of all the arts—poetry, music, painting—and the cult of Beauty in general, and that included the finer emotions like love. These were dismissed as useless pastimes, a form of self-indulgence and self-delusion. 'Beauty', for instance, which could not be proved as a scientific fact, was accordingly the result of optical and other illusions. Philosophical speculation was a futile exercise and deflected man from practical action. The very art of debating 'important' issues was an irrelevance, and the well presented argument, the neatly turned phrase, were dismissed as a waste of intellectual power.

It was the age of a new Rationalism and with it came the theory of 'enlightened egoism', as preached by Chernyshevsky and other Radicals. Convinced of the perfectibility of Man they started with self-improvement and self-interest, since this would lead to the enhanced social usefulness of the individual. To establish a new society along rational lines the old world had to be swept aside, complete with its outmoded ethical and aesthetic assumptions, its ignorance and superstitions, taboos, all forms of escapism, hypocrisy, and self-deception. The New Men knew no hesitations and no doubts; in their boundless self-confidence they felt little need to explain or justify themselves to the 'Fathers'; they knew they were right.

These developments coincided and were linked with the emergence of a new and historically vital generation, that of the '*Raznochintsy*'.[22] Though of non-privileged origin, these men had entered the Intelligentsia and formed the radical, militant wing ('Revolutionary Democrats') of the revolutionary movement. Chief among them were men like the literary critics V. G. Belinsky, N. G. Chernyshevsky, and N. A. Dobrolyubov, whose uncompromising views on aesthetics and socio-political issues provided the ideological base for generations of revolutionary writers and critics, up to and including Soviet times. These men represent a typically Russian combination of socio-political thinker and literary critic. They came from humble backgrounds: Belinsky was the son of a naval surgeon, as Bazarov's father was a retired army surgeon; Chernyshevsky's and Dobrolyubov's fathers were village priests.

The *Raznochintsy* were atheists, materialists, and revolutionaries. Impatient with the eloquent rhetoric of their predecessors, the largely aristocratic and upper-middle class 'Men of the Forties', they were determined above all to act. Their programme was an assault not only on the political structure of Autocracy, but the entire social order. They championed the Russian peasant, still a serf until 1861, but cherished few of their opponents' illusions about him. Their attack on Society was both comprehensive and personalized in a typically Russian way. Respect for, and blind obedience to, authority

and tradition, hypocrisy and conformism with their corrosive effects
on Russian society, were seen as personal failings that had first to be
eradicated if a new, freer Society was to be established. Other
important aspects of their programme for a social revolution were
the emancipation of women and the abolition of the Family, which
they regarded as a reactionary institution. This is what makes
Arkady's concern that his father should marry Fenichka both topical
and faintly comical, for he claims that he has very modern views on
the institution of marriage; while the fact that Turgenev chose to
give a caricature portrait of the 'emancipated woman'—Kukshina—
shows clearly where his own sympathies lay.

Fathers and Sons is essentially the story of Bazarov. As a literary
hero, he was a new departure among the many 'Superfluous Men' in
nineteenth-century Russian fiction—Pushkin's Onegin, Lermontov's Pechorin, Herzen's Beltov, and virtually all of Turgenev's own
major characters. The new hero was no attractive, if weak-willed and
ineffective young aristocrat, no frustrated and introspective army
officer, but a medical student, a Son of the People and committed
revolutionary. He dominates the action throughout and is 'on stage'
for the greater part of the novel. By the sheer force of his personality,
his intellectual power and the cogency of his opinions he exercises an
authority over all other characters, who do not exist in a genuinely
independent sense outside their reaction to Bazarov. If Odintsova is
a magnet, he is a chemical agent that generates strong reactions,
with equal powers to repel and to attract.

Turgenev went out of his way to make the antithesis as stark as
possible. There is an arresting sense of reality about Bazarov; one is
aware of his presence in a more palpable sense than the other
characters who, successful, life-like creations though they are, do not
live on in the reader's mind to the same extent that he does. Generally
he is shown engaged in some physical activity, frequently incongruous in his aristocratic environment. He is out of the house early
in the morning, tramps around the countryside collecting frogs, and
returns to the house fresh and vigorous as the gentry are just
assembling for breakfast. In his room he is cutting up his frogs,
peering through his microscope, consulting a scientific manual,
making notes. He emanates the smell of cheap tobacco and medicine. As he makes his farewell speech to Arkady in Chapter 26, he is
engaged in the prosaic and bizarre activity of stuffing tufts of hay

into his suitcase. He is fully alive, self-reliant, tough and firm in his convictions, energetic and active. For him, living is doing, and he embodies the concept of Man, the Worker. He sees the life of the gentry as a pointless charade, and is aware of the absurdity of himself participating in it on their terms, as in the duel, or by falling in love. For him, life is harsh and offers no rewards. As he says to Arkady, 'you were not made for our bitter, harsh, lonely existence. There's no audacity in you, no venom; you've the fire and energy of youth, but that's of no use for our job. Your sort, the gentry, can't get much further than well-bred resignation and well-bred indignation, and that's nothing. The likes of you won't stand up and fight ... but we insist on fighting. Yes, that's the trouble! Our dust would sting your eyes, our dirt would soil you, ... unconsciously you admire yourself, you enjoy finding fault with yourself. We're fed up with that.' Here there is an abrupt shift in Bazarov's attitude to his former disciple: 'Let's have some fresh opponents! It's others we have to break!'[23] You're a nice lad; but you're too soft, a good little liberal gentleman—*et voilà tout*, as my parent would say' (p. 186). Here, ironically echoing Arkady's words as spokesman for Nihilism earlier in the novel ('We break because we are a force'), Bazarov prophetically sees his former friend as his future enemy, if an insignificant one. 'We want to fight'—but only with an enemy strong and important enough.

Here Bazarov states explicitly the antithesis between himself and the well-bred and self-regarding aristocrats, the revolutionary who fights on aware that he is doomed, both by external circumstances and weaknesses within himself. He perishes 'on the threshold of the future', as Turgenev said of him, while they fade quietly into irrelevance. Both in his life and his death he is physically more real and more vital than those who survive him.

In Bazarov, Turgenev illustrated with remarkable accuracy the essential features of the *Raznochintsy*. 'My grandfather,' he says with pride, 'ploughed the soil.' He flouts the conventions of his aristocratic hosts, horrifying them by the scorn he pours on their life-style and cherished ideals. Turgenev describes his scientific preoccupations with a tinge of irony or incredulity—'he doesn't believe in principles, but does believe in frogs' as Pavel Petrovich sneers. He is impatient of fine talk, of everything he labels 'Romanticism'— Beauty, Art, Love, Sentiment. He does not see the point of explaining his views; when forced to do so, he states his case with a shrug of indifference. He speaks in a series of abrasive, down-to-earth and often incredibly naive aphorisms. For him, Nature is not a temple, but a workshop and man is a workman in it; he looks at the sky only when he sneezes—a tidied-up version of a coarse Russian saying; Raphael's Madonna isn't worth a brass farthing; Pushkin and Schubert are worthless, and so is Logic—you don't need Logic to put a piece of bread in your mouth. The main thing is that two and two makes four ('answered' by Dostoyevsky's Underground Man: 'twice-two-makes-five is also a very nice little thing on occasion'[24]). A decent chemist is worth twenty poets any time. He denies the sanctity and uniqueness of the Individual—people are like trees, there's no sense in studying each one separately. The beautiful Odintsova has such a fine body that he can't wait to get her on the dissecting table.

More important than his anti-romanticism is his rejection of all accepted authority and all general principles, and this includes 'Science as such'. He is self-reliant and filled with arrogance—'the day I meet the man who can hold his own with me, I'll change my opinion of myself' (p. 132). As he appears in the alien milieu of Maryino, he is strong and defiant and, if his behaviour is put on in part 'pour épater les aristocrates', Turgenev was evidently fascinated, horrified, and puzzled by his literary offspring.

Bazarov attempts to iron out the complexities of human nature—including his own—and is resolved to live by the simplistic formulae of the fanatic, who allows nothing about him, apart from his Cause and his work for it, to be of any consequence. He is 'himself' only as long as he fully identifies with and lives out the role he has created for himself. Therefore, he is initially shown as accepting the in-evitability of 'progress' and his own role in promoting it. His views were not unduly sophisticated. Social ills—crimes etc.—could be cured once the diagnosis had been correctly stated; change Society and the distinction between a good man and an evil one will dis-appear. He is not moved by compassion or any other soft emotion for the Russian peasant; in fact, he is offhand with those he meets and certainly does not take their views seriously. Nor does he expect any gratitude from them. He is even sceptical about the ultimate value of working to improve their conditions. He says to Arkady: 'You said that Russia will reach perfection when every peasant will own a house like that one, and each of us must help towards that end . . . But I've developed a hatred for that 'every peasant', that

Philip or Sidor, for whose sake I'm to wear myself to the bone and who won't even thank me for it . . . And why do I need his thanks? All right, so he's going to live in a white cottage and I'll be pushing up daisies. And what happens then?' (pp. 132–3). Here there emerges a strain of the author's own introspective pessimism, which was certainly not typical of the real-life Radicals.

Bazarov, the *Raznochinets*, is at the same time the embodiment of Russian Nihilism. The word was not new. If 'Nihilism' is now defined as 'total negation of everything, total scepticism,'[25] Turgenev popularized it to describe the spirited attitude and ideas of the young generation of the 1860s. As such, the term was badly chosen and one may agree with Venturi and others that it indicates Turgenev's latent disapproval of the 'Sons',[26] whatever he may have said to the contrary. The young radicals believed fanatically in their ideals and were anything but sceptical or apathetic. But the label stuck and throughout the world it became the charismatic synonym for the Russian revolutionary. Turgenev even went to the extent of having one of the characters in the novel give the etymological origin of the word: ' "A Nihilist," said Nikolai Petrovich. "That comes from the Latin *nihil—nothing*, I imagine. The term must signify a man . . . who recognizes nothing?" ' His brother suggests that it is a man 'who respects nothing', which Arkady corrects: 'someone who looks at everything critically. A Nihilist is a person who admits no established authorities, who takes no principle for granted, however much that principle may be revered' (p. 29).

The historical veracity of Turgenev's hero and the whole social picture he created is of crucial importance when establishing his novel as a work of Realism. His own words are pertinent: 'to reproduce the truth, the reality of life, is the greatest happiness for a writer, even if that truth does not coincide with his own sympathies.'[27]

In deciding how valid Turgenev's portrait of the Nihilist generation is, one may compare Bazarov with D. I. Pisarev, the radical extremist and outstanding representative of Russian Nihilism. Indeed, Pisarev's pronouncements come remarkably close to Bazarov's. In his article 'Realists', with its detailed analysis of Bazarov, Pisarev asserted that Turgenev had come closer to understanding the Nihilists than any of the young Realists had.[28]

Pisarev shared Bazarov's exaggerated expectations of Science as providing the solution to social problems, and shared his rejection of all absolutes ('In the natural sciences, everything is in the fact').[29] His concept of Revolution was élitist: the 'People' were to him mere 'passive material' and he asserted that the Intelligentsia 'could extract nothing of importance from popular wisdom.' It was a case not of mobilizing the peasants, but of extending the influence of the Intelligentsia—this was 'the alpha and omega of social development'. For Pisarev, the truly historic figure was the 'Exceptional Individual', foreshadowing the men and women of 'The People's Will' of the late 1870s. Bazarov's 'negation' was to him no mere form of iconoclasm, but became the heroic deed, the exposure of falsehood. Like Bazarov, he denied the importance of the Russian tradition and its cultural heritage; he was contemptuous of his own country and argued that Russia must learn from the superior nations of the West.

He was close to Bazarov not only *in re*, but *in modo*, and some of their statements have a similar ring about them. Pisarev said he would rather be a Russian cobbler than a Russian Raphael; the 'temples' of culture were to become 'workshops of human thought.' He could see no difference between 'the great Beethoven,' 'the great Raphael,' and 'the great chef Dussault.' According to Pisarev, 'we are wrong to enter into pathetic relations with Nature, we lose time in wonder, we obfuscate our minds with all sorts of illusory images, in which some claim to discover beauty, others consolation, still others even meaning and logic.'

However, the main body of Russian left-wing opinion angrily denounced Turgenev's work. Turgenev's own ambiguous attitude to his hero did not go unnoticed. Yet, even if some of the details are arguable, he did succeed in defining this new social type, and Bazarov has been perceived as the prototype of the Bolshevik, became the cult figure for generations of young revolutionaries, who adopted his outlook, behaviour, manner of speech and even his type of clothing; and outstanding Russian scientists, like K. A. Timiryazev and I. I. Mechnikov, acknowledged that they modelled themselves on Bazarov. Thus even his dubious scientific method has found vindication.

Turgenev has Bazarov claim that 'there are quite a few of them', and Sitnikov and Kukshina have apparently known him previously and regard him as one of the leaders of the 'movement'. But this does not compensate for the overall impression that Bazarov has no contact with any other Nihilists, is totally isolated, and, as such, is doomed. Turgenev either did not know or did not want to reveal any information about the activities of the radical student circles in St. Petersburg. From the point of historical credibility, this is a major flaw in the portrait of Bazarov. So, too, is his great emotional crisis after his encounter with Odintsova and the resultant break in his character. These are some of the reasons why the Radicals refused to see themselves in Bazarov. But some of their indignation seems to be misplaced; it was even objected that Turgenev's hero loses the game of cards with Father Alexei in Chapter 21.

Although he recommends Büchner's *Stoff und Kraft* to his host,[30] as a mouthpiece for Materialism Bazarov is less than adequate. One reason for this must be Turgenev's uncommitted political outlook; another, his distaste for Chernyshevsky's 'Peasant Socialism'; a third, his artistic restraint that prevented him from indulging in political pamphleteering. Moreover, the editor of *The Russian Messenger* insisted on reducing the 'apotheosis' of the New Men, and major cuts were made in the text as a result. This is why Pavel Petrovich's statement: 'This Materialism you are preaching . . .' is left suspended in a vacuum—nowhere does Bazarov preach Materialism in a comprehensive way. He does not go beyond uttering a number of telling aphorisms.

These are some of the aspects in which Bazarov is deficient as a portrait of the 'Sons'. But there is another dimension to his personality. In the company of the ordinary men and women around him he is a brooding, alien presence, mocking their trivial deeds and aspirations. Turgenev visualized him as 'a large figure, gloomy and savage, only half-emerging from the soil, powerful, enraged and honest, and yet doomed.'[31] This is a prose equivalent of Milton's Satan, Lermontov's Demon, the Spirit of Negation and Defiance, the Destroyer. As Maurice Baring, somewhat overstating his case, had put it: 'Bazarov is the Lucifer type that recurs again and again in Russian history and fiction. . . . He is the man who denies; . . . he believes in nothing; he bows to nothing; he can break, but cannot bend; he does break, and that is the tragedy, but, breaking, he retains his invincible pride.'[32] Odintsova senses this 'strangeness' in him, is fascinated and frightened by it, as when he declared his love for her and the passion that was struggling within him was 'not unlike rage and perhaps akin to it' (p. 124); or when she recalled with a shudder the 'almost animal-like expression on his face' (p. 125) as he had advanced on her. She is incredulous when he describes himself

as 'a future provincial doctor'—so very different from Turgenev's
other young lovers, and closer perhaps to the 'Possessed' in Dostoevsky's novel. We see this demonic aspect in him when, aware of the
passion arising in him, 'he went into the forest and prowled around
with large strides, breaking branches that barred his way and cursing
her and himself under his breath' (p. 112).

Even while fully committed to the Cause he was serving he was
also aware of the vanity of human existence and aspirations, including his own, and this can go some way to serve as a link between the
two aspects of his personality—Bazarov the purposeful Nihilist and
Bazarov who realizes that he, too, is doomed to oblivion, having
achieved nothing; that he, too, is the 'insignificant creature of a
single day'.[33] And the revolutionary with his programme for social
change gives way to the human being, infinitesimal in the vast perspective of eternity, indistinguishable from his fellow men, as he,
too, completes his pre-ordained cycle and becomes subject to eternal,
unalterable laws. Those whom the gods love, die young, and this
Angry Young Man is spared the humiliation of the steady decline of
ageing (or is it maturing?), the inevitable betrayal, as Turgenev
viewed it, of the ideals of youth. Bazarov's early death is therefore an
act of mercy, an attempt to preserve his image undamaged by forces
that have already sent out their warning shots.

This appears to be Turgenev's view of the tragic destiny of men
who sacrifice themselves in the service of humanity. And his way of
stating his ultimate affection for, and compassion with, his hero, 'the
passionate, sinful and rebellious heart' is shown in the closing lines of
the novel, a moving, if incongruous, requiem in terms of 'all-
embracing peace, the vast repose of "indifferent" Nature, of ever-
lasting reconciliation and life without end.'

After Bazarov, the person of whom Turgenev gave the most complete inner picture is Odintsova. She emerges as a mature, but
complex and enigmatic woman, radiant and triumphant in her
femininity, the type of woman that intrigued Turgenev, though she
does not fully belong in the gallery of dangerous and strong-willed
femmes fatales, like Polozova in *Torrents of Spring* or Ratmirova in
Smoke who destroyed the amorous bliss of young lovers by force of
personality and their overwhelming sexuality. There are several
extensive character studies of Odintsova, notably in Chapters 15 and
16, in terms of her biography and social identity—her first marriage,
her wealth, and success as mistress of a prosperous estate; her per-

sonality is also conveyed in the several descriptions of her estate, that veritable 'Calypso's Island'. She is the only person to measure up to Bazarov and understand him in depth, and she alone could destroy him. She relishes her power over men, but also over her younger sister—the latent tensions between the two women are conveyed with much insight and humour. But her love of calm and order triumphs over the curiosity that Bazarov had aroused in her. 'Bazarov is evidently right—curiosity, mere curiosity, love for peace and quiet, and egoism' (p. 187). Earlier, the author had explained that her conflicting emotions had brought her to the brink; 'and as she peered beyond it, she saw no abyss but only a void . . . a shapeless chaos' (p. 109). Thus she reveals herself as a 'necrophile', to use E. Fromm's term for describing those who need to impose a pattern of order and tidiness upon the chaotic variety of life, which the 'biophile' readily accepts. Turgenev referred to her as representing 'those idle, dreamy, curious and cold epicurean lady aristocrats' and after her flirtation with a dangerous relationship ('stroking a wolf's fur, hoping it won't bite') she returns to 'lying on velvet, washed and dainty'.[34] If she is a social and psychological type she is no stereotype, but a successful portrait of a lady who loses none of her mystery for being revealed. Odintsova is a minor masterpiece of Turgenev's discreet, controlled technique of psychological realism.

A Realist writer is commonly expected to produce 'objective' pictures of reality, with his own bias reduced to a minimum, and Turgenev is no exception. But no writer could wholly surrender his interpretation of the reality he views, or his attitude to the characters he has created. While in this novel, Turgenev does stay outside the action to a remarkable degree, his bias is unmistakable, for example, in his portrayal of Pavel Petrovich, whom he treats with more than a touch of satire. He admitted that he had 'sinned against artistic truth' by endowing him with those more extravagant absurdities— his anglomania, the fez he wears deep in the Russian countryside, the cocoa he drinks, his perfumed whiskers, his affected rhetoric, his life as a *poseur*, his pathetic behaviour during and after the duel, the travesty of a death-bed benediction, the ashtray shaped like a peasant's bast shoe on his desk in Dresden. Yet he did not go so far as to make him grotesque. 'My aesthetic sense caused me to take *good* representatives of the gentry, in order to prove my point: if the cream is bad, what would the milk be like?'[35] He does not seem to dislike Pavel Petrovich. Kukshina and Sitnikov, however, emerge as caricatures of the emancipated progressives, camp-followers that bring noble causes into disrepute. There is a strong sense of distaste both in Bazarov and the author for this 'new woman' with her unsavoury habits and her borrowed and vulgarized 'ideas'. Sitnikov is the incarnation of *poshlost'*, that untranslatable Russian vice that includes ostentatious vulgarity, lack of ideals, preoccupation with material things (Nabokov's rendering as 'Poshlust' comes close to conveying this[36]). Turgenev does not spare the 'young progressive' and reintroduces him almost gratuitously in Chapter 19 as the 'appearance of *poshlost'* merely to pour all his sarcasm on him.

He clearly sympathizes with Nikolai Petrovich and Arkady, whereas his attitude to his hero is ambiguous, as shown above. Though he asserted that Bazarov was his 'favourite child' he was clearly upset by his uncouth manners and his contempt for art, which he dwells on with a dismayed fascination and bewilderment. He watches and listens to him, disagrees with and disapproves of him but is incapable of pronouncing judgement on him. At the same time he is aware that he had created a titan, sensing that this is 'some strange pendant to Pugachov'.[37] Critics have asserted that he only began to feel for Bazarov when he had him fall victim to love. This is an oversimplification, and yet the change in Bazarov from then onwards—his growing self-doubt, his pessimism and his futile death—illustrates the author's ambivalent attitude to him. Turgenev was more at home with failures, idealists who have lost faith in their ideals and Bazarov comes dangerously close to ending his life as another 'superfluous man'. This may have been Turgenev's way of redeeming his hero and he was dismayed to find that his readers appeared to deny Bazarov 'the right to idealization'.

The publication of *Fathers and Sons* produced what was probably the greatest *skandal* in the history of Russian literature. The Radical Left was outraged by the figure of Bazarov, whom they regarded as a spiteful caricature of themselves and denounced Turgenev in unambiguous terms as a traitor to the cause of freedom and progress. A long review of the novel appeared in *The Contemporary*, entitled 'Asmodeus of Our Times'[38] which 'passed a sort of legally reasoned sentence on the author for having falsified reality.'[39] In official quarters the work was received with smug satisfaction: Turgenev had poured ridicule on the 'Sons' in this unflattering portrait and had, moreover, coined a useful label to brand them with.[40] Turgenev was bewildered and dismayed by this reception of his novel, forgetting that in Russia in the heat of literary and ideological controversy views expressed by the fictional characters are too often taken as those of the author, and objectivity and neutrality may be regarded as reactionary.

The action of Turgenev's novel takes place in the agreeable surroundings of a Russian estate; his characters are attractive and likeable persons, except for Kukshina and Sitnikov. The social picture is confined to landowners, though the contrast between the Kirsanovs and the Bazarovs shows how wide and varied the range of that class was. One gets a picture of the household, including the domestic staff, but the action only once moves into the servants' quarters, significantly in the Bazarov home. There is no full picture of the village, the peasants are only encountered in the open, as animated figures in the landscape or as representing problems that Nikolai Petrovich has to cope with. Only Bazarov has any personal encounters with them. The rural setting is a backcloth to the human action and, apart from the *rapport* between Nature and the moods of a few of the characters, especially Arkady's and his cello-playing father, it is not integrated with their lives in any practical sense; again the Bazarov family is the exception. Turgenev's social background and artistic temperament prevented him from writing broad panoramic chronicles of country life, and the absence of the ugly, the sordid, and low-class life necessarily reduces the stature of his novel as a social document of the times.

Yet what in social terms endows the novel with tragic dimensions is not merely Bazarov's death and instant oblivion, but the fact that this parasitical life-style will go on essentially unaltered, regardless of Alexander II's 'Great Reforms'. Turgenev implies that the old order continues, its adherents, like Pavel Petrovich, being driven to disguise their corroding boredom by indulging in futile pursuits and ludicrous poses, while Arkady, the young enthusiast, gradually lapses into the social attitudes of the 'Fathers'. And their 'liberalism' is shown in neat little touches to be little more than skin-deep.

The long-overdue Emancipation of the Serfs—four-fifths of the population—finally took place in March 1861. But this did not relieve social tension. On the contrary, in 1861–2 the political situation became acute. There was mounting unrest both in the countryside and in the major cities. Some of the peasant disturbances were put down by force of arms. In St. Petersburg a number of revolutionary proclamations were published and student activity intensified; some 200 were imprisoned in the Peter and Paul Fortress and elsewhere. In 1862 Chernyshevsky and Pisarev were arrested and their journals, *The Contemporary* and *The Russian Word*, were temporarily closed down (they were finally suppressed in 1866); censorship became more severe than ever. The government had succeeded in gaining some public support by attributing to the Radicals, probably falsely, responsibility for several major fires that had broken out mysteriously in the capital. Within a few years, a number of 'anti-Nihilist' novels had appeared, culminating in Dostoyevsky's *The Possessed* (1871) and the real-life Bazarovs were more and more discredited.

This wider political dimension is signally absent from Turgenev's work. The Act of Emancipation is barely referred to, and barely affects the lives of his characters: in the Epilogue, we are told that Nikolai Petrovich became very busy, travelling around the countryside delivering speeches, but this and a steady improvement in the affairs of his estate is about all, nothing seems to have changed. This despite the fact that Turgenev was working on the novel both during and after March 1861.

In spite of such limitations, the novel is an important historical record. In the Soviet Union *Fathers and Sons* is firmly established as one of the great classics, read and discussed by every schoolchild. Elsewhere, commentators will have us believe, Turgenev's novels are being forgotten. How true is this? It has been asserted that the ideological aspect of the novel has long ceased to interest the modern reader. Such views are unduly complacent, for Bazarov, far from being dead and forgotten, has his descendants today, not only in the Soviet Union but among the Dissident Left in Western Europe and America, in whose statements many of his blunt and aggressive aphorisms are echoed with impressive accuracy. As the controversial Soviet Jewish poet Naum Korzhavin told a Western audience with some feeling: 'Don't tell us again that Russia is always behind the West, is always learning from it. Your young people are now "discovering" some social ideals and are fighting to realize them in life, and you think this is new and original. Here in Russia we went through all this a hundred years ago. Go and read *Fathers and Sons*— it's all there. Bazarov, you know.' This was in 1969, the year after the student revolts in France and elsewhere.

The Nihilist programme was stated more fully and more accurately by Chernyshevsky and others, but it was Turgenev who made it available in palatable and accessible form. The current revival of interest in *Fathers and Sons* has been amply demonstrated (see Notes*). Is it only read by aesthetic highbrows for the beauty of the language and lyrical evocations of the Russian countryside? The ideological battles have not died down. Turgenev may have considered the matter closed, but there have been and will continue to be groups of Angry Young Men determined to pull down the existing edifice and clear the ground for a transformed Society. History proved Turgenev's scepticism wrong. The Russian Radicals, far from being doomed to oblivion, were the spearhead of the movement that culminated in the October Revolution. As Isaiah Berlin persuasively argues, 'it's the Bazarovs who have won'.[41]

Radical criticism holds that every literary work is ultimately a political statement; every novel is a political novel. Even Turgenev, liberal gradualist that he was, stated that 'the entire novel [*Fathers and Sons*] was directed against the gentry as the leading class.'[42] Indeed, *Fathers and Sons* is a political novel written by a political sceptic of scrupulous integrity who was only too aware of the complexity of the saving truth and the inefficacy of simple solutions. The most important and most painful lesson that Turgenev has demonstrated—he was experiencing it in his own life—is that the most bitter fight is not between the extreme Right and the extreme Left, but between political cousins; and in this sense the parting of the two young friends is a moment of greater historical symbolism than the duel between Bazarov and Pavel Petrovich. It is the turning in upon each other of Young Liberal and Young Socialist and foreshadows the bitter strife between Populist and Marxist, Menshevik and Bolshevik, Social Democrat and Communist—all claiming equally to champion the causes of Freedom, Equality, and Justice.

This is but one indication that *Fathers and Sons* is a statement of enduring universal force. What Turgenev has shown in this human drama is at some point true of all mankind—the clash of generations, the power of love, the transience of friendships, the pull of social origin and convention, 'the triumph,' as Eugène-Melchior de Vogüé, the first serious Western student of the Russian novel,[43] had put it, 'of the group over the individual, of the crowd over the hero'; and the intervention in our lives of indefinable and uncontrollable forces. If Turgenev's novel is technically not 'a slice of life', it is much more than 'a summer in the country'; and his characters come alive as unique individuals, while also being recognizable both as perennial human types and as representatives of a particular period in Russian history. As such, they are 'realistic' in the full sense of the term. The fact that Turgenev manipulated his material according to his own artistic principles, that he kept faith with his own vision of reality and political outlook, and that his work is not without its defects and limitations as a historical and social record, in no way reduces its standing as one of the great works of Realism.

NOTES

* Page references after quotations refer to George Reavey's translation (Ivan Turgenev, *Fathers and Sons*, Signet Classics, n.d.), though not always quoted verbatim. Constance Garnett and other honourable exceptions apart, Turgenev has been badly served by his English translators. The first translations in his lifetime were made from the French and not the Russian original, abounding in misunderstandings and mistakes. *Nest of the Gentry* (*Dvoryanskoye gnezdo*) first appeared with the puzzling title 'Nest of the Hereditary Legislators'. Currently three translations of *Fathers and Sons* are available in paperback editions, none of them perfect; the most notorious among them is by C. J. Hogarth in the Everyman Library. Rosemary Edmond's version (Penguin Classics) also suffers from a crop of mistakes, the general flatness of her narrative and a wholly misleading and inaccurate introduction. In G. Reavey's translation, the best of the three, there are minor omissions in the text and a number of annoying inaccuracies. —The novel is commonly known as 'Fathers and Sons', itself a mistranslation of the Russian *Ottsy i deti* —Fathers and Children.

1. Henry James, *French Poets and Novelists*, London, 1878.
2. Maurice Baring, *Landmarks in Russian Literature*, London, 1910, p. 64; reissued as University Paperback, Methuen, 1960.
3. *Sobraniye sochinenii*, XII (1958), 492–3.
4. See above, pp. 10–11.
5. Quoted in V. Shklovsky, *Zametki o proze russkikh klassikov*, Moscow, 1955, p. 222.
6. P. V. Annenkov, *Zametki o russkoy literature proshlogo goda*, 1849. I. A. Goncharov's (1812–91) best-known novel is *Oblomov* (1859).
7. V. G. Belinsky (1811–48), pioneer of Russian 'democratic' criticism, the first to stress the power of literature as a social force; wrote long and perceptive reviews of the works of Pushkin, Lermontov, Gogol, Dostoyevsky, Turgenev, *et al.* Was a close friend of Turgenev's.
   N. A. Dobrolyubov (1836–61), radical critic and revolutionary thinker; wrote on Turgenev, Goncharov, Ostrovsky, *et al.* His fiercely polemical review of Turgenev's *On the Eve* ('When will the actual day come?') preached revolution in a near-overt manner.
   N. G. Chernyshevsky (1828–89), critic, historian, philosopher, novelist and dominant figure in the left-wing Intelligentsia; wrote extensively on socio-political and economic matters and formulated the new utilitarian aesthetics of the Russian Radicals. His most important literary article was entitled 'Essays on the Gogolian period in Russian literature' (1855). Author of the novel *What's to be Done?* (See n. 28). In 1862 he was arrested and exiled for most of the remainder of his life.
8. See below, p. 79.

9. Prosper Mérimée, *Ivan Tourguénef* in *Études de Littérature Russe*, vol. ii, Paris, 1932, p. 244.

10. Yu. I. Aikhenval'd, *Siluety russkikh pisateley*, vol. ii, 5th ed., Berlin, 1922, pp. 208–9. The reverential and romantic attitude to women expressed in Turgenev's novels derived in large measure from his life-long, intense, and probably unconsummated devotion to the Spanish opera singer Mme. Pauline Viardot. Turgenev became a member of the Viardot household, living and travelling with them around Europe. He died in her arms, after being her friend and companion for some forty years.

11. 'Po povodu *Ottsov i detey*' ('A propos *Fathers and Children*') quoted in *Ottsy i deti*, ed. N. L. Brodsky, Moscow, 1955, p. 213.

12. Populism was the dominant movement among the Russian Intelligentsia in the 1870s. The Populists (narodniks) were motivated by a strong compassion and admiration for the Russian peasant. Answering Alexander Herzen's call ('To the People!') they organized two major 'Movements to the People', when young members of the Intelligentsia went to the villages in large groups, intent on studying peasant life and living with the peasants on terms of equality. In 1879 the movement split into two factions, the gradualist 'Black Repartition' and the terrorist 'People's Will', who were responsible for the assassination of Alexander II in 1881.

13. 'Po povodu *Ottsov i detey*', ibid; see n. 11.

14. ibid.

15. Letter to K. K. Sluchevsky, Paris, 14 April 1862. N. P. Ogaryov (1813–77), poet and Herzen's life-long friend. Though residing in London, they were the acknowledged leaders of the Revolutionary Movement during the 1850s and until *c*. 1863. Their publications included the weekly *The Bell* which was smuggled into Russia and was very influential in radical circles.

16. In 'Turgenev at Ventnor', *Slavonic and East European Review*, li (1973), 409–10.

17. 'Spring at Marino', the title of a recent BBC radio dramatization, was on the right lines, even though neither time of year nor location are quite on the mark.

18. Henry James, *Theory of Fiction*, ed. James E. Miller, Jr., University of Nebraska Press, 1972, p. 197.

19. Richard Freeborn, *Turgenev: The Novelist's Novelist. A Study*. Oxford, 1962.

20. His best known plays are *A Month in the Country* (1850) and *The Provincial Lady* (1851).

21. The gaps left in the translation are merely the translator's efforts at improving on Turgenev's original text.

22. The term *Raznochintsy* (lit. 'persons of other ranks') came to be used of members of the Intelligentsia not belonging to the gentry; they included sons of merchants, the clergy, the peasantry, lower officialdom as well as some non-hereditary and déclassé nobelemen.

23. These two sentences (*Nam drugikh podavay! Nam drugikh lomat' nado!*), at first sight puzzling in the context, have bewildered several translators. They are omitted by R. Freeborn when he quotes Bazarov's speech (op. cit., p. 107).

24. *Notes from Underground*, 1864, ch. IX.

25. S. I. Ozhegov, *Tolkovyi slovar' russkogo yazyka*, 10th ed., Moscow, 1973, p. 379.

26. F. Venturi, *Roots of Revolution*, New York, 1966, p. 326.

27. Quoted in *Ottsy i deti*, ed. N. L. Brodsky, Moscow, 1955, p. 201.

28. Rakhmetov is the main character in Chernyshevsky's *What's To Be Done?* (1863), which 'corrected' Turgenev's portrait of the Nihilist. Turgenev left the editorial board of *The Contemporary* in 1859, 'sickened by Chernyshevsky's Peasant Socialism' (Lenin), who, with Dobrolyubov, turned the journal into the mouthpiece of the Radical Left. This break is echoed in the gradual estangement and final break between Bazarov and Arkady, the committed revolutionary and the young liberal veering to conservatism.

29. Quotations here and ff. are taken from E. Lampert, *Sons against Fathers. Studies in Russian Radicalism and Revolution*, Oxford, 1965, ch. V, 'Dimitry Pisarev'.

30. Büchner's *Stoff und Kraft* was a textbook of 'vulgar' materialism, which was translated into Russian in 1860 and was widely read—another instance of Turgenev being very much up-to-date in his details. Büchner ascribed all spiritual, intellectual and emotional experiences to physiological sources. Thus, according to Büchner, the brain secretes thoughts much as the liver secretes juices. Hence Bazarov's assertion that 'everything' is derived from 'sensations', which so dismays his friend Arkady. (ch. 21).

31. Letter to Sluchevsky, as above, n. 15.

32. M. Baring, op. cit., pp. 171–2.

33. R. Freeborn, op. cit., p. 131.

34. Letter to Sluchevsky, as above, n. 15.

35. ibid.

36. V. Nabokov,*Nikolay Gogol*, New York, 1944.

37. Emelyan Pugachov was a Don Cossack who led a major peasant uprising (1773–5). Peasants, Cossacks, Kalmyks, and working people flocked to his army which overran vast tracts of land along the Volga, including the cities of Kazan, Penza, and Saratov; at one point he was expected to reach Moscow. His uprising terrified the gentry and posed a major threat to Tsarist authority. It was finally suppressed and Pugachov was brought to Moscow in an iron cage and executed in 1775.

38. 'Asmodeus of Our Times' by M. A. Antonovich. The title echoes Lermontov's novel *A Hero of Our Times* (1840) and Lesage's *Le Diable boiteux* (1707), translated into Russian as 'Asmodeus' which, along with Lesage's other works was widely read in nineteenth-century Russia.

39. F. Venturi, op. cit., p. 321.

40. The Annual Report for 1862 of the Third Section contains the following: 'Fairness requires it to be stated that a beneficial influence was exerted on the public mind by the novel *Fathers and Sons* by the well-known writer Ivan Turgenev. Standing at the head of contemporary talent and enjoying the affection of educated society, Turgenev has in this work, unexpectedly for the young generation which but recently was applauding him, branded our juvenile revolutionaries with the unpalatable name of Nihilist and has given a jolt to the teachings of Materialism and its representatives.' Quoted by I. I. Veksler, *I. S. Turgenev i literaturnaya bor'ba shestidesyatykh godov*. Leningrad, 1943, pp. 35–6.

41. Isaiah Berlin, *Fathers and Children*. The Romanes Lecture. Oxford, 1972, p. 55 ff.

42. Letter to Sluchevsky, as above, n. 15.

43. Eugène-Melchior de Vogüé, *Le Roman russe*, Paris, 1886, p. xiv.

4

G. Flaubert: *Sentimental Education* (1869)

D. A. WILLIAMS

IT IS something of a paradox that the novelist who is often regarded as the 'father of Realism' should have been so vehement in his denunciation of the ideas of contemporary 'Realist' novelists. Flaubert's antipathy for these ideas was so great that he claimed to have written *Madame Bovary*, his first major novel, 'out of hatred for Realism', yet this same novel is now regarded as a Realist masterpiece. In the course of berating an aesthetic aberration, Flaubert provides a clearer formulation of what Realism ought to entail and a striking illustration of the literary practice which the modern critic associates with Realism.

'Realism' was unacceptable to Flaubert because it was associated in his mind with the view, prevalent in his time, that the novel could and should contain 'absolute truth' or 'absolute reality'.[1] This view led one novelist, Champfleury, to make the patently ludicrous claim that 'what I see enters my head, descends through my arm and becomes what I have seen.'[2] Valuing the aesthetic dimension of literature above all else and believing in the transforming power of the artist, Flaubert perceived and despised the muddled thinking of Champfleury and others which allowed art and reality to be confused. The novel could not, he insisted, give absolute reality since the writer has to select and arrange his material.[3] What he offers is never a straight reproduction of reality but 'du réel écrit',[4] a verbal transcription of the real. Unlike his contemporaries, Flaubert never forgot that what the novelist gives in the first instance is the word not the world.

It is precisely because he did not forget this elementary truth that Realism in his work receives its most profound and lasting expression. More than any other novelist, Flaubert 'lived' Realism as a problematic enterprise, struggling, as Jenkins suggests, to resolve both at a theoretical and a practical level a number of fundamental tensions generated by the contradiction between art and reality.

Although he never abandoned the belief that the basic task of the novelist was to represent or depict human experience, an innocent mirroring of reality was for Flaubert out of the question. A faithful record alone could never be sufficient since art involved a making as well as a matching. These two basic urges are expressed in Flaubert's dual allegiance to 'le Beau' (the Beautiful) and 'le Vrai' (the True). Flaubert's insistence on the importance of the Beautiful—which was connected with the way in which the material for the work was organized at the level both of the phrasing of individual sentences and of the larger patterns and structures that gave shape to the novel—set him apart from Champfleury and Duranty, self-styled 'Realists' who proposed an artless reproduction of unvarnished reality in a transparent style. But to conclude, like Flaubert, that this insistence means that he is not a Realist would be wrong, as the concern for the novel as an aesthetic object in its own right coexists with the notion that the novelist should 'faire vrai', show life in its true colours. If to deny the importance of the Beautiful would be to betray one's artistic mission, simply an artist and ignore the True would be to fail to assume the responsibility Flaubert believed fell on the writer in the modern age.

Showing life in its true colours implied for Flaubert what it implied for many of the other novelists discussed in this volume—a recognition of the uneventfulness of a good deal of experience, the unsatisfactory nature of the lives lived by the largest number, the undoubted mediocrity of the majority of men. For Flaubert, too, this recognition entailed the rejection of literary stereotypes which falsified or idealized existence. Yvetot, an obscure Norman village is as worthy of literary treatment as Constantinople, he declared, and, like Howells, his plea is 'Let's have no more heroes and no more monsters.'[5] But where Flaubert differs from other European Realists is in his intense, though usually contained irritation with the necessary banality of his subject-matter, a chronic exasperation which turns the whole business of writing into a painful cohabitation with characters whom he despises and gives rise to a tonic element of stringent criticism which makes a refreshing change from the self-congratulatory populism into which the Realist can easily slip.

If he must deal with the odious modern world, it was essential, Flaubert felt, to deal with it in depth, revealing what is hidden to the casual observer. Following in the wake of his father, a distinguished surgeon, Flaubert thought of himself as an anatomist, laying bare the secrets of the human heart in a closely dissective art. The emblem which this analytic emphasis calls to mind is not the mirror, the traditional symbol of Realist art, but what Balzac referred to as the 'avid scalpel of the nineteenth century'. The scalpel is a more potent emblem, releasing the novelist from a preoccupation with surface reality and authorizing the concentration on the disagreeable, even painful, side of life and the quest for hidden causes and disreputable motives. The overtly analytic approach, so apparent in the plans Flaubert wrote for his novel, is adopted only intermittently in the novels themselves, however, since it is held in check by the point of view technique which Flaubert favours as a way of restricting the omniscience of a narrator who, if he were too much in evidence, would detract from fictional illusion. The restriction of omniscience does not entail the total suppression of psychological analysis, as some critics have claimed, but it does make for what Maupassant called 'hidden psychology'.[6] Inner states are revealed through significant gestures and descriptive details rather than analysed explicitly and an oblique commentary on the psychological progression of the protagonist is provided by changes in the physical background. Flaubert combines a little telling with a good deal of showing; the narrator's sporadic analysis induces the reader to postulate an ongoing inner life, access to which is gained by a close reading of the mutely suggestive language of externals.

The most important contradiction inherent in Realism to be brought into sharp focus in Flaubert's concept of the novel concerns the nature of the reality which the Realist should seek to delineate. Flaubert lifted Realism above the anecdotal, literal approach of his French contemporaries by insisting that the True lay not in what had actually happened but in what generally occurs, not in what is peculiar to a particular person but what recurrently or typically is the case. The novelist should attempt to discern what is 'universal', the constant features and repeated patterns of human experience; like the scientist,[7] he should begin with the observation of a wealth of particulars which would allow him to induce or infer some general principle—what Flaubert called a generality—governing or underlying human behaviour. Documentation puts the writer in touch with the real but the artistic process of 'generalization' allows the novelist to move beyond the limitations of the actual: 'by imagining one reproduces a generality, whereas if one sticks to an actual happening, what emerges from one's work is merely something contingent, relative, restricted.'[8] Of course, a novelist must of necessity recount the story of individual human beings in a particular situation and at a particular time. But it is possible to show within this concrete and particularized framework the operation of 'generalities' provided that the responses and motives, thoughts and emotions attributed to the characters are in conformity with the general pattern of human behaviour. A precondition of the perception of this general pattern was, in Flaubert's view, impersonality. The novelist must attempt to transcend the limitations of his own subjectivity by refusing to write about his own personal problems: 'art is not meant to depict exceptions . . . the man in the street is more interesting than Mr. G. Flaubert because he is more general, and consequently, more typical.'⁹ He must also avoid writing in an impassioned state: 'passion does not produce verse and the more personal you are, the weaker you are; the less you feel something, the more you are able to express it as it is (i.e. in its permanence, as a general truth, purged of all that is ephemeral and contingent).'¹⁰ This strong insistence on the general is accompanied, however, by an equally strong demand that the fictional world should be entirely consistent with the known or ascertainable facts of the real world. Real places and events, if referred to, must be described exactly as they are. The activity of the characters must be subject to the same conditions as prevail in real life, even in so apparently trivial a sphere as transport. If there was no train service operating between Fontainebleau and Paris in 1848, then the main character of *Sentimental Education* must return to Paris by coach even if this means rewriting several pages.¹¹ 'The difficult thing', Flaubert declared, 'is not to go against nature, not to alienate those who are familiar with the scene of the action.'¹² But why, if the principal task is to deal with the general, should it matter whether insignificant details of the fictional world correspond exactly with the ascertainable facts of historical reality? Flaubert was no more able than other Realists to solve the central contradiction of Realism— the insistence on factual accuracy in the art of the imaginary.

Flaubert's reputation as a Realist was secured, much to his dismay, by the publication of his first novel, *Madame Bovary*, in 1857. But it is his second novel dealing with modern life, *Sentimental Education*, published in 1869, which on several scores constitutes his greatest achievement as a Realist. The central character of this second work is less unusual, less outstanding than Emma Bovary who, as Baudelaire pointed out, is in some ways an awe-inspiring figure, endowed with an energy, passion, and intensity of aspiration which lift her above the ruck of common humanity. Secondly, the references to contemporary social reality in *Sentimental Education* are far more copious than in *Madame Bovary*. Thirdly, Flaubert's aim in *Sentimental Education* is to show the mixed fortunes of a whole generation as well as the psychological development of Frédéric Moreau, whilst in *Madame Bovary* the emphasis is firmly on the destiny of a single individual. Lastly, whilst *Madame Bovary* 'confers on its sufficiently vulgar elements of exhibition a final unsurpassable form',[13] *Sentimental Education* is characterized by a narrative mode and structure which are less conspicuous, less obviously designed to compensate for the novel's equally 'vulgar elements of exhibition'.

All these features of Flaubert's second novel dealing with modern life constitute an intensification of the Realism of *Madame Bovary*— an intensification which extends the form near to breaking point and leaves many readers dissatisfied. In trying to avoid the novel's customary distortion of reality, Flaubert flouts traditional expectations. His choice of a mediocre central character, his studied evocation of an uneventful existence, his presentation of an unusually detailed historical background, his deference to Frédéric's confused awareness, his opting for an extended and curiously unmemorable plot and a deeply concealed structure are all part of Flaubert's deepening commitment to the 'profoundly true'[14] rather than to the entertaining or aesthetically pleasing.

The choice of main character in *Sentimental Education* has often perplexed critics. Flaubert was not obliged to choose 'such an abject human specimen';[15] what then is the purpose of selecting so dull and nondescript a character, or as P. Cortland puts it, 'a faceless man in the crowd'?[16] Even Flaubert had his doubts: 'Do such flabby characters offer any interest',[17] he wonders. The issue is clearly of central importance as Gide realized when he wrote: '*Sentimental Education* raises an enthralling problem; is the least exceptional character the most representative?'[18] The danger of having so disconcertingly null, so uninspiringly mediocre a character is that he will fail to command the reader's attention; but the reward, the possible gain if the Realist wager is accepted, is that such a character, since he so clearly lies closer to the median line of unexceptional averageness than more heroic characters, will be more likely to reflect the pattern and dramatize the problems of the 'average' reader. In such a character's very insignificance lies his significance.

Flaubert once clearly defined the lack of positive qualities in
Frédéric Moreau, by amending the sub-title of the novel to *Histoire
d'un jeune hommet*, using the diminutive form to pinpoint his hero's
rather spineless, apathetic personality and foppish, ineffectual ways.[19]
The actual sub-title—*Histoire d'un jeune homme, Story of a Young
Man*—avoids prejudging the issue, however, leaving the reader to
form his own general conclusions about the inadequacy of Frédéric
from the apparently neutral account of his life. The principal
characteristic of Frédéric—as revealed by his various actions and
utterances—is a relentless passivity, more generally associated with
the heroine of a traditional novel. Frédéric spends most of his life
suspended in a state of expectation. In the opening chapter, we are
told that 'he considered that the happiness which his nobility of soul
deserved was slow in coming.'[20] Happiness for Frédéric is not a goal
which is actively pursued but a reward which he passively waits to
be accorded. Likewise, worldly success. On inheriting a large fortune, he announces his ambition of becoming a minister but makes
it clear that he is prepared to do nothing to achieve this ambition
(p. 107). From the outset, Frédéric renounces all effort in the sphere
of love, too ('As for looking for the woman of my dreams, I've no intention of doing that', p. 28). He expects women to offer themselves
to him and excludes a more forceful approach to the opposite sex.
His typical posture is supine—even in his daydreaming, he sees himself 'reclining on cashmere divans' (p. 64). The opening scene in
which he is seen on the old paddle-steamer richly anticipates his
whole life. Throughout the novel Frédéric seems to drift aimlessly
through life, to be borne along by the tide of circumstance. He will
repeatedly be shown poised motionless in a moving world, surrounded on all sides by the prosaic, bustling activity of the crowd, a
born spectator forever reluctant to participate but drawn into
dubious complicity with the dallying of Arnoux who does what he
does not dare to do, and all the time cherishing the illusion that his
attachment to the idealized 'vision' of the perfect woman sets him
apart from a humanity engaged in more mundane pursuits.

The sinuous course of the river prefigures Frédéric's failure to
'steer a straight course' (p. 418), the way in which he repeatedly takes
the line of least resistance, passively succumbing to his own whims
and desires rather than pursuing a social, political, or artistic objective. The words which recur in connection with his behaviour are
'lâche' and 'lâcheté'; they are usually translated by 'cowardly' and

'cowardice' but the French carries suggestions of flabbiness, pusil-lanimity, lack of energy and moral vigour. 'Cowardice' seems both to descend on Frédéric from outside ('An immense cowardice over-came Madame Arnoux's admirer', p. 260) yet also to form the liquid substance of which his flabby being is composed ('All his virtuous wrath sank in a sea of cowardice', p. 211). When G. Sand attributed the novel's poor reception to 'the lack of control that the characters have over themselves',[21] she was probably thinking principally of Frédéric.

Such lack of willpower and spinelessness cannot be put down simply to the callowness of youth. Even towards the end of the novel, when he is more 'mature', Frédéric continues to give way to his own worst desires; his involvement in politics is interpreted as a sure sign of weakness (p. 298) and, despite the fact that he has now 'won' two women, he is dominated by both of them, meekly carrying Madame Dambreuse's missal when he accompanies her to church (p. 384) and becoming Rosanette's 'chattel' (p. 350). Frédéric some-times judges himself harshly, of course, but the reader is likely to accept his view (p. 357) that it is an act of cowardice to let Rosan-ette drag him away from Madame Arnoux just after he has sworn he loves her as much as ever (p. 354–5). Frédéric's flabbiness emerges clearly from the contrast with other characters. All four women with whom he is involved are more forceful than he is. At the end of the novel, it is Madame Arnoux who seeks to consummate their love; Rosanette is forthright in the offers she makes and in Part III makes a determined attempt to give their relationship perma-nence; Madame Dambreuse precipitates the break by forcing Frédéric's hand at the auction; Louise Roque braves the Paris streets at night (p. 348), having earlier accused Frédéric of not having the courage to take her away from Nogent (p. 253). The other male characters are almost all actively committed to an enterprise of one kind or another; Arnoux to a variety of hair-brained artistic and financial ventures, Deslauriers to launching a political journal, Dambreuse to the consolidation of his fortune, Sénécal to Socialism, Dussardier to the ideal Republic, Pellerin to Art, Martinon to the advancement of his own career. Frédéric, on the other hand, is not committed to anything; a Jack-of-all-trades, he shows no clear pur-pose or consistent effort; he abandons his novel, ignores socially advantageous openings, makes little effort to win votes as a political candidate, betrays each of the women he loves.

Frédéric's lack of direction also contrasts with the more purposeful careers of the young men depicted by Balzac. Although he admired his work and recognized his achievement, Flaubert set out to dedramatize the earlier novelist's presentation of the young man's attempts at making his fortune. Frédéric lacks the boldness and driving ambition of an Eugène de Rastignac or a Lucien de Rubempré; despite the fact that fortune smiles on him in the shape of a substantial inheritance and openings in the fashionable world, Frédéric is, on the whole, indifferent to success and follows an idle and meandering course, unlike Lucien whose character 'urged him to choose the shorter . . . route'.[22] Frédéric does have his frantic moments but these are when he is in pursuit of Madame Arnoux or rushing to see a wounded friend, neither of which advances his social career. The constant implication of *Sentimental Education* is that Balzac's portrayal of the young man's entry into society puts too much emphasis on social ambition which typically, in Flaubert's view, assumes less importance than emotional or sexual matters.

Divergences from Balzacian precedent are numerous and deliberate.[23] Deslauriers makes explicit reference to the fictional model ('Remember Rastignac in *The Human Comedy*,' p. 29) every departure from which we are invited to view as significant. With a relentless concern for the 'ordinariness' of 'average' experience, Flaubert scales down a number of 'classical' scenes (the force of Deslauriers's 'je te dis là des choses classiques', has been lost in translation, p. 29); on the first visit to the Dambreuse (pp. 30–2), there is no immediate evidence of adultery in high places, no faux pas, no outright rejection, no affronted dignity, but merely the dullest and most inconclusive of conversations and the most fleeting of glimpses of the 'grande dame' coupled with Frédéric's rather pathetic attempts to invest the scene with Balzacian drama (cf. his comment about M. Dambreuse, 'A pitiless energy lay in his grey-green eyes, which were colder than eyes of glass', p. 31); the regulation 'orgy' scene is rewritten with brio but is toned down by Frédéric's lack of participation (pp. 121–33); the duel scene (pp. 230–1) is determinedly anti-heroic (since the opposition wilts instantaneously); perhaps most significantly in the suicide scene, Frédéric is prevented from climbing over the parapet by a somewhat anti-climactic 'weariness' (p. 86).

One of the most obvious challenges to Balzacian mythology comes in the sphere of sexual relations. The young man in Balzac is led to believe that the key to social advancement lies in the exploitation of women who are to be regarded as post-horses, to be abandoned as soon as they have outlived their social or financial usefulness. Compared to Rastignac who, as Balzac puts it, soon gets the bit between his horse's teeth, Frédéric is slow to develop 'equestrian' skills. Flaubert, in fact, reverses the pattern, showing in a symbolic dream Rosanette astride Frédéric (who is teamed up with Arnoux) and 'tearing his belly open with her golden spurs' (p. 134). The only woman likely to benefit Frédéric socially is Madame Dambreuse who represents 'the necessary challenge to the post-Balzacian hero'.[24] It is significant, however, that Frédéric for a long time lacks any interest in her despite Deslauriers's injunction that he should set about seducing her (p. 17) and, although at the end he is tempted by her fortune, he makes an un-Balzacian sacrifice when he refuses to enter the symbolic Dambreuse carriage (p. 409).

Lurking in the background in Balzac's novels about young men trying to make their way in society is the criminal, even Mephistophelean figure of Vautrin, aiding and abetting the social ambition of his protégés. Such a figure is conspicuous by his absence in *Sentimental Education*. This means that Frédéric compromises himself in small-scale acts of treachery (as when he writes notes, at Arnoux's request, putting off guests from attending a big banquet launched by a rival, p. 51), whereas Eugène and Lucien, through their association with Vautrin, compromise themselves irredeemably. Whilst Lucien is forced to accept as a last stigmata of Parisian life the money Bérénice has earned by prostituting herself, Frédéric commits the paltry crime of taking the savings of the impecunious Dussardier (pp. 392–3). Flaubert nowhere presents the development of Frédéric in terms of a struggle for his soul between the forces of good and evil; there is no suggestion of some larger cosmic drama which would heighten the significance of the events recorded.

Flaubert is also reluctant to present the young man's career in terms of a conflict between the individual and society, with the latter seen as a quasi-mythical entity against which the young man pits his strength. The reference to 'that vague, glittering, indefinable thing called *society*' (p. 134) casts doubt on the validity of thinking of society in generalized terms and Flaubert substitutes for such a monolithic entity a series of unrelated worlds with sectional interests which never unite to expel the young man from the metropolis. Society is not described as a machine in which one runs the risk of being ground to pieces or as an ocean of mud in which it is impossible not to be besmirched. If the lives of both Frédéric and Lucien follow a downward course, it is for very different reasons. Lucien fails because he has been unable to withstand the pressures of a commercialized world. His downfall is the inevitable consequence of his immersion in a degraded world. Frédéric fails, on the other hand, by virtue of the unfolding of an inner logic; he contains within himself the seeds of his own destruction in the form of totally unreal expectations which makes his final state, 'lost among the ruins of his hopes' (p. 409) a foregone conclusion.

Lastly, the attitude to the whole question of the education of the young man differs. Balzac regards the shedding of youthful illusions as potentially beneficial ('His education was beginning to bear fruit' is the comment in *Old Goriot* when Eugène begins to adapt to the harsh realities of Parisian life). Flaubert, in contrast, associates the loss of illusions not with the achieving of some kind of maturity but with impoverishment and emotional desiccation. One title Flaubert considered for the novel,[25] *Les Fruits secs* ('Withered Fruit') points to the slow organic movement towards sterility which characterizes Frédéric's development. Instead of a pattern of growth and maturation, Flaubert describes a gradual running down of emotional energy, an 'atrophy of the heart' (p. 369), culminating in a state of complete mental and emotional inertia: 'he endured the idleness of his mind and the inertia of his heart' (p. 411).

Flaubert is, of course, not challenging Balzac simply for the sake of it. Many of his rectifications of the Balzacian prototype are a function of his desire to 'represent a psychological state, true, in my estimation, but not yet depicted.'[26] If, in comparison with some of Balzac's heroes, Frédéric seems lacking in energy, it is largely because Flaubert is concerned with 'passion of the kind that can survive nowadays, that is to say, inactive.'[27] Uncomplicated, resplendent passion such as that felt by Mâtho in his previous novel, *Salammbô*, makes for colourful effects but Flaubert feels obliged to forfeit such effects, declaring: 'I see simplicity nowhere in the modern world.'[28] Flaubert is determined to get to grips with the underlying psychological problems of modern man even if this means that his novel, judged by traditional criteria, runs the risk of being considered unsatisfactory.

In conversation with the Goncourt brothers, Flaubert once declared that man is more in need of a 'nervous emission' than a 'seminal emission'[29] and throughout his work he implies that emotional longing takes precedence over physical desire. Flaubert does not, however, set up a false dichotomy between soul and senses, like Balzac in *The Lily in the Valley* or Sainte-Beuve in *Volupté*,[30] for he believes that the 'genital organs are at the root of all passion'[31] and that it is impossible to dissociate sexual and mystical impulses. Flaubert may have declared, at the time of writing *Sentimental Education*, that 'woman, for all men, is the ogive arch reaching up to the infinite'[32] but he was convinced that, although what he called the 'religious adoration of woman',[33] endemic in the modern age, was characterized by the repression of a sexual response, it was, in fact, fueled by sexual energy.

It is these 'generalities' of male sexuality, based more perhaps than he would admit upon his own personal experience, which Flaubert uses in *Sentimental Education* in order to construct his model of a complex form of sexual abstinence. In the opening chapter Frédéric is shown falling involuntarily into a worshipping posture and establishing a pattern that will persist throughout the book. Although he knows nothing about Madame Arnoux at this stage, he bows 'automatically' when she passes and 'with an almost religious impulse of the heart' makes a lavish gift to the harp player. A precondition and a consequence of this worshipping attitude is the suspension of sexual desire: 'the desire for physical possession gave way to a profounder yearning, a poignant curiosity which knew no bounds.' Subsequently, Frédéric insists on regarding Madame Arnoux as a saintly figure, despite the fact that she seems perfectly ordinary to every one else, and this is constantly shown to inhibit a sexual response since to think of her in sexual terms is to profane her image: 'He was restrained by a sort of religious awe. That dress of hers, merging into the shadows, struck him as enormous, infinite, impossible to lift; and precisely because of that his desire increased' (p. 202). An obscure compulsion, compounded of sexual and mystical elements, drives Frédéric to raise Madame Arnoux 'to a position outside the human condition' (p. 174). In a strangely paradoxical manner, the object of desire is pushed further and further away; a harassed middle-class woman of unexceptional appearance is transformed by Frédéric's reverential gaze into an awesome, saintly figure whose inaccessibility guarantees both the strength and the frustration of his desire.

Although both Frédéric and Madame Arnoux, after prolonged

acquaintance, seek to put their relationship on a different footing, they are unable to shake off the idealized images they have built up. Even when he believes Madame Arnoux is about to yield, Frédéric is shown incongruously preparing the apartment in the rue Tronchet 'more reverently than somebody decking out an altar of repose' (p. 275). If Madame Arnoux were to have attended the rendezvous, it would have been psychologically impossible for Frédéric to consummate his passion. This is made clear at the end of the novel when he rejects the offer Madame Arnoux makes of herself. All external obstacles have now been removed to reveal an underlying resistance to sexual contact in Frédéric, a resistance which is in part explained by the apotheosis of Madame Arnoux as a mother-figure.[34]

'Religious adoration of woman' is shown both to shape and distort Frédéric's whole life. It makes for continuity—the 'golden thread' running through his otherwise base existence—but also has disruptive and damaging side-effects. On the one hand, the image of Madame Arnoux is the lodestar of his mental universe, the unmoving obsessional centre around which his world is made to revolve. In the first chapter she dominates an expanding world ('His world had suddenly become larger. She was the point of light on which all things converged') and throughout Part I remains the focal point of his metropolitan world: 'Paris depended on her person, and the great city, with all its voices, thundered like an immense orchestra around her' (p. 78). All that is contiguous with the commanding centre is invested with significance; since the centre itself is taboo and Frédéric can rarely bring himself to look her in the eye, his attention digresses metonymically[35] to her immediate surroundings, possessions, casual utterances, with the result that all the Realist detail becomes charged for him with quasi-mystical significance (cf. 'He looked at her work-basket with eyes full of wonder, as if it were something out of the ordinary', p. 18). One thing his passion does achieve—the rehabilitation of the commonplace.

In Part II a more complex organization comes into existence as Frédéric sets the sacred object of religious adoration in rigid opposition to the profane object of sexual desire, Rosanette. Madame Arnoux's image is enhanced and strengthened by the repeated contrast Frédéric makes with Rosanette, and, inasmuch as he believes he has found in her a focus for carnal desire, his response to Madame Arnoux is 'purified'. The beneficial effect of Frédéric's thralldom to the idealized image of the Madonna is perhaps most clearly illustrated in Part III for, once Madame Arnoux has been removed from his life, he undergoes a rapid moral deterioration. Frédéric, it becomes clear, has preserved a kind of integrity and a relative 'decency' by worshipping at Madame Arnoux's shrine. But Frédéric's obsession also has undeniably deleterious effects. His basic passivity is compounded, if not explained, by his adoration of an idealized image, an adoration which is felt to be a kind of imprisonment: 'Incapable of action, cursing God, and accusing himself of cowardice, he turned restlessly about in his desire, like a prisoner in his dungeon' (p. 79). Secondly, it puts everything else into the shade, impoverishing his relationships with others, undermining his friendship with Deslauriers and leading him to undervalue Rosanette and attempt to restrict narrowly his response to her ('if, in Rosanette's company, his heart happened to be stirred he promptly remembered his great love', p. 149). Thirdly, it eclipses all his social and intellectual ambitions. Frédéric stakes everything on his relationship with Madame Arnoux with the result that other sides of his life suffer from neglect.

This would be less of a tragedy if Madame Arnoux's image survived untarnished but in fact it is repeatedly degraded and profaned. On several occasions Frédéric interprets his involvement with Rosanette as a form of treachery (cf. the scene at the races, p. 209). Although he attempts a rigid compartmentalization of his responses to the two women, the pure woman is contaminated by the impure one. Sacred objects such as the casket are exposed to 'sacrilege' (p. 259) when moved into the orbit of the impure woman and it seems that an 'atrocity' (p. 406) is committed when Madame Arnoux's precious 'relics' are auctioned. But the urge to defile is also deeply rooted in Frédéric himself; when Madame Arnoux fails to turn up at the rendezvous, he substitutes Rosanette for her 'in order to degrade Madame Arnoux more completely in his mind' (p. 283). The closest Frédéric ever gets to the ideal is when profaning it but, ironically, this also means that it is destroyed. *Sentimental Education* gradually reveals the way in which sacred and profane love are interdependent. A rigid opposition between the two is set up in Frédéric's conscious mind but there is a strong suggestion that at an unconscious level they are complementary rather than antithetical. At the source of Frédéric's erotic life is the brothel episode, though it is not described in full until the very end of the book. The reason why the episode is regarded as 'the happiest time we ever had' (p. 419) is that the two adolescents were able to combine two attitudes which later become mutually exclusive—on the one hand, the 'poetic', reverential attitude to woman implicit in the offer of 'big nosegays', on the other the practical realization that money is required to purchase her favours. The subsequent polarization of Frédéric's response to the opposite sex causes considerable psychological damage. Love and desire become mutually exclusive and he reacts to Madame Arnoux and Rosanette in a hopelessly partial manner. The psychological need to complete the incomplete and restore the ideal unity experienced in the brothel now gives rise to the painful drama of profanation; if Frédéric is to add the missing element, inevitably he will detract from her idealized image. *Sentimental Education* offers a sustained and perceptive study of the complex and problematic nature of male sexuality.

Flaubert's exploration of the religious adoration of woman is not conducted in a vacuum. Frédéric's reactions are not analysed in isolation; Flaubert is typically Realist in his assumption that 'human life is most truthfully presented in terms of the individual's milieu, of the particularity of social situation and historical circumstance.'[36] 'Generalities' relating to male sexuality are illustrated in the context of a life which itself provides an excellent illustration of what Auerbach considers indispensable to Realism—'the embedding of random persons and events in the general course of contemporary history, the fluid historical background.'[37]

References to contemporary history fall thick upon the page in *Sentimental Education*, as compared with the sparseness of historical allusions in *Lost Illusions*[38] or *Madame Bovary*. Flaubert wished to evoke the historical background in a systematic, exhaustive manner. One critic has compared the work to a mosaic of which the tesserae are all authenticated happenings[39] and, despite the fictional nature of the main events, the novel is still regarded by historians as an invaluable source of information about the period extending from 1840 to 1851 and in particular about the year 1848.

Flaubert's documentation of the historical background involved a labour of heroic proportions. He read 132 historical works on the period; he took extensive notes[40] from the papers and periodicals of the time; he went to the Bibliothèque Nationale and consulted the manuscripts which still form the basis of the historian's study of 1848; he was in correspondence with eye witnesses of the events of the February and June Revolutions; in short, he sought to know all that could possibly be known about the period, from the fashions in clothes of each year to the sort of menu that was available in 1847 in the Café de Paris. In the end Flaubert had accumulated far more information than was necessary; does it really matter, for instance, that the clothes worn by the various characters are those that might have been worn had they actually been alive in that particular year and how many readers, anyway, are in a position to appreciate Flaubert's manic exactitude? Many of the allusions to contemporary events, found mainly in conversations, now require a footnote if their accuracy is to be appreciated and, since they are integrated into a fictional system the validity of which is not that of historical writing, they may do no more than produce intermittent 'history' effects.[41] There is a danger that Flaubert's slavish preoccupation with topicality—which takes the Realist concern for the particularity of social situation and historical circumstance to its logical conclusion—will push the novel towards that realm of ephemeral circumstance he believed it should transcend.[42]

Documentation, however, provides the basis for the novel's 'grasp' of historical reality; whilst the passing references to minor historical figures, trivial events, and changes in fashion are of questionable value, the fuller evocation of the upheavals of 1848 and after, the February Revolution which led to the overthrow of the bourgeois monarchy of Louis-Philippe and the setting up of the Second Republic, the June days which saw the brutal repression of the Parisian proletariat, and the *coup d'état* of 1851 with which Louis Bonaparte brought the Second Republic to an end and paved the way for the Second Empire, is, precisely because it is more detailed, artistically successful. The full-scale depiction of the course of history did, however, pose considerable problems. Flaubert felt that the background risked swallowing up the foreground, as 'the historical personages are more interesting than the fictional characters, especially when the latter have only moderate passions.'[43] In fact this does not happen although the first chapter of Part III almost cracks under the strain. Flaubert, in the event, provides only partial coverage of the events of 1848. He justifies keeping the narrative focus firmly on Frédéric by intensifying his emotional life at the three turning-points in history. On the eve of the February insurrection, Frédéric is absorbed in his preparations for meeting Madame Arnoux. At one point he is shown scurrying into hiding in order to avoid being swept away by his friends (p. 276) and when the fighting breaks out the next day he is completely bound up in his agonized disappointment at Madame Arnoux's failure to turn up at the rendezvous. In June, an unexpected idyllic interlude in his relationship with Rosanette leads Frédéric to react with 'disdainful pity' to the distant rolling of drums 'for all the excitement struck him as trivial in comparison with their love and eternal nature' (p. 235). Similarly, in 1851, he is again caught up in his own problems: 'Politics left him indifferent, he was so preoccupied with his own affairs' (p. 409).

Not that history is given short shrift. Flaubert manages to achieve a balance between fictional and historical elements; the intensification of Frédéric's emotional life enables him to tone down the interest of the colourful historical events which threaten to eclipse his colourless hero but the reader does not lose sight of these events since Frédéric is made a witness of history. Even when preoccupied with his own affairs, he is not completely impervious to external reality. The key historical events impinge upon his consciousness in a paradigmatic fashion, in the form of distant sounds such as the 'crackling noise' of rifles being fired on the Boulevard des Capucines (p. 283) and distant sights such as that of the dense crowd which 'looked like a field of corn swaying to and fro' (p. 276). Frédéric is not always a reluctant witness; on each occasion there is a phase when he is fascinated by what is taking place and used to register both important historical events and 'peripheral oddities'.[44] In February, he wanders around Paris on the second day of the Revolution, witnessing the storming of the Château d'Eau and the ransacking of the Tuileries by the Parisian mob, as well as observing a host of revealing or curiously insignificant incidents, from the working-class man arguing with his wife that he must fight (p. 286) to the howling of a stray dog (p. 287). In June, he returns to Paris too late to witness the major events but, when arrested by the National Guard, he has direct experience of the confusion of the last night of the insurrection and the 'impressive traces' (p. 331) which it has left, before learning of the dilemma of Dussardier who, like many people committed to the Republic, had not known on which side of the barricades he should be fighting (p. 333). In 1851, before the *coup d'état* Frédéric is made to gather that the proletariat has now learnt its lesson ('We're not such fools as to get ourselves killed for the rich', p. 409) and he returns in time to witness the dragoons intimidating the Parisian crowd and Sénécal's shooting of Dussardier, which is dictated not by an actual historical event but by Flaubert's desire to score a point against early Socialism, showing how it contains an element of authoritarianism which leads it to usher in a totalitarian régime.

Throughout the novel Frédéric's attitude to political developments is representative and to have made him more involved would have been to fly in the face of the 'generality' that political commitment tended to be inversely proportional to personal wealth. The contrast with other characters and Frédéric's reactions in 1848 reveal, however, that he is not completely uninvolved. The complete lack of principle of Dambreuse, the cynical detachment of Hussonnet, the prudent withdrawal of Martinon, the querulous dissatisfaction of Regimbart highlight Frédéric's instinctive sympathy for the unfortunate and a capacity to respond generously to the revolutionary fervour of the Parisian proletariat. The contrast between Hussonnet's arrogant dismissal ('I find the common people revolting') and Frédéric's uncritical admiration ('I think the people are sublime', p. 290) is particularly marked and not altogether to Frédéric's disadvantage. On the other hand, his failure to translate the right sentiments into concrete political action is underlined by the contrast with Dussardier who 'had been on his feet for the past forty-eight hours' (p. 291) during which time Frédéric had been engrossed in other things. Frédéric's lack of real political commitment, clear political views, and strong political ambition emerge forcefully from the comparison with Dussardier's unfailing devotion to the Republican cause, Sénécal's doctrinaire Socialism and Deslauriers's self-seeking activity as an electoral agent.

The number of people who actually fought at the barricades in February has been estimated at around 7,000. Frédéric's absence in the early, most dangerous phase of the revolution is both socially significant and part of an attempt to deflate the 'barricade mythology' of Hugo's *Les Misérables*. But if self-absorption and self-preservation prevent the bulk of the bourgeoisie from participating in the actual fighting, other motives—curiosity, naive acceptance of utopian visions of the future, opportunism—soon draw them out of hiding and into the political arena. Here again, Frédéric's behaviour is profoundly symptomatic. Though basically inoffensive and a man of considerable means, he is fired by the general enthusiasm and considers standing as a Republican candidate, advocating in the speech he prepares a whole series of reforms, including a tax on

unearned income, which would be detrimental to his own interests
as a wealthy man (p. 301). Coming from him, the advice to the upper
classes ('Spare nothing, you rich men! Give! Give!', p. 297) is as
incongruous as the notion he entertains that he, of all people, is cut
out to help the political movement forward (p. 297). His recommendations are purely theoretical and his candidature the result of
opportunism and a frivolous attraction to 'the uniform which the
people said the deputies were going to wear' (p. 297). Sénécal's
objections to his candidature (p. 306) are entirely justified and
Frédéric's lack of commitment in the past catches up with him in a
revealing way, preventing him from climbing onto the political band-
wagon. In contrast, his lack of participation in June wins approval—
not from Sénécal who has now been deported but from the influential figure of Monsieur Dambreuse who takes his place—since
'after all, those who had combatted the insurrection had in fact been
defending the Republic' (p. 343). Typically fickle, having first considered standing as a Republican, he now stands as a Conservative.
The people whom he had in February considered 'sublime', are now
seen as 'immature' and in need of direction from above (p. 365). However, even when adopting political views more in keeping with his
social and economic position, Frédéric is too desultory and allows
success to be snatched from him, suggesting that the *coup d'état* of
1851 is in part the result of the failure of more moderate elements
of the bourgeoisie to offer effective resistance to the reactionary
movement which began in June.

Frédéric's lack of involvement in the historical crises described
limits the extent to which he is affected by them. Despite his impressionable nature, causal connections are rare. The gay atmosphere
in February (p. 282) contributes to his light-hearted behaviour with
Rosanette but this change of mood would not have taken place if
Madame Arnoux had not failed to attend the rendezvous which in
turn is the result of chance (the illness of her child). Subsequently
his relationship with Rosanette is coloured by the prevailing joyous-
ness of the Parisian crowd but, for historical events to have had a
more direct effect on the course of the life of the protagonist, they
would have had to have been seen from the point of view of a
Dussardier. Is this to say that the historical material simply provides
a groove along which Frédéric can slide and that Flaubert fails to
show 'the inner life of man, its essential traits and conflicts . . . in
organic connection with social and historical factors'?[45] Before

jumping to hasty conclusions,[46] it is as well to recall that it was part of Flaubert's ambition in writing the novel to 'show that sentimentalism . . . follows politics and reproduces its phases.'[47] Although he does not set up a direct causal relationship between public events and private emotions (which arguably would run counter to the way things are[48]), the development of Frédéric's emotional life and the development of historical events are linked in significant ways.

There are a number of obvious parallels between the two spheres. The slow build-up of emotional frustration in Frédéric corresponds to the build-up of political exasperation and Frédéric's veneration of Madame Arnoux resembles in some ways the utopianism of Socialist and Republican thinkers. By 1848 Madame Arnoux's life is entering its mature phase ('she was approaching the August of a woman's life', p. 272) and the moment is psychologically ripe for her to cede (in his notes Flaubert uses the phrase 'when everything is ripe'[49]). This parallels the political situation (cf. Deslauriers's note 'the "pear" is ripe', referring both to Louis-Philippe and to the opportune moment, p. 276). Whilst one ripe pear falls, the other is spared indignity. Frédéric's relationship with Madame Arnoux is turbulent at this juncture but it stops short of the cataclysm that racks the body politic. The contrasts within the parallels are as significant as the parallels themselves. Later Frédéric himself jokingly draws a parallel ('I'm following the fashion—I've reformed', p. 282) and goes on to profane Madame Arnoux's image in a way that anticipates the mob's profanation of the Queen's bedroom (p. 289). Subsequently his relationship with Rosanette goes through an idyllic phase (in Fontainebleau) which corresponds to the earlier era of extravagant hopes and political illusions following the February Revolution. Frédéric will be no more able to maintain his emotional harmony with Rosanette than the bourgeoisie social harmony with the proletariat as the counterpointing of the June days with the Fontainebleau episode suggests. Finally, Frédéric's relationship with Madame Dambreuse involves the same kind of compromising and opportunism as takes place in the period after the June days. Flaubert shows that in politics as in love ripeness is not all; after ripeness comes desiccation.

The network of parallels and oppositions invites the reader to judge politics and love each in terms of the other. Louis-Philippe's régime lacks the solidity and dignity of Madame Arnoux. The political optimism of 1848 is as frothy and insubstantial as Frédéric's feelings for Rosanette. Napoléon is stretching over France the same cold autocratic hand as Madame Dambreuse over Frédéric. Or, reversing the comparison, the betrayal of republican ideals is a reminder of Frédéric's betrayal of his sentimental ideal. Dussardier's life is spent in the service of republicanism (although he fears he may have unwittingly betrayed it in June) and he is a martyr to it whilst Frédéric, although he is an idealist like Dussardier, cannot sustain his initial dedication.

The parallels between the public and private spheres are not simply contrived for aesthetic effect but reflect a common underlying causality. Like other Realist novels, *Sentimental Education* is a critique of the Romantic outlook whose impact is shown to be as deleterious in the sphere of personal life as in the collective life of the nation. In Flaubert's view the Romantic movement had blocked the development of the rational, scientific tradition inaugurated by Voltaire and the *philosophes*, resulting in what amounted to a reactionary or regressive over-emphasis on the emotions, religious revelation, and unattainable ideals. The sentimentality inherent in Frédéric's 'religious adoration of woman' is balanced by the irrationality of the Socialists' 'adoration of humanity for and by itself'.[50] Early Socialist thought, Flaubert noted, was deeply impregnated with the values of primitive Christianity, essentially anti-rational and unscientific, committed to the ulcerating pursuit of unrealizable utopian schemes.[51] The consequences of the pursuit of the ideal which for Flaubert lies at the heart of Romanticism are the same in both spheres. Flaubert shows that grandiose political visions result in the same sterility and inactivity[52] as are associated with Frédéric's passion for Madame Arnoux. The failure of the Socialists to achieve a perfect society in 1848 is as inevitable as Frédéric's attempt to grasp the ideal figure of Madame Arnoux. In love as in politics, the pursuit of the ideal leads to a fatal neglect of reality which manifests itself in a number of ways. Just as Frédéric's idealized vision entails a refusal to recognize the sexual component in his response to Madame Arnoux, so the vision of an ideal Republic stands in the way of an awareness of the reality of class conflict. Frédéric thinks of the ideal woman as a figure of saintly purity but becomes involved with a woman of easy virtue who represents the reality of woman as determined by a particular social and economic system. The revolutionary purity which the Socialists ascribe to the proletariat is similarly mocked by the spectacle of the prostitute posing as a statue of liberty (p. 290).

Socialism, Flaubert claimed, believes in miraculous changes and fails to take account either of the passing of time or the 'fatal evolution of things'.[53] The men of 1848 awake from their dreams when the beautiful revolution of February is followed by the ugly revolution of June and the decisive setback of the *coup d'état*. History takes its course and their political illusions have prevented them from doing anything about it. Likewise Frédéric cannot arrest the slow disintegration which takes over both his personal life and the Arnoux household and he too has a rude awakening to the ravages of time when he is finally confronted with Madame Arnoux's white hair (p. 414). The generation of 1840 try to live their lives under the sign of the mother, cocooning themselves in a state of passive expectancy, blinded by visions of perfection but they simply facilitate the coming of the repressive father who blocks their aspirations and sweeps away their idle visions. Flaubert insists, therefore, that there is no radical break between the two spheres since in both the deleterious consequences of sentimentalism are apparent. The life of Frédéric and the historical development of France are two facets of what is basically a single cultural phenomenon—a lack of adjustment between ideal and reality.

The critique of the pernicious effects of the Romantic outlook is not as direct as has perhaps been so far implied. The technique of impersonality, entailing as it does the withdrawal of the novelist from the novel, precludes, Jenkins argues, the presentation of an explicit world-view. Even more than in *Madame Bovary*, Flaubert wishes to keep a low profile and avoids, on the whole, statements which could be construed as emanating from an opinionated, fallible human being, or what are usually referred to as authorial interventions. This does not mean, however, that the events of the novel cease to be narrated or that the device of omniscient narrator is rejected. The narrator in *Sentimental Education* may not be easily identifiable since he rarely refers to himself or expresses an opinion or a value-judgement which would allow him to assume some kind of character in the reader's mind but approximately 11 per cent of the novel can be ascribed to a narrator who, though depersonalized, is nonetheless the source of reliable information and perceptive insights.[54] It is easy to overlook the existence of the omniscient narrator in the novel because, for most of the time, Frédéric's point of view is adopted. The technique of point of view does not involve Frédéric 'speaking' but simply requires the narrator to restrict himself to a presentation of his experience, lifting the lid off his mind and reporting briefly in summaries or more extensively in free indirect style on the way events impinge upon his consciousness. The postulate of a narrator endowed with the superhuman capacity to see into another person's mind is, in fact, confirmed rather than negated by the use of point of view technique. Flaubert is restricting not dispensing with the omniscience of the narrator.

The extent to which Flaubert uses point of view does, however, pose problems. First, there is a danger that the reader will take Frédéric's impressions on trust, failing to appreciate the extent to which reality is distorted by him. Secondly, there is the opposite danger that he will take nothing on trust, refusing to accept that anything that Frédéric sees or thinks has any validity. In both cases, however, there is always the possibility of summoning the omniscient narrator either to make clear that Frédéric is falsifying reality or to corroborate his view of events. It could be argued that if Flaubert did not call upon the narrator from time to time, the Realism of the work would be impaired. The unbroken use of point of view may be epistemologically sound (since everyone perceives reality in his own way) and aesthetically rewarding (as Henry James first showed) but if Flaubert had adopted Frédéric's point of view throughout the novel, he would inevitably have failed to provide the understanding and range of experience which are characteristic of Realist writing.

The thematic significance of *Sentimental Education* is not conveyed solely or even primarily by the omniscient narrator's sporadic analysis of the characters and events though his residual authority does lend the fictional world a certain solidity. As Jenkins has argued, meaning in Flaubert emerges from an elaborate orchestral and suggestive structure. In *Sentimental Education*, however, this structure shares the same unobtrusive quality as is conferred upon the narrator. It is part of Flaubert's Realist strategy to avoid imposing on the novel an overall form which is too crudely contrived, too patently manipulated to achieve neat symmetrical effects. It was precisely this refusal of the aesthetically obvious which, in his view, accounted for the poor reception of the novel:

It is too true and, aesthetically speaking, lacking in distortion of perspective. By dint of having arranged the plan well, the plan disappears. Every work of art should have a point, a summit, form a pyramid shape, or the light should fall on one area of the sphere. But there is nothing like that in nature. No matter! I believe nobody has taken probity further.⁵⁵ The apparent shapelessness of *Sentimental Education* stems from Flaubert's fidelity to the slow hesitant rhythms, the self-defeating repetitiveness and liquid continuity which he believed lay at the heart of human experience. When writing *Madame Bovary*, Flaubert had already found that his deference to the psychologically 'true' prolonged incubation period of passion ('people harbour passions for twenty years which are only translated into action for one day and then die'⁵⁶) made for a novel which was all exposition and little action but the dramatic contrasts between Emma's early experiences and her decline and suicide provide the basis for a strong pyramid structure with corresponding 'blocks' on each side of the clubfoot chapter which forms the apex of the work. *Sentimental Education*, on the other hand, as Brombert points out, is 'a novel of steady flow and indefinite expectation. No final catastrophe ever interrupts the fluidity of existence. Tragedy here stems not from the brutal interruption of life, but from its hopeless and self-destructive continuity.'⁵⁷ The image which most richly evokes the dilatory, hesitant quality both of Frédéric's delayed development and the protracted plot is that of the river. Viewed in its totality, Frédéric's existence is a meandering, aimless, riverlike succession of unspectacular events, trivial crises, and shabby emotions which creates an impression of steady flow and flatness. The reader has the vertiginous impression of somehow being inside time itself as it slowly passes, bearing along and wearing down a whole generation. Flaubert has captured brilliantly the 'slow, irregular rhythm of life', a rhythm based on the intermittent devotions of love and friendship, the flagging of passion and idealism, an alternation between vast expanses of boredom and bursts of frantic but vain activity. Whilst in *Lost Illusions* events are packed dramatically into a short timespan, in *Sentimental Education*, Flaubert extends the action over a period of eleven years (longer if one counts the last two chapters), opening up vistas of drab monotony and dreary continuity, and stressing the hollowness and meaninglessness of life in a series of anti-epiphanies (along the lines of 'His return to Paris gave him no pleasure', p. 254).

Water is a destructive element in Flaubert. Within its liquid confines *Sentimental Education* records the slow dissolution of ideals and aspirations, the disintegration of illusions and ambitions, the collapse of personal integrity and political regimes. The novel is like a battlefield, littered with ruins and broken objects, moving from the pathetic debris of Dussardier's pipe ('he gazed at these ruins of his happiness', p. 43), through the central ruins of Frédéric's hopes (p. 409) to the apocalyptic 'ruins of some vanished city' suggested by the landscape of Fontainebleau (p. 349). The level at which everything seems to be collapsing is that of content rather than form. The ruination of hopes is as amenable to aesthetic manipulation as any other subject and the long linear development of the novel conceals a multitude of patterns, an underlying order and harmony. Complementing the lack of clear dramatic outline is a deeply concealed structure which rests on the same deep-rooted tendency Flaubert described in his early, autobiographical work, *Novembre:* 'in human actions I would suddenly perceive relations and oppositions whose luminous precision dazzled me.'[58] The reader has, therefore, a dual sense of form being destroyed and achieved, of experience dissolving into chaos and falling into an overall pattern.

The patterning of *Sentimental Education* is extensive, from the symphonic organization of the main theme—the erosion of the hopes and ideals of a whole generation—to the controlled oppositions and parallels between the various characters. The aesthetic impact of these patterns is, of course, not felt by Frédéric. Although his point of view is adopted for much of the time, Flaubert is able to overcome the limitations of his consciousness by the occasional use of omniscience, the distribution of clues from which the reader can make crucial inferences, the skilful arrangement of scenes and relationship in internalized paradigms which invite systematic cross-reference. For some critics the relationship with Madame Arnoux provides the central, co-ordinating element in the novel but Frédéric's involvement with other women, the tangential pull of friendship, the colourful nature of the historical events all threaten to undermine such a simple postulate. A rich network of parallels and oppositions link all four women in Frédéric's life.[59] Although rigid oppositions between the saintly figure of Madame Arnoux and the loose figure of Rosanette, and between the sophisticated Madame Dambreuse and the gauche Louise Roque are set up in Frédéric's mind, all four have much in common and behave at various points in a similar fashion. For instance, all four women are frustrated victims of a patriarchal society who believe that Frédéric can afford them some relief from their unsatisfactory lives but each one is let down by him. In each case, after prolonged reconnoitring, there is a brief period of

emotional harmony and subdued ecstasy, followed by disenchantment and treachery. All four women have an over-generous view of
Frédéric, believing him to be more noble or considerate than he is
and seeking to reward him for what they take to be his devotion.
Each relationship is intertwined both with his friendship with
Deslauriers who, as unabashed as Frédéric is reticent, attempts to
seduce all four, and with historical material, taking on a colouring
which corresponds to a phase of history. In a similar fashion,
Frédéric's friends and friendships are compared and contrasted and
the hegemony of his relationship with Deslauriers undermined.

The surreptitious patterning of the novel can also be seen in the
placing of similar or related episodes at strategic points. For instance,
each of the three parts of the book ends with a scene in which
Frédéric is kissed or embraced by a woman whom he does not desire
and in each case great distress is generated, marked twice by tears.[60]
Flaubert stresses in this way the failure of human beings to synchro-
nize their feelings. The novel also begins and ends with scenes which
are linked. The opening scene in which Frédéric has his first 'vision'
of Madame Arnoux is balanced by the penultimate chapter in which
she reluctantly takes her leave of him. The second chapter in which
the friendship of Frédéric and Deslauriers is presented before they
go their separate ways contrasts with the final chapter where friendship is shown surviving all else. In both cases the wheel has come
full circle. Frédéric has lived his passion prospectively until he is
finally brought to the point where it can be celebrated only retrospectively and, since the brothel episode which Frédéric declares to
be the happiest time of his life occurred before the book begins, he is
finally made to realize that he had, in fact, arrived even before he had
set off. The beginning and end of Frédéric's long linear development
are finally joined to form a circular pattern which seems to negate all
purpose and progression. Typically, however, the scene which
undermines the value of Frédéric's life, is an aesthetic *tour de force*.
Whilst Frédéric has postponed indefinitely the consummation of his
desire for Madame Arnoux, Flaubert brings the novel to a satisfying
conclusion by finally underlining the undoubtedly seminal significance of the brothel episode and allowing the reader to reach a
fruitful understanding of Frédéric's fruitless existence.

Despite his vehement disclaimers, Flaubert should be considered
as a Realist. His claim to the title rests securely on his penetrating
understanding of the relationship between literature and life in an

age in which it was frequently misconstrued, on his readiness to take as a central character someone as significantly insignificant as Frédéric, on his skill in projecting into this character's development a number of recurring features of male sexuality, on his depiction of Frédéric's life against a colourful historical background which is more than a mere backdrop and on the achieving of an artistic form so finely contrived that it expresses both the shapeless liquid continuity in life as well as the pattern beneath it.

NOTES

1. Balzac, *La Comédie humaine*, Pléiade, Paris, 1949–59, xi. 244; Champfleury, *Le Réalisme*, Levy, Paris, 1957, p. 87.
2. Quoted in P. Martino, *Le Roman réaliste sous le second empire*, Paris, Hachette, 1913, p. 83.
3. Cf. *Correspondance*, Paris, Conard, 1926–33, iv. 92, and viii. 224.
4. *Correspondance*, iii. 268.
5. *Correspondance*, iii. 249 and vii. 281.
6. In the Preface ('Le Roman') to *Pierre et Jean*, ed. G. Hainsworth, Harrap, London, 1966, p. 42.
7. Cf. B. F. Bart, 'Flaubert's Concept of the Novel', *Publications of the Modern Language Society of America*, lxxx (1965), 86.
8. *Correspondance*, iii. 401.
9. *Correspondance*, v. 253.
10. *Correspondance*, ii. 462.
11. *Correspondance*, v. 409.
12. *Correspondance*, iii. 88.
13. Henry James, 'Gustave Flaubert: 1902', *Selected Literary Criticism*, ed. M. Shapira, Heinemann, London, 1963, p. 221.
14. Cf. 'The subject, as I have conceived it, is, I think, profoundly true but precisely because of that, not amusing', *Correspondance*, v. 158.
15. H. James, op. cit., p. 222.
16. P. Cortland, *The Sentimental Education*, Mouton, The Hague, 1967, p. 64.
17. *Correspondance*, v. 331.
18. *Journal*, Pléiade, Paris, 1951, i. 805.
19. Cf. Introduction to the Penguin translation referred to in n. 20, p. 8.
20. *Sentimental Education* (translated by R. Baldick), Penguin Books, London, 1964, p. 16. All future quotations will be followed by page references to this edition.
21. In an article quoted in the Conard edition of the novel.
22. *Lost Illusions*, Penguin, London, 1971, p. 252.
23. Cf. A. Vial, *Faits et significations*, Nizet, Paris, 1973, pp. 55–107.
24. Alison Fairlie, 'Some Patterns of Suggestion in *L'Éducation sentimentale*', *Australian Journal of French Studies*, vi (1969), 279.
25. R. Dumesnil, *Flaubert et L'Éducation sentimentale*, Société des belles lettres, Paris, 1943, p. 132.
26. *Correspondance (Supplément)*, ii. 65.
27. *Correspondance*, v. 158.

28. *Correspondance*, v. 331.
29. *Journal*, ed. Ricatte, Éditions de l'imprimerie nationale de Monaco, 1956–8, vi, 173.
30. Cf. *Le Lys dans la vallée*, Pléiade, Paris, 1949, viii. 948–9; *Volupté*, Charpentier, Paris, 1927, p. 44.
31. *Correspondance*, iii. 24.
32. *Correspondance*, v. 274.
33. Goncourt, *Journal*, vi. 173.
34. It is significant that Madame Arnoux should bestow her parting kiss 'like a mother' (p. 415). The oedipal element in the relationship has been discussed in P. Cogny, *L'Éducation sentimentale de Flaubert*, Larousse, Paris, 1975, pp. 177–87.
35. Cf. R. Jakobson, *The Fundamentals of Language*, Mouton, The Hague, 1956, pp. 53–4.
36. Cf. Chapter I, p. 5.
37. *Mimesis*, Doubleday Anchor Books, New York, 1957, p. 434.
38. Cf. Chapter on *Lost Illusions*, p. 18.
39. A Cento, *Il Realismo documentario nell' Éducation sentimentale*, Liguori, Naples, 1967, p. 44.
40. A selection has been published in *Œuvres complètes*, Club de l'honnête homme, Paris, 1973, viii.
41. Akin to the 'reality effects' discussed by R. Barthes in 'L'effet de réel', *Communications*, ii (1968), pp. 84–9.
42. *Correspondance (Supplément)*, ii. 118.
43. *Correspondance*, v. 363.
44. A. Fairlie, art. cit., p. 270.
45. G. Lukács, *Studies in European Realism*, Merlin Press, London, 1972, p. 8.
46. Cf. Fischer's contribution to a Colloquium on Flaubert, *Europe*, xlvii (1969), 139.
47. *Œuvres complètes*, iii. 418.
48. Cf. J. Proust, 'Structure et sens de *l'Éducation Sentimentale*', *Revue des sciences humaines*, 1967, p. 71.
49. *Œuvres complètes*, iii. 417.
50. *Correspondance*, iii. 208.
51. *Correspondance*, v. 344 and v. 383.
52. *Correspondance*, iii. 178.
53. *Correspondance (Supplément)*, iv. 275.
54. Cf. the chapter on *Sentimental Education* in R. J. Sherrington's *Three Novels by Flaubert*, O.U.P., Oxford, 1970.
55. *Correspondance*, viii. 309.
56. *Correspondance*, ii. 202.
57. *The Novels of Flaubert*, Princeton University Press, Princeton, 1966, p. 149.
58. *Œuvres complètes*, xi. 621.
59. A. Fairlie, art. cit., pp. 275–87.
60. Cf. L. Cellier, *Études de structure*, Archives des *Lettres Modernes*, No. 56, Minard, Paris, 1964, pp. 2–20.

5

G. Eliot: *Middlemarch* (1871–2)

PATSY STONEMAN

IN HIS introductory chapter to this book, Jenkins associates the
Realist movement in literature with the growth during the nineteenth
century of scientific and sociological rationalism—a movement which
can conveniently be called 'scientism'. On the other hand, he
questions whether many of the Realist writers thoroughly understood the scientific principles they invoked: 'the fact is that the
Realists tended, as innocently as we ourselves might do today on a
similar basis of second-hand scientific knowledge, to justify their
activity, to themselves as well as to others, in the intellectual terms
which had come to dominate their culture' (p. 9).

George Eliot, like Flaubert, had perhaps a more serious claim to a
scientific understanding. She wrote no fiction until she was thirty-
nine, and the years before this were spent in consolidating an
extraordinary range of knowledge, including science. She was an
intellectual giant, recognized as such by her contemporaries, and as
assistant editor of the learned *Westminster Review*, she dealt with
works on philosophy, theology, history, geography, sociology, and
the natural sciences.

Her life-long partner, George Henry Lewes, was also a polymath;
actor, novelist, astute literary critic, he was also an eminent man of
science, especially in the fields of zoology and physiology. His *Sea-
side Studies* was still used by undergraduates into the twentieth
century.

George Eliot thus had access to more than the layman's knowledge
of science, and it is appropriate to begin a consideration of Realism
in one of her novels with a scientific holiday which she spent with
Lewes at Ilfracombe in 1856—fifteen years before *Middlemarch*—
where they spent their days clambering over wet rocks collecting
sea-anemones, polyps, and annelids for *Sea-side Studies*.[1] At night,
in lodgings piled high with jars full of aquatic creatures waiting to
be dissected and viewed under the microscope, George Eliot con-

tinued with work for the *Westminster*. Under the influence of this zoologizing, she noted 'a tendency that is now constantly growing in me to escape from all vagueness and inaccuracy into the daylight of distinct, vivid ideas'.[2] One of the articles written during this holiday was a review of two works by the German writer Wilhelm Heinrich Riehl, which she called, significantly, 'The Natural History of German Life'. Riehl's books[3] are what we would now call sociological, and George Eliot roundly praises his patience and accuracy in recording detailed observations, especially of

small shopkeepers, artisans, and peasantry—the degree in which they are influenced by local conditions, their maxims and habits, the points of view from which they regard their religious teachers, and the degree in which they are influenced by religious doctrines, the interaction of the various classes on each other, and what are the tendencies in their position towards disintegration or towards development.[4]

This sort of subject-matter is close to that of Realist fiction, as described for instance in another *Westminster Review* article, possibly by Lewes, three years earlier:

It has been the tendency of modern writers of fiction to restrict themselves more and more to the actual and the possible . . . The carefully wrought story, which details events in orderly chronological sequence; which unfolds characters according to those laws which experience teaches us to look for as well in the moral as in the material world; and which describes outward circumstances in their inexorable certainty, yielding to no magician's wand or enchanter's spell, is essentially the function of a complex and advanced state of society.[5]

Realism, then, as suggested in these passages, was a kind of corollary to the prevailing scientism of the age, and as G. J. Becker puts it, 'the basic ideal of the movement was and is rigorous objectivity'.[6] Becker goes on, however, to point out that this approach inevitably involves a contradiction, since 'while there was no official position philosophically maintained by Realists, it was inescapable that if they looked around them, if they subjected traditional views to the rigorous test of experimental method and observation, they would collide headlong with the concept of the ideal and would be forced to deny it.'

In most Realist writers this contradiction remains implicit, but in George Eliot it becomes immediately apparent. We need look no further than 'The Natural History of German Life' to see it at work. Having praised the 'rigorous objectivity' of Riehl and suggested that novelists should adopt the same method, she goes on, 'Art is the nearest thing to life. . . . All the more sacred is the task of the artist when he undertakes to paint the life of the People' (p. 54). In a review of Ruskin, also written in 1856, she writes, 'The truth of infinite value that he teaches is *realism*. . . . The thorough acceptance of this doctrine would remould our life; and he who teaches its application to any one department of human activity with such power as Mr. Ruskin's, is a prophet for his generation.'[7] Realism, therefore, is not simply a 'scientific method' but a 'doctrine', and the Realist not simply a scientific observer, tracing laws of causality in the physical world, but a teacher, a prophet, a man with a sacred task. George Eliot's enthusiasm for the Realist position leads her to proffer it, paradoxically, as an ideal in itself, to be adopted not simply for the sake of objectivity, but for a moral reason. On the other hand, as Becker points out, the logic of the Realist view 'entailed an absolute denial of the principle of idealism' (loc. cit.). The whole issue is complicated by the fact that in the 1850s many critics respectably maintained that the only moral method in literature was Idealism, conceived as presenting models of irreproachable excellence for readers to imitate. George Eliot, in espousing Realism for a moral reason, was thus putting herself outside the camp not only of traditional Idealism, but also of the majority of Realists who believed that objectivity precluded any moral dimension to their writing.

The contradiction is, however, inescapable, as Becker shows, and George Eliot and George Henry Lewes were perhaps less naive than other Realists in facing up to the problem. Lewes countered the difficulty in two ways. Firstly he recognizes that Realism is limited by the medium of the work of art—the words on the page or the paint on the canvas—so that what is in question is not an absolute, but at best an illusion of reality.[8] Secondly, since all ideals originate from experience, he insists that Idealism is not the antithesis of Realism, but a special kind of Realism: 'The true meaning of Idealism is a vision of realities in their highest and most affecting forms, not a vision of something removed from or opposed to realities.'[9]

In practice, this 'moral' Realism differs from a supposed photographic Realism mainly in the selection of material, not in its treatment, although it certainly predisposed George Eliot to retain the intrusive method of narration, which allowed her to draw attention to the morally important aspects of her story, and to draw the reader into a moral involvement with the fictional events. Both Lewes and George Eliot are vehemently opposed to 'falsification' of a subject once chosen. 'We want to be taught to feel', says George Eliot, 'not for the heroic artisan or the sentimental peasant, but for the peasant in all his coarse apathy, and the artisan in all his suspicious selfishness'.[10] On the other hand Lewes disapproved of Balzac because he allowed the wicked to triumph and the innocent to perish,[11] and both Georges disapproved of Nathaniel Hawthorne for the same reason.[12] The distinction seems to be that while the selected material must be faithfully presented in accordance with the laws of cause and effect, the overall course of events in the novel must not outrage the reader's sense of poetic justice. George Eliot felt that 'the art which leaves the soul in despair is laming to the soul, and is denounced by the healthy sentiment of an active community.'[13] If the function of art is moral, the readers of fiction must not be crippled with pessimism. The same moral appropriateness can be seen in the events of *The Rise of Silas Lapham*, written, like *Middlemarch*, in a predominantly Protestant country where moral earnestness tended to survive even in those who, like George Eliot, had abandoned any formal creed.

What may seem like naivety in George Eliot's approach is the direct result of her meliorist world-view. She believed, in default of religion, in the value of human life and the duty of every individual to improve its conditions. It is because she believes life to be sacred that she can call Realist writing a 'sacred task', since it sets out to reproduce not only the outward conditions, but also the values, of the real world. George Eliot would argue that even the most hardened egoist has a keen sense of the value of his own life, and it is from this sense of value that morality can be developed, for if my life is valuable to me, then by an effort of the imagination I can see that your life is valuable to you. At the other end of the scale, she attacked the hardened cynicism of the complete determinist, and argued in a letter to Mrs. Ponsonby that although she believed our actions to be determined by physical laws, it was of the utmost psychological and social importance not to allow this belief to undermine morality:

As to the necessary combinations through which life is manifested, and which seem to present themselves to you as a hideous fatalism, which ought logically to petrify your volition—have they, *in fact*, any such influence on your ordinary course of action in the primary sphere of your existence as a human, social, domestic creature? And if they don't hinder you from taking measures for a bath, ... why should they hinder you from a line of resolve in a higher strain of duty to your ideal, both for yourself and others? But the consideration of molecular physics is not the direct ground of human love and moral action, any more than it is the direct means of composing a noble picture or of enjoying great music. One might as well hope to dissect one's own body and be merry doing it, as take molecular physics (in which you must banish from your field of view what is specifically human) to be your dominant guide, your determiner of motives, in what is solely human. That every study has its bearing on every other is true; but pain and relief, love and sorrow, have their peculiar history which make an experience and knowledge over and above the swing of atoms.[14]

George Eliot's Realism is thus an attempt at balance between scientific devotion to a true record of things as they are, and the ethical evaluation of those events which arises from subjective consciousness. This attempt at balance characterizes not only a literary theory, but a whole philosophy, derived from Comte, Feuerbach, and other rationalist writers of her time.

These thinkers rejected theology on the grounds that it was an attempt to explain the universe in terms of subjective vision—that of a God formed in man's own image. This vision makes the cosmos a comfortable home for mankind, since he sees himself as of central importance in it, but it fails to provide truth, since it does not take account of non-human, physical laws. Complete objectivity, on the other hand, while it provides truth, reduces mankind to an insignificant speck in a hostile environment, and ignores every man's urgent sense that he is important, if only to himself. Thus 'without objectivity there is no truth; but without subjectivity . . . there is no human value or meaning.'[15]

Nineteenth-century science provides a link between these two orders of knowledge. Bernard Paris explains how, according to Darwin, Spencer, Lewes and Huxley,

the cosmic process, which has no relation to moral ends, produced human society, or what Huxley called the ethical process, by virtue of the survival value of social union. Since those societies whose members were most devoted to the common welfare were naturally selected, the cosmic force, whose principle is aggressiveness and competition, gave rise to the ethical process, the moral order, whose principle is co-operation (loc. cit., p. 421).

George Eliot attempts to show both the 'cosmic' and the 'ethical' processes in her novels, by giving both an objective view of the laws which govern human society, and a subjective view of the human value within it. Her views on Realism did not radically alter during the fifteen years and five novels between 'The Natural History of German Life' and *Middlemarch*, and the balanced and connected claims of objective and subjective views can be seen in many aspects of this work.

The presentation, for instance, is divided between an objective, or 'dramatic' rendering of action, and subjective, or evaluative, passages of comment and interpretation. The choice of marriage as one important theme in the novel is connected with this principle of balance, for while George Eliot deplored the gross neglect of women's intellect in the nineteenth century, she still believed that the sexes were biologically determined, towards a preponderance of the subjective, sympathetic faculties in women, and towards the objective, analytical faculties in men. Marriage could redress this inevitable imbalance, the partners complementing one another.[16]

The most important balance, however, lies in George Eliot's concept of the human situation, somewhere between the total subjectivism of the new-born baby, for whom existence is no more than a series of vivid desires, and the total objectivity of the determinist, which, as she says in the letter to Mrs. Ponsonby (p. 105), 'ought logically to petrify your volition'. In Chapter 21 of *Middlemarch* George Eliot explains that 'we are all of us born in moral stupidity, taking the world as an udder to feed our supreme selves.'[17] The ethical process leads the individual out of this state of crude subjectivity—the humanist's version of original sin—by making him recognize both external necessity and the 'equivalent centre of self' in others, upon which morality can be based.

By explicitly considering how this subjective/objective balance is, or is not, achieved within the characters of the novel, George Eliot manages to combine the 'rigorous objectivity' of the Realist aesthetic with the form of a *Bildungsroman*, following the moral development of the characters, and designed to have a moral impact on the reader. This *Bildungsroman* aspect has encouraged critics to analyse the novel on a simple linear pattern, and although I shall argue later that complexity is of the essence of George Eliot's Realism, it is

interesting to see how rigorously she herself evaluates her characters on a subjective/objective scale.

Every character in *Middlemarch* shows egoism, or unbalanced
subjectivity, in some form—Dorothea in desiring a grand destiny;
Lydgate in assuming that he should naturally have the best of everything; Casaubon in making his own dignity take precedence over
humanity; Bulstrode in supposing that Providence singled him out
for special favours; Fred in feeling that the world owes him a living.
The variations and processes of egoism can be seen conveniently,
however, in the three heroines, Rosamond Vincy, Mary Garth, and
Dorothea Brooke.

Rosamond is an unmitigated egoist, having 'a Providence of her
own who had kindly made her more charming than other girls' (p.
297, Ch. 27). She learns nothing from experience because she is
shielded from having to recognize external necessity—in the shape
of financial pressure, for instance—and she has no inclination to
imagine what other people are feeling except in relation to herself.
She is an example of the aggressive instinct in spite of her passive
behaviour, showing 'that victorious obstinacy which never wastes its
energy in impetuous resistance' (p. 630, Ch. 58), and she effectually
destroys her husband, who attempts to co-operate and has to end by
yielding.

Mary Garth, on the other hand, is a good example of balance:

having early had strong reason to believe that things were not likely to
be arranged for her peculiar satisfaction, she wasted no time in astonishment and annoyance at that fact . . . Mary might have become cynical if
she had not had parents whom she honoured, and a well of affectionate
gratitude within her, which was all the fuller because she had learned to
make no unreasonable claims [p. 349, Ch. 32].

Mary is thus equally far from egoism and from cynicism. The favourable circumstances in her case seem to be a realistic acquaintance
with economic facts, and an affectionate family life which predisposes
her to sympathise with others outside the family. When Rosamond
dismisses her governess as 'so uninteresting', Mary retorts that 'she
is interesting to herself, I suppose' (p. 141, Ch. 12). Whereas
Rosamond is trapped within egoism by her subjective view of life,
Mary is able to make positive use of subjective responses by 'putting
herself in the place' of others. Her attitude to the governess is not
simply objective, nor is it altruistic, since altruism implies a denial

of self; it is a sort of extended subjectivity, an imaginative 'feeling with' the other person, which is what George Eliot means by 'sympathy'. As a result of her balanced outlook, Mary is not only able to live in a tolerably happy way despite external difficulties, but she also engages with the lives of other people in a positive way, forming what George Eliot calls a 'theatre' for the actions of others, especially Fred Vincy. 'Even much stronger mortals than Fred Vincy', we are told, 'hold half their rectitude in the mind of the being they love best.' (p. 274, Ch. 24). In the same way Dorothea provides incentive to Will to persevere in his 'bit of work, though it was not that indeterminate loftiest thing which he had once dreamed of as alone worthy of continuous effort' (p. 501, Ch. 46).

The progress of Dorothea is of course much more complicated than the almost static picture of Rosamond and Mary. She moves from an illusory ideal of a grand destiny to a realistic appraisal and humane sympathy for her husband, and from this, after his death, to an extended sympathy for humanity at large. Her development depends almost equally on an increased objectivity in her assessment of her own situation in relation to other people, and on the increased ability to 'put herself in the place' of others, imagining what it feels like to be them. In a striking image at the climax of her development, Dorothea looks out of her window and feels both 'the largeness of the world' and that she is 'a part of that involuntary, palpitating life' (p. 846, Ch. 80). It is as a result of this dual recognition that she is able to make the crucial visit to Rosamond which marks her transcendence of egoism. Of course this process is shown with a minute attention to cause and effect, which I cannot begin to demonstrate in this small space, and in fact all these linear patterns of moral development operate in the context of an infinitely complex reality. It is in indicating this complexity that I feel George Eliot to be most truly a Realist.

In *The Mill on the Floss*, published in 1860, George Eliot uses the idea of complexity to defend her choice of humble subjects:

The suffering, whether of martyr or victim, which belongs to every historical advance of mankind, is represented . . . in every town, and by hundreds of obscure hearths; and we need not shrink from this comparison of small things with great; for does not science tell us that its highest striving is after ascertainment of a unity which shall bind the smallest things with the greatest? In natural science, I have understood, there is nothing petty to the mind that has a large vision of relations, and to which every single object suggests a vast sum of conditions. It is surely the same with the observation of human life [Book IV, Ch. 1].

Thus human life is seen as 'a vast sum of conditions'. Science is a 'striving after . . . a unity which shall bind the smallest things with the greatest'; ethics, a 'historical advance' 'represented' in hundreds of examples; and in 'the comparison of small things with great' there is a suggestion of the aesthetic principle on which *Middlemarch* is based. George Eliot has warned us that this complexity cannot easily be unravelled, saying that 'for getting a strong impression that a skein is tangled, there is nothing like snatching hastily at a single thread',[18] and a governing image in *Middlemarch* is that of a web, or net, connecting every element with every other. Nevertheless some sort of dissection seems necessary if we are to see how, in Caleb Garth's words, 'things hang together' in *Middlemarch*, and, bearing in mind that the categories will not always allow themselves to be kept separate, I propose to consider how complex reality is rendered in *Middlemarch* first under the aspect of science, or sociology, secondly in the moral sphere, and finally in the aesthetic structure of the novel.

In 'The Natural History of German Life', George Eliot insists that 'a wise social policy must be based not simply on abstract social science, but on the Natural History of social bodies' (p. 72). Thus the kind of sociology she is interested in is both particular and complex. She is opposed to interpretations by rule of thumb, whether it takes the form of convention, religious dogma, or political science of a too abstract kind. All possible techniques of investigation must be brought to bear on all the available information, in the service of 'rigorous objectivity'.

In his chapter on *Sentimental Education* (p. 77) Williams uses the image of a scalpel to suggest the kind of Realism which is not content with surface appearances. George Eliot uses the image of a microscope. In Chapter 6 of *Middlemarch*, having shown Mrs. Cadwallader interfering in the life of Sir James Chettam, she stops to question what her motives were. These could not, she assures us, be derived from a mere surface observation of her activities:

Even with a microscope directed on a water-drop we find ourselves making interpretations which turn out to be rather coarse; for whereas with a weak lens you may see a creature exhibiting an active voracity into which other smaller creatures actively play as if they were so many animated tax-pennies, a stronger lens reveals to you certain tiniest hairlets which make vortices for these victims while the swallower waits passively at his receipt of custom. In this way, metaphorically speaking, a strong lens applied to Mrs. Cadwallader's match-making will show a play of minute causes producing what may be called thought and speech vortices to bring her the sort of food she needed [p. 83, Ch. 6].

The immediate purpose of this passage is to explain why George Eliot needs to give us more than the 'dramatic' or surface rendering of a scene—why, in fact, authorial explanation is called for. But it also provides justification for other, quasi-scientific, aspects of the novel which also work towards revealing the 'play of minute causes'.

The novel is sub-titled 'A Study of Provincial Life', and the economic structure of the town of Middlemarch provides a system of connections within which the 'minute causes' can play. The characters are chosen as if they were a part of a sociological survey, and it is possibly for this reason that the novel is set back forty years in time, to the period of the Reform Bill of 1832. It has become a modern dogma that the Realist novel deals with contemporary life, but in fact most of the novels dealt with in this book distance their subject-matter by something like a generation. *Middlemarch*, with its forty-year gap, is set back further than any except *Mastro-Don Gesualdo*, which deals with events even before the novelist's birth. In some cases the novel covers the events of a lifetime, and is brought up to date at the end. In many cases the novelist uses autobiographical material from his own childhood and youth, as George Eliot used memories of election riots which she witnessed in Nuneaton as a child, and this inevitably sets the action back into the period of the writer's childhood. But this is only part of a larger compulsion, which all the Realist novelists seem to have shared, towards documentation and archive work. In Chapter 40 of *Middlemarch* George Eliot states that 'in watching effects, if only of an electric battery, it is often necessary to change our place and examine a particular mixture or group at some distance from the point where the movement we are interested in was set up' (p. 434). The research which George Eliot, and to a greater or lesser degree the other Realists, felt to be necessary, was more easily accomplished at a distance in time, when records were more easily available and judgement had the benefit of perspective. In this she is most comparable with Flaubert, who, as Williams points out (p. 88), became a marvel of information on the 1848 revolution, and like her kept notebooks of background data. George Eliot also spent infinite pains on accurately representing the background to her novel. Her working notebook, *Quarry for Middlemarch*[19] contains scores of notes taken from the *Lancet* of 1830-3, and from other medical sources, containing information on the cholera epidemic, the distinction between typhus and typhoid, heart disease, and the treatment of delirium tremens, as well as on the state of medical education and practice in general, the taking of fees, dispensing of drugs and so on. All this ensured that Lydgate appeared as a genuinely enlightened man, ahead of his time, and in the case of Raffles an important moral dilemma is made to turn on an innovation in medical practice. The *Quarry* also contains lists of political dates, including many, like the 1830 revolution in France, which are not used at all in the novel, and others, like the progress of the cholera, which are used in a subdued and peripheral fashion. There is even a note of the terms and periods of examination at Oxford and Cambridge, presumably to authenticate the movements of Fred Vincy. The fictional 'events' are similarly noted and dated, often to the month, and the fictional geography of the town plotted out. This scrupulous preparation bears fruit in the characters; it is generally acknowledged as the main excellence of Realist fiction that its characters have the added conviction which comes of being accurately set in a particular environment.

George Eliot did not, however, like Balzac and Pérez Galdós, use scarcely altered real personages in her novels. Robert Evans, George Eliot's father, served as the source for Caleb Garth, but few other characters can be identified so easily. Dr. Clifford Allbutt of Leeds, who started one of the earliest fever hospitals in the country, may be an original for Lydgate, but his brother, while accepting the possibility, noted that 'nothing in their careers was common, save the training and the high aspiration.'[20] George Henry Lewes is an obvious original for Ladislaw, but Richard Ellmann argues persuasively that his characteristics were well blended with those of John Walter Cross, who became George Eliot's husband after Lewes's death.[21] Likewise Casaubon has been attributed to the scholar Mark Pattison, and to George Eliot's girlhood friend R. H. Brabant, but Ellmann produces at least three other possibilities, and quotes a revealing story recorded by F. W. H. Myers in *The Century Magazine* of November 1891, to the effect that when George Eliot was asked where she found Casaubon, 'with a humorous solemnity, which was quite in earnest nevertheless, she pointed to her own heart'. Ellmann continues:

This remark deserves to be considered. She meant by it exactly what Flaubert meant when he said '*Madame Bovary, c'est moi.*' Flaubert, too, had his Brabants and Mackays, and secured a few useful details from actual events and persons, but in his writing he had other things to think about. What must be sought is not a Casaubon, but casaubonism, and this George Eliot found, as Flaubert found *le bovarysme*, in herself [loc. cit. p. 166].

What we have here is in fact another aspect of the blending of subjective and objective information. George Eliot doubtless began with observations of particular people, but her finished characters draw their significance and life partly from a 'scientific' process of abstraction, by which the observed originals shed inessential characteristics and contribute only those features which fit them for a particular self-consistent role in the novel, and partly from the subjective identification and sympathy of the author. The abstracting process gives truth, or probability, but it is the feeling of the author which prevents the picture from being dry and statistical, and provides what Lewes called 'a *vision* of realities in their highest and most affecting forms' (my emphasis). George Eliot makes this point in 'The Natural History of German Life':

Appeals founded on generalizations and statistics require a sympathy ready-made, a moral sentiment already in activity; but a picture of life such as a great artist can give, surprises even the trivial and the selfish into that attention to what is apart from themselves which may be called the raw material of moral sentiment [p. 54].

This has George Eliot's characteristic moral slant, but the Marxist critic Georg Lukács, in *Studies in European Realism*, makes essentially the same point about the characters of Realist fiction. He objects equally to the 'pseudo-objectivity of the naturalist school' and the 'mirage-subjectivism of the psychologist ... school'. Realism, distinct from either, recognizes

that a work of literature can rest neither on a lifeless average, as the naturalists suppose, nor on an individual principle which dissolves its own self into nothingness. The central category and criterion of realist literature is the type, a peculiar synthesis which organically binds together the general and the particular both in characters and situations. What makes a type a type is not its average quality, not its mere individual being, however profoundly conceived: what makes it a type is that in it all the humanly and socially essential determinants are present on their highest level of development, in the ultimate unfolding of the possibilities latent in them, in extreme presentation of their extremes, rendering concrete the peaks and limits of men and epochs.[22]

Thus in George Eliot's work the 'real-life counterparts' of her characters are much less important than their 'typical' quality, which gives a sense of individual existence, fused with a sense of social representativeness.

Each of the older generation of characters in *Middlemarch* represents a certain economic interest. Mr. Brooke is landed gentry, with Sir James Chettam a shade nearer aristocracy. Mr. Vincy is the urban, bourgeois manufacturer. Mr. Bulstrode is finance and trade. Caleb Garth is a combination of the new 'managerial classes' and the old yeoman class.[23] There is a sufficient representation of clergymen and doctors for the professional class. The lower classes, in spite of the notion that Realist novels must have low subjects, do not feature prominently in the shape of individuals. This is in fact true of most of the novels dealt with in this book, although of course there are important Realist novels of working-class life, and later Naturalism became engrossed with this subject. George Eliot probably confined herself to the middle classes because, as she says in 'The Natural History of German Life', among the lower classes 'custom . . . holds the place of sentiment, of theory, and in many cases of affection' (p. 61). This means that when they do appear, they voice the attitudes of habit or tradition, rather than any individual perception. The 'lower orders' are certainly present, as in the scene where the railway surveyors are routed; where Mr. Brooke's tenant Dagley gives him a piece of his mind; or where Mrs. Dollop of the Tankard inn opposes Lydgate's dangerous innovations in medicine, and, as can be seen from these examples, it is by their 'interference, however little we may like it, [that] the course of the world is very much determined' (p. 448, Ch. 41). Their instinct is to oppose change. George Eliot's remark about 'custom' was actually made in reference to the peasantry, but it seems likely that her own rural background predisposed her to take the rural working class as representative of the working class in general, and in any case her liberal humanist world view made her distrust the possibly disruptive power for social change within the working class, which was certainly present at the time she is writing of. Given her commitment to a historical advance which she thought would evolve through the enlightened consciousness of individuals, it was inevitable that George Eliot should give most attention in her novel not to the mass, whose inaccessibility to ideas she saw as part of their oppression, but to those who were most open to the kind of ethical transformation she envisaged.

For this reason she concentrates on the more individual and detachable members of the middle class; the younger generation, who are less firmly anchored than their elders to economic functions and who cry out in a chorus 'What can I do ?'[24]

Fred Vincy is the most ordinary of them, struggling with the decision whether or not to enter the Church, which seems the only respectable opening for a young man of his class with no private means. The case of Dorothea is at the centre of the novel, and the Prelude prepares us for the theme of aspiration in an age where 'no coherent social faith and order could perform the function of knowledge for the ardently willing soul'. Will Ladislaw, confident of genius but seeing no fit channel for its development, simply places himself 'in an attitude of receptivity'—including drunkenness and the taking of opium—'to all sublime chances' (p. 109, Ch. 10). In spite of the irony in this exposure, and to a lesser extent in the treatment of Dorothea too, George Eliot is here investigating a genuine historical phenomenon, observable throughout Europe as the middle-class intelligentsia found the heroic energies which had been appropriate to an age of Romanticism and revolution, stranded in an age of commercialism, reduced to 'aspiration without an object'.[25] It is a common theme for Realist writers (for instance Balzac, Flaubert, Strindberg), who tend to expose their idealist heroes to an atomistic society in which their ideals are shattered. The mechanistic processes of the market in particular provide precisely the inhuman environment in which ideals wither and the affections die. Thus Balzac called his novel *Lost Illusions* and Flaubert toyed with the title *Withered Fruit* for *Sentimental Education*. Lukács argues that Realism arose precisely in response to the irony inherent in the 'tragic self-dissolution of bourgeois ideals by their own economic basis, by the forces of capitalism' (op. cit., p. 47).

George Eliot, because she tends to construe historical problems in ethical terms has a less pessimistic reading of the idealist's fate in society than either Balzac or Flaubert, but she does show this economic determinism at work—not primarily in the case of Dorothea or Will, however, but in that of Lydgate, who at the outset seems superior to either in that his lofty ideals have a practical and humane outlet in the practice of medicine. Nevertheless it is

Lydgate who is made to feel most keenly 'the hampering thread-like
pressure of small social conditions, and their frustrating complexity'
(p. 210, Ch. 18). The finely plotted course by which a disinterested
desire for good actions leads Lydgate into a humiliating dependence
on Bulstrode and the social establishment is a track which I have no
space to follow through, but it does show the 'mesh' of social prejudice and economic pressure in a very complex interaction. It is
typical of George Eliot that Lydgate's eventual failure is, however,
relative; he suffers nothing worse materially than 'an excellent
practice, alternating . . . between London and a continental bathing-
place', but 'he always regarded himself as a failure: he had not done
what he once meant to do' (pp. 892–3, Finale). Foster, in her chapter
on *The Rise of Silas Lapham*, sees this 'relative' failure of characters
like Lydgate, Frédéric Moreau, and Lapham himself, as characteristic of Realist novels, whereas a more crushing defeat, like that of
Lucien in *Lost Illusions*, has the flavour of Romance, in spite of its
'determined' nature.

George Eliot is, I think, true to this spirit in that even her 'success
stories' are so relative that modern readers have often taken Dorothea's fate, for instance, to be tragic. Nevertheless Dorothea, and
Will, and Fred Vincy, do not fail in the same way as Lydgate or
Frédéric Moreau, and this does mark George Eliot off from the
more wholly deterministic writers. The reason why Dorothea, Will,
and Fred, who all start out so aimlessly, do not fail, while Lydgate,
with his promising beginning, does, is that George Eliot wants to
demonstrate the power of the individual will as a counterbalance to
environmental determinism and as a means of reconciling the ideal
with the actual. The loss of illusions in Flaubert leads to personal
collapse; there is no prospect of attaining a 'wider vision'. The collapse, moreover, is seen as an inevitable process. In Balzac there is
some suggestion that a character may learn from experience, but
there is still no doubt of society's ultimate crushing of the individual.
George Eliot, however, sometimes speaks as if the individual could
avert disaster by an unsupported, heroic effort: 'It always remains
true, that if we had been greater, circumstances would have been less
strong against us' (p. 632, Ch. 58). Lukács, speaking of Balzac, identifies such 'heroic' statements as this as 'a core of idealist illusions'
which 'inevitably still persists even in' writers dedicated to the
Realist position. 'Nevertheless', he continues, 'these illusions contributed to the continuation of the great struggle of mankind for

freedom,' helping 'to preserve the great heritage of *bourgeois* humanism and save what was best in it for the future benefit of mankind' (op. cit. p. 63). George Eliot's letter to Mrs. Ponsonby (quoted on p. 105), certainly makes her insistence on individual heroic effort seem more like a deliberate moral strategy than an illusion in any more pejorative sense, and her handling of the theme of lost illusion, and of the reconciliation of the ideal and the actual, shows considerable subtlety.

George Eliot's investigation of a historical problem ('aspiration without an object') has thus led her to an ethical solution (heroic individual effort), and this leads us, in our consideration of her Realism, from the 'scientific', 'Natural History' aspect of her novel to its personal, moral aspect; from the recording of social cause and effect to the individual's attempts to influence the process. Here again we find that complexity is essential to George Eliot's treatment. Moral perceptions are necessarily complex, firstly because the enlightened consciousness must take account of what George Eliot calls 'hard non-moral outward conditions', which are themselves complex. The obscure ramifications of connection between Ladislaw, Bulstrode, and Lydgate are, I think, meant to demonstrate an aspect of 'outward conditions' which George Eliot calls 'the stealthy convergence of lots', 'a slow preparation of effects from one life to another, which tells like a calculated irony on the indifference or frozen stare with which we look at our unintroduced neighbour' (p. 122, Ch. 11). Secondly, the ethical process involves an attempt to imagine the inner states of others, which are again complex. Even the simple-seeming Mrs. Cadwallader reveals hidden motives to the 'strong lens' of the inquiring novelist.

The main need for a complex vision, however, lies in the process, which George Eliot saw as central, of reconciling the ideal with the actual. She saw clearly how often people fail to integrate various aspects of their own lives. Lydgate, for instance, suffers from 'the creeping paralysis apt to seize an enthusiasm which is out of adjustment to a constant portion of our lives' (p. 632, Ch. 58). In this case his work was 'out of adjustment' with his domestic life. But the dislocation can operate in many spheres and is far from unusual—'is it not rather what we expect in men, that they should have numerous strands of experience lying side by side and never compare them with each other?' (p. 634).

Say that, for our rather crude purpose, we divide the life of a man or a woman into four departments: ideals, daily life, source of income, and personal relationships. The perfectly integrated person would recognize a connection between them all. Caleb Garth is such a person. This happy man, drawn from George Eliot's own father, draws his ideals from a sense of wonder in practical work well done; the practical work is his daily life, from which he draws his income; his personal relationships are either connected with his work, or else within his family, who share his ideals, his income, and his practical activity. This thorough integration means that they can think clearly, act firmly, and react to misfortune, whether financial hardship or personal sorrow, in a straightforward way which makes it more bearable; they do not experience that wry anguish which comes when misfortune exposes unsuspected weakness in our own past actions or present attitudes which is often more difficult to cope with than the misfortune itself, since it can destroy self-reliance and paralyse action.

Almost every other character in *Middlemarch* suffers some sort of dislocation, causing distress which the characters themselves are often unable to identify. The commonest gaps, in this era of gentility and unearned income, are related to money. Fred Vincy, for instance, in spite of his warmly affectionate nature and his gentleman's code of honour, is sent seriously astray, pressured as it were into dishonourable behaviour, by expecting to inherit Peter Featherstone's estate. He recovers when he abandons the ideal of genteel ease and embraces real human affection and practical work instead.

Will Ladislaw, again, suffers at the beginning of the novel from a dislocation of ideals from practical life which is sustained by an allowance from Mr. Casaubon. As soon as he gives up the allowance and turns his hand to practical work, connected with his radical ideals but also bringing him an earned income, he gains a sense of integrity which later enables him to reject Bulstrode's conscience-money, which he feels would carry contamination with it.

Dorothea herself is not free from this dislocation of ideals which derives ultimately from her unearned income. At the conceptual level she wants ideals that must 'frankly include the parish of Tipton', and where practical schemes like housing and the hospital offer themselves, she eagerly embraces them. But Celia is as usual perceptive when she calls these activities 'fads', 'notions', and 'schemes'. They cannot determine the quality of her daily life. What she suffers from in fact is the stifling oppression of that gentlewoman's world, where everything was done for her and none asked her aid—where a sense of connection with a manifold pregnant existence had to be kept up painfully as an inward vision, instead of coming from without in claims that would have shaped her energies.—'What shall I do?' 'Whatever you please, my dear': that had been her brief history since she had left off morning lessons [p. 307, Ch. 28].

Her marriage to Casaubon, as an attempt to fill the daily blank of this 'oppressive liberty', was a dismal failure, because his work proved to be totally disconnected from any ideals of her own. In fact it is only when she abandons part of her income to become the wife of Will Ladislaw, now an 'ardent public man', that she achieves a life filled 'with a beneficent activity' (p. 894, Finale).

It is important to realize that none of these people are actively mercenary. Even the materialistic Rosamond 'never thought of money except as something necessary which other people would always provide' (p. 301, Ch. 27), and Bulstrode, who shows the grossest dislocation between ideals and income, buys Stone Court in order to throw 'more conspicuously on the side of Gospel truth the weight of local landed proprietorship' (p. 563, Ch. 53). And George Eliot is careful to tell us that 'this was not what Mr. Bulstrode said to any man for the sake of deceiving him: it was what he said to himself' (p. 565). In a society where unearned income was the norm for an influential class of people, such dislocation must be endemic.

Other 'failures of adjustment' are unconnected with money, but just as serious. Mr. Casaubon certainly demonstrates the 'unearned income' syndrome since he performs almost none of the functions of a parish priest and his daily life is absorbed by his aspiration, to produce a 'Key to all the Mythologies'. But his more serious lack of adjustment is towards people, especially Dorothea. He sees the function of marriage as 'to adorn his life with the graces of female companionship . . . and to secure in this, his culminating age, the solace of female tendance for his declining years' (p. 87, Ch. 7). He thus thinks of a wife as a kind of superior servant, not at all a person with whom he could enter a reciprocal relationship, or, at first, integrate in any way either in his daily preoccupations or his larger ideals.

Lydgate, too, in spite of medical progressiveness, sees his wife as 'an accomplished creature who would venerate his high musings and momentous labours and would never interfere with them . . . in-

structed to the true womanly limit and not a hair's breadth beyond—
docile, therefore, and ready to carry out behests which came from
beyond that limit' (p. 387, Ch. 36). Both with Rosamond and in the
earlier episode with Madame Laure, he sees love as an interruption
to his real life, which is work. Impatient with the unsettled state of
courtship, he looks forward to marriage as 'the best thing for a man
who wants to work steadily' (p. 383). In practice this means that
Rosamond is relegated to a totally background role, while his real
energies are devoted to scientific research:

bringing a much more testing vision of details and relations into this
pathological study than he had ever thought it necessary to apply to the
complexities of love and marriage, these being subjects on which he felt
himself amply informed by literature, and that traditional wisdom which
is handed down in the genial conversation of men [p. 193, Ch. 16].

It is interesting that Bazarov, in *Fathers and Sons*, also a doctor, who
shares Lydgate's passion for scientific research and has a similar
grand conception of general benevolence, is, like Lydgate, destroyed
because the pattern of his life has no place for warm personal relationships.

Dorothea, as well as mistaking Mr. Casaubon's work for something
which could fill her life, shows another 'lack of adjustment' in marriage which is not covered by my four categories. A gap in her own
self-knowledge allows her to overlook the sensual disparity between
her and Mr. Casaubon. Whereas he is constantly presented as dry,
withered, almost mummified, she is healthy and vigorous, enjoys
riding 'in a pagan sensuous way' and walking through the woods at a
'rather brisk pace'; she glows 'from her morning toilette as only
healthful youth can glow'. 'Ardent' is an adjective very frequently
applied to her, and it can apply to physical as well as spiritual fervour:

she had ardour enough . . . to have kissed Mr. Casaubon's coat-sleeve,
or to have caressed his shoe-latchet, if he would have made any other
sign of accepting it than pronouncing her, with his unfailing propriety,
to be of a most affectionate and truly feminine nature, indicating at the
same time by politely reaching a chair for her that he regarded these
manifestations as rather crude and startling [p. 230, Ch. 20].

By the end of Chapter 21, when they are still on their honeymoon,
'she had begun to see that she was under a wild illusion in expecting

a response to her feeling from Mr. Casaubon' (p. 243). Will Ladislaw, with whom she achieves her integrated life at last, is by contrast
'like an incarnation of the spring', and they finally come together
against a background of storm which seems to represent 'the flood' of
'young passion bearing down all obstacles' (p. 870, Ch. 83).

The gaps are filled and the adjustments made, if at all, through the
process of disenchantment, often presented in the novel through the
image of a daylit room. After Dorothea's return from Rome, for
instance, her blue-green boudoir has quite a different aspect from
before: 'The very furniture in the room seemed to have shrunk since
she saw it before. . . . The duties of her married life, contemplated as
so great before, seemed to be shrinking with the furniture and the
white vapour-walled landscape' (p. 306, Ch. 28). It is interesting that
the view should be shut out by the snowy weather, for it is the ex-
pansive view from the window which comes to symbolize later what
I am tempted to call a more realistic idealism—idealism which has
been shorn of its fantastic elements and retains only, in Lewes's
words, 'a vision of realities in their highest and most affecting forms'.
In a letter of 1848 George Eliot describes disenchantment as a
necessary stage in the growth of the spirit, and seems to envisage a
kind of permanent ethical revolution in which the spirit must constantly shed illusions and replenish ideals. The image of the daylit
room features here too:

Alas for the fate of poor mortals which condemns them to wake up some
fine morning and find all the poetry in which their world was bathed
only the evening before utterly gone—the hard angular world of chairs
and tables and looking-glasses staring at them in all its naked prose. It is
so in all the stages of life—the poetry of girlhood goes—the poetry of
love and marriage—the poetry of maternity—and at last the very poetry
of duty forsakes us for a season and we see ourselves and all about us as
nothing more than miserable agglomerations of atoms . . . This is the
state of prostration—the state of self-abnegation through which the soul
must go, and to which perhaps it must again and again return, that its
poetry or religion, which is the same thing, may be a real ever-flowing
river fresh from the windows of heaven and the fountains of the great
deep—not an artificial basin with grotto work and gold fish.[26]

George Eliot's zoologizing led her to wish for 'the daylight of distinct, vivid ideas'. But the 'daylight' of objective science can become
'the hard angular world' of disenchantment, revealing nothing but
'miserable agglomerations of atoms' unless re-humanized by

'poetry', by the 'vision of realities in their highest . . . forms'. In *Felix Holt* George Eliot says that 'what we call illusions are often, in truth, a wider vision of past and present realities—a willing movement of a man's soul with the larger sweep of the world's forces—a movement towards a more assured end than the chances of a single life' (Ch. 16). Illusions, then, are harmful if they cannot be integrated into the life of an individual, but, corrected by the processes of disenchantment, they may be seen as 'a wider vision', a means of integrating the individual in the larger life of humanity. In the life of Dorothea, as I have briefly indicated, we can see this corrective process going on. But George Eliot also suggests the 'larger sweep' through the structure of the novel, especially in the use of analogies.[27]

Jenkins writes that the Realist novelists began to use 'internal structures'—'the symphonic organization of themes, the controlled parallelism and opposition of characters and events, subtle shifts of narrative tense, a clever modulation of point of view, ironical juxtaposition'—because 'surface effects are clearly not enough' to render the 'depth and order' of reality (p. 11). George Eliot's aesthetic theory shows this tendency very clearly, together with the insistence on complexity which marks every aspect of her work. In 'Notes on Form in Art', George Eliot states that the 'highest form' is 'the most varied group of relations bound together in a wholeness which again has the most varied relations with all other phenomena'.[28] Thus not only does the work of art—the 'wholeness' in question—become more perfect in proportion to the number of functional relationships it bears within itself, but it must also relate in as many ways as possible to the world at large. In *Quarry for Middlemarch* George Eliot lists eleven 'relations to be developed' between major characters, and after reading her definition of form in art it is no surprise to find that in Chapter 15 of *Middlemarch* she describes the universe as a 'tempting range of relevancies' (p. 170).

Various characters in *Middlemarch* attempt to unite the one with the many, the general with the particular. Casaubon's 'Key to all the Mythologies', Lydgate's search for the 'primitive tissue' which would provide a key for pathology, Dorothea's search for a grand social aim which would 'frankly include the parish of Tipton'—these can be seen as aspects of the same search.[29] It is appropriate, then, that the structure of the novel should be dominated by parallelism and analogies which also attempt to link the one with the many, the general with the particular. I have already mentioned many parallels in the choice of subject-matter—many characters are involved in coping with idealism, with money, with marriage. The headings to the eight books also suggest parallels and contrasts: 'Old and Young', 'Three Love Problems', 'The Widow and the Wife', 'Two Temptations', 'Sunset and Sunrise', and 'The Dead Hand', which refers both to Featherstone and to Casaubon.

There are also parallels between private and public life, for as George Eliot says in *Felix Holt*, 'there is no private life which has not been determined by a wider public life'. Numerous half-hidden references link the progress of the main characters with the progress of the first Reform Bill. For instance, the beginning of Chapter 19: 'When George the Fourth was still reigning over the privacies of Windsor, when the Duke of Wellington was Prime Minister, and Mr. Vincy was mayor of the old corporation in Middlemarch, Mrs. Casaubon, born Dorothea Brooke, had taken her wedding journey to Rome' (p. 219). This may seem merely a pompous way of saying 'Once upon a time', but it, and other similar passages, establish a link between the older generation in Middlemarch and the anti-reform movement in the country. It thus neatly suggests that Dorothea, in marrying Mr. Casaubon, was not really taking a step towards freedom as she thought, but allying herself with the forces of reaction. Similarly Mr. Casaubon is associated with Peel, Peter Featherstone is 'dead and buried some months before Lord Grey came into office', and Mr. Vincy wonders 'whether it were only the general election or the end of the world that was coming on, now that George the Fourth was dead, Parliament dissolved, Wellington and Peel generally depreciated and the new King apologetic.' (p. 321, Ch. 30, p. 375, Ch. 35, p. 392, Ch. 37). Casaubon's death coincides with the dissolution of Parliament in April 1831, and the match between Will and Dorothea follows the vicissitudes of Lord John Russell's Bill. Will himself, of course, is an active advocate of reform.[30]

While the analogical structure is characteristic of most Realist novels, *Middlemarch* is unusual in the scope of its material. Many of the novels dealt with in this book are in effect fictional biographies. *Middlemarch*, however, covers only a short period in its characters' lives, while its lateral spread is greater than anything except Tolstoy and, perhaps, Balzac. The omniscient, even intrusive, mode of narration which George Eliot uses is important in establishing these wide connections. It enables her to change focus rapidly from a close-up of particular people to the town of Middlemarch or to the whole of England, and often by a sleight of hand includes the reader also. A sentence that begins with 'Lydgate' or 'Dorothea' will end with 'you' or 'we', creating the sense of an unbroken series of connections between the events of the novel and those of the real world. As Lydgate says, 'a man's mind must be continually expanding and shrinking between the whole human horizon and the horizon of an object-glass' (p. 690, Ch. 63).[31] It is interesting that in George Eliot the instinct towards analogical structures, which Jenkins sees as characteristic of the impersonal mode of Realism, is combined with the more old-fashioned technique of the intrusive narrator, which enables her to include the reader in the analogies.

The ability to change focus is also used over the range of time, and George Eliot evaluates and compares her characters by reference both to explicit historical analogies and to the conventions of the present time, which act like 'frozen' history, the patterns of the past exerting an influence on the present. We have seen how the rural lower classes are limited by habitual modes of thought (p. 114). Formal codes of behaviour and dress limit, in the same way, those members of the middle class who do not put themselves in 'attitudes of receptivity' to new ideas. Thus Rosamond's education consists almost entirely of learning rules of etiquette, 'even to extras, such as the getting in and out of a carriage' (p. 30, Ch. 11), and Mr. Casaubon is dominated by cut-and-dried rules: 'The deeper he went in domesticity the more did the sense of acquitting himself and acting with propriety predominate over any other satisfaction. Marriage, like religion and erudition, nay, like authorship itself, was fated to become an outward requirement' (p. 314, Ch. 29). After the passage in which Dorothea thinks of kissing Mr. Casaubon's coat-sleeve, we are told that 'having made his clerical toilette with due care in the morning, he was prepared only for those amenities of life which were suited to the well-adjusted cravat of the period' (p. 230, Ch. 20). On the other hand we are told of Dorothea's 'direct simplicity' of manner, how, in discussing Mr. Casaubon's illness, she threw off bonnet and gloves 'with an instinctive discarding of formality' (p. 322, Ch. 30), and how she becomes 'her old self' when Celia robs her of her widow's cap, which had become, as she confesses, like a protective shell (pp. 292 and 294, Ch. 55). Will displays more marked unconventionality by giving picnics to groups of ragged children, and by lying full-length on the rug in houses where he became familiar (p. 503, Ch. 46).

History in a more explicit form plays a part in the story when Dorothea makes her wedding journey to Rome. We are told that she had never been able to relate the pictures at Tipton to anything in her own life, and Rome, 'the city of visible history', affects her as 'stupendous fragmentariness'; 'All this vast wreck of ambitious ideals, sensuous and spiritual mixed confusedly with the signs of breathing forgetfulness and degradation . . . took possession of her young sense, and fixed themselves in her memory' (p. 225, Ch. 20). The 'fragmentariness' is an echo on a larger scale of her own disenchantment, the sensation of becoming 'a miserable agglomeration of atoms'. At this stage she feels that the pressure of the past prevents her from realizing her own identity, though as we have seen her development leads her to accommodate a sense of the larger processes of history. Sue Bridehead, in Hardy's *Jude the Obscure*, has a similar sensation in the 'ancient dwelling' she lives in at Shaston: ' "Such houses are very well to visit, but not to live in—I feel crushed into the earth by the weight of so many previous lives there spent. In a new place . . . there is only your own life to support" ' (Part IV, Ch. 1). Sue's attempt to support only her own life, without reference to history or convention, is the result of her indignation 'that the social moulds civilization fits us into have no more relation to our actual shapes than the conventional shapes of the constellations have to the real star-patterns' (ibid.). Marx had a similar perception that men act only in the arena prepared by the past: 'Men make their own history, but they do not make it just as they please; they do not make it under circumstances chosen by themselves, but under circumstances directly found, given and transmitted from the past. The tradition of all the dead generations weighs like a nightmare on the brain of the living.'[32]

'The weight of unintelligible Rome' presses on Dorothea and reduces her sense of her own identity, but Mr. Casaubon seems at home in history. He pays for this comfort, however, by losing touch with the present. 'Such capacity of thought and feeling as had ever been stimulated in him by the general life of mankind had long shrunk to a kind of dried preparation, a lifeless embalment of knowledge' (pp. 228–9, Ch. 20). Whereas Dorothea sees Rome as 'ruins' and 'fragments', 'poor Mr Casaubon . . . was lost among small closets and winding stairs' (p. 229), and his mental state is constantly

compared with labyrinths, mazes, closed rooms, tombs, and cata-
combs. He too is disenchanted, but he refuses to accept it as a phase
of growth. 'With his taper stuck before him he forgot the absence of
windows, and in bitter manuscript remarks on other men's notions
about the solar deities, he had become indifferent to the sunlight'
(p. 230).

Will Ladislaw provides a contrast to them both. With his 'piety' of
spontaneous delight, he enjoys 'the very miscellaneousness of
Rome, which made the mind flexible with constant comparison, and
saved you from seeing the world's ages as a set of box-like partitions
without vital connection' (p. 244, Ch. 22).

George Eliot herself makes 'vital connections' between 'the world's
ages' by means of allusion, providing another example of how she
combines what Jenkins calls 'internal structure' with the technique
of the intrusive narrator. Thus Dorothea is compared with St.
Theresa and Antigone, and Mr. Brooke compares Will with Burke,
Shelley and Byron. But a more fundamental connection is established by reference to the ancient myths of imprisonment and
release.

In particular, Mr. Casaubon, associated as we have seen with dark-
ness, tombs, and labyrinths, becomes Pluto to Dorothea's Per-
sephone, while she, seized from the sunshine to live 'in a virtual
tomb' becomes in another place Eurydice, and Will Ladislaw
Orpheus, 'receding' as 'she stood at the door of the tomb' 'into the
distant world of warm activity and fellowship—turning his face
towards her as he went' (p. 516, Ch. 48). Again in several places
Dorothea is Ariadne, whom Theseus rescued from the labyrinth of
the Minotaur (p. 220, Ch. 19, p. 253, Ch. 22).

In Will's mind the same image takes on the aspect of folk-lore: he
sees Dorothea imprisoned by fire-breathing dragons, or by Mr.
Casaubon as an ogre growing grey 'crunching bones in his cavern'
(p. 395, Ch. 37), and generally casts himself as knight errant to
Dorothea's damsel in distress. But of course real action is barred by
the mesh of social conditions: Mr. Casaubon 'was something more
unmanageable than a dragon; he was a benefactor with collective
society at his back' (p. 241, Ch. 21).[33]

In her patient display of 'minute causes' George Eliot attempts to
show not only the thwarting effects of social determinism but also
the gradual evolution of the ethical process. The historical analogies,
and the human archetypes embodied in the myths, enable us to see

the tiny achievements of one generation against a larger time-scale. They also allow George Eliot to emphasize the necessary conflict between deadening conservatism and the rebelliousness of youth, without having to specify any politically radical programme. In Will in particular the doubtful qualities of bohemianism become more positive when he is identified with Orpheus, or even Dionysus, who in some versions of the myth is the eventual mate of Ariadne. Thus hope in a stronger guise than gradualness is proffered by making large connections, while the social surface of events retains the texture of reluctant actuality. The case of Will Ladislaw shows up the extent to which the 'internal structure' in *Middlemarch* forms part of what I have called George Eliot's 'moral strategy'. As Eagleton puts it in *Criticism and Ideology*, 'the novel's difficulty in "realizing" him springs from its incapacity to see how this desirable ideological conjuncture, yoking prudent gradualism to visionary Romanticism, can be achieved in the historical conditions it describes' (p. 121). His acceptability has therefore to be reinforced within the novel by all its battery of aesthetic organization.

It has become obvious in the course of this study that what seems to be the Realists' first priority—'rigorous objectivity'—will not take us very far in understanding *Middlemarch*. George Eliot's 'objectivity' is itself motivated by an ethical intention, and even historically formulated problems in the novel are given an ethical solution, in terms of inter-personal relations, of the individual's 'heroic effort' towards an objective/subjective balance, and an integration of disparate experience. Moreover, the fact that these ethical solutions are seen in terms of balancing opposites, or of making 'large connections', means that they are reinforced, even authenticated, by the aesthetic patterns of correspondence and contrast which we have seen in the novel. This means that there is a much closer connection than would at first seem possible, between the claimed 'objectivity', the ethical scheme of value, and the aesthetic structures.

Jenkins argues that because their 'objective' goal was a kind of mirage, 'the artistic achievement of the Realists is best perceived not in terms of the unattainable objectivity . . . but in terms of the technique of impersonality to which the forces making for an objective rendering of the world almost inevitably led them' (p. 10). In George Eliot, however, a conscious moral intention mediates between the 'objective' and the 'aesthetic'. In her work, moreover, the impulse towards 'internal structure', which Jenkins sees as peculiar to the impersonal mode, is combined with an intrusive narration, in which the narrator 'shows his hand', for instance by making classical allusions, or by making explicit the bearing of the events of the novel on the reader's own life.

I would argue that the success of this combination in *Middlemarch* shows that while aesthetic structures are indeed of unexpected importance in Realist novels, the impersonal mode is not the only way of resolving the objective/subjective contradiction which, as Jenkins argues, is the main 'problem' of Realism. What George Eliot has done is to establish a narrator with such breadth of knowledge and experience, such depth of feeling, and such 'wisdom' (to use a now discredited Victorian word),[34] that she is able to set up an objective/subjective balance within the narrator. When the narrator moves with ease over a wide range of modern and ancient history and literature, science, religion, and politics, we are more prepared to accept his statements as, not impersonal, but impartial, which is another route to objectivity. On the other hand, it is through the emotional reactions of this narrator that we are invited to share the subjective experiences of the fictional characters, and through the narrator's 'wisdom' that we can reconcile the outer and inner views. In the person of the narrator, in fact, we have the paradigm for the balanced consciousness which the characters of the novel strive towards, and the readers are invited to emulate. This is what Eagleton means when he says 'the problem of totality within the novel is effectively displaced to the question of aesthetic form itself ... Only the novelist can be the centred subject of her own de-centred fiction, the privileged consciousness which at once supervenes on the whole as its source, and enters into empathic relation with each part' (op. cit., p. 120).

It is the tremendous flexibility of this narrative mode which allows George Eliot to present her characters at the same time as insignificant units in a phenomenal social and cosmic web, and as vitally important, autonomous human beings. The Finale of *Middlemarch* shows this subtle combination of an objective recognition of limited possibilities with the hopefulness which arises from subjective identification; we are told of Dorothea:

Certainly those determining acts of her life were not ideally beautiful. They were the mixed result of young and noble impulse struggling amid the conditions of an imperfect social state, in which great feelings will take the aspect of error, and great faith the aspect of illusion [p. 896].

This description fits many Realist heroes and heroines from Lucien de Rubempré to Effi Briest, though George Eliot perhaps betrays more sympathy than usual for˙her heroine's 'young and noble impulse'. The closing words of the novel, however, are surely unique in their peculiar quality of balance. The recognition of 'hard, non-moral, outward conditions' is modulated by ethical meliorism so that although the words are muted and qualified, the narrator's voice has the achieved tone of wisdom, neither strident nor apathetic, neither enthusiastic nor discouraged, but calm, sure, and persuasive:

But the effect of her being on those around her was incalculably diffusive: for the growing good of the world is partly dependent on unhistoric acts; and that things are not so ill with you and me as they might have been, is half owing to the number who lived faithfully a hidden life, and rest in unvisited tombs [ibid.].

NOTES

1. For the connection between Realism and science in George Eliot, see A. J. Sambrook, 'The natural historian of our social classes', *English*, xiv (1963), 130–4.
2. 'Recollections of Ilfracombe 1856' in *The George Eliot Letters*, edited by G. S. Haight, 7 vols., Oxford University Press, London, Yale University Press, New Haven, 1954–6, ii. 251. Subsequent references will be to *Letters*, and will be included in the text. Dean Howells also uses the phrase 'honest daylight' in connection with Realism. (See p. 4).
3. *Die burgerliche Gesellschaft*, 3rd edition, 1855; *Land und Leute*, 3rd edition, 1856.
4. 'The Natural History of German Life', *Westminster Review*, N.S. x (July–Oct. 1856), 51–79 (p. 56).
5. 'The Progress of Fiction as an Art', *Westminster Review*, N.S. iv (July–Oct. 1853), 342–74 (pp. 343–4).
6. G. J. Becker (ed.), *Documents of Modern Literary Realism*, Princeton University Press, Princeton, N.J., 1963, p. 34.
7. 'Art and Belles Lettres', *Westminster Review*, N.S. ix (Jan.–April 1856), 626.
8. See G. H. Lewes, 'Realism in Art: Recent German Fiction', *Westminster Review*, N.S. xiv (July–Oct. 1858), 488–518 (p. 493).
9. G. H. Lewes, *Principles of Success in Literature*, 1856, edited by F. N. Scott, 3rd edition, Boston, 1894, p. 82. Quoted by Alice R. Kaminsky in 'George Eliot, George Henry Lewes, and the Novel', *Publications of the Modern Language Association of America*, lxx (1955), 997–1013 (p. 1001).
10. 'The Natural History of German Life', pp. 54–5.
11. See Kaminsky, op. cit., pp. 1004–5.
12. e.g. in a review of Hawthorne's *The Blithedale Romance*, *Westminster Review*, N.S. ii (July–Oct. 1852), 594, quoted by James R. Rust in 'The Art of Fiction in George Eliot's Reviews' *Review of English Studies*, N.S. vii (1956), 164–72 (p. 164).

13. 'Notes on *The Spanish Gipsy*' in J. W. Cross, *George Eliot's Life as Related in her Letters and Journals*, 3 vols., Blackwoods, Edinburgh and London, 1885, iii. 48.

14. *Letters*, vi. 98–9, 10 Dec. 1874.

15. B. J. Paris, 'George Eliot's Religion of Humanity', *English Literary History*, xxix (1962), 418–43 (p. 436).

16. See Lloyd Fernando, 'George Eliot, Feminism and Dorothea Brooke', *Review of English Literature*, iv (Jan. 1963), 76–90.

17. *Middlemarch*, 4 vols., Blackwoods, Edinburgh, 1871–2; Penguin edition, Harmondsworth, 1965, 243 (Ch. 21). Subsequent references will be to this edition, and will be included, together with chapter references, in the text.

18. Quoted by W. J. Harvey in 'Idea and Image in the Novels of George Eliot', *Critical Essays on George Eliot*, edited by Barbara Hardy, Routledge and Kegan Paul, London, 1970, pp. 151–198 (p. 160).

19. *Quarry for Middlemarch*, edited by Anna Theresa Kitchel, University of California Press, Berkeley and Los Angeles, 1950.

20. *Quarry* p. 3.

21. Richard Ellmann, 'Dorothea's husbands: Some biographical speculations', *Times Literary Supplement*, 16 Feb. 1973, 165–8.

22. Georg Lukács, *Studies in European Realism*, Hillway Publishing Co., London, 1950, p. 6.

23. Terry Eagleton, in *Criticism and Ideology*, N.L.B., London, 1976, suggests that the characters of *Middlemarch* are similarly representative of ideological positions. Thus Casaubon represents 'idealism, Lydgate scientific rationalism, Bulstrode Evangelical Christianity, Dorothea Brooke Romantic self-fulfilment' (p. 119).

24. For this perception I am indebted to Barbara Hardy, *The Novels of George Eliot*, Athlone Press, London, 1959, reprinted 1963, pp. 104–5.

25. See Lukács, op. cit., pp. 47–64; also Ian Milner, *The Structure of Values in George Eliot*, Prague, 1968, pp. 67–9; Eagleton, op. cit., p. 111.

26. *Letters*, i. 264, quoted by David Carroll in 'An Image of Disenchantment in the Novels of George Eliot', *Review of English Studies*, N.S. xi (1960), 29–41 (p. 30). Barbara Hardy has an earlier treatment of this theme, op. cit., pp. 189–200.

27. See Eagleton, op. cit., p. 120.

28. *Essays of George Eliot*, edited by Thomas Pinney, Routledge and Kegan Paul, London, 1963, pp. 431–6 (p. 433).

29. I am indebted for this material to David R. Carroll, 'Unity Through Analogy in *Middlemarch*', *Victorian Studies* ii (1959), 305–16.

30. See Jerome Beaty, 'History by Indirection: the Era of Reform in *Middlemarch*', *Victorian Studies* i (1957), 173–9. *(See pp 93–4 and p. 187 for discussion of a similar technique in Flaubert and Galdós.)

31. For a discussion of the 'author's voice', see Hardy, op. cit., pp. 155–84; also Derek Oldfield, 'The Language of the Novel', *Middlemarch: Critical Approaches to the Novel*, ed. Barbara Hardy, Athlone Press, London, 1967, pp. 63–86.

32. Karl Marx, *Selected Works*, edited by V. Adoratsky, 2 vols., London, 1942, ii. 315.

33. See Brian Swann, '*Middlemarch* and Myth', *Nineteenth Century Fiction* xxviii (Sep. 1973), 210–14.

34. See Isobel Armstrong, '*Middlemarch*: A Note on George Eliot's "Wisdom"', *Critical Essays on George Eliot*, pp. 116–32.

6

A. Strindberg: *The Red Room* (1879)

IN THE autobiographical work *The Son of a Servant* (1886–99) August Strindberg tells us that he wrote *The Red Room* during the early morning hours of the spring and summer before leaving for work at the Royal Library in Stockholm. Certainly the opening scene of the novel is imbued with a morning freshness which does not accord well with the narrator's opening words that 'It was an evening early in May.'[1] In 1879 Strindberg was thirty years old and was at a turning-point in his life. His historical drama *Master Olof* had been hawked around the theatres, repeatedly rejected and rather obsessively re-written. He had just married Siri von Essen and his existence was at least temporarily harmonious; he was working at this time in the academic sanctuary of the Royal Library. His bohemian days and his early failures as a dramatist were now things of the past, as were the financial problems that had recently beset him. These were in the past but were not forgotten, for they form the stuff of a novel which brought Strindberg if not fame at least considerable notoriety and established him as a writer to be reckoned with.

The Red Room was a new departure for Strindberg; he had already published a collection of short stories in 1877, entitled *From Fjär-dingen and Svartbäcken*, which are based on his experiences at university in Uppsala and satirize the academic life, but it was a large step from these sketches to the treatment of a broader spectrum of Swedish society in a full-length novel. The work also marks a new phase in Swedish writing generally, for the novel as a mirror of contemporary society was a rarity in Sweden at this time. Probably the only Swedish prose work previously to discuss social problems in a serious way is C. J. L. Almquist's *Det går an* (1839). (The title is virtually untranslatable; the novel has been published in English as *Sara Videbeck* after its heroine.) This work, which is by no means typical of Almquist, is an attack on the conventional views of marriage. *The Red Room* therefore constitutes a breakthrough for Realism in Swedish literature, and marks the beginning of *Åttitalet*, the Eighties, which was a major period of realistic and naturalistic writing in Sweden. With its exuberant and racy style it was to inject new life into the Swedish novel.

Although there are few Swedish forerunners, it must not be assumed that *The Red Room* was conceived in some sort of cultural vacuum. Strindberg was a voracious and omnivorous reader and it is clear that he was familiar with the literary trends on the Continent. He had certainly read *Madame Bovary* and *Sentimental Education* in the mid-1870s and at one time planned a Swedish translation of *Madame Bovary*.[2] In *The Son of a Servant* he denies, however, that he had read Zola when he wrote the novel, and hits back at those critics who had presented him as merely a Zola imitator.[3] Unfortunately Strindberg has not himself provided us with much help in placing *The Red Room* in a literary context since he wrote little about literary matters during the 70s. Nevertheless, some critics have spent considerable time and effort in tracing literary influences upon the novel. These are only reviewed briefly here.

Martin Lamm stresses the importance of Dickens, and sees in his method of characterization a model for Strindberg's method in *The Red Room*. Lamm also makes particular mention of Alphonse Daudet's novel *Le Nabab* (1877), which in theme at least—the big business of the capital and its grand frauds—would seem to have features in common with Strindberg's novel.[4] Algot Werin claims similarities in characterization with Turgenev, whose *Fathers and Sons* had been translated into Swedish while Strindberg was working on *The Red Room*.[5] Both Falander and Borg in Strindberg's novel possess traits in common with Turgenev's nihilist Bazarov. Smedmark, who both assesses and adds to this list, claims that other critics have overemphasized the importance of Dickens, Victor Hugo, and others, and writes that 'In all basic respects Strindberg is much nearer to the new literature'.[6] Strangely, Smedmark omits Balzac from his survey, and an attempt is made below to indicate his significance for the work. *The Red Room* must also be seen in a Scandinavian context: Ibsen had just published *Pillars of Society* in 1877, a work which, like Strindberg's, tries to allow fresh air to penetrate a stagnant and complacent Scandinavian society; also at this time the influential Danish critic Georg Brandes was publishing his lectures on *Main Currents in Nineteenth Century Literature* in which he urged that 'literature should make problems a matter of debate.' The reality on which Strindberg's novel is based is easy to identify. Arvid Falk's experiences are based on Strindberg's own, those of a young man struggling for acceptance as a writer in the harsh cultural climate of Sweden in the 1870s. But some critics have stressed only the similarities between Falk and the young Strindberg and have virtually equated the two. It must be remembered that Falk is a literary construction and thus has other functions to perform in the novel than merely reflecting his creator. Strindberg's moods are, however, reflected to some extent in Falk's, in for example, the fluctuation between fanaticism and despair, but Falk does not have the same drive and will-power as the young Strindberg. The emphasis placed on financial speculation and corruption in the novel may perhaps be explained by Strindberg's own bankruptcy during the economic crisis of 1878: the narrator appears to be motivated by revenge in this case, a reaction which is also evident in the portrayal of publishers and literary critics as rogues and charlatans who do not appreciate good writing. Strindberg and Falk also share many of the same experiences: both are civil servants; both spend periods as journalists and cover parliamentary debates and shareholders' meetings; both undertake menial literary tasks.

Other situations in the novel reflect the Stockholm of the 1870s: the scene at the Workers' Association Northern Star attempts to depict the situation in the Stockholm Workers' Association. The conversion of the newspaper *Grey Cape* from liberal to conservative is based on a similar change of policy in the paper *Aftonbladet*. In a letter to Edvard Brandes, Strindberg writes of *The Red Room*: 'As far as the satires are concerned, they are based on reality—to some extent. All the figures in the Second Chamber are taken from Parliamentary minutes. The Triton Company's report is partly a copy of the published report of the Neptune Company etc. That is why the enemies of light cried that "it was lies", for, behold, it was truth!'[7]

The members of the Red Room coterie—so called because it meets in the Red Room at Berns Restaurant—are also based on Stockholmers of Strindberg's circle: Struve, Borg Lundell, Olle Montanus, Rehnhjelm, and Ygberg are all modelled in this way, whilst Falander, Pastor Skåre, and the Chairman of Triton also possess counterparts in real life.[8] The depiction of Rehnhjelm's period as a drama student is drawn from Strindberg's own disastrous experiences. Of course the characters are disguised, but sometimes only very thinly: Olle Holmberg points out that Sellén paints sunsets in Halland (on Sweden's west coast), whereas his counterpart in real life, Per Ekström, painted sunrises on Öland (an island off the east coast).[9] *The Red Room* is thus a *roman à clef:* characters, institutions, and situations were easily recognizable to many of its readers. But in his criticism of these social institutions, Strindberg softens the blow by employing outrageous caricature and satire. He allows his opponents the opportunity of claiming that he could not possibly intend the novel to represent real characters and institutions, because of these exaggerations.

The setting is also based closely on reality: from the very first page Stockholm comes alive in a bustling panorama, with its church bells, its streets, its parks, Berns Café, Carl Nicolaus' little shop in the narrow alley in the Old Town. The topographical references are as familiar to Swedes now as they were a hundred years ago.

In the opening scene of the novel Arvid Falk is presented as an outsider. He has tried to adapt to society but is too much of an idealist to fit in. He has seen through the sham of the Board for Payment of Civil Service Salaries and recounts his humiliations at the hands of the bureaucrats to the wordly-wise Struve: innocence encounters experience. Now Falk plans to throw himself into the arms of literature. Struve warns him that he must conform in order to survive and promptly goes off to write up Falk's story for his reactionary newspaper. On the heights of Mosebacke Falk is defiant—he raises his fist to the city beneath him. Yet he is also a weak and sensitive individual with ideals to which the reality of life is destined never to correspond. Now he enters the city and acts as our guide. We follow him first to his brother's shop. Carl Nicolaus Falk is a bourgeois, a small capitalist who is respected by his fellow bourgeois but is a bully to Arvid whom he has cheated out of part of his inheritance. Having been duly browbeaten, Arvid flees the city and, leaving civilization behind him, seeks peace in nature. In the idyllic setting at Lill-Jans he falls in with the Red Room circle, and here he finds solace. He is among friends, people who speak his language, and he also introduces us to the collective hero of the story. This is 'The Red Room', the group of artists who form the focus of the novel, the pivot around which it turns. The members of the group are struggling in their various ways to retain their artistic integrity and yet make headway in a philistine world. The bohemians of The

Red Room are contrasted sharply with the establishment figures whom Falk encounters. The bohemians present a rough uncivilized exterior which conceals in each case an honest, sensitive, spiritual nature. The members of the establishment, on the other hand, present a respectable façade which conceals only greed, falsehood, and brutality. Red Room's skirmishes with the establishment, its defeats and victories, form a major theme in the novel. Yet Red Room has its own internal conflicts: its members conduct, for example, heated arguments on the nature of art.

Falk's next foray is to the publisher Smith, whose ignorance of major Scandinavian poets, to say nothing of Swedish history, is astonishing. Arvid is crushed by the publisher in much the same way as he has been crushed by his brother. The chapter 'The Imitation of Christ' provides a parallel to the visit to the publisher. Another pillar of society is presented here: the very modern priest Pastor Skåre, who looks like a sea-captain and speaks like a big businessman—which is what he is. Both Skåre and Smith are only concerned with making money; Smith seems uninterested in Arvid's poems, Skåre in the spiritual nature of the work he offers Falk. So Falk takes to journalism and becomes a reporter on the radical *Red Cap*. By choosing this particular employment Strindberg gains access for Falk and his readers to a range of social milieux. In his new job Falk's first port of call is Parliament, where he manages to sound like the boy in Andersen's story of the Emperor's new clothes when he asks 'Where is the opposition?' The answer comes: 'The devil alone knows. They agree to everything' (p. 81). When Sven Svensson rises to speak on the Poor Law, everyone hurriedly departs in search of lunch, except Falk, who stays to hear 'a man of honour whose life was irreproachable voicing the complaints of the oppressed and downtrodden—while nobody listened' (p. 84). We are treated during the debate to the hair-splitting of the university member, the financial self-interest of Anders Andersson and the sabre-rattling patriotism of Count von Splint.

But there are greater frauds for Arvid Falk to expose. His next visit, to the shareholders' meeting of that philanthropic institution the Triton Marine Insurance Company, marks a change of tone in Strindberg's social criticism. Thus far caricature has largely dominated these exposés; the criticism has been indirect, good-humoured or outrageous, but never harsh. In the chapter dealing with the newspaper syndicate *Grey Cape* a note of bitterness begins to creep in. The beginning of the chapter about Triton is narrated in a similarly caustic tone. Here the young businessman Levi is given a lesson in high finance: how to float an insurance company without capital and without risk. The narrator draws a picture of a grand fraud in the making. The avariciousness of the shareholders of Triton, scandalized by their small dividend, contrasts markedly with the pompous rhetoric of the chairman: 'Not that we want any reward . . . for our small services, which are given—I must make this quite clear—simply out of goodwill, pure goodwill' (p. 118).

When the narrative returns to Stockholm after the events at the theatre in X-köping and we once again meet Falk, he has become thoroughly disillusioned by his experience of man as a social animal. But he is to encounter greater inhumanity as he penetrates into the lower layers of society. At Vita Bergen he is introduced to the working classes and faced with real poverty and great squalor: one room shared by three squabbling families. Yet, despite the crushing sense of helplessness which pervades this scene, one man at least retains some pride. The carpenter, Eriksson, addresses the two bourgeois ladies, Mrs. Falk and Mrs. Homan, who have come on an errand of mercy: 'Well, if there's to be any charity now, let it be while my back's turned, for true charity works secretly—Give us some work if you like, and see that you pay us for the work, then you needn't go running round like this' (p. 163). In this scene there is a pathos which takes on a lyrical quality in the chapter 'From Churchyard to Eating House', in which Falk attends the funeral of the wretched Struve's illegitimate child.

Few of Falk's illusions about his fellow man remain now. At the meeting of the Workers' Association Northern Star he hopes to 'see the working man at close quarters' (p. 216). What he finds, however, is a lack of free speech, an association which has been infiltrated by the establishment, another sham in fact. Nevertheless, he retains a desire to fight for the oppressed and joins the *Worker's Banner* only to discover that its brutal editor is also in league with the establishment, its policy totally prejudiced and his own ideals seriously compromised. He is dejected and desperate and is then suddenly whisked away from his empty life by Borg. But he has traversed a cross-section of Stockholm society from Parliament to working-class slum, and in a series of finely-studied scenes, a string of pearls, the narrator has captured the humbug, the greed and corruption of that society. Incidentally, it is noticeable how at times our guide tends to disappear from view: at Vita Bergen, for example, he enters the tenement with Ygberg and is then shunted off into a back room to become only a passive observer of the confrontation between charity and the deserving poor.

There are, however, two threads of the narrative which are not observed through Falk's eyes. One is the picture of bourgeois morality presented by Carl Nicolaus Falk's household. The scene in which Carl Nicolaus feeds his 'dogs', the rebellious debtors Levin and Nystrom, must surely rank as one of the finest Strindberg has written, for its evocation of the stages of drunkenness and for Carl Nicolaus' careful stage-managing of the sentimental orgy. Also, irresistible and essentially modern is the picture of the prototype woman's liberationist Eugénie Falk twisting her husband around her little finger but failing disastrously in her carefully laid plan to up-stage her rival Mrs. Homan. The other thread is the depiction of the theatre, which is shown to be as cruel and shallow an institution as any of the others. The young Rehnhjelm, Falk's stand-in in these scenes, is humiliated by Falander as Falander himself had been when he was a young novice.

How accurate, then, is Strindberg's picture of Swedish society at the beginning of the 1870s? In Strindberg's own words this was a 'Time of Ferment'. Sweden underwent its agricultural and industrial revolutions very late and the growth of urban industry was rapid during the latter half of the nineteenth century. This brought with it all manner of social problems including cramped living conditions and a very high mortality rate in the insanitary slums, especially from tuberculosis; this is reflected in the novel in the scenes at Vita Bergen. Strangely, workers were slow to organize: the labour movement proper dates in fact from the 1880s. Socialism of the kind expounded by carpenter Eriksson was not yet a force in Sweden and 'the idlers who live off the work of others' (p. 163), as he describes them, clearly had nothing to fear at this time. During the 1860s so-called 'Workers' Associations' had grown up, mostly with the aim of forming sickness and pension funds for their members and organizing lectures of the kind Olle Montanus is invited to give. But one historian describes these associations in these terms: 'In so far as any political positions were adopted these were mostly in a liberal direction, many of the prominent figures belonged to the petite bourgeoisie or intellectual groups, and the real workers were in a minority of the membership.'[10] So what might be thought of as an exaggerated scene at the *Northern Star* in fact corresponds clearly to historical reality.

The Representation Reform of 1865, which forms the political background for the novel, abolished the Four Estates and instituted a Bicameral Parliament, but four-fifths of Swedish men and all Swedish women were still deprived of the vote, and the urban proletariat fared worst. The results of Reform disappointed the reformers: a property qualification for electors resulted in domination of the Second Chamber by the farmers, to the great disappointment of the urban middle classes, and soon an enmity grew up between farmers and civil servants: we can see this in Falk's description of the Salary Board where the 'farmers were called traitors' (p. 11). Strindberg himself supported the Agrarian Party at the beginning of the 70s, and in the opening sequence of the novel Falk is heard to praise the journalist Struve for his articles in the *Peasants' Friend* and is naïvely optimistic about the Reform Parliament. Carl Nicolaus finds in Reform an excuse for his lack of business success, but in general the middle classes did very well, enjoying a considerable increase in wealth in the 70s: we have only to think of Mrs. Falk showing off her possessions to Mrs. Homan. The bourgeoisie were becoming increasingly reactionary and with a booming economy came financial speculation—businessmen like Levi of Triton discovered 'that it is cheaper and more agreeable to live on other people's money than by one's own work' (p. 112). But the fermenting opposition to the government and all the radical activity on an intellectual and economic plane seem to have had little effect on Parliament itself, which remained untouched by progressive ideas. Two other important social movements of the period are glimpsed briefly in the novel. One is the movement for Female Emancipation, and it is obvious from the irony employed in the depiction of Mrs. Falk's Society for Womens's Rights that Strindberg was, for a radical, perhaps surprisingly anti-feminist. The other movement is a Free Church Revival, similarly ridiculed in the portrait of Pastor Skåre.

Let us now see what has happened to Falk on his way, how he has changed during the course of his education, and what changes are discernible in his friends. For, like *Sentimental Education*, *The Red Room* combines an account of a young man's education with a critical analysis of the ills of society. When Falk meets the group at Lill-Jans he encounters individuals who have refused to compromise their principles, with one exception: Lundell, that 'practical man', the artist who paints to 'meet the public's taste and demand' (p. 30). He alone has already sold out. Significantly we come across him later, in the chapter 'Audiences', where he is discovered painting Carl Nicolaus Falk's portrait. He has become a tool of the establishment it seems, just another of Carl Nicolaus' 'dogs'. But is this really the case? Strindberg leaves us in some doubt; perhaps he is merely concealing his true, more rebellious nature. Contrasted with Lundell is Sellén, the man who paints landscapes—barren coastlines from Halland—and refuses to take the practical Lundell's advice and 'put a cow in the foreground' (p. 58), that is make any concessions to public taste. Olle Montanus, the philosopher of Red Room, is contrasted with Falk: Falk is well-read but unoriginal, whereas Olle is uneducated but clever, and has abandoned sculpture temporarily for philosophy, which he is taught by the gaunt Ygberg. The latter is a rather mysterious figure who appears to starve most of the time when not supported by friends such as Falk, and who finally appears in the offices of the *Red Cap*. Then there is Rehnhjelm, who is an aristocrat attempting to become an actor, and Falk of course, a civil servant trying to become a poet.

At first Falk retains his idealism and refuses to compromise. He returns the work which Smith has foisted on him and throws Pastor Skåre's literary crumbs through a convenient window. Then he admits to authorship of Struve's article about the Salary Board and becomes a social outcast. But he has to live, and his experiences as a journalist leave him despondent. By the time he returns to Mosebacke and meets Ygberg he has begun to feel 'old, tired and disillusioned, he had seen inside those houses there below him, and they were quite different from what he had expected' (p. 153). But he forgets that he has only seen man 'as a social animal', and that there is 'another animal which in privacy is very amiable' (p. 153). Ygberg, like Struve before him, tries to persuade Falk to give up his convictions. 'Only stupid people have them' he tells Falk, 'One's first and foremost duty is to live—to live at any price' (p. 155). Ygberg has already compromised earlier, writing that history of Ulrika Eleonora which Falk refused. But Falk proceeds to greater dejection. He has realized that his poems are worthless and his love affair is a disaster. His nadir is reached in the coffin-like cellar of the Star Inn, drinking with a couple of hack journalists. Borg then rushes him off to the islands to toughen him up, to imbue him with the same

cynical view of life which *he* has developed, and after a while to re-
introduce him into society. When he re-appears it is difficult to
recognize this new Arvid Falk as he trots between his government
offices and presents himself to the Red Room as a cynic. The development in his character is too dramatic. Yet is this conversion really
a permanent one? For Olle Montanus's tragic fate is seen to cut
through this pose of indifference. At Sellén's levity about Montanus's death, Falk bursts out with 'How heartless you are! How
crude! Damn your frivolity!' (p. 266), and admits to being 'sentimental'. In the 'Review' Borg himself doubts Falk's capacity to conform permanently: 'Falk is a political fanatic, who knows he'd burn
up if he fanned the flames, so he smothers them with hard dry
work—but I don't think he'll be successful in this. Because of his
restraint I fear an explosion some time' (p. 274).

Next to Falk's fate that of Olle Montanus is the most interesting.
Olle's development is only very briefly sketched in the novel. He is
at the peak of his happiness when he has found work, probably on
the wood carvings in Träskåla Church, and flirts with the unfortunate Marie. He keeps in touch with Falk by letter and seems
content. Yet when he returns to Stockholm he is penniless and
desperate. Like the others he will have to abandon his art for a job
to stay alive. In the freezing cold of Sellén's studio he asks 'I wonder
why one doesn't put an end to one's life when it is as cold as this?'
(p. 229), and later we learn that he has drowned himself. The decision is not perhaps so surprising. Olle is made of sterner stuff than
Falk; he is more uncompromising and has the will-power to take the
logical step which his nihilism leads him to—suicide.

Rehnhjelm is the member of Red Room who most successfully
conforms to the ways of society. After his treatment at the hands of
the bitter cynical Falander, Rehnhjelm abandons his art and returns
to commerce; in the 'Review' Borg describes him as the 'manager of a
large factory'.

All the members of Red Room have a belief, a calling, and all are
involved in a struggle. Most of them are fighting for their art, Falk
perhaps to retain a particular view of society. They all encounter an
uncomprehending world, are repulsed and experience despair and a
feeling of helplessness. They move from idealism to scepticism and
finally they all make the best of the situation and follow their various
natures. Most conform whilst Olle, who finds this impossible, seeks
peace in death.

In the discussion which follows, *The Red Room* is examined in relation to three aspects of Realist method, those of *subject-matter*, *technique*, and *organization*. Jenkins has listed those features of Realism which the French theorists held as most obvious, that is 'the need for observation and documentation, for fictional characters to be constructed as typical or representative, and for the writer to regard as his rightful territory the whole range of society and experience, not excluding the working classes or sexual relations.'[11] Despite its subtitle, 'Scenes of artistic and literary life', *The Red Room* does encompass a broad range of social milieux and character types: there are prostitutes and parliamentarians, bohemians and bankers. The narrator does admittedly in the early chapters present a gallery of portraits of establishment figures—Carl Nicolaus Falk, Smith, Skåre, the editor of *Grey Cape*, the chairman of Triton—but the book is by no means concerned exclusively with the bourgeois world. Though middle class himself, Arvid Falk feels he ought to champion the cause of the working classes, to be their voice, and he introduces us to the sordidness and banality of real poverty. But the narrator also provides scenes of uncomplicated happiness, such as those early idylls with Red Room, and of sadness, as when Struve buries his child. Nor is sex entirely missing from the range of human experiences: Agnes's scene with Falander has considerable erotic undertones.

In its setting the novel is specific, in time contemporary, though Strindberg thought it wise to set the events a few years earlier. It is, as has been demonstrated above, a depiction of reality within the author's own field of observation and is based partly on documentary evidence. Yet the way in which the narrator treats his characters, who are based on real figures or types, is problematical. The difficulty here is the extent to which he may adjust the balance in his characterization and representation of society and retain any vestiges of the hallowed objectivity of the Realist. For he overemphasizes the black and white in his depiction to the detriment of the shades of grey, exaggerating particular features of his establishment targets. What is more, he makes them not only despicable but also extremely funny. Strindberg the satirist and caricaturist may and does sacrifice a realist portrayal of character when it does not suit his purpose. Also, his favoured characters, such as Falk and Olle Montanus, evoke a great deal of sympathy from him and from us. We do not admire them for they are not heroic figures, but we sympathize with their

plight. Strindberg seldom shows a clinical detachment from his subject. In *The Red Room* the Realism in subject-matter would appear to have been compromised by Strindberg's method. Both in his use of caricature and by setting the events some ten years earlier he has pulled his punches and this is detrimental to his social criticism.

If we turn for a moment to the details of the action, it is possible to find much that is familiar from the French Realists. The young idealist, who in Balzac and Flaubert is a provincial and in Strindberg is rather uncertainly cast as a Stockholmer, tries to make his way in the capital, encounters duplicity, greed, and humbug at every turn, and quickly loses all his illusions about his fellow men. He languishes in the wilderness for a while, overcomes some opposition, gains acceptance socially and gets on. At the same time he introduces the reader to life in the capital, revealing the true nature of its hallowed institutions. The young man may encounter a representative group of artists—idealists like himself—who are struggling for recognition and who share his vicissitudes. There is such a group in Balzac's *Lost Illusions*, *Le Cénacle*, a circle of starving artists whom Lucien de Rubempré comes into contact with on arriving in Paris, and who congregate at times at the same restaurant. Like Arvid, Lucien tries to place his poems with various publishers but is everywhere turned down because he is not an established author.

Lucien falls in with some unscrupulous journalists who lecture this neophyte in the ways of their trade, teaching him, for example how to write a damning review of a work followed by a glowing one under a pseudonym. This is exactly the method employed by Struve to rehabilitate Sellén's painting and cover up the newspaper *Grey Cape*'s *faux pas*. Astonished to see his journalist friend Étienne Lousteau selling his review copies, Lucien enquires innocently 'But . . . how will you write your reviews on them?'[12] Arvid Falk, dining with the hack journalists at the Star restaurant, asks his companions 'Perhaps you don't read the books you review?' 'Who do you think has time to read books?' comes the reply, 'Isn't it enough to write about them?' (p. 242). Despite his initial innocence, Lucien is soon involved in the corruption of the world of journalism, and appears to possess fewer moral scruples than Falk. Balzac seems to regard the corrupting influence of this world as inevitable, whereas Strindberg sees some hope for society from idealists like Falk. The cynicism and materialism of the publishing world, and of journalism in particular, were part of Strindberg's personal experience as they were of Balzac's, but the parallels between the two works are too detailed to be mere coincidence. What is more, both Lucien and Falk's *alter ego* Rehnhjelm are introduced to the world of the theatre and to young actresses, of whom Agnes is described in much the same terms as Florine. The young men are at first dazzled by the theatre but later become horrified as the corruption behind the scenes: Étienne Lousteau's use of Florine in his financial skulduggery and Agnes's seduction of Falander in order to obtain a role for Rehnhjelm. Both Lucien and Arvid come eventually to the brink of suicide—though for different reasons—and are rescued at the last moment by the intervention of a diabolical *deus ex machina* figure. The action of Borg in stiffening Falk's sinews and blunting his sensibilities has more than a passing resemblance to the influence of Carlos Herrera (Vautrin) upon Lucien, and ultimately both young men are re-introduced into the life of the capital.[13]

Next we turn to Strindberg's *technique* in *The Red Room*. Jenkins observes that the removal of the author from the stage, the achievement of an 'apparently impersonal illusion of reality' must ideally be brought about by contriving 'a coherent and apparently autonomous structure of persuasion which will of itself . . . say what the writer wants to say without his actually having to intervene directly to say it.'[14] In *The Red Room* it does happen that we find ourselves listening to the *ex cathedra* voice of the narrator: the rather ill-fitting chapter about 'The Newspaper Syndicate Grey Cape' is narrated in this way—Strindberg abandons his 'autonomous structure of persuasion' and attacks the cultural policy of the paper directly. It is more usual, however, to find the narrator manipulating viewpoint so as to present his opinions and feelings through the characters. Arvid and Rehnhjelm reflect the young Strindberg's idealism and optimism. Other characters reveal different aspects of his personality and history: like Falander, Strindberg struggled for ten years before his talents were recognized, and, like Struve, he was forced to compromise and abandon his art in order to live. Borg reflects Strindberg's general view of society in his derisive exposure of its ideals as humbug.[15] It is perhaps worth underlining that it is Borg's viewpoint, not Arvid's, which dominates the final chapters. Strindberg uses other indirect means to say what he wants to say without intervening directly: the letters in the novel, and particularly the 'Review', are vehicles which allow him freedom of expression.

One obvious result of impersonality is the increased importance of scene. Strindberg's approach is a very scenic one: some chapters, such as those set in X-köping and 'Audiences', are little more than a set of stage directions followed by dramatic dialogue, and it is interesting that, when Swedish Television made their film version of *The Red Room* in 1970, the director was able to lift these scenes virtually intact from the novel.[16] Certainly dialogue is extensive in the novel, although individual lines of dialogue are very short and pithy. There are few long speeches to slow down the proceedings, and where a speech is made, for example at the Triton meeting and the Northern Star, it is enlivened by the insertion of the audience's reactions and criticisms. Dialogue is given a considerable characterizing role: Strindberg reveals his characters in this way rather than by plumbing the depths of their minds or by means of lengthy passages of biographical background. A few hurried details are all we are told about a character until he opens his mouth to speak. The characterization in *The Red Room* is by necessity very sketchy, there is a large cast after all, and there are some inconsistencies, for example: how is the intelligent, vivacious actress Agnes so dramatically transformed into the slovenly prostitute Beda? Again, is a crude cynic like Borg not a little unlikely as the saviour of Falk?

While the materials of the novel conform broadly to Realist theory and practice, while the detailed correspondences with at least one major Realist novel seem clear and the technique employed demonstrates some of the novelties of Realism, the *organization* of the work poses more of a problem. The dilemma for the practitioner of Realism was that too obvious a shaping of the materials—for example, the provision of a striking correspondence between beginning and end, the use of patterning, or a neatly conclusive ending to the plot—is not true to the seemingly haphazard or untidy nature of life, and is therefore unrealistic. Such structuring also reveals all too clearly the hand of the artist at work, yet nevertheless impersonality of presentation paradoxically results in this method as one of the ways in which meaning is effectively conveyed. Now it cannot be said that *The Red Room* has a particularly unrealistic opening sequence, though the first scene may be a little clichéd. Young men may have acted in the way Falk acts. The author does not, however, in this opening chapter launch into a history of his times or a detailed account of Arvid's background and parentage. What kind of a man Falk is emerges from what he tells us himself, or rather tells Struve, and from the action into which he is plunged almost immediately. But what of the ending of the novel? Can the 'Review' be said to be true to life? The form of the last chapter is that of a letter from Borg to Sellén, who is in Paris, telling him all the news from Stockholm. We may consider, then, that the fiction of the report itself is sufficiently motivated. But its effect is artificial: it ties up very neatly all the loose threads of the narrative, describes the fates of Triton, Levi, Agnes Rundgren, and, not least, of Falk himself. Borg reports that Falk has married and marriage is after all a traditional way of bringing down the curtain. Yet, as has been shown above, Falk's future is a problem: has there really been any change in his attitudes? Will he be able to repress his true feelings? So as far as Arvid Falk is concerned the ending of the novel is by no means conclusive.

There is a great deal of ordering, of patterning in *The Red Room*. Although in the past the novel has been criticized for its 'looseness of structure',[17] and there are some apparent deficiencies in its integration, these are in fact more apparent than real. Falk himself has drawbacks as a unifying agent in the work because he is 'on stage' in only nineteen of the twenty-nine chapters, and Stockholm presents the same problem: five chapters are set in the provincial town of X-köping. This aspect—the setting—is the most striking discontinuity in the work: these chapters on the theatre seem at first sight to break away from the main body of the narrative. But the X-köping narrative is not totally isolated. There are links between Stockholm and X-köping; the most obvious is Rehnhjelm who appears in both settings, and then there is Agnes, Rehnhjelm's great love in X-köping, who later appears to torment Falk in Stockholm. There is a further parallel in so far as Rehnhjelm's treatment at the hands of Falander is similar to Borg's treatment of Falk. So it is possible to see the X-köping narrative as less a digression and more a projection of one of the main themes in *The Red Room*, namely the struggle for artistic success.

There are some obvious structural links in the novel which have thematic significance: there is the cyclic course which Arvid Falk follows in the course of a year from the heights of Mosebacke down into the city and back to Mosebacke—despite his trials nothing has really changed for him—there is the use of the seasons, spring, summer, autumn to emphasize the changing moods of the characters from optimism to disillusion. Triton's business dealings and Carl

Nicholaus Falk's impinge upon virtually every aspect of the narrative, demonstrating the all-pervasive nature of business. Similarly, characters from one social milieu have a tendency to materialize in others in some rather strange places: Lundell is seen at work on Carl Nicolaus's portrait and Ygberg has business dealings with Smith. At the Falks' dinner Arvid feels that there are 'invisible bonds' holding the company together, and, incidentally, Levi and Borg make brief appearances at this dinner. These bonds have already been hinted at in the chapter 'Poor Country': in Parliament Arvid discovers Carl Nicolaus together with Smith, and Olle Montanus is strangely out of place in this setting. An explanation of these coincidences is only forthcoming much later. There are also a number of extras in the novel—an army of civil servants—whose representatives fill all the important posts on the Salary Board, in Parliament, at Triton and—this is a shock for Arvid who is constantly running into these people—also in the Workers' Association Northern Star.

One symbolic motif which has recently been shown to run through the novel is the contrast which Strindberg employs between images of the city and captivity on the one hand, and nature and freedom on the other. The images of doors and windows abound, underlying the barriers which society places in the path of aspiring young men.[18] A typical scene reveals a character in a fusty room gazing out at the fresh countryside, as when Falk is seen at the *Worker's Banner*: 'Falk was left alone. The sun cast its rays over the steep roof opposite and the room grew warm. He opened the window and put his head out for a breath of fresh air, but was met by stupefying fumes from the gutters. He turned his eyes to the right . . . and saw far away in the distance part of a steamer, a few waves on the Mälar, glittering in the sunlight, and a ravine over on Skinnarviksbergen, which was just beginning to show a little green here and there in its crevices' (p. 237).

What *The Red Room* lacks in depth and perhaps in unity of theme and purpose is compensated for by its range, not only the panoramic view which Strindberg provides of his own world, but also the range of tone and mood: here is the innocent happiness of the bohemians in 'Happy People' and the hilariously funny satire of bureaucracy in the Salary Board, but also the bitter indignation at social conditions in 'At Vita Bergen'. In the space of a single chapter, 'From Churchyard to Eating House', we are moved by the sublime pathos of Levi's burial prayer for Struve's child and disgusted by the coarseness of the outrageously drunken Borg.

As in other works of Strindberg, the reader is left with the vague feeling that the book is somehow incomplete, that the finishing touches remain to be made, but this is a personal trait rather than a characteristic of the genre. The narrator of *The Red Room* is certainly not devoid of ambition, but does fall short on consistency and thoroughness in that the novel provides no truly rigorous examination of social problems of the time. What is provided is a host of sparklingly witty impressions of a particular milieu in a minor European capital.

The significance of *The Red Room* as a work of literature lies both in its links with the tradition of European Realism and in its value to Scandinavian writers as a pointer to new paths which the novel might follow in future.

NOTES

1. Quotations are taken from the translation by Elisabeth Sprigge published by Dent, London, 1967 in the Everyman Series, No. 348. Page references are to this edition.
2. Carl Reinhold Smedmark, *Mäster Olof och Röda rummet*, Almqvist and Wiksell, Stockholm, 1952, p. 155.
3. August Strindberg, *Tjänstekvinnans son*, Samlade skrifter xix, Bonniers, Stockholm 1913, p. 164.
4. Martin Lamm, *August Strindberg*, Aldus/Bonniers, second edition, Stockholm, 1963, p. 64, pp. 66–7.
5. Algot Werin, 'Karaktärer i Röda rummet', in *Synpunkter på Strindberg*, edited by Gunnar Brandell, Aldus/Bonniers, Stockholm, 1964, pp. 88–9.
6. Smedmark, p. 170.
7. August Strindberg, *Brev* ii, edited by Torsten Eklund, Bonniers, Stockholm, 1950, 166 (29 July 1880).
8. For a key to the *roman à clef* see: Olle Holmberg, *Lovtal över svenska romaner*, Bonniers, Stockholm, 1957, pp. 49–52.
9. ibid., p. 52.
10. Sten Carlsson, *Svensk historia* ii, Tiden after 1718, Bonniers, Stockholm, 1961, p. 506.
11. See p. 7 above.
12. Honoré de Balzac, *Lost Illusions* (1837–43), Penguin Classics edition, translated by Herbert Hunt, Harmondsworth, 1971, p. 255.
13. Stellan Ahlström indicates a number of similarities between *Lost Illusions* and *The Red Room* in his 'Balzac och Röda rummet', *Svensk litteraturtidskrift*, xvii (1954), 175–9.
14. See p. 12 above.
15. Smedmark, p. 255.

16. See, Gunnar Hallingberg, 'TV-versionien av Röda rummet', in *Perspektiv på Röda rummet*, edited by Erland and Ulla-Britta Lagerroth, Rabén & Sjögren, Stockholm, 1971, pp. 204–23, especially p. 215.
17. See, for example, Brita M. E. Mortensen and Brian W. Downs, *Strindberg. An Introduction to his Life and Work*, Cambridge U.P., 1965, p. 160, and Eric O. Johannesson, *The Novels of August Strindberg*, University of California Press, Berkeley, 1968, pp. 29–30.
18. Erland Lagerroth, *Svensk berättarkonst*, Skrifter utgivna av Vetenskaps-societeten i Lund 61, C.W.K. Gleerup, Lund, 1968, p. 54 ff.

7

W. D. Howells: *The Rise of Silas Lapham* (1885)

S. FOSTER

DISCUSSIONS OF nineteenth-century Realism as a movement tend to centre on the European innovators and practitioners and it may seem somewhat anomalous to include an American novelist in a book devoted primarily to Continental realists. The inclusion is nevertheless well-justified, partly because it shows how the impetus towards realistic writing in fiction spread from the Old World to the New and led to a continuing relationship between European and American literature during the latter part of the nineteenth century and the early part of the twentieth century, and partly because it demonstrates the way in which American Realism, as exemplified by one of its most notable pioneers, adapted the modes of European inspiration and experimentation to its own circumstances and materials. In the work of a writer such as W. D. Howells, we can see how the common assumptions and concerns of a widespread literary trend are taken up and implemented to create a new native tradition.

Howells himself has been called the founder of and spokesman for the Realist school of fiction in America—a claim which, though somewhat sweeping, rightly draws attention to his life-long interest in Realism as a literary development, and to his earnest efforts to promote what increasingly seemed to him the only artistically valid mode of writing. Always a wide-ranging and penetrating reader, soon after he had joined the staff of the *Atlantic Review* in March 1866 Howells was introduced by Thomas Sargeant Perry to many of the great nineteenth-century European Realists. Convinced that these writers represented a new spirit in literature, Howells printed many reviews of their work in the *Atlantic* between 1866 and 1881 (he was editor from 1871 to 1881), and later in other major American periodicals with which he was connected, including *Harper's Weekly*, *Harper's Monthly*, and the *North American Review*. His recognition of their literary achievements led him not only to bring them to the notice of his own country's readers and to recommend their often radical-seeming methods and subject-matter, but also to encourage similar writing in America; his unflagging enthusiasm for Henry James, J. W. De Forest, Mark Twain, Stephen Crane, and Frank Norris, for example, helped to introduce them as native exponents of a new movement in fiction and to establish the principles they represented. For Howells, the flowering of Realism was not merely a passing phenomenon, but a major cultural advance which, he felt, demanded his personal championship as well as emulation.

It is significant that, like his friend and compatriot Henry James (whom he so much admired and who not only acquainted him with the works of the French Realists, but actually suggested that by striving to realize in fiction the essence of America Howells could become the American Balzac[1] or 'the Zola of the U.S.A.'[2]), Howells was both critic and novelist, since the one role considerably affected the other. Indeed, he saw the functions of criticism and novel-writing as similar in many respects: both ascertain and discover facts and principles in a dispassionate and analytical spirit of truthfulness, through accurate observation, comparison, and close investigation; both, by challenging a false representation of life, offer a constructive commentary on the development of different and better artistic standards. Howells's deep involvement with the progress and critical issues of Realism has a particular effect upon his own creative work. In its assertion of the artistic criteria which he demanded and sought to promote in the writings of others, his fiction is illustrative of his professional commitment to the Realist school. His own treatment of 'the real' is inspired to a large extent by literary motives; it is not the result of an interest in purely scientific scrutiny, nor is it primarily aesthetic experimentation, an attempt to create a wholly new art form or to capture the exact feel of individual experience; neither does it seek to demonstrate a philosophical theory about existence and human behaviour, like the Naturalists whom, significantly, Howells regarded as too concerned with specific issues as well as with certain subjects better omitted from fiction. Taking as his basic axiom that the business of art is to represent life (he said that 'no author is an authority except in those moments when he held his ear close to Nature's lips and caught her very accent'[3]) Howells employed his Realism both as protest and as positive recommendation. It was protest in that it sought to oppose fiction which he considered not

only inferior, but also morally harmful because it told lies; it recom-
mended itself since it aimed to show that by giving a faithful and
objective picture of life the novelist is able to reveal the beauty
which exists in everyday experience and in the play of social relations, and which needs no heightening or artificial embellishment
to make it interesting and meaningful.

As Howells was aware, in seeking to put such a programme into
practice he was indicating the great responsibility of the Realist
novelist, but it was a responsibility which he was constantly stressing
in his critical writing. In his *Criticism and Fiction*, published as a
single work in 1891, but including many extracts from his earlier
pieces in the 'Editor's Study' column in *Harper's Monthly* which he
took over in January 1886, and representing the culmination of many
years of critical thought and commentary, he insists, in very Jamesian
accents, on the central importance of 'the good or bad faith of the
novelist'[4] in dealing with his material:

I cannot hold him to less account than this: he must be true to what life
has taught me is the truth . . .[5]
I do not care to judge any work of the imagination without first of all
applying this test to it. We must ask ourselves before we ask anything
else, is it true?—true to the motives, the impulses, the principles that
shape the life of actual men and women?[6]

Realism thus becomes a matter of conscience for the literary artist,
who has a duty to render faithfully. We can detect here a certain
earnest and declamatory tone, which, as will be shown later,
appears in Howells's creative writing, not explicitly but in the general
shape and direction of his novel.

A preliminary examination of the nature and grounds of Howells's
literary objections and recommendations will help to clarify his aims
as revealed in *The Rise of Silas Lapham*. It is generally agreed that the
most consistent impetus behind his work, both critical and creative,
was his antipathy towards the romance and romantic writing, in as
far as these implied distortion and sentimentality. In his well-known
disagreement with James, he puts forward his view that 'the romance
and the novel are as distinct as the poem and the novel',[7] objecting
that in his book on Hawthorne the younger novelist seems to disregard the distinction. For Howells, the novel is a growth out of the
older romance, and, as a higher evolutionary species, inevitably
superior. Acknowledging that at the beginning of the century,

romance, in seeking to break with tradition and widen the bounds of
sympathy, 'was making the same fight against effete classicism which
realism is making today against effete romanticism',[8] he argues that
the novel is now the only kind of fiction commensurate with a
democratic era:

Romanticism belonged to a disappointed and bewildered age, which
turned its face from the future and dreamed out a faery realm in the past;
and we cannot have its spirit back because this is the age of hopeful
striving ... when the recognition of all the facts in the honest daylight
about us is the service which humanity demands of the humanities.[9]

Not surprisingly, Howells attacks romanticism not only because it
is outmoded, but also because in dealing with superstitions and the
'make-believe', it presents a view of life which is untrue and which
encourages the exaggerated prejudices of its readers. Romance
writers, he claims, show us 'images of false gods and misshapen
heroes';[10] their characters are impossible stereotypes, and their plots,
complicated and mechanical, are full of strange incidents and melodramatic effects. The romantic spirit 'worshipped genius, worshipped heroism' and 'its error was to idealize the victims of society,
to paint them impossibly virtuous and beautiful';[11] it was thus false
to life and to art. In a provocative attack upon English fiction,
Howells includes among the nineteenth-century writers who have
succumbed to 'the mania of romanticism . . . the taint of their time'[12]
Scott, Thackeray, Charlotte Bronte, and Dickens. He felt that even
Balzac, whose pioneer attempts at Realism Howells highly applauded,
was, at his worst, not free from the romantic tendency to falsify
nature, and in a novel such as *Old Goriot*, his characters seem
'figures jerked about by the exaggerated passions and motives of the
stage'.[13] Howells also maintained that Zola, for all his pseudo-
scientific theories, was really a 'romanticist', who was always 'taking
realities and placing them in romantic relations',[14] and whose
powerful and epic imagination overruled his Realist ideals.

   Howells recognized that the romance, as a separate literary genre,
had its own value. Moreover he was prepared to give some credence
to that value. He admired the 'romantic spirit' with which the
Norwegian writer Björnsterne Björnson dealt with 'the plainest
fact', making it true 'to the real as well as the ideal';[15] and he felt that
Henry James's 'best efforts' were 'those of romance',[16] somewhat
regretting that his later work moved so distinctly into the realm of

the novel. But if Howells enjoyed the poetry of pure romance, it was not a path which he himself could ever take in his mature art, though his earliest creative efforts were to some extent influenced by current sentimental trends. His creed may be said to encompass a certain kind of moral idealism, as will be suggested below, but it is not the distorted idealization of romanticism. In his own work, he consciously aimed at a different (and, as far as he was concerned, superior) mode of writing. So he wrote to James Osgood in 1884 that 'I don't believe in heroes and heroines, and willingly avoid the heroic',[17] and throughout his criticism and fiction he strove to show up the sentimentality which he so disliked.

Since Howells's antagonism to the literature of falsification was exacerbated, if not solely inspired, by his awareness of the high standards which fiction could achieve, as seen in the work of the new generation of European Realists (he thought that in England only Jane Austen was worthy to be put beside them), it is predictable that he should have adopted and implemented many of their principles and techniques. At the root of his thinking, as of theirs, was the belief that the primary function of art is to portray life in its normal and recognizable aspects, without distortion or exaggeration, and without restricting its field of vision. For him, all experience was valid material for the novel:

[The] true realist . . . cannot look upon human life and declare this thing or that thing unworthy of notice, any more than the scientist can declare a fact of the material world beneath the dignity of his inquiry.[18]

The analogy with the scientific mode of observation—an important criterion of the Realist school—is significant here. From his earliest reviews, Howells showed preference for works which fulfilled the demands of faithfulness to life and human nature, and he considered the greatest novelists to be those such as Jane Austen, Mark Twain, Verga, and Henry James, who treated their subjects with complete truthfulness and accuracy. 'Truthfulness' here, of course, means that which can be measured against the senses and against individual experience—thus, fidelity to place and situation, life-like characters (preferably ordinary people with the virtues and vices of all humanity), and incidents and circumstances not 'too far out of the common'.[19] Howells also maintained that plot should be subordinate to character: not only did he reject the contrived and highly-coloured 'moving accident'[20] as part of the romanticist's machinery, but he also demanded that the course of events be determined by the motivation and actions of the protagonists and not the other way round.

Howells was echoing, too, one of the major preoccupations of Realism—though one which presents more problems and practical differences—in his emphasis on the objective approach. The sense of reality will be conveyed by the author's withdrawal from any evident manipulation and by his refusal to make any direct commentary on his work. Failure in this respect was to Howells, as it was to James, a betrayal of the 'sacred office' of the novelist. He was highly critical of Thackeray for 'stand[ing] about in his scene, talking it over with his hands in his pockets, interrupting the action, and spoiling the illusion in which alone the truth of art resides',[21] whereas one of his greatest literary heroes was Turgenev, who 'never calls on you to admire how well he does a thing; he only makes you wonder at the truth and value of the thing when it is done. He seems the most self-forgetful of the story-telling tribe'.[22] As Jenkins has pointed out in his chapter on Realism, almost all the major exponents of the genre at this time were led to the technique of impersonality in some form or other as a means of resolving the apparent contradiction between objectivity and subjectivity; and objectivity of method, with its corollary, dramatic presentation, was one of Howells's most constant artistic demands. It accounts for his admiration of Verga, Galdós, and De Forest, among others, as well as for his dislike of 'the whole English school in which the author permits himself to come forward and comment on the action and things in general, and subjects the drama to himself'.[23]

Armed with such artistic convictions and principles, Howells was eager to do battle with the sentimentalists and their false picture of life, particularly as his critical ideas grew more assured and well-formulated. He obviously thought that one of the best modes of attack was through the very form which the writers of romance, with their idealized and stereotyped love stories and their glamorized historical tales, had abused, and he sought to use the novel itself (perhaps because it commanded a wider readership than criticism, popular though periodicals such as *Harper's* were) to speak for the criteria it was bound to embody. So, paradoxically, we have in Howells the Realist who, adhering firmly to the importance of objectivity in fiction, and arguing that the novelist must not be too concerned with specific grievances, actually pleads for a particular artistic creed in his own fiction, in a way which has the ring, if not the overt manner, of didacticism. His novels frequently not only reveal the strength of Realism as a method, but also treat directly the mistake of looking at life through literary glasses, and the falsifying effects of sentimentality. This is observable at all stages of his literary career: his first nationally published story, 'A Romance of Real Life' (1871), for example, is a comic portrayal of the gap between the real and the romantic view of the real, while his last novel, *The Vacation of the Kelwyns* (1920), satirizes the sentimentalist's treatment of the relationship between the sexes.

The Rise of Silas Lapham, perhaps Howells's best-known novel, demonstrates most clearly the connection between his practical and his theoretical realism, and the nature of the literary motivation behind them. Published in book form in 1885 (it was previously serialized in the *Century Magazine* beginning in November 1884), the work was produced at a time when Howells's demands for Realism were becoming noticeably more direct and pronounced in his criticism. Two years before, his controversial essay 'Henry James, Jr.', in the *Century* of November 1882, which had praised the new and 'finer art'[24] of fiction exemplified by James—the analysis of character rather than mere story, artistic impartiality instead of overt commentary, and the engagement of sympathy through depth of detail, not insinuation—had helped to set off lengthy discussion about the novelist's art, especially its relationship to the romance. Now his novel could take its part in the debate, both as an exemplum and as a commentary on the principles and techniques of earlier European Realists which Howells had had time to absorb and develop in his own writing.

Howells did not conceive of his propagandist intention as in any way undermining the supreme need of truth to life, but it involved the conscious exploitation of certain realistic devices in order to express his call for literary reform and innovation. Without violating his own belief in authorial impersonality, Howells permits his views to enter the book in various ways. Firstly, several of the characters make references to other fiction, real and imaginary, which point either directly or implicitly to the criteria which Howells himself seeks to uphold. Tom Corey, discussing *Middlemarch*, remarks that George Eliot seems too hard on those characters she dislikes;[25] and Penelope Lapham complains that this novelist is too evidently in control: ' "I wish she would let you find out a little about the people

for yourself" ' (p. 82). Both comments clearly reflect Howells's own
reservations about George Eliot's direct intrusions into her story and
her obvious preferences for certain characters, and show his commitment to authorial impersonality. The observations of Nanny
Corey, who, unfortunately lacking the attentions of an admirer, 'had
read a great many novels with a keen sense of their inaccuracy as
representations of life, and had seen a great deal of life with a sad
regret for its difference from fiction' (p. 144), indicate Howells's
concern for the realistic portrayal of life. Her cousin, Charles
Bellingham, speaks even more unequivocally for the Realist position
in his proposal for a new and more suitable kind of material for
novelists:

'The commonplace is just that light, impalpable aerial essence which
they've never got into their confounded books yet. The novelist who
could interpret the common feelings of commonplace people would have
the answer to "the riddle of the painful earth" on his tongue' [pp. 187–8].

More importantly, the main sub-plot of the novel, the Tom/Irene/
Penelope triangle, serves primarily to illustrate the substance of a
literary argument. At the Coreys' dinner-party, one of the guests
mentions a novel she has been reading, called *Tears, Idle Tears*,
which she finds ' "perfectly heartbreaking" ' (p. 182) since its
heroine sacrifices herself for her ideal of love. Another guest, Mr.
Sewell, the minister who later acts as adviser to the Laphams,
expresses his objection to such works, and suggests that:

'The novelists might be the greatest possible help to us if they painted
life as it is, and human feelings in their true proportion and relation, but
for the most part they have been and are altogether noxious ... The
whole business of love, and lovemaking and marrying is painted by the
novelists in a monstrous disproportion to the other relations of life'
[pp. 183–4].

The spectacle of romantic self-sacrifice is, he claims, ' "wholly
immoral" ' (p. 183). We do not need the evidence of Howells's own
disapproval of the emphasis on false duty and sacrifice in novels,
expressed in several of his *Harper's* 'Editor's Study' columns, to
recognize that Sewell is here speaking for his creator. Words alone,
however, do not point the message strongly enough. His remarks are
made to prove prophetically relevant, for when Penelope, the elder
Lapham daughter, discovers that Tom Corey loves her, and not, as

all had supposed, her sister Irene, her response is both exaggerated and foolish; although she, like Mr. Sewell, agrees that in *Tears, Idle Tears* the heroine's action of giving up the man she loves to another woman just because this 'other' loved him first, is ' "silly . . . wicked" ' (p. 201), in her own case reason fails her, and by indulging in misplaced heroism she makes herself a burden and causes unhappiness to all concerned.

Thus, despite Howells's dislike of plot contrivance, he has here created and implemented an incident purposely to demonstrate a literary thesis. This seems to be the most valid way of regarding the sub-plot. Howells is making the point that even an intelligent and perceptive girl like Penelope has become so imbued with the standards of the novels she has read that she acts out the very principles which she theoretically despised. To view it in any other way is to see Howells as muddled and confused, on the one hand allowing Sewell to speak for him, and on the other presenting a story which appears to support those attitudes which Sewell is opposing. As has been suggested, this kind of propaganda does not preclude realistic presentation. But the thematic framework of literary reference in the novel implies the extent to which Howells's Realism was not only the exemplification of a mode, but also an obvious and conscious protest.

The main plot of *The Rise of Silas Lapham* is less patently illustrative, and is, furthermore, not specifically concerned with literary issues. But here, too, Howells is concerned with opposing the sentimentalist approach. He puts forward his 'anti-romantic' views by deliberately denying the expectations which would result from an addiction to sentimental novels. The book has the form and pattern of much romance fiction: the hero, risen from obscurity and become highly successful, has to endure suffering and disappointment before finally discovering his true self in spiritual re-birth; the love-affair, having passed through a series of vicissitudes and misunderstandings, ends happily with the 'right' people marrying each other. Within this pattern, however, Howells carefully puts to work his belief that fiction must 'portray men and women as they are, actuated by the motives and the passions in the measure we all know'.[26] In the first place, the central character is very different from 'the stock hero'[27] of romance. Silas Lapham, a native Yankee, is a hard-headed, successful businessman, who has made his money through paint, and whose lowly antecedents are still only too obvious in his lapses of grammar, his vulgarity, and his social ineptitude; he is boastful, stubborn, and self-engrossed, and has execrable aesthetic tastes. The revelation of his faults is part of the author's scheme of portraying imperfect humanity; whenever Lapham seems limited or ridiculous, this is an intentional effect, and not because he is the absurd embodiment of a romantic concept. Silas's good qualities are inextricably mixed with his bad ones. He is not inhumane (he maintains the wife and daughter of the man who saved his life, for instance), but he reveals sad deficiences of tact and sympathy in his personal relationships; his pride distorts his concern for his daughters' welfare; his good business sense is marred by a weakness for speculation and display; his moral awareness is often blurred or muddled.

Catastrophe, too—the overwhelming tragedy of melodramatic fiction—is qualified according to normal experience. As in many of the other Realist novels, misfortune seems here merely a part of the cycle of life, temporarily crippling for certain people, but without a sense of utter and irremediable disaster. Even at the lowest depths of his fortunes, caught between conflicting impulses and desires, Lapham's mood fluctuates between optimism and gloom, and the process of his financial disintegration is

like the course of some chronic disorder which has fastened itself upon the constitution, but advances with continual reliefs, with apparent amelioration, and at times seems not to advance at all, when it gives hope of final recovery not only to the sufferer, but to the eye of science itself [p. 282].

Again, the scientific-medical analogy is particularly interesting here. It is significant that at this point Howells himself makes one of his infrequent appearances in the book to protest against the theory, presented by poets and novelists, that disaster, sorrow, and affliction are absolute and incessant: he explains that Lapham's adversity 'was not always like the adversity we figure in allegory; it had its moments of being like prosperity' (p. 282). Furthermore, if Lapham's final renunciation is heroic, it is a stumbling and muted heroism, unattended by any of the positive blessings of romance. When he returns, at the end of the novel, to his birthplace in Vermont, financially defeated and morally chastened, this is no idyllic return to a state of pre-lapsarian innocence. He has clearer vision, but other benefits are by no means assured, as he himself recognizes:

For his nerves there was no mechanical sense of coming back; this was as much the end of his proud, prosperous life as death itself could have been. He was returning to begin life anew, but he knew as well as he knew that he should not find his vanished youth in his native hills [p. 325]. On the other hand, it is important to notice that if this is not a glorious beginning, neither is it the complete end. Howells's hero is not reduced to utter degradation by suffering; in contrast to Hurst-wood in Dreiser's *Sister Carrie*, whose defeat leads him to suicide, Lapham, like Frédéric Moreau or Lydgate, endures, even though his triumphs are over and his highest hopes unrealized.

The achievement of personal happiness through love is not presented as an absolute in the novel, either. The affection between the two young people does not have to go to the extreme expedient of defending itself against parental opposition. When Tom Corey announces his intention of marrying one of the Lapham girls, his father (as the older man himself jokingly remarks) acts quite unconventionally in accepting the fact instead of cutting him off with a shilling in paternal fury. Moreover, though Penelope and Tom love each other, when the marriage takes place it is not the instrument of general reconciliation so dear to romance writers. The disparity in social status, experience, and ideals between the Coreys and the Laphams remains ineffaceable, and even if Tom's career in Lapham's paint firm represents a potentially healthy business alliance between aristocratic culture and proletarian shrewdness, his union with Penelope in no way draws together the two families. The point is made ironically both by Penelope herself when, having bidden farewell to her new in-laws before leaving for South America, she comments ' "I don't think I shall feel strange among the Mexicans now" ' (p. 332), and by Nanny Corey who is glad of the separation because ' "At that distance we cannot correspond" ' (p. 332).

The Rise of Silas Lapham also seems to be countering another tendency which Howells disliked in sentimental fiction—the superimposition, through a contrived plot, of a rigid and artificial pattern upon life. The novel is not unstructured, and is in fact built around four main climaxes: the 'revelation' in the Penelope/Irene/Tom triangle, the burning of the house, the affair of the mills, and the financial disaster which overtakes Lapham's business, all of which are stages in Lapham's progress towards humility and self-knowledge. But Howells manages to incorporate them within his overall scheme of showing life as a natural and recognizable process. Firstly, like many of the other Realists, Howells accepts a connection between chance and causality, and so although there is a sense of 'necessity' in his novel, it is what Lukács has called a 'poetic necessity'[28] and not an obviously contrived fatality. Thus the stages of disaster have been prepared for and are accountable for in terms of character and circumstance, while at the same time they are illustrative of the 'bad luck' which can happen to any individual. As in *Lost Illusions* Balzac makes us see that, given Lucien's personal qualities, he will inevitably come to grief in a world full of allurements of wealth and prestige, yet also shows us the unpredictability of experience and the power of fortune at certain crucial moments— such as Lucien's chance meeting with Vautrin at the end of the novel, which is clearly going to affect considerably his future career —so Howells demonstrates that fate and recognizable cause-and-effect are not incompatible. Tom's preference for the witty and amusing Penelope, instead of for the lovely but somewhat insipid Irene, is perfectly credible, and the revelation seems an incomprehensible blow to all concerned only because they have been viewing the affair according to preconceived assumptions. The burning of the house (a week after the insurance has run out), perhaps the nearest Howells comes to obvious manipulation of plot for ethical purposes, is the direct result of Lapham's carelessness, and even though the element of chance is closely involved, the 'accident' is appropriate to character and situation. Similarly, the series of financial disasters which overtake Lapham are related both to his personal irresponsibility (his initial treatment of Rogers and his material over-ambition) and to natural contingencies which include the discovery of gas in West Virginia and a fall in the demand for paint. Secondly, the misfortunes create a pattern only in as far as they contribute to a general downward trend in Lapham's career; they are not linked according to an obviously superimposed plan. The distress caused by the unexpected love-affair contributes to the family's suffering but is not connected with the final disaster, and the house-burning and the sale of the mills are separate elements in the gradual collapse which leads to the crash. Howells has sought to replace the artificiality of romance with the arbitrariness of real life.

In suggesting that Howells's Realism was to a considerable extent inspired by literary protest, I have indicated what seems the particular purpose of some of the thematic and structural elements of the novel. Examination of the work in more general terms reveals that despite Howells's urge to propagandize he implements his aim largely in accordance with the principles established by the writers he so much admired. To reiterate an earlier point, his desire to combat tendencies which he considered inimical to true art may have led him into a kind of 'telling', but it did not alter his firm intention to make his own work practically illustrate the required standards. Even though parts of the book may have a slightly literary flavour—some of the exchanges between Mr. and Mrs. Corey, and the incident of the mistaken suitor, for instance, have a certain affinity with the novel of manners as represented by Jane Austen—as a whole it reveals the author's commitment to a new mode of writing. So as well as seeing *The Rise of Silas Lapham* as a deliberate 'anti-romance', we must recognize it as an accomplished example of nineteenth-century Realism, in an American setting. One of its most noticeable features is its truth to life, revealed firstly in its fidelity to place. Centred almost entirely on Boston, the novel, like James's *The Bostonians* (published the following year), gives a convincing picture of the city with its narrow streets, its thronging crowds, and its splendid views across Back Bay to the spires and roofs of Cambridge 'in a black outline, as if they were objects in a landscape of the French school' (p. 287). It also pays careful attention to the physical appearance of buildings; the contrasting details of the Laphams' house with its mixtures of wall colourings, its chandeliers of 'massive imitation bronze' and its carpets 'of a small pattern in crude green' (p. 199), and the Coreys' house with its classic proportions, its 'slim and fluted' columns, and its staircase climbing 'in a graceful, easy curve from the tesselated pavement' (pp. 173–4) especially reminds us of Flaubert's painstakingly specific descriptions of domestic interiors. Howells further seeks to render reality accurately by reproducing the peculiarities of individual speech: the Laphams' provinciality is revealed by their use of colloquialisms and their grammatical lapses, while the Coreys' refinement and education is revealed in their more measured, formal language.

The Rise of Silas Lapham illustrates the Realist's aim for 'truthfulness' in a historical sense, too. Like many of the novelists discussed in this book, Howells is concerned with a specific period as well as an actual place, and with the representative qualities of his characters and circumstances within this period. In his dual concern with both the human and the historical significance of his protagonists he fulfils Lukács's criterion that the truly great realists were those who recognized the organic and indissoluble connection between man as a private individual and man as a social being, thus synthesizing the particular and the general.[29] Apart from the last few pages which take us forward several years, the action of the novel occurs between 1875 and 1877, at the end of the Grant administration—a complex period of industrial expansion and social change, during which the capitalistic and materialistic values of the Gilded Age were at their strongest, business and financial success were the great ideals, and the entrepreneurs or 'Robber Barons' flourished. The retrospective setting enables Howells to view his world dispassionately and analytically. Like Balzac, whose *Lost Illusions* portrays the corruption of bourgeois society by the emergent forces of capitalism in post-revolutionary France, seen in the destinies of his characters, or Turgenev, whose presentation of the relationship between generations in *Fathers and Sons* shows the clash between conservatism and radicalism in the Russia of his day, so Howells seeks to convey as accurately as possible, in his hero's story, the changing environment of nineteenth-century America, where traditional values are confronted by and have to confront a new spirit of commercialism—a confrontation most marked and extreme in the isolationist and reactionary Boston. In contrast to writers such as Flaubert or, to a somewhat lesser extent, George Eliot, he does not incorporate any actual events into his story and his social documentation is both less detailed and less panoramic than theirs, but he creates a sense of social and historical reality by having a relatively small group of characters act out their roles against a background recognizable in time as well as place.

Lapham himself is not only an individual linked to 'real life' by his similarity to his creator (Howells was of humble origins, though he came from Ohio, not Vermont, and his family was considerably more cultured than the Laphams; he, too, bought a house 'on the water side of Beacon Street', and in fact jokingly told James that the proceeds of the novel might pay for it[30]); he is also 'typical'. It is significant that we first see him as a subject for the 'Solid Men of Boston' series in a local newspaper, since this in many ways establishes him as one of a species or group. Like another self-made man, Verga's Gesualdo, in whom, as a new capitalist motivated by the principle of material self-interest, a whole historic process is typified, Lapham is a representative figure. In his rise from lowly beginnings, through a mixture of good luck and hard work, to commercial success, he is reminiscent of the great millionaires of this era such as Rockefeller and Vanderbilt, even if his achievements are not so spectacular as theirs. This kind of representativeness was clearly foremost in Howells's mind, for as early as 1869, he wrote that 'the history of a man's rise from poverty and obscurity to distinction' is a 'perpetual romance' which 'delights and touches all, for in this nation it is in some degree the story of every man's life or the vision of his desires'.[31] Lapham's succumbing to the business ethics of the age is further indicative of a general trend. The relationship between the Laphams and the Coreys also has a representative significance: the awkwardness and misunderstandings which never completely disappear on a personal level illustrate the conflict between the older Boston aristocratic society and the new brash world of business which demands acknowledgement from it.

None of the characters, however, embodies a single aspect of the social reality with which Howells is concerned. All are 'real' in the way that Howells found so admirable in Galdós's work, where the people are 'typical of a certain side of human nature . . . but not exclusively of this side or that. They are . . . of mixed motives, mixed qualities'.[32] Not only is Silas himself, as has already been suggested, a commonplace, average hero, combining wisdom and foolishness, altruism and self-centredness, but his wife is also a mixture of qualities. She is both practically astute and socially naïve; her sense of moral responsibility, coloured by 'her helpless longing, inbred in all Puritan souls, to have someone specifically suffer for the evil in the world, even if it must be herself' (p. 255), leads her to insist on Lapham's guilt in his treatment of his former partner, Rogers, yet later she is unable to distinguish between economic reparation and basic dishonesty; on slight evidence she suspects her husband's relationship with his typist, Zerilla; and she fails him in his hour of greatest need when he is agonizing over whether or not to sell the mills. The Lapham daughters are not mere stereotypes, either. Indeed, they reveal qualities of life-like unpredictability which may surprise us. The pretty, somewhat empty-headed Irene turns out to be much more resilient to disappointment than would be expected, whereas it is the apparently more perceptive and self-sufficient Penelope whose reasonableness fails her at a time of crisis.

Howells's treatment of the Coreys also shows his method of bringing out the many-faceted complexity of human nature. Though perhaps Tom Corey, in his dogged loyalty to both Lapham and Penelope and his heroic willingness to try to save the failing paint firm, is too good to be true (a comparison with, say, Fred Vincy in *Middlemarch* would not be to the former's advantage), other members of the family are convincingly drawn. Broomfield Corey, for example, is an intelligent and considerate man who recognizes the need to preserve cultivated and civilized standards in an age devoted to materialism, but he himself takes refuge in a sterile detachment; he regards his son's business aspirations with complacency, yet his ironic vision can find only entertainment at the spectacle of human suffering:

His standpoint in regard to most matters was that of the sympathetic humorist who would be glad to have the victim of circumstance laugh with him, but was not too much vexed when the victim could not [p: 246].

Even in their socially representative roles, the characters are of 'mixed qualities'. If the Laphams are vulgar, materialistic, and muddled, they are also energetic, resourceful, and refreshingly frank; if the Coreys are elegant and cultured, they are also snobbish and cruel. We are given in the novel a clear-eyed, though not unsympathetic, view of an imperfect world in which our attitudes towards humanity have continually to be revised.

Another essential element of Howells's artistic credo, which is closely linked to his ideal of truthfulness, is objectivity of narration. He felt that it is neither possible nor desirable totally to exclude the writer's personal vision, but that the author must not be in evidence 'to moralize openly and badly . . . to "sympathize" with certain of his people, and to point out others for the abhorrence of his readers'.[33] Like Verga who 'meant to let the people show themselves with the least possible explanation or comment from him'[34] (Flaubert and Fontane could also have been used as examples here), Howells aimed at freedom from authorial interference, allowing his characters to develop naturally and to speak for themselves. Writing to Hamlin Garland in 1888, he indicated that the 'message' of his books could never be directly stated:

To infuse, or to declare more of my personality in a story, would be a mistake, to my thinking: it should rather be the novelist's business to keep out of the way. My work must take its chance with readers.[35]

The influence of Turgenev was probably particularly strong in this respect, since in his discussions of the Russian novelist Howells frequently draws attention to the way in which Turgenev gives psychological depth to his characters without commenting or interfering or demanding final judgements from the reader.

Objectivity is clearly a predominant aim in *The Rise of Silas Lapham*, even if it is not wholly consistent in practice. Howells does not in fact entirely abandon the use of direct authorial commentary, but, as I shall show later, his remarks tend to be reflective and speculative, directing attention from the specific to the more universal aspects of human experience, rather than narrowly prescriptive or moralistic. For the most part he is the conventional narrator who tells the story, but he often assumes an ironic tone which distances him from the action. He frequently disclaims omniscience about characters' motivation or intentions by using words and phrases such as 'perhaps', 'maybe', or 'it may have been' to describe their actions. Information about his protagonists is often conveyed from within the story itself, instead of by the more obvious method of straightforward narrative. The opening of the novel is a good example of this: Silas Lapham is being interviewed by Bartley Hubbard, a Boston journalist, who interrogates him about his career and business achievements. This question-and-answer device not only introduces us to Lapham without any explicit 'telling' from the author himself, but it also presents us with a double viewpoint: Hubbard's cynical and unscrupulous reporter's eye seizes on Lapham's naïvety, his sentimentality, and his tasteless self-assertion, but it also indirectly reveals his idealism, his openness, and his magnanimity. Later in the book, other characters comment on Lapham, thus building up a composite picture. Walker, his head book-keeper, tells Tom Corey of his employer's tireless energy, his devotion to his work, and his absolute rule in his office, while in contrast Tom's uncle, James Bellingham, who tries to sort out Lapham's financial muddles, gives an indication of the latter's confused and somewhat flexible business ethics:

'Lapham doesn't strike me as a man who's in the habit of acting from the best in him always . . . I suspect that a hopeful temperament and fondness for round numbers have always caused him to set his figures beyond his actual worth. I don't say that he's been dishonest about it, but he's had a loose way of estimating his assets' [p. 276].

The extensive use of conversation in the novel, enabling people both to reveal themselves and to cast light on their fellows, helps to create the sense of Howells's essentially free and impartial view of his characters. Penelope Lapham, for instance, is variously referred to by others as a pert young thing, a wise and witty observer, and an ideal partner in marriage, and the reader must assimilate and distinguish between all these ways of regarding her. Conversations between groups of characters, too, show up contrasts and similarities in particular situations. The discussions between Mr. and Mrs. Lapham, and between Mr. and Mrs. Corey about their children's matrimonial plans are structurally paralleled and provide a dramatic way of suggesting a mutual concern for filial welfare, despite differences of emphasis and expression.

Howells sometimes combines an apparently impartial presentation of his protagonists and their attitudes with an ironic gloss on them, thus managing to reconcile a sense of distinctions with objectivity of method. Though by no means as skilful or consistent in this as James, he seems to be experimenting with the Jamesian 'point of view' technique, which allows the author to make or suggest evaluations without directly inserting his own opinions, while giving the illusion that his characters are free agents. In the following passage, we are shown the Coreys' reluctant acknowledgement that they owe some kind of 'return' to the Laphams for their kindness in helping the sick Mrs. Corey the previous summer:

[Mrs. Corey] opened the matter with some trepidation to her daughters, but neither of them opposed her; they rather looked at the scheme from her own point of view, and agreed with her that nothing had really yet been done to wipe out the obligation to the Laphams helplessly contracted the summer before, and strengthened by that ill-advised application to Mrs. Lapham for charity. Not only the principle of their debt of gratitude remained, but the accruing interest [p. 160].

This is a fine example of the Realist's method of refusing to comment overtly on his characters, yet at the same time drawing attention to certain aspects of their behaviour. The passage seems on the surface a simple description of the Coreys' attitudes, using reportage instead of direct speech, and with no evident authorial evaluation. But by suggesting that they look on 'their debt of gratitude' in essentially financial and calculating terms, and by the use of words such as 'helplessly' and 'ill-advised' (which represent the Coreys' reactions, not the author's), Howells makes us see not only the

Coreys' snobbish regret at forming such an unfortunate acquaintance, but also their desire to conclude it as quickly and conclusively as respectability and self-esteeem will allow.

As I implied earlier, Howells's ideal of objectivity included stress on the dramatic mode. By this he seems to have meant the rejection of verbose and elaborate description, the direct presentation of character, and an 'organic' plot depending on a natural and unheralded progression of events. His emphasis on this method recalls James's constant reminder to himself to ' "Dramatize it, dramatize it!" '[36] Unlike James, however, Howells was not concerned with the more formal aesthetic aspects of dramatic technique, such as unity of action or tightness of narrative structure, since these might actually work against his particular realistic aims. 'Drama' in his novels in fact usually consists of placing characters in certain scenes and allowing them freely and directly to express themselves through their subsequent behaviour, giving the illusion that they are acting independently and not according to the author's intentions towards them. One of the best illustrations of this in *The Rise of Silas Lapham* is the Coreys' dinner party. This occasion, during which the Laphams feel themselves at a strong social and cultural disadvantage, contrasts effectively with the previous confrontation between members of the two families—Broomfield Corey's visit to Lapham's office—when Lapham, feeling himself in the secure position of employer and successful businessman, assures Corey with embarrassingly patronising condescension that all are not fortunate enough to have an aptitude for business and that ' "The idea is to make the most of what we *have* got" ' (p. 131). At the dinner-party these roles are reversed. The Laphams are hopelessly inept: Mrs. Lapham announces bluntly and unexpectedly that Penelope is not coming after all, and Silas, worried about social proprieties and uncomfortably conscious of his large hands which 'looked, in the saffron tint which the shop girl said his gloves should be of, like canvassed hams' (p. 174), fiddles with the glasses at table, talks with his cigar in his mouth, and drinks too much. He ends the evening by boasting wildly, treating all the other guests (the Boston élite) like old friends whom he can help to better things, and taking leave of all 'with patronising affection' (p. 192). The scene is finely executed, and Howells's skill is evident in the manner in which not only do we see the pitiable gulf between the Laphams and these 'old Bostonians', but we also recognize the complacent superiority and clannishness of the Coreys and their ilk, as they debate aesthetic questions and make sweeping assumptions about social hierarchies. This is truly dramatic presentation, character unfolding itself in action. As with the other instances of Howells's objectivity, the reader is not required to do more than observe, but finds himself becoming involved, paradoxically because of the lack of imposed authorial judgements.

The Rise of Silas Lapham, then, sets out to focus on the Reverend Sewell's objections that ' "those novels with old-fashioned heroes and heroines in them . . . are ruinous" ' (p. 183), and by direct polemic and exemplification of the anti-romantic position to reinforce Howells's plea for fiction which paints life as it really is. Using many of the techniques of other nineteenth-century Realist novels, it strives to show the strength of accurate and uncontrived presentation of familiar material. But when we consider the novel as an example of Howells's Realism, we are inevitably made aware of the ambiguities or conflicts intrinsic in the genre, not only in his explicit promotion of it as a literary method, but also in the nature of the book as a whole. If the work of the other Realists demonstrates the impossibility of 'pure' realism, Howells's fiction is no exception; like theirs, his novel is inevitably coloured and shaped by his own vision of the world and his sense of its significance. As we have already seen, he felt that the novelist had a responsibility to tell the truth, partly because this was an artistic merit, but more importantly because in this way he could demonstrate to his readers the meaning and value of life in its most ordinary aspects. In his insistence that the artist must reveal the poetry of everyday experience—the beauty and nobility which 'lie within the realm of reality . . . and . . . nowhere else'[37]—and that the purpose of literature is to enable men to know themselves and each other better, Howells is trying to resolve the eternally problematic relationship between art and morality which troubles all writers concerned with Realism. Committed to the principle of veracity, yet with an unmistakeable streak of idealism in him (which accounted for his slightly apologetic pleasure in romance as well as for his view that certain subjects such as the profoundly tragic or 'the passion of guilty love'[38] were better omitted from American fiction), Howells attempted to strike a balance between scientific devotion to faithful recording and a more subjective evaluative approach. So although he objected to overt didacticism, he argued that the essence of Realism was to interpret its material:

When realism becomes false to itself, when it heaps up facts merely, and maps life instead of picturing it, realism will perish too. Every true realist instinctively knows this, and it is perhaps the reason why he is careful of every fact, and feels himself bound to express or to indicate its meaning at the risk of over-moralizing.[39]

This quality of ethical idealism (if we may so term it) enters more noticeably into Howells's fiction of the mid-80s and later, at a time when he was becoming increasingly aware of the deterioration of standards, moral and social, in American life. It is interesting, too, that this is the period when he first read the work of Tolstoy (in 1885), whom he came so much to admire and who seemed to confirm the importance of the prophetic function of art:

Here for the first time, I found the most faithful pictures of life set in the light of that human conscience which I had falsely taught myself was to be ignored in questions of art, as something inadequate and inappropriate.[40]

The recognition of moral concern in the work of the great Russian—a concern which, in Howells's eyes, set him above his compatriot, Turgenev—was perhaps responsible for his own view that

no conscientious man can now set about painting an image of life . . . without feeling bound to distinguish so clearly that no reader of his may be misled between what is right and what is wrong, what is noble and what is base, what is health and what is perdition, in the actions and the characters he portrays.[41]

The Rise of Silas Lapham clearly shows the result of Howells's growing commitment to the idea of conscience and ethical clarification, both in its themes and its structure. Its critical or evaluative emphasis in the social sphere—its portrayal of the changing values of a materialistic age in which the lure of money and the desire for upward social mobility are pervasive, and the individual is caught up in the temptations and corruptions of a capitalist society—has already been suggested. But there is more than this: we are not only made to realize the particular significance of the central character in this general theme, we have also to regard his involvement to a considerable extent in ethical terms. Although Howells is not directly didactic, by giving his novel a traditionally Christian framework—a pattern of sin, guilt, retribution, and regeneration—he compels us to recognize a moral relationship between cause and effect, and

a difference between 'good' and 'bad' behaviour, even while he
implies that these are relative distinctions. 'What is' in the novel is
accompanied by a definite suggestion of 'what should be'.

Interestingly, in this awareness of a moral dimension beyond the
mere recording of events and consequences, Howells has much in
common with George Eliot. As has been mentioned above, he
criticized her for failing to meet the requirements of objectivity and
dispassionate observation, and argued that her immense sincerity and
psychological truthfulness were marred by her intrusion into her
story. But as he grew older, he came increasingly to believe that one
of her greatest strengths was her insistence on ethical considerations,
and attributed 'the consciousness of right and wrong implanted in
me'[42] largely to her influence. In fact, in 1901, re-reading *Middlemarch* after many years, he now acknowledged that it 'is as large as
life in those moral dimensions which deepen inwardly and give the
real compass of any artistic achievement through the impression
received.'[43] Though these opinions date from a decade or more later
than *The Rise of Silas Lapham*, we can sense George Eliot's influence
in the novel, especially her recognition of the relationship between
the individual and the social environment, and her interest in moral
deterioration through a combination of personal guilt and external
circumstances. Howells shares with George Eliot the belief that the
lives of ordinary people contain lessons for all humanity; of particular relevance is the emphasis both writers place on the insidious
effects of past sin; in this respect there are some interesting points of
comparison between Bulstrode and Lapham. Sometimes, too, her
sage-like voice can be detected in the occasional direct pronouncements which Howells makes in the novel. For example, he remarks
of the Laphams' distress that 'each one of us must suffer long to
himself before he can learn that he is but one in a great community
of wretchedness, which has been pitilessly repeating itself from the
foundation of the world' (p. 221).

Howells saw no conflict between George Eliot's moralism and her
Realism (he spoke of her 'clear ethical conscience which forced [her]
to be realistic when probably her artistic prepossessions were
romantic'[44]) and indeed her reconciliation of the ideal and the actual
through sympathetic analysis and stress on self-awareness probably
seemed to him the best way of combining involvement and clear-
sightedness. As Stoneman has argued, George Eliot's 'moral'
Realism stems from her belief that art must reflect the value of life,

and she attempts to find the balance between an accurate presentation of things as they are and an ethical assessment of them, through subjective awareness. Howells, too, must have hoped to fuse Realism and morality in his work in a similar way, by portraying the known 'facts' of his world as objectively as possible, while at the same time offering some kind of judgement on them. In this, however, he is not completely successful: unlike George Eliot, he cannot entirely convince us that a belief in a fundamentally ethically-based system is compatible with a conviction that unequivocal moral conclusions about life are impossible.

The central moral idea of the novel seems to be that by wronging a fellow man an individual will himself suffer spiritual injury, which must be atoned for before health can be restored. At the beginning of the story, we are told that Lapham has acted badly towards his former partner, Rogers, in forcing him out of the business when it was prosperous and he no longer needed him: his guilt is established not only by Mrs. Lapham, who tells him that he 'took an advantage' (p. 45) of a man who had previously helped him, but also by Howells himself, who, in one of his direct statements, comments:

As he said, Lapham had dealt fairly by his partner in money; he had let Rogers take more money out of the business than he put into it; he had, as he said, simply forced out of it a timid and inefficient participant in advantages which he had created. But Lapham had not created them all. He had been dependent at one time on his partner's capital. It was a moment of terrible trial. Happy is the man forever after who can choose the ideal, the unselfish part, in such an exigency! Lapham could not rise to it [p. 47].

To repair this wrong, Lapham lends Rogers some of the money which he was going to spend on the new house, and we are obviously meant to see this both as an admirable act of conscience and an appropriate way for Lapham to assuage his wife's long-standing unease about the affair. From this point on, however, the moral focus becomes less clear. On the one hand, we see that Lapham is by no means free of blame for what subsequently happens to him—he speculates in the financial world, he is eager to promote the marriage between Tom and Irene because it will offer him social advancement, and he is proud and boastful—and that therefore to some extent the code of guilt and expiation, stressed by his wife, is applicable to him. On the other hand, Howells makes it quite evident that Mrs. Lapham has serious limitations as a moral guide: though she often keeps her husband straight by her shrewd common sense, she is helpless and confused when the trouble over Tom and her daughters arises, and she continues to view Lapham's relationship with Rogers in terms of sin and atonement even after reparation has been made. In fact Howells strongly suggests that her need to attribute blame and to find a discernible cause for misfortune and pain are not to be taken as unqualified wisdom, and that crime, punishment, and re-birth are not simple concepts but need modification according to individual circumstances.

At the end of the novel, Lapham is presented with what seems an intolerable choice: he can either sell the mills and save Rogers from financial ruin, or act with uncompromising uprightness and forgo the deal. Mrs. Lapham, who originally saw the potential dishonesty in the proposed sale, now fails him at this crisis, and he is left to make the decision on his own. Though he has been tempted to do business with the Englishmen, and though he himself is aware of the ostensible absurdity of his scruples, his actual choice (and even though the letter from the G.L. & P. comes before he has spoken to Rogers, we know which way he is drawn) has to be seen as an act of absolute moral value. We recognize this as the climax of his moral 'rise' (as spelt out in the title), an indication that through suffering he has reached a state of spiritual health; and his honourable refusals—to sell the mills either directly to the Englishmen or via Rogers, since he knows the purchase will be worthless, or to accept help for his business without telling the prospective investor about the West Virginia company—clearly have authorial approval. For Lapham to have capitulated to 'temptation' would have been to have enacted that 'potential immorality which regards common property as common prey, and gives us the most corrupt municipal governments under the sun' (p. 300). Significantly, Mrs. Lapham herself comes to realize her mistake in this respect:

she had now to confess . . . that she had kept her mind so long upon that old wrong which she believed her husband had done this man that she could not detach it, but clung to the thought of reparation for it when she ought to have seen that he was proposing a piece of roguery as the means [p. 308].

We have here, then, the apparent anomaly of the Realist who wants to portray life in all its natural and normal aspects imposing a pattern of moral imperatives on his work. The appeal to such imperatives need not, of course, be at odds with the Realist's aims—after all, virtuous behaviour is as much part of 'real' life as weakness and vice—but *The Rise of Silas Lapham* seems a less than satisfactory fusion of Realism and morality because of the way in which the ethical elements are introduced. It would be simple to argue that the ambivalence created by the contrasting moral viewpoints in the novel represents the Realist's refusal to acknowledge ethical absolutes, were it not for the fact that at the end, despite Sewell's uncertainty about the operation of evil in the spiritual world, a definitive moral statement does seem to have been made. This statement affects the book in three main ways. Firstly, the resolution seems both socially and psychologically unconvincing. It not only asserts Howells's positive faith in the spiritual integrity of the American businessman, by asking us to accept that Lapham, as a representative of his class and kind, in an age of compromised values, would pass up an opportunity to avert financial ruin when no law-breaking is involved, and this surely in the face of much contemporary evidence to the contrary, but it is also inadequate in terms of character and motivation. Given that Lapham was behaving 'normally' (that is, according to his natural impulses) in his initial treatment of Rogers, and given the view we have of him for much of the novel, with his moral uncertainties and his shifting attitudes, it is hard to see why he should be so virtuous at the end. The progress of his growth to this position is not shown clearly enough, and his final declaration that ' ". . . it seems to me I done wrong about Rogers in the first place; that the whole trouble came from that" ', and his feeling that if ' "the thing [the refusal to sell] was to do over again, right in the same way, I guess I should have to do it" ' (pp. 336, 337), seem scarcely commensurate with his character as it has been drawn.

Secondly, the moral emphasis affects the novel's structural significance. Though earlier it was suggested that the major crises of the book are essentially in accordance with 'natural' chance—apparently random and fortuitous circumstances which are yet probable because of the nature of the people and situations concerned—they must also be seen as stages in the hero's spiritual development. Hence, they may seem somewhat contrived, 'message pointers' rather than merely steps to financial ruin, and standing out from the general naturalistic quality of the plot. Thirdly, the pattern of guilt/

atonement/regeneration, with the hero attaining moral victory and with character ultimately defined and evaluated by a kind of ethical idealism, gives the novel something of the flavour of the very genre which Howells was trying to counteract—the romance. As in the case of the almost impossibility virtuous Tom Corey, the essentially romantic vision tends to undercut the other successful elements of Realism in the work.

A very interesting comparison can be made here with Balzac's *The Rise and Fall of César Birotteau* (1839). As has been indicated, despite his reservations about the more highly-coloured elements of the Frenchman's fiction, Howells much admired Balzac as a pioneer of Realism and was clearly influenced by him. The parallels between this particular novel and *Silas Lapham* are so striking, in fact, that Howells must have had Balzac's work in mind when he wrote his own. Birotteau, like Lapham, is a self-made man, who has achieved success from the invention of a new product—in this case a per-fumed cosmetic—which has been brought to birth partly by accident (he finds an old book about preserving beauty), partly by his hard work, and partly through the help of a renowned chemist, Vauquelin, who gives him a formula for the cosmetic and allows him to style himself its inventor. Like Lapham, too, Birotteau is country-born, ill-educated, and without social graces, but also shrewd, industrious, and honest; he is married to a woman who is in many ways his superior, and who acts as his adviser and mentor when she feels he is in danger of over-extending himself. He is socially ambitious, and spends large sums of money on renovating his house (as with Lapham, his appallingly bad taste is overruled by a skilfully persuasive architect) in order to give a great ball whose expense is partly responsible for his downfall; when he finally succumbs to economic ruin, he abandons all his previous pretensions and sets to work to repay his creditors. The sub-plot, too, corresponds to that in Howell's novel: the Birotteaus' only daughter, Césarine, is courted by a young man who works for Birotteau and who, when his employer gets into difficulties, offers him the proceeds of his own part of the business. In plot and background, then, the two novels are very similar, and Taine probably had this particular similarity in mind when he remarked of *Silas Lapham* :

I have read it in English with the greatest pleasure and with much admiration; it is the best novel written by an American, the most like those of Balzac, the most profound and the most comprehensive.[45]

Yet in many ways, *César Birotteau* is a more successful example of Realism. Although Balzac frequently enters his work to make large social and moral generalizations, and although there is an obvious moral dimension to the book, since Birotteau achieves true heroism and spiritual refinement after his fall by resigning himself to misfortune and working incessantly to repay all he owes, the overall pattern is more in accordance with Realism's aims than is *Silas Lapham*. Birotteau has committed no sin, apart from some foolish and slightly dubious speculation; his fall is to a large extent engineered by a previous employee, du Tillet, who has vowed implacable enmity towards Birotteau because the manufacturer found out that he had stolen money from him. Birotteau is therefore mainly the victim of a plot against him which he is too naïve to suspect. He dies at the end, honoured for his financial probity and an exemplum of honesty and uprightness, but because there is no emphasis on guilt and atonement, the progression of events seems more natural and inevitable, and there is less sense that a definitive ethical statement is being made.

It is interesting that Howells recognized the weaknesses of *César Birotteau* which, he felt, 'stood at the beginning of the great things that have followed since in fiction'.[46] He objected to Balzac's ending:

It is not enough to have rehabilitated Birotteau pecuniarily and socially; he must make him die spectacularly, of an opportune hemorrhage, in the midst of the festivities which celebrate his restoration to his old home . . . It is very pretty; it is touching, and brings the lump into the reader's throat; but it is too much.[47]

He conceded that the story was beautiful and pathetic, 'full of shrewdly considered knowledge of men, and of good art struggling to free itself from self-consciousness', but he also considered that

Balzac, when he wrote it, was under the burden of the very traditions which he has helped fiction to throw off. He felt obliged to construct a mechanical plot, to surcharge his characters, to moralize openly and badly; he permitted himself to 'sympathize' with certain of his people, and to point out others for the abhorrence of his readers.[48]

And yet, though these comments were written only the year after the publication of *Silas Lapham* (they were originally in the June 1886 edition of *Harper's*), and Howells must have read the French novel sometime earlier, he does not seem to have extended his critical

awareness to similar weaknesses in his own work. His conclusion is
far less melodramatic, and he tries to avoid an obvious division of his
characters into good and bad, but his dislike of Balzac's plot construction and his overt moralizing has not prevented the intrusion
into his novel of an ethical idealism which risks being destructive of
Realism. Perhaps he is a more direct ancestor of Balzac and his
romanticism than he would have imagined or wished.[49]

In his determination to examine the moral implications of man's
behaviour, then, Howells perhaps comes closest to the appearance of
didacticism. But we cannot say that this nullifies the achievement of
the novel as a whole. Its portrayal of its chosen world is well-detailed,
perceptive, and sympathetic, and by making us understand human
nature, Howells gives us a sense of values without demanding our
allegiance to one particular interpretation of the world. Such an
approach is, as one of the novel's early readers recognized, both
honest and enlightening:

It is admirable portraiture, realistic in the best sense of the word. It
must touch the consciousness of a great many people, and . . . it will teach
the much needed lesson that money cannot do everything.[50]

Though, to some extent, *The Rise of Silas Lapham* looks back to the
tradition of didactic and romantic literature, in many ways it
represents reform and innovation. Adapting the interests and techniques of European Realism to the native American material which
Howells grew to believe was the only material for the novelists of his
country, it is an excellent example of the move towards a new kind of
writing in the United States. Despite the fact that Howells was
regarded by later and more revolutionary Realists as outmoded,
tame, and prudish, it is undeniable that without his lead the
development of Realist American fiction would have been far less
rapid and self-confident.

NOTES

1. *The Letters of Henry James*, ed. Percy Lubbock, Scribner's, New York, 1920
   i. 73–4.
2. Unpublished letter to Howells, 22 July 1879. Quoted in Olov W. Fryckstedt, *In
   Quest of America: a study of Howells' early development as a novelist*, Harvard U.P.,
   Mass., 1958, p. 208.
3. *Criticism and Fiction and other essays*, ed. Clara and Randolf Kirk, New York U.P.,
   New York, 1959, p. 14.

4. ibid., p. 43.
5. ibid., p. 43.
6. ibid., p. 49.
7. From review of James's *Hawthorne*, *Atlantic Monthly*, xlv (Feb., 1880). In Edwin H. Cady, W. D. *Howells as Critic*, Routledge, London, 1973, p. 53.
8. *Criticism and Fiction*, p. 14.
9. From 'The Editor's Study', *Harper's Monthly*, Sep., 1889. In Cady, p. 158.
10. *Criticism and Fiction*, p. 15.
11. ibid., p. 86.
12. ibid., p. 38.
13. ibid., p. 18.
14. ibid., p. 155.
15. From review of Björnson's *Arne, The Happy Boy*, and *The Fisher Maiden*, *Atlantic Monthly*, xxv (April, 1870). In *Criticism and Fiction*, pp. 109, 106.
16. From 'Henry James, Jr.', *Century Magazine*, November, 1882. In Cady, p. 68.
17. *Life in Letters of William Dean Howells*, ed. Mildred Howells, Doubleday, Garden City, New York, 1928, i. 361.
18. *Criticism and Fiction*, p. 15.
19. *Life in Letters*, i. 281.
20. From 'Henry James, Jr.', Cady, p. 70.
21. *Criticism and Fiction*, p. 39.
22. From review of Turgenev's *Liza*, *Atlantic Monthly*, xxxi (Feb., 1873). In *Criticism and Fiction*, p. 111.
23. Review of Aldrich's *Prudence Palfrey*, *Atlantic Monthly*, xxxiv (Aug., 1874), p. 229.
24. Cady, p. 70.
25. *The Rise of Silas Lapham*, Signet, New York, 1963, p. 104. All subsequent page references will be to this edition.
26. *Criticism and Fiction*, p. 51.
27. ibid., p. 48.
28. G. Lukács, *Studies in European Realism*, Merlin Press, London, 1972, p. 56.
29. ibid., p. 6.
30. *Life in Letters*, i. 366.
31. *Atlantic Monthly*, xxiii (Feb., 1869), p. 260. Quoted in Fryckstedt, p. 230.
32. From review of Galdós's *Doña Perfecta*, *Harper's Bazaar*, 2 November, 1895. In *Criticism and Fiction*, p. 136.
33. *Criticism and Fiction*, p. 16.
34. From introduction to Verga's *The House by the Medlar-Tree*, transl. Mary A. Craig (1890). In *Criticism and Fiction*, p. 120.
35. *Life in Letters*, i. 410.
36. Preface to *The Altar of the Dead, The Art of the Novel*, Scribner's, New York, 1963, p. 251.
37. From review of Valdés's *Marta y Maria*, *Harper's Monthly*, Apr., 1886. In *Criticism and Fiction*, p. 126.
38. *Criticism and Fiction*, p. 74.
39. ibid., p. 15.
40. From 'The Philosophy of Tolstoy', *The Library of the World's Best Literature*, ed. Peale and Hill (1897). In *Criticism and Fiction*, p. 172.
41. *Criticism and Fiction*, p. 48.
42. *My Literary Passions*, Harper and Bros., New York, 1895, p. 185.
43. *Heroines of Fiction*, Harper and Bros., New York, 1901, ii. 77.
44. *My Literary Passions*, p. 194.
45. Reported by John Durand to Howells, 10 April 1888. Quoted in Edwin H. Cady, *The Road to Realism*, Syracuse U.P., Syracuse, 1956, p. 240. My translation.

46. *Criticism and Fiction*, p. 16.
47. ibid., p. 16.
48. ibid., p. 16.
49. A more extended discussion of the relationship between the two novels—which also argues that Howells's work is more fundamentally 'romantic' than Balzac's, despite his criticism and avoidance of the French writer's exaggerations and simplifications —is to be found in Elaine R. Hedges, '*César Birotteau* and *The Rise of Silas Lapham*: a study in parallels', *Nineteenth Century Fiction*, xvii (Sep., 1962), pp. 163–74.
50. *Life in Letters*, i. 373.

8

B. Pérez Galdós:
Fortunata and Jacinta (1886–7)

J. J. MACKLIN

BY THE time Galdós came to write *Fortunata and Jacinta*,[1] which appeared in four parts between January 1886 and June 1887, his position as the leading novelist in Spain was already well established. During the 1880s he began publishing his novels of contemporary life, initiated in 1881 by the appearance of *La desheredada*, which marked a shift away from the ideologically-conceived novels of the previous decade, typified by *Doña Perfecta* (1876), *Gloria* (1876–7) and *La familia de León Roch* (1878). This new period in Galdós's career is commonly referred to as the 'Naturalist phase' and the novels of the 1880s are characterized by an increased interest in the more sordid and unattractive aspects of reality and in the influence of heredity and environment on human personality. But Galdós, as we shall see, is a very different kind of Naturalist from Zola not least because he sees the relationship between man and environment as one of reciprocal influence in which individual personality develops dynamically through struggle and challenge, and circumstances, in turn, are changed by individuals. Moreover, by the time *Fortunata and Jacinta* was being written the Russian novel was beginning to make an impact in Spain, coinciding with a rejection of a determinist viewpoint in favour of an increased awareness of man's spiritual and psychological complexity. What makes the novels of contemporary society a new departure for Galdós, however, are changes in technique. First and foremost, he abandons imaginary provincial settings for the real world of Madrid. His novels portray a broad spectrum of society which is seen, not simply in terms of polarities, but as a fluid and complex whole. The polarities do not completely disappear of course (*Fortunata and Jacinta* is based on the polarity suggested in the title) but they are tempered by being submerged in the greater whole. The tone he adopts is no longer that of the polemicist but rather that of a detached, bemused, and frequently ironic observer. The movement away from partisanship and didacticism is reflected in a decrease in dramatic conflict, to the extent that conflicts are as much within characters as between them. Moreover, Galdós is concerned to show that a character cannot exist in isolation, and by exploring a large web of relationships, both private and public, he reveals a whole world to the reader.

Galdós developed no systematic theory of the novel but his broad position outlined in his scattered critical writings identifies him unmistakably with Realism.[2] In his 'Observaciones sobre la novela contemporánea en España' (1870) he states his belief that the modern novel should be a novel of characters and of manners based on direct observation, and should be faithful to the reality it describes. It should find its raw material in contemporary society, especially among the middle-classes whose problems, activities, and aspirations epitomize the character of that society. In 'La sociedad presente como materia novelable', delivered as a lecture to the Real Academia Española in 1897, Galdós reiterates his belief in the need for observation of society but dwells at length on the changes that have taken place in that society in the latter part of the nineteenth century. In Galdós's view, the monolithic class structure is breaking down and is being replaced by one amorphous middle class. The novelist, therefore, should abandon portraying generic types in favour of fully delineated individuals. In fact, Galdós's practice in *Fortunata and Jacinta* shows the limitations of such a view. Fortunata herself, with no loss of individuality, conforms to the Realist concept of the type as embodying an emergent social force at a given moment in history.[3] By stressing individual experience, however, Galdós identifies himself with a view of Realism that will deal with a multifarious, diverse, and complex reality. At one level, Realism concentrates upon the everyday experience of the real, tracing out meticulously the small and seemingly trivial events that make up the texture of ordinary people's lives. It will record details of the social contacts and physical surroundings of individuals. At another level, it will recognize that any one conception of reality is, by its very nature, limited and will strive, therefore, to present a pluralistic view of the world. It is precisely Galdós's awareness of the relativity and complexity of reality that makes him adopt a mixed approach to narrative presentation.

Realism made a relatively late appearance in Spain and explanations for this are most commonly sought in the economic and political backwardness of the country itself. The fundamental traditionalism of Spanish society and its inherent resistance to new ideas produced a reaction to Realism akin to that provoked by Romanticism earlier in the century. This resistance, and the opposition to it, forms part of the 'two Spains' conflict between reactionaries and liberals which Galdós's early didactic novels reflect. Progressives as well as traditionalists produced biased and partisan novels, so that whereas the first important Realist novels were produced in the 1850s, in Spain they do not appear until the 1880s and are strongly influenced by the theories of Naturalism. The influx of these theories and other new ideas from abroad was favoured by the more liberal climate in Spain in the years following the 1868 Revolution.

There was, moreover, another factor in Spain which contributed to the growth of Realism: the literary movement known as *costumbrismo*. Largely an attempt to conserve in literature traditional and picturesque customs of Spanish life in a period of rapid change, *costumbrismo* provided a precedent, in its portrayal of the way of life of ordinary people, for a literature based on direct observation of everyday reality. However, the approach of the *costumbristas*, which was to praise and idealize the Spanish way of life, was basically conservative and uncritical in its approach to social reality. Moreover, *costumbrismo* differs from Realism in that it was concerned with idealized typical characters rather than with individuals who are memorable in themselves and capable of character development. In an important sense, then, the origins of the true Realist novel lie in a reaction to *costumbrismo* as much as in following any precedent that it offered. The critical strain in Realism applies certainly to social questions but also more widely to any idealized pictures of man. Realism has as its most fruitful theme the shattering of illusions, the rejection of romantic views of life. One of the most interesting features of *Fortunata and Jacinta* is the way in which the complacent, almost bland, vision of society put forward in Part I is gradually eroded until it has disintegrated completely by the time the novel ends.

Fortunata and Jacinta is generally acknowledged as Galdós's masterpiece and as the outstanding novel of Realism in Spain. Galdós's method is to follow individual lives within a realistically described social environment, in order to provide the reader with an insight into what are predominantly social values. Underlying the social aspects are broader philosophical themes, particularly with regard to the conflict between Nature and society, and the dynamic and assimilative workings of personality. One of the chapter titles of the novel is 'Spiritual naturalism' and this may well sum up the scope and intention of Galdosian Realism. Spiritual naturalism, broadly speaking a marriage between Hegelian optimism and Darwinian evolutionary theory, attempted to provide an alternative to the more grimly pessimistic form of determinism in which the individual is dominated by the species. This alternative 'naturalism' conceived of the individual as the leader of the species, and evolution as a process of self-realization through competition and co-operation. The individual, instead of being dragged down by circumstances, makes a slow and steady advance and helps the species to evolve. The emphasis is less on man's past than on his future. Thus, though the themes of *Fortunata and Jacinta*—adultery, sterility, madness, impotence, prostitution—are markedly Realist, the novel presents neither a sordid nor a completely depressing picture of man. In the light of contemporary circumstances there are reasons why this should be the case. Although the progressive-traditionalist debate was acrimonious, there was a latent desire for reconciliation which found its best expression in Krausism, a philosophy aimed at harmonizing the demands of religion and reason which influenced Spanish literature at least until the end of the nineteenth-century. On the political front, the Restoration represented an attempt to ward off revolution by reconciling the different forces in society, and such an attempt readily found favour in a population weary of commotion and civil strife.[4] It is easy to see, therefore, why Galdós should have been interested in ways whereby conflict and struggle could be seen as potentially creative. However, his attitude to 'Spiritual naturalism' is ambivalent and his double-edged vision of the implications of such an outlook underlies the balance of qualified optimism and tragic awareness in the novel.

Fortunata and Jacinta is a love story and a study of class distinctions. Though it begins as the chronicle of two upper middle-class families, the Santa Cruz and the Arnáiz, united by the marriage of their children, Juanito and Jacinta, the novel broadens out to become a complicated love triangle transcending the bounds of class to bring in the proletariat in the person of Fortunata, Juanito's mistress, and the petty bourgeoisie in the person of her husband, Maxi Rubín. The working out of these relationships produces an exploration of class conflict together with a powerful novel of personality in which individual impulse and aspiration collide with social convention and restraints. Galdós deals with the problem in moral, psychological, and philosophical terms in which social and natural laws are found to be in conflict. This conflict is expressed, above all, in the rivalry between Fortunata and Jacinta for the love of Juanito Santa Cruz.

The narrator of *Fortunata and Jacinta* acts as the reader's guide into the world of the novel. Of course, the 'I' of the novel is not to be equated with Galdós himself but exists almost as another character through whose eyes events are seen but who does not intervene in the action. In this sense, Galdós can be said to have created an autonomous fictional world. But more importantly, the use of a personal narrator increases the illusion of the real in the work. The narrator remains as an observer though not from without for he is part of the society he describes. He is well acquainted with Madrid, whose streets and buildings are described with faithful accuracy and although the exact nature of his relationship with the other characters is not made known he is clearly on close terms with them. Jacinta, for example, is recorded as having confided her feelings to him (e.g. p. 608). His omniscience on these matters, therefore, is partly justified. As the novel progresses authorial intrusions become less frequent. Although the narrator delves into minds and reveals motives, he rarely passes moral judgement. The exception here is when he is dealing with Juanito Santa Cruz. A frequent technique in the early part of the novel is to give a character as the source for a particular piece of information, as in the very first sentence of the novel. In this way the author is at pains to limit his omniscience and often admits to lapses of memory: 'I do not know if it was into Novar's class or Uribe the metaphysics lecturer's' (p. 31), 'The exact date has escaped me' (p. 34), and so on. This parade of non-omniscience reinforces the authenticity of what is being recounted. It also establishes the genial, almost casual, tone of the novel which increases our sense of familiarity with what is going on. Ultimately, though, the reader is deceived, for this non-omniscience in matters of inconsequential detail gives way to complete omniscience later. He can tell us of Barbarita's inner anxieties (p. 35), or state quite categorically, 'To be quite truthful, it must be said that Santa Cruz did love his wife' (p. 175).

What we find in *Fortunata and Jacinta* is variety in narrative presentation through the use of multiple points of view ranging from the almost complete identification between narrator and character to the documentary approach of the social historian presenting a wide panorama of Madrid life. This latter approach is that adopted in Part I, in which Juanito Santa Cruz predominates, and its effect is to keep the reader detached from this world which is presented extensively rather than intensively. However, we experience reality in varying degrees of depth so that out of this broader spectrum certain characters and situations are given more relief. The viewpoint changes from social to individual. In Part I of the novel there are numerous background characters, who are largely seen from the outside through the narrator's comments. One way in which Galdós does individualize even minor characters is through speech. As S. Gilman has observed,[5] there is an abundance of oral situations in *Fortunata and Jacinta*. We see people at home, in Church, in shops, in cafés, and the language used is social. Guillermina is clear and comes straight to the point; the cleric, Nicolás Rubín, uses a pompous, sermon-like style; doña Lupe changes her style of speech when she is talking to her social superior Guillermina; Estupiñá is consistent in the way he talks throughout the novel. Galdós reproduces child-language: in Pituso and the street-urchins of the lower classes, but also the words of the doting Feijóo and the exchanges of Juanito and Jacinta on their honeymoon. Language, too, is used to undermine a character's pretensions: the speech of José Izquierdo does not match his lofty ambitions.

If minor characters are seen largely from the outside, in the cases of the major characters Galdós's mode of characterization is more varied as can be seen from his very different approaches to Juanito and Maxi, for example. One aspect of characterization relevant to point of view is the manner in which events are seen through the eyes of the characters themselves. Thus when Fortunata and Jacinta are at the bedside of the dying Mauricia la dura, although the narrator is describing the scene, the words he uses are those of Fortunata. Jacinta, for example, is termed the 'saintly lovely' (p. 753). This adoption of limited omniscience makes the narrator less obtrusive by giving precedence to the consciousness of the character. The same process can be seen in the description of Fortunata's death where, as S. Bacarisse has observed, Galdós does not inform us of what is going on but rather presents 'a picture which would be seemingly available to *our* senses as we read, just as reality was available (or failed to be available) to Fortunata.'[6] But while the narrator

makes his own presence less obtrusive by giving precedence to
the consciousness of the character at the same time, however, by
giving the flow of impressions of a character he is going beyond the
limits of what he could reasonably, objectively know. Yet if he were
to limit himself to a strictly outside view, he would fail to render
adequately the 'feel' of experience which is by its very nature subjective. These contradictions are a problem for the Realist and what
Galdós does is to use language in such a way as to avoid the conceptual precision of which it is capable so that the reader becomes
less aware of his role as author. By using what Bacarisse calls 'the
language of perception', he strives to achieve that 'apparently
impersonal illusion of reality' which Jenkins sees as the aim of
Realist fiction.

There is a further problem here for the Realist in that writing a
novel imposes a need to order and arrange material in a way that
could legitimately be said to falsify it. Here again, Galdós's partial
abandonment of the illusion that the story is unfolding itself before
the reader's eyes enables him to acknowledge that selection and
ordering are inevitable. At the end of Chapter II of the First Part he
mentions Jacinta's marriage, then adds: 'At this point, I must cut
this particular thread, and go on to relate certain things that should
come before Jacinta's marriage' (p. 72). He goes on to tell us about
Plácido Estupiñá, as he had promised earlier (p. 60). Such remarks
make the reader accept quite naturally that a story is being recon-
structed from a much greater mass of information than he is being
given in the novel. But he implicitly accepts the existence of that
information.

Neither the display of non-omniscience nor the admission that
material is being patterned for the purposes of narration solve by
themselves the problem of making the fictional world appear as a
plausible model of the real world, but by inviting the reader to participate in the illusion that these are real people, Galdós encourages
him to accept that the laws and circumstances operating in the
fictional world are the same as those in the real world. Thus by
putting the characters on the same footing as the narrator, he confers
on them something of the status of real people. The narrator got to
know Baldomero and Barbarita in 1870 and they are still alive when
the novel is being written. He examined a portrait of Juanito's
grandfather at their home. Unsophisticated devices such as this
engender in the reader a sense of familiarity with these people and

for those who know the *Novelas contemporáneas* as a whole this familiarity is increased by the use of recurring characters. José Ido del Sagrario, for example, would be familiar to anyone who had read *Tormento* (1884). The moneylender Torquemada, not much more than an associate of doña Lupe in this novel, will appear in a series of later novels. The sepulchral figure of Villaamil, the out-of-work government official who makes a brief appearance in *Fortunata and Jacinta* seeking a recommendation for a job, becomes the main character in *Miau* (1888).

Jenkins, in his chapter, observes how the reader of a novel accepts the illusion of reality being offered to him because of a 'tacit assumption that a human life is most truthfully presented in terms of the individual's milieu, of the particularity of social situation and historical circumstance' (p. 5). *Fortunata and Jacinta* is firmly set in the period 1868 to 1876 though most of the action occurs between 1873 and 1876. Galdós takes great care to record dates precisely. The novel opens with the student riots on the night of 10 April 1865 but goes back even further than this to 1796 when the Santa Cruz business was established. This tracing of events back to their origins is important for it implies a belief in causality, a conception of the present growing out of the past. What is involved here is a whole vision of human social evolution, its victories and its casualties. Thus the long introduction adumbrates an important theme of the novel, progress, for which Baldomero is the first spokesman:

Nature cures itself; you just have to leave it alone. The powers of regeneration do it all, helped by the air. Man is educated only by virtue of absorbing influences that determine consciousness in his mind, and this is aided by social environment. Don Baldomero did not put it like this, but his vague ideas on the subject were condensed into a fashionable and very useful phrase: 'the world goes on' [p. 60].

Precise dating, like the marriage of Barbarita and Baldomero in May 1835, the birth of Juanito in September 1845 and his marriage to Jacinta in May 1871, adds authenticity to the chronicle of family life. Galdós goes far beyond this, however, by relating individual lives very closely to historical occurrences, a technique used first of all with the characters Estupiñá and Isabel Cordero.

Estupiñá was born on 19 July 1803, the same day as the *costumbrista* writer Ramón de Mesonero Romanos, to whose *Panorama matritense* (1835) and *Escenas matritenses* (1836–42) Galdós was indebted for much of his material on the commerce of Madrid in the early part of the nineteenth century. This character has an important structural role in the novel: it is his illness which brings Juanito to the Cava de San Miguel where he first encounters Fortunata and at the end of the novel it is he who brings Fortunata's baby to Jacinta. His first important function, however, is to outline the recent history of Spain for 'His boast was that he had seen all Spanish history in this century' (p. 74). Isabel Cordero de Arnáiz, Jacinta's mother, coincides in her confinements with important dates in the reign of her namesake Isabel II: ' "My first son", she used to say, "was born when the Carlist troops came right up to the walls of Madrid. My Jacinta was born when the queen married, or within a few days. My Isabelita came into the world on the very day that priest Merino stabbed Her Majesty" ' (pp. 67–8). Isabel herself died on the same day as the leading opponent of the Bourbons, Juan Prim, was assassinated, 30 December 1870, just as Juanito's and Jacinta's engagement was being arranged. This establishes a parallel between the turbulent political life of Spain and the unstable and unsettled marriage of Juanito Santa Cruz. Whereas Spanish history is simply revealed through the characters of Estupiñá and Isabel Cordero, in the case of Juanito it is used as a means of characterization. Public and private mirror and comment on each other. The parallel is also reflected in the structure of the novel. Juanito's oscillations between mistress and wife are an image of Spain's swing from order to revolution, from anarchy to peace.[7]

From the outset, Juanito is presented as fickle and capricious, seen in his neglect of his studies, then his fresh dedication to them, followed by his subsequent abandonment of them (pp. 32–3). The narrator does not directly criticize Juanito at first and may even appear to find praiseworthy his preference for practical rather than theoretical knowledge: 'To live is to have close relationships with life, to enjoy and suffer, to desire, hate and love. Reading is artificial life lent to the reader, profit gained, by means of a cerebral function, from the ideas and feelings of other people' (p. 36). But already the author's irony, the chief instrument by which he imparts his judgements to the reader, is at work. The banality and superficiality of Juanito's philosophy is made apparent in the example he uses to illustrate it: eating a chop.

Juanito is the most predictable of the four main characters. The son of a rich and established bourgois household, he is the new aristocrat, the idle *señorito* with time on his hands to enjoy himself and seduce the women of the *pueblo*. The suggestion that this new class—the *nobleza del dinero*—forms a new dynasty is contained in Juanito's nickname, the *Delfín* (dauphin) and the use of quasi-regal numerals to distinguish between father and grandfather, Baldomero I and Baldomero II. In fact, the father takes great pleasure in comparing his own youth, full of hard work and subject to strict moral codes, with that of his son, free from work and moral restraint. Juanito embodies the values and attitudes of a whole class, the hero of Restoration society: 'He was a good-looking boy, master of the art of pleasing people and dressing well, the only son of rich parents. He was intelligent, educated, capable of an attractive conversational phrase, quick in response, sharp and witty in his opinions. In short, he was a boy whom society could well label brilliant' (p. 36). But there is an ironic contrast between all the promise that surrounds Juanito at the beginning of the novel and the insignificance that enshrouds him at the end.

The first significant historical reference, the abdication of Amadeo in February 1873, occurs at the end of Chapter 7. The event is discussed in the Santa Cruz house, but Jacinta is more concerned about her husband's behaviour. The political theme and the theme of fidelity are thereby linked, and just as Juanito was seen to have changed his political stance many times, the narrator now comments on the same fickleness in his marriage: 'At the root of human nature, just as on the surface of social life, there lies a succession of fashions, periods when one just has to change one's tastes. Juan had periodic and almost predictable spells when he loathed all his escapades, and then his gorgeous, loving wife bewitched him as if she were someone else's wife. Thus the familiar and well-known is transformed into something new' (p. 174). The actual political happenings of 1873 are not recounted in the novel and the public–private parallel does not reappear until the last chapter of Part I. Villalonga reports to Juanito, who is in bed with a cold, on the coup of General Pavía who turned the deputies out of the Chamber on 3 January 1874. The report of the incidents in the Chamber is mixed with news that Fortunata has returned to Madrid. Spain's political instability and Juanito's marital instability are linked as Spain begins a year of chaos and Juanito sets off to find his mistress.

The next significant historical event is to be found in Part III in the ironically entitled chapters 'The Revolution suppressed' and

'The victorious Restoration'. The public event is the restoration of the Bourbon monarchy in the person of the young Alfonso XII. As with the case of Amadeo's abdication, the family discussions on the implications of this turn of events are of less importance to Jacinta than her anxieties about Juanito. What Baldomero has to say about Spain's 'alternate or intermittent fevers of revolution and peace' (p. 610) is reflected in the behaviour of his son: 'Ever since the last days of 1874 the Delfín had entered that calm period that invariably followed his debaucheries. In fact, it was not virtue, but being weary of sin; the feeling was not one of pure, normal order, but rather a loathing of revolution' (p. 613). In the character of Juanito Santa Cruz Galdós reveals the nature and role of a whole class, a class which had, in essence, come to dominate society itself.[8]

The parallel drawn between Juanito Santa Cruz and Spanish public life is an obvious one, as is the basic political pattern of the novel. The Santa Cruz and Arnáiz families are conservative; Fortunata and her friends from the lower classes are associated with the republican cause. The opposition between Fortunata's fecundity and Jacinta's sterility reinforces this pattern, and while we are increasingly made aware as Part I progresses of Jacinta's longing for children as a feature of her rivalry with Fortunata, that rivalry is predominantly one based on class. Jacinta is very much a product of the middle-class and a large amount of space is devoted to describing her family background and the values it embraces. In contrast, Fortunata appears spontaneously in the novel: she has no background, is an orphan and in all probability is illegitimate.

The upper-middle-class world of the Arnáiz and Santa Cruz families is portrayed from within for the narrator seems to be at home in it. Villalonga, for example, is called his friend. He appears to share many of the values and assumptions of this class and arguably his criticism of Juanito can be seen as a condemnation of the way in which certain middle-class ideals, such as thrift, honesty, hard work, belief in progress, have been corrupted. This is a society which regards Fortunata, who aspires to enter it, as an outsider, despite the narrator's views on the intermingling of classes in Spain:

It is strange to see how our age, so unfortunate in some of its other ideas, presents us with a happy fusion of all classes, or rather the concord and reconciliation of them all . . . Unobtrusively, with the help of bureaucracy, poverty and the academic education all Spaniards receive, all classes have been intermingling, and their members have mixed with each other, weaving a thick net which anchors and solidifies the mass of the population. Birth means nothing among us, and whatever may be said about what is written on parchment is just chatter. The only differences are the basic ones, those arising from good or bad education, from being stupid or wise, from differences of the mind, eternal as the attributes of that same mind. The other positive determination of class, money, is founded on economic principles as immutable as physical laws, and to try to alter this is the same as setting out to drink the ocean dry [pp. 136–37].

This is, of course, simply an acknowledgement of the fact that money is the most important determinant of class and that the absence of an aristocratic background is no obstacle to social advancement. It is a promulgation of the ethic of the self-made man, the commercial bourgeois. The distinction between those who have and those who have not is still the same and the middle-class house described in Chapter 6 (pp. 142–3) is a world away from Fortunata's aunt's egg and poultry store (pp. 85–6). The author uses the street names of Madrid as a clear indication of class: the fact that Fortunata lives in the Cava de San Miguel leaves us in no doubt as to what class she belongs. At several points in the novel there are generalizations on the role of the common people, the *pueblo*, in society voiced by different characters. Villalonga says, 'The people are like a quarry. From them come great ideas and great beauty. Then comes intelligence, art; the workman's hand draws out the block of stone, works it' (p. 306) and here he is echoing Juanito's words. Juanito himself later exhibits this sentimental middle-class attitude to the people: 'The people ... the basis of humanity, the fundamental material, because when civilization allows itself to lose its finer feelings, its supreme philosophies, then it has to turn to the stone-quarry of the people' (p. 546). Guillermina voices a similar view: 'You have all the brutal passions of the common people, like rough hewn rock'. The narrator is quick to concur: 'in our society, the people preserve all the basic feelings in their coarse, rich abundance, just as a quarry contains marble, the material for the moulding of form. The people have the great truths of the world en masse, and civilization turns to the people as it wastes itself on trifles, for it lives on the common people' (pp. 796–7). The image of the quarry is significant in that it suggests a pattern of exploitation with the bourgeoisie at the receiving end. The *pueblo* represents vitality and primitiveness, the very qualities which first attract Juanito to

Fortunata. The giving of Fortunata's son to Jacinta will symbolize
the fecundation of the bourgeoisie by the *pueblo*. Without this, the
Santa Cruz family would have no heir. The middle classes, for their
part, see the *pueblo*—in the person of Fortunata—as something to be
shaped according to their designs. Juanito wants to make her his
mistress; Maxi wants to make her honourable; Guillermina wants to
reform her in a religious sense; Nicolás sees her as a challenge to his
priestly powers; doña Lupe wants to make her respectable. Fortunata's triumph in the novel is that she breaks out of this passive
role others have created for her. Her success, however, is only a qualified one and it is achieved through the assimilation, albeit not in the
way her middle-class educators intended, of the values with which
she is in conflict.

Galdós wastes no opportunity to describe as many facets as
possible of the rich world of Restoration Madrid, a world in which
the gap between appearance and reality offers a fertile theme for the
Realist writer to exploit. Chapter I of Part III takes us into the world
of Madrid café life, inhabited by the administrative petty bourgeoisie
and reveals the hypocrisy that governs Spanish political life of the
time. Principles have been sacrificed for expediency as loyalties are
switched in return for the security of political office:

there was friendship between the Carlist and the Republican, the hard-
headed progressive and the implacable moderate ... A tacit collusion
exists (and not so well hidden that it may not soon be found when a
politician is lightly scratched) by which the change of power is established ... Political morality is a cloak with so many patches on it that
nobody knows which is the original material [p. 580].

Or as Feijóo more bluntly states: 'it's all a farce and the only thing
that matters is knowing who to crawl to and who to avoid' (p. 580).
The best illustration of this attitude is Juan Pablo Rubín who has
been in almost every political camp at one time or another and
ends up with the governorship of a province. In like fashion, his
brother, Nicolás, ends up a canon. Galdós tries to portray completely the reality of Spain in the 1870s: the lottery, life in a convent,
charities, money-lending, life in a factory. But these are not simply
reproduced for contradictions and incongruities are made apparent.
For example, Guillermina's efforts for charity, her construction
of a home for orphans, are partly financed from the proceeds of
slum-letting.

It is in the sphere of finance and commerce that *Fortunata and Jacinta* is particularly rich in information. Galdós omits no significant detail about the development of business life, especially as this affects the textile trade: the tariff reforms of 1849 and the importation of foreign materials; the rise of England as a trading nation; Catalan 'dumping'; the lobby for protectionism; the use of banknotes; the effects of foreign investment; the development of the railway system. Smaller changes are noted as well: the first matches; the introduction of gas-lighting; changes in fashion. Recording changes in style of dress helps reveal the particularity of a historical period, and additionally reinforces the underlying theme of evolution and progress. In *Fortunata and Jacinta* it also acts as a barometer of the fortunes of commerce and underlines the more dominant and increasingly self-conscious role of the bourgeoisie, who more and more are detaching themselves from the working class. This is seen first in the abandonment of the Manila shawl and then of all bright colours which become the exclusive property of the *pueblo*. The bourgeoisie now favour the more sombre tones of French fashion, and this is an illustration of the narrator's point about the real vitality of society residing in the common people.

The wealth of detail which Galdós provides adds to the density of the world he is creating. The essentials of human life—clothes, food, and houses—are minutely depicted. Physical surroundings and personal relationships are the contexts of character; a character will be more or less real to the extent to which he is integrated into the greater whole. Galdós traces a complex web of relationships across Madrid and likens it to 'a vast, labyrinthine tree, which is more like a creeper, and whose roots cross, rise, fall and are lost in the hollows of the densest foliage. . . . The most assured mind is not capable of following the labyrinthine intricacy of the offshoots of this colossal tree of Madrid families. The threads cross, are lost and reappear when least expected. After a thousand turns above and as many below, they are joined, separate and from their conjunction or division come new intertwinings or tangled skeins' (pp. 137 and 141). Individual lives and social trends are seen together. Galdós adds name upon name to his list of people. Some remain only as names; others have minor roles in the novel; some have major roles. In this way foreground and background are made to coalesce and out of this very varied and complex whole, whose ramifications are only sensed, a few characters emerge. It is the creation of a convincing social dimension which in the first place gives the novel its authenticity, while the manner in which character is rooted in social circumstances is a powerful feature of its Realism. As J. P. Stern observes, 'in a novel like *Fortunata and Jacinta*, the chosen form puts the social milieu on the plane of the main action and not merely behind it'.⁹

Galdós's treatment of social reality goes beyond a surface reproduction, however, for he probes the values which underlie the superficial appearances, and it is clear that much of middle-class morality is little more than a façade. It amounts to a concern for respectability, and here we begin to see that the narrator's 'happy fusion of all classes' represents an idealized vision of contemporary society. Juanito protests that he suffers pangs of conscience for having abandoned Fortunata and when he goes to seek her out he protests that he is really trying to save her from a life of depravity. When she marries Maxi Rubín he is pleased for this helps her keep up appearances, seem respectable. By a further twist, it is his preoccupation with respectability which is the final excuse for breaking off with her. In all cases the same principle is perverted to achieve the desired end. The reality is that he seeks her out driven by passion and he abandons her out of boredom. Juanito is the only character who is directly criticized by the narrator because his morality is unashamedly cynical and self-interested, but there are other characters whose moral stances are conditioned by their class and circumstances. Guillermina Pacheco is consistently referred to throughout the novel as 'the saint' but Galdós suggests in all kinds of ways that her religion is conventionally middle class with an emphasis on externals. Just as she sees no conflict between her faith and her activities as a slum landlady, she has no scruples about making some profit out of the money deal for the false Pituso. The convent of Las Micaelas for fallen women is the natural product of her religious views and in the case of its two most important inmates the treatment it provides proves to be ineffective. It is the very rigidity of Guillermina's views, both religious and social, that make her incapable of giving to Fortunata the support she needs. Her exhortation to self-sacrifice is totally inadequate to the reality of Fortunata's situation. Galdós's attitude to this character, however, is ambiguous for he sees much that is good in her and, as L. V. Braun has shown, she is based on a character whom Galdós knew, admired, and wrote about elsewhere.¹⁰ In the novel, he endows Guillermina with enthusiasm, joyfulness, good humour, and tolerance. After Fortunata's death she says: 'we shouldn't laugh at anything, and everything that happens, just because it does happen merits a certain respect' (p. 1058).

Materialism is seen to permeate all levels of middle-class life. In the scene where Estupiñá and Barbarita are in church, money and religion are again linked: the words of the prayers are interspersed with details of the latest food prices in the market (pp. 152–3). Isabel Cordero's efforts to marry off her daughters are likened to a trader hawking his wares. The narrator refers to the 'case of samples', to the need for the vendor to 'promote the merchandise' (p. 71). The very sale of the false Pituso illustrates the way people can be considered almost as objects.

Materialism can devalue and dehumanize individuals. But the ground between condemnation and sympathy is a very shifting one and Galdós's irony is gentle.[11] If commercialism can debase human beings, it also generates commendable energy and resourcefulness, as Isabel Cordero's efforts to save the family business testify. At the other end of the social scale a character like José Izquierdo, uncle of Fortunata, is portrayed as the working-class agitator, full of bombast but basically ineffectual. Guillermina puts his romantic illusions about his own past into perspective as she mercilessly cuts him down to size (p. 251). Yet Izquierdo provokes sympathy, for, in the midst of all the political expediency and compromise of the times, his out-pourings represent the bewilderment of many ordinary adherents to the republican cause sold out by their affluent and intellectual leaders and neglected by the State.

One way in which Galdós conveys a sense of reality in *Fortunata and Jacinta* is to multiply certain themes by working them out in a series of variations. The theme of romantic idealism which forms the basis of the treatment of Fortunata and Maxi is explored through other characters and situations. If José Izquierdo's idealism is political, Jacinta's manifests itself in her exaggerated desire for a child. Her barrenness is an important theme, of course, and it is made to contrast with the seemingly boundless fertility all around her: her mother bore seventeen children; her sister Candelaria, much less well-off than she, is fertile and this irony is magnified in the picture of the numerous children brought up in the slums. Galdós mildly ridicules her in the scene where she attempts to save the kittens drowning in the gutter: 'All the maternal ambition within her, all the tenderness that the emotions of the woman who longs to be a mother had been building up in her soul, became an active force to respond to the *miiii* from beneath the ground with a *miiii* that was just as anguished' (p. 148).

The interweaving of reality and illusion is seen in the honeymoon of Juanito and Jacinta. Planned as an idyllic journey around Spain, it comes to be dominated not by the two spouses but by Fortunata. The later honeymoon of Fortunata and Maxi is similarly dominated by Juanito. Fortunata's relationship with Juanito is gradually revealed as they travel through Spain, as Jacinta becomes more and more obsessed with knowing and owning her husband's past. The beginnings of her inner conflict are apparent here: pride that the other woman has been rejected, protest against the injustice of such a rejection. The moral superiority of Jacinta over Juanito is apparent: 'Jacinta could not think of the betrayal in any other way, although it represented the triumph of legitimate love over illicit love, of marriage over living together as lovers' (p. 131). The character's conflict is part of a wider conflict between nature and society, seen first in the rivalry between the two women and within each of them. 'Jacinta begins to see this while Juanito adheres to the false values of middle-class morality: 'My dearest love, you must be realistic. There are two worlds, the seen and the unseen. Society is not governed by pure ideals. . . . Differences of education and class always establish a great difference in the conduct of human relationships' (p. 132). In her own way, Jacinta collides with society. She fails to provide the Santa Cruz family with an heir and this, together with her obsession with her rival, leads her on a melodramatic quest for Juanito's son by Fortunata. The manner in which this episode is treated is in accord with a view of Realism as a rejection of romance. The whole affair is narrated amidst frequent references to romantic literature: 'Only in bad novels do unexpected babies appear' (p. 194), 'theatrical effect', 'dramatic interest', 'novelistic details' (p. 259), 'like something out of a novel' (p. 266), 'badly conceived plots . . . an inflated artistic inspiration' (p. 287). Moreover, Jacinta is introduced to the Pituso story by the romantic writer, whom Galdós had satirized in earlier novels, *El doctor Centeno* (1883) and *Tormento* (1884), José Ido del Sagrario. Another variation on the theme of romantic idealism, Ido sees his ugly wife as a great beauty who is unfaithful to him. He casts himself in the role of the wronged husband of Spanish Golden Age drama and wishes to avenge his honour with blood. The Pituso story does not conform to the literary model for it ends in a realistic way: the child is proved to be false and is put into Guillermina's orphanage. This pattern—reality making inroads into illusion—is the fundamental pattern of Realist fiction, and attempts to transform the banal tragedies of everyday life into something heroic come to nothing. The core of *Fortunata and Jacinta* deals with this clash between aspiration and reality as represented in the lives of Maxi Rubín and Fortunata. The struggle to attain an ideal, to fulfil an aspiration, and the way in which circumstances conspire to thwart it, give rise to a continual process of self-adjustment. Galdós's portrayal of this process whereby the individual collides with reality and evaluates the moral implications of that collision makes of *Fortunata and Jacinta* more than a novel of class conflict. It becomes a powerful novel of personality, and underlying it is a philosophical theme.

Maxi Rubín is beset with physical and social disadvantages from the start. In the first place, some doubt is cast upon his ancestry: the Rubíns may have had Jewish blood and therefore would have been out on the fringes of traditionalist Catholic society. Moreover, his own family background was an unstable one and such stability as is provided by his paternal aunt, doña Lupe, is offset by his excessive dependence on her. With these details Galdós begins his study of an abnormal personality overwhelmed by a sense of inferiority induced by a physical unattractiveness and constant ill-health. Maxi compensates for his inferiority by daydreaming, idealistically imagining his defects remedied and himself in situations where he displays courage and confidence. One of his most persistent dreams is to be loved by an honourable woman so that when he encounters Fortunata he sets himself the ideal of redeeming her. The process by which he breaks away from his aunt's protectiveness culminates in the destruction of his money-box, an apparently trivial event given extended treatment by Galdós. The episode is seen through the eyes of the character who visualizes the money-box as victim and himself as a murderer carrying out a crime and covering up the traces. As M. Nimetz observes,[12] the account reads like a sensational newspaper report on a murder. As well as conveying Maxi's immaturity and ridiculousness, Galdós underlines his sense of guilt and anxiety at breaking the bonds which unite him to his aunt. Most importantly, vivid rendering of this type constitutes a variation in narrative presentation: the scene is viewed not from the outside and recorded after the event but is actualized so that we experience it as immediate and real.

A great deal is revealed in this way about the inner workings of the mind of Maxi as Galdós, with much sensitivity, traces his attempts through illusions and subterfuges to keep a painful reality at bay: the attraction of philosophical thought; a religion of death and suicide as a liberation; the progress of logic. Maxi struggles desperately to preserve the balance of his mind, disrupted by his marriage to the unfaithful Fortunata. Progressively, his experience of reality is so fragmented that he can no longer perceive it correctly. His life becomes a series of alternations between lucidity and insanity. His first defence mechanism is to deny Fortunata's adultery. Then he experiences a terrible need for her to confess and confirm what he has suspected. The dualism of his conception of Fortunata suggested at an early stage, 'Two Fortunatas existed then: one, the Fortunata of flesh and blood; and the other whom Maximiliano bore imprinted on his mind' (p. 346), in which the mental representation is divorced from the reality is at the root of this oscillation between the two states. When Fortunata is pregnant he invents the illusion of her fecundation by Pure Thought, but readily admits in his more lucid moments that this was a necessary deception to keep him going. It is a more developed version of the defensive neurotic symptoms he used in adolescence. He can say to José Ido del Sagrario, whose delusions are analogous to his own, 'calm yourself and learn to look at life as it really is. It's stupid to believe that things are as we imagine them to be and not as they wish to be' (p. 994). He can even talk rationally to Fortunata and say that their marriage was doomed to failure from the start. Despite these moments of rationality and lucidity, Maxi's psyche is in a process of disintegration and the loss of Fortunata through death is the final blow which leads him into complete madness as he retreats voluntarily from the world into an asylum.

The character of Maxi Rubín shows a remarkable degree of understanding on the part of Galdós of the dynamics of mental health, and references to medicine and psychiatry are to be found in many of his works. Maxi himself has recently been studied as a case history, described as a 'borderline psychotic personality' who, after being for a time in 'an intermittent paranoid delusional state', moves on to 'overt schizophrenia'.[13] Interesting as this type of study is in itself it does not constitute literary criticism and from the point of view of Realism what is important about Maxi's, and the other characters', developing psychology is how Galdós sees it as a process of frictional contact between self and environment characterized by gradual change and imperceptible advances and regressions. There is a pattern of causality here, of course, but Galdós does not rely on a cause-and-effect relationship alone to create a convincing illusion of reality. He also has recourse to a series of analogies. Thus Fortunata's conflict between a desire for respectability and the force of her passion are paralleled in Mauricia la dura's craving for self-esteem and her reversion to instinct and near-savagery. These, like Juanito's oscillations between order and anarchy, Maxi's alternations of sanity and insanity, and other analogous patterns create multiple images of similar experiences. Minor characters, in addition to adding depth to the picture of a fully drawn society, echo the conflicts and problems of the protagonists. Ido del Sagrario's self-deception, Moreno-Isla's lonely isolation, José Izquierdo's acceptance of his vocation as artist's model and not as a public figure, all find their full expression in the figure of Maximiliano Rubín who is finally broken by the conflicting and irreconcilable demands of society, love, philosophy, idealism and reality. Through him we are made to realize and experience the stresses placed upon personality by its having to adjust to others and to circumstances. Thirty years later the same theme is given its most disturbing treatment in the novels of Miguel de Unamuno where these stresses are given a cosmic dimension. In the world of the Realist novel, these stresses are primarily conceived in social terms and in *Fortunata and Jacinta* it is Fortunata herself who is made to bear their full impact.

Fortunata comes into the novel only indirectly in Part I. What we know of her after her first appearance, when she is described simply as 'a pretty, tall young woman' (p. 86), we learn from Juanito Santa Cruz. However, she becomes the main interest of the novel from Part II onwards and much of what takes place is seen largely from her point of view. Abandoned by Juanito, she has led a life of near-prostitution with the misguided intention of thereby taking revenge on him but is now beginning a slow ascent from a trough of despondency. Despite her repugnance for Maxi, the prospect of respectability held out by his offer of marriage is enough to induce her to follow a course of regeneration in Las Micaelas. Just as her life of depravity had singularly little effect upon her in the long term, now the regime of the convent fails to stifle the strength of her passion for Juanito.

At the same time, it is part of a process whereby she assimilates, in a distorted form, bourgeois attitudes and aspirations which, though temporarily overthrown, re-emerge later. When she is abandoned by Juanito for a second time there is a perceptible shift in her aspirations as her feelings become directed towards Jacinta and away from Juanito. Her illusion is to be honourable like her rival, yet she is morally and socially inferior to her. Part III finds her in a state of moral confusion, stabilized for a time by the benevolent protection of don Evaristo Feijóo who encourages her to be practical, to 'accept the law of reality' (p. 655) and to keep up appearances.

Two important encounters with Jacinta in Part III help her define her situation more sharply. On their first encounter by Mauricia's death-bed, Fortunata reveals who she is, sure in the knowledge that Jacinta 'would be like me if she were in my place' (p. 754). Her outburst, a sign of her inferiority, is regretted almost immediately: she had demeaned herself in front of her rival. Fortunata is now more deeply torn between her natural impulse and her instinctive sense of what is hers, and a desire to be accepted into Jacinta's circle, not to be considered 'a worthless slut' (p. 755) and excluded.

The second important episode is her interview with Guillermina while Jacinta is listening hidden behind glass doors. Fortunata's rebelliousness contrasts with her earlier acceptance of Guillermina's advice, for she is gradually developing what will become known as her 'idea': she will use nature in the sense of being able to have a child by Juanito as a means of asserting her physical superiority over her rival (pp. 792–3). Galdós's insistence on Jacinta's sterility in the early stages of the narrative gives added force to this idea when it comes. The growth of the idea had been gradually traced through the stages of her competition with Jacinta. When she first saw her in Las Micaelas, Jacinta, like Guillermina, has become part of Fortunata's consciousness, as the narrator makes clear: 'She could feel her deep inside, as if she had swallowed her, as if she had taken her like the Host at Communion' (p. 782). It is this relationship of the self to others that interests Galdós much more than the workings of environmental or hereditary determinism. Indeed, for him, environment includes influences in the form of ideas and personal relationships. In a sense, Fortunata's struggle with passion and society is represented in Mauricia la dura and Guillermina Pacheco, but interestingly at several points in the novel (for example, pp. 772, 782–3, 794), the faces of the 'saint' and the 'devil' merge bringing the two forces into an incomprehensible relationship. As S. H. Eoff points out, Galdós is fond of portraying the paradoxical appearance of life:

defiance of moral rules is in reality an expression of the value attached to approval by others, which brings the ever-increasing need of a more respected moral status . . . Paradox . . . is fundamental to the novel's structure . . . The turning to Juanito is in reality a turning from Juanito to Jacinta; the attainment of superiority is the expression of inferiority; the desire to triumph over an enemy is a desire to win her respect and friendship; the ascendancy of natural forces is a concession to social forces.[14]

Fortunata transcends moral categories of good and bad as she uses nature to realize a social aspiration. Juanito's son will guarantee her—or her flesh and blood—acceptance into the Santa Cruz family. This conditions her developing relationship with Jacinta which is no longer based on rivalry and competition but on something akin to identity and co-operation. Thus when she attacks Aurora—Juanito's new mistress—she does so in the name of the Santa Cruz family and most especially of herself and Jacinta. More significantly, her earlier relish at the possibility that Jacinta might not be virtuous after all is converted into a need that she should be indeed saintly and that she should be like her. It is on this understanding, which Guillermina convincingly gives, that she hands over her child. Thus the pattern of relationships established at the beginning of the novel is re-arranged. *Fortunata and Jacinta* began as a bourgeois novel, seen from the standpoint of that class, with Juanito as its 'hero'. By the end, Juanito has all but disappeared. Fortunata, by her gesture, stakes her claim to the title of 'angel' and Jacinta, in her mind, grants her an equality with her:

she was amazed to feel in her heart sentiments that were rather more than pity for the luckless woman, for she nurtured something akin to companionship, a sisterly affection founded on common misfortunes . . . With death between them it could well be that the two women, one in the life that was visible, the other in the unseen life, were looking at each other across the void, intending and desiring to embrace each other [p. 1059].

The novel shows how individuals develop psychologically and morally through conflict. S. H. Eoff sees a wider symbolic meaning 'in the author's contraposition of nature and society as beneficially antithetical'. Fortunata and Jacinta, representing nature and society are mutually dependent:

Undoubtedly the author meant the two women, when symbolically viewed, to be mutually complementary in a moral sense; but the moral import can easily be extended to harmonise with a philosophical concept of universal law. From a comprehensive viewpoint ... *Fortunata y Jacinta* is the account of the co-operative activity on the part of natural and social forces working itself out in individual psychology along a line of moral invigoration.[15]

Fortunata and Jacinta, then, centres on the portrayal of a woman of the lower class grappling, on a moral and psychological plane, with the problems posed by her association with the middle class. It is a novel of developing social awareness in which questions of morality, especially with regard to sexual relations, are measured in relation to accepted social and religious standards. On a social level, the novel appears to be saying that though the middle class appears dominant, it needs the vitalization which the *pueblo* can offer it. This would be the meaning of the dénouement and in keeping with the general theoretical statements about the common people scattered throughout the pages of the novel. Thus the fusion of nature and society seen in individual relationships, can be seen as applicable to the whole question of class distinctions. The novel would be unmistakably optimistic in which, as D. L. Shaw suggests, 'A wise and benevolent Nature presides reliably over human destinies'.[16] But such a neat reconciliation of opposites, though discernible, cannot be accorded the status of the whole truth about this extensive and complicated novel. A more ambivalent view can be seen in the metaphor used to describe Moreno-Isla's death: 'He was torn away from humanity; a completely dead leaf fell from the great tree, a leaf only held together by scarcely visible fibres. The tree felt nothing in its great mass of branches. Here and there more and more useless leaves fell at the same moment, but the following morning fresh new buds would burst forth into the light' (pp. 901–2). It is Galdós's tone more than the outcome of events which attenuates the tragic implications of the novel. Fortunata has provided a son for the bourgeoisie, but she herself has died. Had she lived, would the same resolution have been possible? Moreover, there is no reason to believe that Juan Evaristo will be raised as anything other than as a bourgeois.

Feijóo's ambition to have Fortunata settled in a life of respectability before his death is frustrated. She dies before him. The other principal victim, Maxi, finds his conflicts resolved not by death, but by insanity, and humanity's advance through the co-operation of nature and society is not fulfilled in his case. Society merely compounded the disadvantages visited upon him by nature. And around these two characters are ranged a host of minor tragedies: the lonely life and death of Moreno-Isla, the ruined marriage of Juanito and Jacinta, the death of Mauricia la dura, of Feijóo, the unrequited love of Ballester, the unfulfilled ambitions of José Izquierdo. Other characters are more fortunate: Juan Pablo and Nicolás Rubín ascend to positions of influence but the portrayal of the political background of the period would suggest that such success can only be temporary. Against this gallery of unfulfilled hopes and wasted lives Fortunata's life has its moment of triumph and she can claim to be an angel. But the criteria by which this claim can be tested are not of this world. Significantly, none of the Santa Cruz family are at the funeral of the woman who provided them with an heir.

Galdós, then, balances a broadly optimistic account of human development and achievement with a recognition of life's more unpleasant possibilities. These, rather than being the inevitable result of some malign or deterministic force, are seen to spring from an incompatibility between the characters' own inherent natures and the type of world they are required to inhabit. *Fortunata and Jacinta* is a Realist novel by virtue of its main theme, the individual's struggle against a hostile society, and the techniques used to create a fictional world which acts as a plausible model of a social and historical reality. Central to Galdós's treatment of the conflict between individual and society is the theme of adjustment or adaptation, in which it is significant that the failures tend to outweigh the one partial success, Fortunata. Galdós's double-edged vision is summed up in Maxi's meditations in the cemetery with which the novel ends, and its tragic potential is underscored by Maxi's own failure to adapt. Thus the comfortable view of society as a coherent and integrated whole which the narrator presented in Part I is fragmented by the force of individual experience. It is this shift from an objective and relatively stable viewpoint to a multiplicity of perspectives, together with a pattern of analogies, that creates the sense of the diversity and complexity of the world presented in the novel. Galdós, in *Fortunata and Jacinta*, combines sympathy with condemnation as he steadily reveals the achievements and failures of characters submerged in a reality that is too complex to understand and in a society whose values frequently conflict with their own aspirations. It is this vision, at once ironical and tolerant, that lies at the heart of Galdosian Realism.

NOTES

1. All references are to Lester Clark's translation, Penguin, London, 1973. The translation has serious deficiencies but it is, unfortunately, the only one available.
2. Galdós's critical writings are most easily consulted in Benito Pérez Galdós, *Ensayos de crítica literaria*, ed. L. Bonet, Península, Barcelona, 1972.
3. Georg Lukács, *Studies in European Realism*, Hillway, London, 1950, p. 6.
4. For the historical background to *Fortunata and Jacinta* see R. Carr, *Spain, 1808–1939*, O.U.P., Oxford, 1966, especially ch. VIII, pp. 305–46.
5. S. Gilman, 'La palabra hablada en *Fortunata y Jacinta*',*Nueva Revista de Filología Hispánica*, xv (1961), 542–60.
6. S. Bacarisse, 'The Realism of Galdós: Some Reflections on Language and the Perception of Reality', *Bulletin of Hispanic Studies*, xlii (1965), 239–50.
7. For a full treatment of this aspect of the novel see G. Ribbans, 'Contemporary History in the Structure and Characterization of *Fortunata y Jacinta*', *Galdós Studies*, Támesis, London, 1970, pp. 90–113, to which the present writer is greatly indebted.
8. The whole question of class in the novel is considered by J. H. Sinnigen, 'Individual, Class and Society in *Fortunata y Jacinta*', *Galdós Studies II*, Támesis, London, 1974, pp. 49–68.
9. J. P. Stern, *On Realism*, Routledge & Kegan Paul, London, 1973, p. 110.
10. L. V. Braun, 'Galdós' Recreation of Ernestina Manuel de Villena as Guillermina Pacheco', *Hispanic Review*, xxxviii (1970), 32–55. A more critical view of Guillermina is put forward by J. L. Brooks, 'The Character of Guillermina Pacheco in Galdós' Novel *Fortunata y Jacinta*', *Bulletin of Hispanic Studies*, xxxviii (1961), 86–94.
11. For a very fine study of Galdós's irony in the early chapters of the novel see J. Whiston, 'Language and Situation in Part I of *Fortunata y Jacinta*', *Anales galdosianos*, vii (1972), 79–91.
12. M. Nimetz, *Humor in Galdós. A Study of the 'Novelas contemporáneas'*, Yale University Press, New Haven and London, 1968, pp. 122–3.
13. J. C. Ullman and G. H. Allison, 'Galdós as Psychiatrist in *Fortunata y Jacinta*', *Anales galdosianos*, ix (1974), 7–36.
14. S. H. Eoff, *The Modern Spanish Novel*, Peter Owen, London, 1962. pp. 134–5.
15. Eoff, p. 140.
16. D. L. Shaw, *A Literary History of Spain: The Nineteenth Century*, Benn, London, 1972, p. 142.

9

G. Verga:
Mastro-Don Gesualdo (1888)

JOHN GATT-RUTTER

IN A letter to his friend Luigi Capuana, on 25 February 1881, Verga wrote:

I kept telling myself that the simplicity of line, the uniformity of tone, that certain fusion of the whole which was intended to result in the most vigorous impact possible, the care I took to smooth down the corners, almost to veil the drama beneath the most human events, were all things that I had wanted and deliberately tried to bring about and were certainly not calculated to excite interest at every page of the narrative, but that the interest should spring from the whole, when the book has been shut, when all those characters have emerged so plainly as to come back before your eyes as people you have known, each through his own action. The confusion caused in your mind in the opening pages by all those characters brought before you face to face without introduction, as if you had always known them and as if you had been born and had lived in their midst, should disappear little by little as you advanced into the book and as they returned before your gaze and emerged through new actions but without *mise en scène*, simply, naturally. This too was an artifice, deliberately striven after—pardon the quip—to avoid all literary artifice, to give you the complete illusion of reality.[1]

The author is referring here to *The House by the Medlar Tree* (*I Malavoglia*), which had just been published.[2] However, the passage describes *Mastro-Don Gesualdo*[3] just as well. There, too, the dramatic moments are subdued and subordinated to the overall effect in a rigorous unity. There, too, as with all the most systematically Realist novels, the reader is bewildered to find himself surrounded from the outset by a host of characters whom the author takes for granted as they do one another. In fact, the author himself is invisible and inaudible. A complete ventriloquist, he lets you hear only the voices of his characters. This, as Verga sums up, is 'the complete illusion of reality'—the illusion which, as Jenkins emphasizes, is the very heart of Realism in literature.[4] Verga had seen the paradox.

Verga regularly talks of this perfect illusion as being the supreme end of his Realist fiction. Realism thus appears to have an aesthetic aim, as opposed to a moral, social, or educational aim. In this sense, the integrity and autonomy of the work of art, rather than its truth, are what seem to matter (though, as we shall shortly see, truth *is* held to be at least equally important). So, in the well-known letter to Salvatore Farina which prefaces his story 'Gramigna's Mistress' (referred to by G. Becker[5]), Verga writes:

When in the novel the affinity and cohesion of its every part will be so complete that the creative process will remain a mystery, like the development of human passions, and the harmony of its elements will be so perfect, the sincerity of its reality so evident, its manner of and its reason for existing so necessary, that the hand of the artist will remain completely invisible, then it will have the imprint of an actual happening; the work of art will seem *to have made itself*, to have matured and come into being spontaneously, like a fact of nature, without retaining any point of contact with its author, any stain of original sin.[6]

Art here tries to outdo Nature, or God. Technique turns into miracle. In the original 1880 edition of the preface, Verga was even more insistent and explicit, and ended by describing such a work of Realist art as 'throbbing with life and immutable as a bronze statue whose author has had the divine courage to eclipse himself and disappear into his immortal work.'[7]

Yet the other side of the paradox remains. In the same preface (as well as in numerous other passages) Verga insisted on authenticity in terms of the observed world, not merely as being necessary to the illusion, but as a value in and for itself. Like the Goncourts, he appeals to the authority of the 'human document', of 'what *has really been*', of the 'simply human fact', of 'true tears', of the 'psychological phenomenon', of 'scientific precision'. And the authenticity is not only that of observation and accurate transcription. It depends also on an analytical method, on tracing the 'logical and necessary development of the passions and of the facts', 'the obscure link between causes and effects'. It aspires to become 'the science of the human heart'—an aim which progressively fascinated the great French Realists, Balzac, Flaubert, and then Zola and his contemporaries.[8]

The references to causality and science are a tribute to the formidable influence in the 1870s of Zola and other French Naturalists and Realists—an influence conveyed particularly through the agency of the most advanced Italian literary thinkers of the time, De Sanctis and Capuana.[9] Verga embraced the 'scientific' notions that helped to constitute Naturalist theory (though retaining his critical independence and remaining within the mainstream of Realism): social environment as a major causal factor, if not a determining one, in human behaviour; social evolution as a slow but vast forward and upward Progress achieved at untold cost in the human suffering of the unfit; and (but with severe reservations) the influence of heredity. These notions are contained in the preface to the *House by the Medlar Tree* in which Verga laid out his plans for a cycle of five novels, of which *Mastro-Don Gesualdo* was to be the second, and in fact turned out to be the last when Verga found himself unable to continue. His plan was first announced in 1878 in a letter to Salvatore Paola.[10] He then proposed to entitle the cycle *La marea*, referring to the tide of Progress, which he saw as a 'phantasmagoria of the struggle for life', offering 'a thousand representations of man's grand grotesque'. In the preface, the title has changed to *I vinti* ('The Vanquished', or 'The Losers'), but the scheme remains the same.[11] It echoes Balzac's *Human Comedy* and Zola's Rougon-Macquart cycle in that the last four projected novels (that is, beginning with *Mastro-Don Gesualdo*) were to be linked by the family relationship between their respective protagonists. It also echoes Edmond de Goncourt's preface to *The Brothers Zemganno*[12] in proposing that each novel in turn should move up one social level from the lowest to the highest, impelled by 'the quest for something better'. In the first, set in a Sicilian fishing-village, 'it is still nothing but the struggle for material necessities'. In the second, *Mastro-Don Gesualdo*, set in a Sicilian country-town, it is the 'greed for wealth' of the self-made man. 'Then it will become aristocratic vanity in *La duchessa di Leyra*', to be set in the Sicilian capital of Palermo, and political ambition in Rome, in *L'onorevole Scipioni. L'uomo di lusso*, the pinnacle of mankind, who subsumes all the suffering of the species, is to be the artist in Florence, whose ambition is the most over-weening of all. Following Edmond de Goncourt, Verga envisages a higher degree of psychological, and hence stylistic and formal, complexity at each stage.

Verga never got beyond the first chapter of the third novel of the series, *La duchessa di Leyra*,[13] though he was to write other plays and stories. But his scheme for *The Vanquished* is as interesting as his failure to complete it, for it shows the profound contradiction in him —a contradiction rooted in the whole of Italy's literary culture of the age and for a long time to come. Nothing shows Verga's hierarchy of values better than this scheme in which the suffering of the artist subsumes that of all his fellow-beings and art is presented as the highest human activity and the loftiest ambition. And nothing shows better how far—for all his pretensions to scientific positivism and literary Realism or *verismo*—Verga was from being cured of his ineradicable idealism, his aesthetic subjectivism. In his godless universe, art has become a sort of secular religion, the only form of transcendance. The artist is ready to assume godhead.

However, we have seen from the preface to 'Gramigna's Mistress' that Verga's artistic godhead can realize itself only by becoming immanent in a work of art, hiding within it, incarnating itself without leaving any residue of explicit, 'transcendent', self-revelation. The work of art achieves its perfection only when the author's presence has been eliminated. Realism is the necessary mode of Verga's aestheticism. This means that the godhead (the artist, the novelist himself) cannot be approached directly, for it exists only in its creation. The Realist mode could not permit Verga to write *L'uomo di lusso*. The scheme of *The Vanquished* was a contradiction in terms. The third and fourth novels could be written within the Realist canon, and one could argue that they were written by other Sicilian novelists, in Federico De Roberto's *I Vicerè* (*The Viceroys*) and in Giuseppe Tomasi di Lampedusa's *Il gattopardo* (*The Leopard*)[14]. But the fifth novel could be accommodated only within the considerably altered aesthetic of a Thomas Mann, a Joyce or a Proust, or in the totally different genre of Orphic poetry.

Verga was from the first drawn towards presenting heroic or tragic versions—whether male or female—of himself. With these, the reader, depending on his or her degree of naivety, was tacitly invited to identify. One way of looking at Verga's later and greater *veristic* or Realist works is to see them as the most sophisticated projections into the objective world of the author's self-image, with which only a minute number of contemporary readers were able to identify. This is certainly the case with Gesualdo, and with the female triptych of Bianca, Diodata, and Isabella. Even with some of these (Bianca in particular), Verga's endeavour to objectivize, to dissociate himself from his creation, is not always successful, and we shall see how, in spite of all the discipline of Realism, he is occasionally tempted by the prospect of a feast of tragic emotion and pathos. Verga was never able to write his *Sentimental Education*. Always, the closer he came to autobiographically based characters, reflecting his own ideals, desires, aspirations, the less able he was to present a convincing reality. It was left to Italo Svevo, totally neglected for over thirty years, whose first novel, *Una vita* (*A Life*), was to appear in 1892,[15] a mere three years after the publication in book form of *Mastro-Don Gesualdo*, to carry Realism in Italy inward into the self. Verga's tussle with this problem in *Mastro-Don Gesualdo* can be measured, partly at least, by comparing the two published versions of the novel. For this was first serialized in the Florentine journal *Nuova Antologia* between July and December of 1888 and was published as a book by the Milan publisher Emilio Treves, late in 1889. There is also a manuscript, owned by Livio Garzanti, showing the process of correction and re-writing by which Verga produced the very considerably altered text which we now read. We can interpret the consensus of the critical studies which have compared these versions[16] as being that Verga has come closer, in the final version, to Gesualdo, treating him with more sympathy and sensitivity, and has detached himself from Bianca, cutting down her part in the novel quite considerably and giving far less rein to the expression of her emotions, so that she now becomes the least talkative character in the novel, indeed almost silent, and the real pathos of her life is enhanced and all the more effectively conveyed because the hand of the artist has become more completely invisible.

There is just one passage in the novel where Verga's hand slips and we catch sight of it. This comes at the end of Chapter 3 of Part 1. Bianca, pregnant by Niní Rubiera, has managed to speak to him *tête-à-tête* at the Sganci house on the occasion of the celebrations for the local patron saint, and has realized that her lily-livered lover is going to leave her in the lurch. She also discovers that a move is afoot to marry her off to the rich plebeian, Gesualdo. As Gesualdo and the scheming Canon Lupi accompany Bianca home, Lupi reminds Gesualdo of the proposed match. Gesualdo evasively replies that he will sleep on it. 'Night brings counsel, my dear Canon,' he remarks. Now Verga shows his hand:

Bianca, who was walking with a tight heart, listening to the indifferent small-talk of her uncle, beside her silent, emaciated brother, heard those last words.

Night brings counsel. The dark, desolate night in her wretched little room. The night which carried away the last sounds of the festival, the last light, the last hope—like the vision of him who went away with another woman, without turning, without speaking, without replying to her who called him from the bottom of her heart, with a moan, with a sick lament, burying her face in her pillow wet with hot and silent tears.

The tugging at heart-strings, the attempt to work directly on the reader's emotions, goes against the Realist canon of impersonality, impassibility, and objectivity, and spoils the effect Verga has already produced by the incident which the passage refers to—where Niní turns his back on Bianca and walks off with Donna Fifí Margarone.

It is of course those hot and silent tears that Verga wants us to savour. 'True (i.e. real) tears', as in his prefatory letter to 'Gramigna's Mistress', are for him the very essence of reality, and therefore of Realism. *Sunt lachrymae rerum. Mastro-Don Gesualdo*, like all Verga's strictly Realist works, produces tears of the most authentic sort in abundance. But it does so precisely by not inviting the reader to join the writer in savouring them. Given Verga's weakness for the lachrymose and for self-dramatization, the discipline of Realism was absolutely essential to his literary achievement, and he had to apply it in its most 'scientifically' rigorous form. That is, he had to adhere literally to the method of positive science, which is to record only what can be observed. It will be noticed that the passage about Bianca's hot and silent tears is one of the rare passages in the novel where Verga looks 'inside' one of his characters. The greater part of the novel is made up of dialogue—that is, recorded speech. For speech constitutes scientifically valid data—something external and observable—about what is going on in people's minds and hearts. Thus the reason why this novel is such a garrulous one is not only one of subject-matter—that rural Sicilian society is itself garrulous. The garrulousness is dictated by Verga's choice of method, by his particular form of Realism.

Of course, people do not necessarily reveal their motives or feelings in their speech directly or honestly. They certainly do not usually do so in *Mastro-Don Gesualdo*. This is what calls for all the novelist's skill. Not only must he characterize all his figures through the way they talk, and therefore take pains to produce dialogue of convincing authenticity in terms of the observed society. He must also allow the characterization to emerge gradually through a whole series of comparisons—the comparison between what the character says in one situation and what he says in another, to another person or at another time; the comparison between what he says and what he does; between what he says and what he fails to say. The effect of the book springs therefore, as Verga claimed in the letter which is my opening quotation, from the book as a whole, and not from its individual moments. The details of this process are plain enough, and there is no lack of examples, as the book is made up of such details. So, in the first chapter, we are not told exactly what else, besides a fire, has been going on in the Trao household. All we are told is that Don Diego re-emerges from Bianca's room 'having aged ten years in a minute, embarrassed, rolling his eyes, with a terrible vision in the depths of his grey pupils, a cold sweat on his brow, his voice choked with an immense grief . . . ' (Incidentally, the English reader must make allowances throughout for the ineptness of D. H. Lawrence's translation. Here, for instance, Verga does not describe Don Diego as 'embarrassed' and 'rolling his eyes', but with 'face turned white, eyes staring', while his grey pupils contain a terrible image or picture, rather than a 'vision', and the pain which chokes him is not exactly grief.) We have heard Bianca say, 'Kill me, Don Diego!— Kill me then! But don't let anybody come in here', and Don Diego exclaiming, 'You? . . . You here?', and, like the rest of the townsfolk, we can only speculate on what this signifies and on the Traos' cries and Nanni l'Orbo's report that he has seen a thief. In other words, we are put into the same position as the characters in the novel, who have to rely on gossip to piece together what is going on. Only in the next chapter do we learn that Niní Rubiera was in Bianca's room, and only when one of the characters, Don Diego, says so to another character, Baroness Rubiera. This, of course, maximizes not only the narrative suspense, but also the drama and pathos of Don Diego's situation. Likewise, in the first chapter of Part 4, we are not told what to make of the kindness of the Zacco family, former enemies of Gesualdo, in tending the ailing Bianca, in the teeth of the whole town's hostility to Gesualdo. But Bianca expresses irritation at Lavinia Zacco's attentions, and then jealousy, accusing the Zaccos of wishing her dead, so as to marry their daughter to Gesualdo. It is not until two chapters further on that Baroness Zacco attempts the classic stroke and the family storms out when Gesualdo refuses the match. A writer need not be a Realist to avoid giving his characters' game away from the start, but all the weight of Realist method helps to push him in this direction.

Of course, these procedures are in part simply an ingredient of all good story-telling or dramatic composition. Key information is artfully withheld until the moment when its revelation is most effective or its significance most far-reaching. But in Verga it forms part of a systematic method in which the withholding of information is less important than the manner in which the information is conveyed. Dialogue, then, and the barest bones of narrative or description of a dynamic sort—not the static, set-piece descriptions of a Balzac or a Flaubert—form the fabric of the novel within which the author disappears, in keeping with his 'scientific' method of external observation. There are a few passages of 'internal observation', which we shall come to shortly, but first something must be said about what I have called the bare bones of narrative and description, for this is the most remarkable part of Verga's disappearing act.

How can the novelist disappear from the irreducible minimum of narration and description ? 'Objectivity' or 'impersonality'—in other words, refraining from extraneous direct comment or palpable bias or distortion in presentation—is an important first step, a step taken by every novelist with serious claims to being a Realist, including all those represented in this volume. But it is not enough. Narration and description still demand an 'omniscient' narrator who transcends the text and the subject-matter and whose godhead is therefore still too visible. If the work of art is to appear 'to have made itself', the story must appear 'to have told itself'. In other words, the style and point of view of the narrative must be *internal* to the world contained in the narrative, and must be circumscribed in every way by the horizons of that world—psychological, cultural, ethical.

The simplest (which is not necessarily the easiest) point of view internal to a narrative is that of one of the participants or close onlookers of the action narrated. The story is told by, or from the point of view of, one of the characters, with all the limitations and distortions that this might involve. This is not the path chosen by the typical Realist, though it has frequently been used by novelists on the margins of Realism who want to keep some sort of objective control on the intensely subjective or otherwise extraordinary experiences and events which they wish to relate. In these cases, it is really used as an *external* point of view. Other writers (Svevo, Proust) use a first-person or *quasi* first-person point of view to explore a subjectivity in depth. This is a later mutation of Realism. For the typical Realist, such a point of view is too limited, too exposed to the perils of a facile author-narrator-reader identification, not lending itself readily to the sort of free-ranging, multi-faceted presentation of social relationships and of numerous and varied characters that the Realists were most interested in.

Tolstoy, in *War and Peace* and *Anna Karenina*, maintained a point of view internal to the narrative, whilst allowing himself the freedom of a wide social canvas, by his 'infinitesimal' method of narrating the story through the consciousness of one particular character, strategically chosen, in each chapter. A looser form of this method, frequently used by nineteenth-century Realists, and notably by Flaubert, is the *discours indirect libre* or *erlebte Rede*: the author presents what a character is thinking or saying, in a form of indirect speech, but without explicitly attributing the indirect speech to the character, so that events can be narrated from the point of view of the character most appropriate to narrate them, without the shifts of the narrative becoming unduly perceptible to the reader, who is thus drawn in to the story, sharing the reactions of different characters by turn without the danger of uncritical identification which is inherent in a fixed point of view, and with rich ironic possibilities arising 'impersonally' and 'objectively' from the juxtaposition of conflicting points of view.

Verga, the first thorough-going technician of Realism, applied a highly sophisticated, though apparently naïve, form of this *erlebte Rede* in his first great Realist novel, *The House by the Medlar Tree*. Here the entire novel is narrated through the speech, direct or indirect, of the whole village in a shifting succession or virtually in chorus. The village therefore tells the story, including that essential minimum of narration and description which in most other Realist novelists would have to be provided by an omniscient narrator, the objective observer standing outside the action.[17]

Attempts have been made to explain Verga's 'discovery' of this style of writing in simple terms of this or that model.[18] He himself recounted that his eyes (or ears) had been opened by reading an account of a storm at sea as recorded in the unschooled prose of a schooner captain's log-book. Attention has been drawn to the influence of his friend Capuana's dialect ballad, *Lu cumpari*, later turned into a short story in Italian entitled *Comparatico*.[19] Certainly, both of these will have had their effect on a Realist author casting about for a suitable narrative form in which to convey the experience of Sicilian peasants and fishermen. Equally or more important must have been the lessons which De Sanctis—in a series of unsurpassed interpretative and appreciative articles on Zola—drew from his readings of the great French writer.[20] These articles appeared just before the great flowering of Verga's Realism, and contain all the ideas on which Verga based his Realist theory and practice. De Sanctis sees Realism as both perfect artistic illusion and high morality. He even quotes *Sunt lacrimae rerum.* Most pertinent to the present point, he draws attention to dialect as the great reservoir of linguistic vigour. All this, as well as his own reading of Zola and the other French Realists and Naturalists, undoubtedly helped Verga to travel in the direction which he was to take. Above all, Verga's tenacious study of his Sicilian subject-matter, undertaken in accordance with the Naturalist canon of first-hand observation from life, must inevitably have led him to this 'discovery'. 'Listen, listen, if you wish to learn how to write.' Verga listened to his Sicilians, but wanted to write for Italians. He evolved, therefore, his own narrative idiom, which was not Sicilian dialect, nor a translation from Sicilian into Italian, but a skilful Italian rendering of the idiom, syntax, and cadences of Sicilian speech.[21] The result was a far cry from the high style and linguistic formality and purism that most impressed the Italian reading public, and this, along with the stark subject-matter, was one of the main reasons why Verga's great Realist novels and stories found so much less favour than his earlier tales of passion in high society or the bohemian fringe.

Verga develops the method of choral narration in *Mastro-Don Gesualdo*, though the changed subject-matter and social milieu necessitate some changes. The description of the Trao house (p. 13) is not only perfectly functional to the event being narrated. It is also couched in terms of the spoken word, rather than in the syntax of narrative prose. 'A perfect hole that house ...' Not a word or expression in the description—and hardly one in the whole book— goes outside the style or mentality of the inhabitants of this small Sicilian town. Moreover, the description is directly related to Gesualdo, who is concerned to prevent the fire from spreading to his own house next door. To him, the decrepit state of the Trao house appears mainly as an impediment to saving his own. Also, to a builder who has risen to wealth from nothing, as is Gesualdo's case, it must typify, vividly, the very antithesis of all that he stands for.

Much of the novel is related in this way from a point of view that approximates to that of Gesualdo but cannot usually be pinned down to him. More usually, in the crowded scenes that form the bulk of the novel, the point of view is less definite, and approximates to that of a typical witness on the spot, or else amounts to a sort of synthesis of all the different first-hand reports on the episode, or pieces of hearsay, that might be imagined to be circulating around the town.

In all these cases, the narrative point of view is therefore *internal* to the story being told and the social milieu portrayed, but *external* to the more intimate levels of the psychology of the individual characters. This more private dimension of unspoken or inarticulate experience poses the great problem for a novelist using a thoroughgoing Realist method, such as Verga.

Briefly, it can be said that Verga gets round this problem by two different devices, as appropriate to the circumstances. That he does so testifies yet again to the importance he attached to those 'hot and silent tears', and shows the efforts he made to get as close as possible to them.

The first device is to keep the tears silent. The reader is left to sense from the situation what the suffering character must be feeling. The silence of authentic anguish is made more eloquent by contrast to the callous or insincere talkativeness of other characters. The tragic characters in the novel—Bianca, Diodata, Isabella, and, in Part 4, Gesualdo himself—are essentially silent characters, and most silent in their most tragic moments. This applies particularly to the scenes involving Bianca in Chapters 3 and 6 of Part 1, and those between Diodata and Gesualdo, in Chapters 5 and 7 of Part 1, where he discusses his projected marriage to Bianca quite oblivious of Diodata's own affection towards him (or perhaps with a bad conscience), and bawls at her for weeping.

The other way in which Verga ventures into the perilous regions of subjectivity is by a sort of interior monologue or extended *erlebte Rede*. This fits in well with the spoken character of the narrative as a whole, and is carefully managed so as to merge into the narrative flow naturally and imperceptibly. The best example of this is the final chapter, where the ailing Gesualdo, close to death, is a guest in his son-in-law's palace in Palermo. The ambience is presented through Gesualdo's own eyes, so the transition from the description of the expensive pomp of the palace to Gesualdo's recollection of the beloved lands for which he has laboured so hard, and whose fertility and industry sustain that useless pomp, occurs without any narrative break or shift. The interior monologue is couched in the same rough-and-ready, but vigorous, language that Gesualdo always uses, and that is characteristic of the whole narrative, and in fact, that same interior monologue leads on to a dialogue, indistinguishable from it in style, when Gesualdo pleads with Isabella to look after his estates which have cost him so dear. Here we may say of Verga something akin to what De Sanctis wrote about Zola: that his passion for the real made him the greatest French stylist since Proudhon.

Isabella's cultivated sensibility, taking Verga close to the Romantic subjectivity which had swamped the novels he had written before his great Realist works, presents more of a problem. Adolescence, her expensive education, and the poetic influence of Corrado La Gurna combine to produce in her a feverish, almost swooning or dream-like infatuation fed by the mysterious suggestions of moonlight and nature. Already, in Chapter 2 of Part 3, Verga had ventured into her state of mind on returning to her home town and finding it, to her disappointment, so much less enchanting and impressive than she had pictured it. (This is in itself a typical Realist procedure, by which the author produces a new characterization of the milieu, at the same time as he renders a characterization of Isabella, by presenting her reactions to the milieu.) Now, in two passages, the first on pages 228–30 in the same chapter, and the second on pages 246–7 of the following chapter, Verga stretches his narrative resources near to breaking-point to chart in all its intimacy the girl's progress from the vague restlessness and yearning of her solitude to the first awakening of her love, or infatuation, for the young La Gurna, culminating, as she rushes to bid her lover her last farewell, in a sentence that must echo a hundred nineteenth-century romances:

Only among the weeds of the path along which he must come were humble thistle-flowers glinting in the sun, and green berries bending and swaying softly, saying 'Come! Come! Come!' [p. 247].

The dividing line is extremely thin here between a Realist's objective rendering of a romantically-inclined nineteenth-century girl and a romantically-inclined nineteenth-century novelist's naïve version of the supreme love-experience and accompanying semi-mystical transports. On this occasion Verga has given us dis-passionate history, not sublimated subjectivity. This is all the more remarkable in that the authentic self is the real object of his interest. He is saved by his Realist method, which is essentially a *critical* method, like all true realism, all true science, and all true knowledge.

The author dwells on all that is *inauthentic*, and the authentic is arrived at by a process of reduction or elimination. That is, when everything inauthentic has been taken into account, what is left is the authentic.

In this particular case, Isabella's infatuation, which might contain something authentic, is expertly subordinated to, or balanced with, quite extraneous and opposed elements, in fact, all the other narrative concerns then afoot: the cholera; Bianca's condition; Gesualdo's generous, yet carefully measured hospitality; and, most dramatically, his father Nunzio's death, which coincides with, and makes possible (because of Gesualdo's absence), the adolescent courtship, and involves Gesualdo in a frightful property feud with his sister Speranza; and also Nanni L'Orbo's interested spying on the young lovers. Gesualdo, obsessed with his wealth, can see Corrado La Gurna only as a fortune-hunter, and his remarks put the young lovers in a most un-Romantic and critical perspective:

the youth's slyness as he pretended not to look at her, like one at a fair who passes and re-passes in front of the heifer he wants to buy, without so much as glancing at her . . .

'Ha!—poetry! That stuff won't fill anybody's belly.'

We don't know about Corrado's real motives. Gesualdo *may* be right, as he may be right in treating Isabella's passion as mere calf-love, or idle and dangerous fancy. The Realist author, critical in his approach, has warned us about all the possibilities of inauthenticity, and has left us to gauge what is left that is authentic: Gesualdo's passionate defence of his daughter and his property and of his daughter *as* his property (a defence which is authentic enough, no matter how mistaken we may think it to be); and his daughter's equally passionate need for a dimension of life which Gesualdo cannot give her, and which, rightly or wrongly, she associates with the poetic young Corrado. Equally authentic—and one of the major themes of the book—is the aching gulf that separates Gesualdo from the daughter who is not his own.

The reader may be disappointed to find the love-affair between Isabella and Corrado not gone into more fully and directly. But Verga has told us all we need to know. Isabella, like her mother Bianca, is denied the man she loves and whose child she is carrying (as is clearly hinted in Limoli's words to Gesualdo on p. 265), and, for reasons of wealth and status, forced into a loveless marriage. Verga is even more parsimonious in vouchsafing a presentation of Bianca's passion for Niní Rubiera. The Realist writer might be expected to explain how a girl of such proud family, and so vulnerable in her poverty, as Bianca, could have so fatally risked her honour. Instead, Verga is at pains to explain how, with all her family pride and her passion for Don Niní, she is persuaded to do such an unthinkable thing, given the social attitudes of baronial Sicily which Verga stresses particularly in the third chapter of the book, as to marry a workman, however rich he may be. What finally persuades her is an argument presented in true Realist fashion. The poverty-stricken Bianca, newly with child, and with no prospects of anything but haughty squalor, is faced with an image of her own likely future self in the person of Grazia, the wife of Don Luca, the sacristan:

Donna Bianca had stopped arrested [i.e. had stopped short], her head high, on her cheeks a sudden flame that seemed as if it were cast by the lifting of the door-curtain at that moment, as someone entered the church. Appeared a skinny [thin] woman with her ragged skirt lifted from her thin legs by her stomach that was big with child, dirty and unkempt, as if she had done nothing else all her life but carry that belly in front of her; the look of a mother-hen stupefied by brooding her young, with two round little eyes on her pointed, parchment-yellow face, and an invalid's torn handkerchief tied under her chin; nothing else on her shoulders, being quite at home in the house of the Good God. From the doorway she began to moan as if her travail pains were upon her [p. 100].

There are times however when Verga, a Realist for the sake of self-discipline, and against his inmost tendencies, takes the Realist method too far. From impersonal irony, emerging organically from the complete and many-sided presentation of his subject-matter, he can descend to more or less open satire at the expense of his subject-matter or his characters. To reject too strongly is again to be too involved, though negatively. There is a tendency towards caricaturing his sleepy provincial town. If Palermo is in revolt, we must put up a good show, too, cries Baron Mendola. The local conspirators of 1820 (not 1821, as Verga erroneously has it), including Gesualdo himself, appear in comic terror. Caricature is most marked in the episode of Niní Rubiera's amours with the actress Aglae, starting with the egregious *billet-doux* which opens Chapter 4 of Part 2, and culminating with the remark which interrupts Aglae's high-flown and lengthy declaration of her dedication to her art: ' "Hey!" they heard the deep voice on the stairs. "Do you want them fried or with tomato sauce?" '(p. 189).

The Realist felicities of the novel, however, greatly outnumber and outweigh its occasional lapses or excesses. The opening—the chapter on the fire in the Trao house—is a virtuoso performance that tells us clearly that we are in for a well-made novel. Verga plunges us straight into a hectic, crowded scene, in which nearly all the characters are electrified into activity in the sleeping village. The confusion of the reader at being surrounded by so many strange faces all at once matches the confusion of the scene of the fire itself, and the confusion of the Trao brothers at finding their squalid but proud ancestral home suddenly invaded by all the rabble of the town. The scene has not been set, and yet we are right in it, and know it almost without realizing it. This *is* dynamic presentation.

And Verga has not only plunged us into the middle of a scene. He takes us *in medias res*, by the time-honoured canon of narrative art, right into the middle of the plot. Already, Bianca is dishonoured, by the conventions of her society. Already, by those same conventions, she is unmarriageable, because dowryless, barring the extraordinary circumstance, which the plot will bring about, of marrying below her class. Already, in this scene, her lover's discovery decides him to abandon her.

Curiosity and gossip, hints and innuendoes, emerge right away as the currency of social intercourse in this provincial community. By the end of the chapter, word has got to the reader, who is put in the middle of this gossip and speculation, that Bianca has had a lover and may be looking for a husband.

One of the main virtuosities of this opening, almost an extravagance of concealed art, is the casual appearance of the novel's protagonist. Casual, but significant, in that it introduces us immediately, and with such artful artlessness, to two of his foremost characteristics— his energy, and his exclusive concern for his own property.

This sidelong introduction is carried on in the second and third chapters. In the second, Gesualdo does not even appear. But we hear of his multitudinous affairs and undertakings, and of his seemingly irresistible advance towards dominance in the local economy. More tellingly, Don Diego's interview with Baroness Rubiera about her son's responsibilities towards Bianca is framed within an incident which is trivial in itself, and yet many-sided in its significance for the novel: for the chapter starts with the Baroness congratulating herself on having sold dear to Gesualdo, and ends with her disgruntlement at finding that Gesualdo has outwitted her by buying Baron Zacco's cheaper grain and leaving hers on her hands upon some trumped-up pretext. Gesualdo's business methods and his ability to beat the opposition have thus been quite adequately brought home to us without the author having to open his mouth.

A brief aside—this chapter also examplifies the technique of carrying along two episodes or incidents almost concurrently, or interweaving them together, so as, at one and the same time, to give a lifelike impression of randomness, while actually achieving a greater concentration and economy of narrative. This compositional skill, moreover, is not merely its own reward: in the juxtaposition of the two incidents, Verga gives rise, using 'impersonal' means alone, to an irony of the sort which we colloquially call poetic justice. Baroness Rubiera, having cheated the Traos, through refusing to hear of her son wedding Bianca, of their honour, is herself cheated by Gesualdo. That her loss, in this instance, is so trivial compared to that of the Traos, only reinforces the morality which seems to arise from things 'objectively' observed. The incident foreshadows a rich crop of similar ironies involving the Traos, the Baroness and Gesualdo throughout the novel.

The third chapter more clearly extends the characterization of Gesualdo, though from a perspective which still makes him appear relatively insignificant. And, still, the characterization is *dynamic*. His very appearance among the society of the nobles is a dramatic, even a historic, event. He develops before our eyes through the various reactions of the other characters and through the way he behaves—unassuming and slightly ill-at-ease, yet quietly assured in saying what he has to say. Through apparently unconnected incidents, through hearsay and innuendo, and through direct scenes between Bianca and Niní, the action develops as we hear that matches are being plotted, Niní Rubiera is to marry Fifí Margarone and Bianca to marry Don Gesualdo, and the chapter ends with Canon Lupi making Gesualdo the 'golden' proposition. Only after Gesualdo has been shown to us from the perspective of the nobles does he appear in his own right in the following two chapters, which thus have all the effect of climax.

Verga's method of achieving artistic immediacy by dramatizing his narrative as much as possible in the form of dialogue or through choral narration largely determines the way in which the novel is structured as a series of chapters each forming a continuum in itself. This also explains why so much action is packed into each chapter, several important events often occurring simultaneously. For the apparently casual choral procedure, to preserve its naturalness, would fill many hundreds of pages if all the events narrated were strung out in time. A real 'slice of life' should take as much time as the actual living. So, in Chapters 2 and 3 of Part 2, Gesualdo goes into hiding as a Carbonaro conspirator, Don Diego dies, and Bianca prematurely gives birth, all at the same time. To some extent this heightens the drama of the several events narrated—particularly, as we saw, in the case of Mastro Nunzio's death interrupting the progress of Isabella's amour with Corrado La Gurna. But—again as in the Isabella episode—Verga is also being a good Realist in another way, in following a strict causality as the inner logic of events. This causality is the organizing principle of the whole book. It underlies both the apparently haphazard or aimless procedure and succession of chapters, and the interference of apparently fortuitous events. There are two important coincidences, however, which help to structure the plot. The first is Don Diego's death in the midst of the town's Carbonari conspiracy. The second is Mastro Nunzio's death from malarial fever in the midst of the cholera epidemic of 1837.

Other events which do not seem obviously related to the main thread of the plot, turn out to be essential links in the causal chain. As he avowed was his intention, in his letter to Capuana, Verga has worked the causal connections in so naturally as to seem inconspicuous. One instance of this is the collapse of the bridge in the fifth chapter. What looks like a chance misfortune is actually the effect of a previous cause, and the cause of a new effect: it is the result of Mastro Nunzio's interference in Gesualdo's affairs, and decides Gesualdo to break with his family (in order to avoid similar mishaps in the future) and marry Bianca Trao (in the hopes of getting the support of the local nobility in evading payment of caution-money incurred).

Similarly, other events in the book can be explained not only in terms of its *internal* aesthetic economy, but in terms of an objective causality, for, in Verga's Realist canon, the two principles, of aesthetic coherence and of causation, are one and the same. One chapter which has caused some argument is the first in Part 2, the celebrated scene of the auction of the lease on the common lands.

Romano Luperini has seen this as an unnecessary *tour de force* on Verga's part, merely reiterating his already proven skill in handling crowded and disorderly scenes, and also reiterating Gesualdo's already proven dominance over his rivals.[22] But there is more to it than that. Having married into the nobility to gain their support and enhance his status, Gesualdo finds that he has achieved neither. In any case, he is not interested in equality with the nobles, but dominance. His plan, as he explains openly (p. 140), is to control the supply of wheat, and hence its price, over the whole county. We have here, not a *bourgeois gentilhomme*, but a modern capitalist, aiming, through competition, towards monopoly. For the first time here we see him taking on, and beating, the whole baronial class. Yet, Gesualdo's triumph in this scene is also his undoing. Refusing to play the barons' game, he sets them all against him. He has already broken with his family by marrying Bianca. The manner in which he increases his wealth sets peasants and workers against him. This leaves him with a tiny handful of faithful dependants, and others, like Nanni L'Orbo, who are only greedy and calculating—parasites on his own ambition. The way is clear for his downfall.

To embark on this brief analysis is already to show how concrete and sure is Verga's presentation of social relations. He shows not only the powerful class-consciousness of the nobles (over the question of admitting Gesualdo into their ranks, or denying to the peasants the common lands which are rightfully theirs), but the economic, social, and ultimately political dynamics of Gesualdo's rise from Mastro to Don.

A weaker chapter, perhaps, is that which recounts Ninì's amorous fortunes and misfortunes with Donna Fifì and the actress Aglae (Part 2, Chapter 4). We may feel here that Verga is filling in time between one great crisis and the next, for sixteen years must elapse between Isabella's birth in the 1820–21 turmoil and her initiation in the 1837 cholera epidemic.

The Aglae episode does of course provide a welcome comic interlude. It also brings some necessary developments in the plot: Ninì's amours put him heavily in Gesualdo's debt, paralyse his mother the Baroness with a stroke, and at last turn the philanderer into a dogged defender of his own wealth and, because of the debt, into Gesualdo's most dangerous enemy. The ironies of reality at the expense of the Baroness, Ninì, and Gesualdo, thus continue to unfold. Yet, on the whole, the dynamic of the novel does seem to falter at this point, and it is strange that we hear no more of the progress of Don Gesualdo's grandiose economic schemes.

The Naturalists attracted the criticism of 'respectable' society by their uncompromising exposure of scabrous areas of reality. Verga seems restrained in the way he deals with the most sensitive areas of sex and squalor. And, yet, his picture of human degradation is no less stark than Zola's. What appals us in Verga's presentation of life is its meanness and pettiness, its narrowness of horizon, and his almost overwhelming insistence on disease and death. Disease and death are, in one sense, the ultimate realities, and the Realist is bound to have a good look at them. Where the Romantic might have been tempted to squeeze the last drop of sentimentality out of them, Verga is the more effective and moving in remaining the precise and *apparently* detached observer.

Verga does not, however, give us an arid perspective in which it is death that defeats Gesualdo. That was indeed the theme of a short story, 'La roba', about a similar type.[23] In this sense, we are all defeated by death. But in many of Verga's earlier Realist stories his peasant protagonists die, or damn themselves, like heroes for their passions and their inner compulsions. Death is not defeat, but the triumph of their authenticity. Gesualdo, on the other hand, is defeated before he dies, before he is ever ill. He has bought and failed to win his wife, and lost the daughter who was never his. He has sold the woman who loved him, Diodata, repudiated his sons, and seen them turn against him. He has seen his whole life's work squandered away. He is his own victim, as well as the victim of the society whose values he lives and whose hostility, in the last resort, he has not managed to conquer. He is defeated by Sicily, the baronial Sicily of the nineteenth century.

This Sicily is the essential component and condition of Verga's Realism. He did also write Realist stories which are based in Milan. He also wrote several novels about Sicily or with Sicilian protagonists that fail markedly to match up to the standards of Realism, and fail equally to convince as art, even though they fly the banner of *verismo*, and claim to tell the frightful truth about passion. The difference is that in these works of Verga's earlier *verismo* (as opposed to the later Realist works in which he applied the lessons he had learnt from Zola, especially through De Sanctis) the author treats characters with his own literary and romantic sensibility, characters of his own class and culture and of his own aspirations, identifying

with them naïvely, incapable of seeing them critically from the outside, as the Realist–Naturalist method of telling the story from
different social viewpoints later enabled him to do. The humble
Sicily that is *least* Verga's is what enables the writer to remain objective and retain his grip on terrestrial reality.

We have mentioned causality. In the context of Naturalism,
causality inevitably brings to mind heredity and environment.
Verga treats both with discretion. There is no theorizing about
either. Consumption and aloofness are hereditary in the Trao line.
Children inherit something from their parents—though no explanation from heredity is provided for the *differences* between Gesualdo,
his brother Santo and his sister Speranza. Nor does the physical environment explain why Gesualdo works with seemingly inexhaustible
energy, while his brother Santo drinks and games. Rather, it is
used as a poetic element, to convey aspects of a character: Gesualdo
is heroically pitted against beating rain and beating sun, but also
enthroned in the fertile lands of his industry; Isabella has the moonlight, and the lush semi-wilderness of the hillside at Mangalavite.

On the other hand, the social environment is all-pervading and
all-conditioning, not in the sense that it absolutely determines any
specific action, but in that it defines the parameters *within which*
individuals can act. Being a negative and uniform influence, it is
hard to illustrate with examples, except by stating one's impression
of the book as a whole. But we might think of Gesualdo's attempt to
treat Bianca Trao with exactly the same working-man's rough and
ready joviality he had shown Diodata. Isabella, who has been taken
out of this environment, brings out its character by contrast. It is a
dual contrast: a contrast of styles, as between the metropolis,
Palermo, and the province; and a contrast of *goals*, as between the
avidity for property and wealth, common to both province and
metropolis (embodied in the Duke of Leyra), and the affections of
the heart. For Verga, this latter is the vital contrast, the contrast
between the authentic and the inauthentic. The affections of the
heart in this novel are clearly represented by Bianca, Diodata,
Isabella, to some extent by the disinterested amiability of Marquis
Limoli, and ultimately, and most vitally of all, by Gesualdo himself.
Just as for Fontane in *Effi Briest*, the sufferings of these characters
are evidence to Verga both of the strength of social pressures, and of
their inhumanity, of their antagonism to all that is authentic in
ourselves. And it is the discovery of this authentic something that

constitutes Verga's 'science of the human heart' and the real goal of his Realism. It is the subject of his novel—a tragic subject. As I have said, he achieves this by a process of elimination. When Niní Rubiera starts a whole chain of misery by abandoning Bianca, it is because of considerations of property and wealth. He is afraid that his mother will cut him off without a penny. These considerations *are* shown to be determinant in the novel in the sense that they actually crush individual freedom. Bianca and Isabella may be *internally* free to value love above wealth or security. But, in practical terms of what they do with their lives, they have to bow to the logic of property and status which their society, very concretely embodied in such persons as Baroness Rubiera and Gesualdo, imposes on them. Women, in fact, have not even reached the status of sexual objects: they are treated as property. Verga is much more ruthless than Fontane, perhaps even simplistic, in showing up such considerations as being the all-pervasive logic of society (a society, in each case, undergoing an uneasy and uncertain transition from the feudal principle of caste and landed wealth to the capitalist or bourgeois principle of liquid money and industry). It is his exploration of the workings of this inescapable principle of material self-interest as the motive force in society that is, overwhelmingly, the most important instrument of Verga's Realism. Against the hard, irreducible, rigorously 'scientific' facts which this principle throws up, Verga measures all that is undefinably human. Again, he does what De Sanctis admired Zola for doing. In De Sanctis' terms, he allows the Ideal to emerge by showing us only the Real.

How property considerations determine everything in the novel, and are the very structure of the 'social environment', every reader can see and explore both in the general design and in the details of the narrative. Property considerations act like an acid to dissolve all other considerations: even bonds of kinship, so strong in Mediterranean society; even that other great driving force of human activity, also 'scientifically' verifiable and dear to the Naturalists—sex—as we see by the abrupt termination of the amorous Niní's courtship of Aglae. Even the poverty and pride of the Traos are due to the fact that they live in hope of obtaining six hundred years' compound interest on a sum owed them by the King of Spain. They have failed to make the at least partial transition from feudalism to capitalism which the other nobility, trading in grain and buying the lease on the common lands to rent to the peasantry, have made.

The political upheavals, too, are shown as being materially motivated—the peasants demanding their rightful share of the common
lands allotted to them by feudal tradition and by royal decree—and
manipulated by various sections of the wealthy, each trying to increase its own holding while keeping it out of the hands of those that
actually work the land. This comes to a head in the first three
chapters of Part 5 (see especially page 280, and also page 282, where
Lawrence has a disastrous mistranslation of 'good-for-nothings' for
'have-nothings'). In the third chapter, the 'liberal' party, who have
been inciting the peasants against Gesualdo, grow afraid that the
agitation may get out of hand and rebound against themselves, and
are at pains to check it, the adroit Canon Lupi bringing all the
resources of religion and the watchword of universal brotherhood to
bear on the confused peasants.

The most powerful embodiment and representative of the economic principle is of course Gesualdo. He is not, however, its *typical*
representative, but its most advanced one. As I have remarked, he is
the character in the book closest to being a modern capitalist. He is
not merely a rentier, contractor, trader and speculator in foodstuffs,
all on a grand scale; he is after monopoly control of prices. Verga is
being here an accurate and profound Realist in capturing the essence
of a broad historical process (though his dates, as we shall see, may
not be quite right), just as he is being accurate and profound in
portraying the new capitalist, Gesualdo, being swamped by the
strong baronial caste—which is the essence of the economic, social,
and political history of Sicily from the eighteenth century, through
the nineteenth, and at least until the end of the last war.[24]

Mastro-Don Gesualdo thus has a very special interest in literary
history, in the evolution of literature as a means of understanding the
reality we live in. It is not simply a study of greed, of the type that
goes back, say, to Ben Jonson's *Volpone*. Nor is it a social morality,
such as we might see in the figure of Bulstrode in *Middlemarch*, nor
does it give us only a typical and colourful figure out of a particular
epoch, like Arnoux in *Sentimental Education*. Nor have we here a
comparative moral study of different social classes such as Silas
Lapham is involved in—though some similarities between Gesualdo
and Silas are apparent. Far less is Gesualdo yet another satire of the
parvenu, of the *bourgeois gentilhomme* (though there are some satirical
touches), typical of a static, aristocratic literature. He is a heroic
figure. He towers above the other characters in the novel for sheer

energy, physical endurance, astuteness and resourcefulness, courage and ambitious economic vision, and even generosity and loyalty, within the limits of the outlook he has drawn from his social environment, towards his family and friends; as well as for driving a hard bargain and disposing callously of people (particularly Diodata and his own unacknowledged offspring). Verga portrays in him the positive, as well as the negative, side of capitalism on the rise: its creativity, its bold and intelligent grasp of both the real and the possible, its disdain for vain and useless pomp. Gesualdo is not characterized merely in terms of individual psychology, nor as a traditional 'type', nor yet as a simple combination of the two. In him a whole historic process is made human (in keeping with another of De Sanctis' remarks about Zola's protagonists). The economists call it 'primitive accumulation' or 'capital formation'. Verga calls it Mastro-Don Gesualdo Motta and characterizes it precisely in time and place. The novel is one of the very few true epics of the rise of capitalism.

In his presentation of Gesualdo, as well as of all the 'minor' characters in his novel, Verga is both following and furthering one of the major advances brought about by Realism and Naturalism. The Realists and Naturalists demolished the notion, central to both the classical literary tradition and to the Romantics, to both Christian and non-Christian writers and cultures from the Renaissance onwards, of the individual as an independent entity, making moral or practical choices in full freedom, and thus fully responsible for himself and for others. Without direct argument, this is now revealed as an abstraction. Individual and species, individual and environment, individual and society—in each of these antinomies, neither term can be conceived without the other, for each exists only in relation to the other, and without the other is a pure abstraction.

The greatest writers had always been tragically, because not 'scientifically', aware of the problematical nature of the individual considered as an autonomous universe. This notion, being the very centre of their view of man and of themselves, could not be shaken without profoundly disturbing them, or else radically altering their whole view of things. The autonomy of the individual is still central to Balzac, though not without strongly problematical and tragic implications. His characters are still moral entities. It is already in doubt in Flaubert and Turgenev, where the whole historical climate of an age, or the changed mental outlook of one generation succeeding another, *contains* individual volitions. In Italy, Manzoni's *The Betrothed* (1827)²⁵ had very clearly paved the way, but it found no true followers until Verga.

Gesualdo, then, transcends the individualism of a pre-Realist era of character presentation. He would be inconceivable outside the specific historical stage of development of Sicilian society, or outside the economic forces and forms which had arisen, then and there, and which Gesualdo himself, as an individual expressing some of the most advanced possibilities of his society, will carry forward and attempt (unsuccessfully in this case) to bring to fruition. History—as the dynamic process of interaction of individuals within their society and within their time—is now the locus of understanding and judgement. Only within that context can the responsibilities of individuals be meaningfully studied, and, by the same token, the responsibilities of society. Verga has taken us a long way, even if not all the way, towards this realization. This makes Gesualdo a historic figure: the drama is not only in the relations between persons, and their private emotions—the area into which the novel, even the social novel, is constantly in danger of shrinking and confining itself; but also in public action, in economic endeavour, in raw political struggle. And yet this brings no loss of intimacy or depth. The character is not impoverished, but enriched. Gesualdo is the most successful and greatest inward characterization in Italian literature.

Actually, living in a time when economic and social history had barely begun to be written, and when men of letters did not in any case regard such a study as their concern, Verga seems to have put the rise of Mastro-Don Gesualdo a decade or two too far back in history, relying on his own first-hand observation and on memories of his childhood.²⁶ We may perhaps regard this as nothing more than a slight slip, an insignificant departure from the Naturalist's scientific accuracy. But it might be an indication that the historical authenticity of *Mastro-Don Gesualdo* owes more to Verga's diligent and faithful observation of what was going on around him than to a fully-developed historical sense on his part. He may himself see his protagonist as a particular historical embodiment of a timeless and universal figure, 'economic man', rather than as the embodiment of a unique moment in the evolution of society. Verga did have an evolutionary notion of Progress, which reports about the great Universal Exposition in Paris in 1878 must have forcibly impressed on him, as on many of his friends who visited the exhibition. His preface to *The*

House by the Medlar Tree and the cycle of *The Vanquished* refers to
the grand inexorable onward march of Progress and to the in-
numerable obscure lives which it tramples underfoot, and which are
in fact his subject. In his preface to *Eva* he had also talked of his era
as the age of Industry. Yet he seems to envisage Progress on the one
hand in terms of scientific and technical discoveries, inventions, and
achievements, and on the other hand in moral terms. He seems not to
have understood the new forms of economic and social organization
except in terms of their visible results and symptoms—urban squalor
and social unrest. And yet, these had always existed: Naples and
Palermo could testify to that. So, although he hits on the drive towards monopoly as the brand-new characteristic of the brand-new
class represented by Mastro-Don Gesualdo, he does not seem to
grasp its historical significance.

Verga's carelessness towards history is also betrayed by the fact
that he assigns the disturbances of 1820 to 1821.[27] This is more surprising, though hardly more important. (Verga also has Bianca
married in July and her child born the following month. He does not
explain how Gesualdo fails to notice that Bianca was already with
child at her marriage. Flaubert's pen records a similar miracle in
Sentimental Education. Maternity is not the strongest field for male
writers, however Realist.) But it might suggest that the historical
setting of the novel is not done with complete seriousness, that it is
really a *pseudo*-scientific, a decorative element, part of the fashionable paraphernalia of Realism, calculated to foster the *illusion* of
authenticity, rather than essential to the internal authenticity of the
work. (One might suspect this also—but with a difference—of
Sentimental Education, where period atmosphere, to the casual reader,
seems to count for more than the historical processes—the difference
being that Verga seems to have caught the historical processes
independently of 'factual' history, reflecting the limitations of contemporary historiography.)

There are ways, then, in which *Mastro-Don Gesualdo* is a historical
novel, which was the very genre which the *veristi* in Italy had started
by rebelling against. Of course, it is a very different sort of historical
novel from those which were written in Italy before *verismo*. Nevertheless, the events described in the novel come to an end some two
score years before Verga was writing, and most take place before his
own date of birth.[28] If completed, the cycle of *The Vanquished*
would have brought Verga up to his own time (and *L'uomo di lusso*

would have brought him to his own person). But both Sicily and Progress would have been left behind—or so we must surmise from Verga's existing schemes for the work.

Now, for a Realist novelist, this is surprising. For it means that Verga was avoiding the critical period of Sicily's union with Italy after Garibaldi's famous expedition of 1860. Garibaldi's followers led the Sicilian peasants to believe that Unification would give them the rights which they and the Bourbon monarchy had for so long been striving to wrest from the usurpation and oppression of the baronage. In many parts of Sicily, bloody class war broke out in the wake of the Garibaldian advance, and was bloodily suppressed by Garibaldi's lieutenants, notably at Bronte.[29] As we have seen, Verga gives a foretaste of this in his account in the novel of the 1848 'revolution'. After Unification, the peasantry found that the new Kingdom of Italy showed *more* favour to the nobility than the Bourbons had done. Not only did it do nothing to restore to the peasants their land rights, but it increased the taxes that most hurt the peasants, and, worst of all, introduced conscription, which the gentry were able to evade through payment (as Verga himself did, ardent patriot though he was), but which the peasants could escape only by becoming outlaws. The result of all this was endemic revolt and lawlessness, culminating in a fresh full-scale uprising in Palermo in 1866, which took a naval bombardment and forty thousand troops to quell.[30] A full-scale civil war—nominally to suppress brigandage—was fought in Sicily and Southern Italy which lasted for two decades and cost more lives than all the wars for the Unification of Italy put together.[31] The barons and the brigand *squadre* between them gradually evolved that characteristically Sicilian form of organized anarchy which we call the Mafia. The novel exemplifies the first germs of this in the killing of Nanni L'Orbo, which serves the dual purpose of getting rid of the most dangerous peasant leader and of enabling the barons to turn the peasants' wrath against the supposed author of the crime, their rival, Gesualdo. There was little chance of escape or improvement for the unhappy island except through mass emigration.

Most of this was brought to public attention by two celebrated and soberly factual documents—the reports by Sonnino and Franchetti in 1877 and by Jacini in 1886. These were angrily dismissed by middle- and upper-class Sicilians as a slanderous conspiracy against their island by the northerners. It is hard to tell how far Verga shared the general view of his fellow-countrymen. It seems clear from *Mastro-Don Gesualdo* that he was critically aware of the rapacious and cynical machinations of his peers, and it seems more than likely that the Sonnino and Franchetti report was a cardinal influence on his development as a Realist.

On the other hand, he retained till the end of his life an unshakable faith both in the Kingdom of Italy and in the rightness of the social order. He was forthright in his views on the latter:

We were to leave today, but we are fortunate enough to have a strike here too, and there is no cab to take us to the station. The children are furious, but I ask myself what sort of freedom is this and what sort of civilization where the mob, that is the inferior, rule and command. Still, let them amuse themselves until the day comes when the *comrades* of one party and one country and those of another gobble each other up, as is logically bound to happen.

This tragically accurate prophecy comes in a letter of 1904 from Verga to his mistress³² (for he believed in love, but not in marriage—at least not for himself; just as he believed in nationalism, but not in military service, at least not for himself).

Holding these views, it is perhaps not surprising that Verga should avoid any direct Realist confrontation with that most troubled period in Sicilian history, which would have forced him into a radical critique of those notions and values which he held most dear. His Realist works never do more than tread the edges of this dangerous territory, coming closest to it in *The House by the Medlar Tree* and the short story *Rosso Malpelo*. Here are rivers of very real tears he was not Realist enough to tap. This is in keeping with Verga's table of social classes in the preface to *The Vanquished*, which purports to give a complete cross-section of society, and is quite odd even for the Sicily of his day, omitting the two largest classes—peasantry, and industrial or urban labourers. In 'ascending' order, he includes self-employed fishermen; the entrepreneur; the *parvenu* aristocrat; the politician; and 'l'uomo di lusso', the artist. Such a view of society was bound to draw the author's attention away from the class war and repression going on during his own life-time. And yet Verga's picture of baronial Sicily in *Mastro-Don Gesualdo* is already enough to explain that island's unhappy history, and it has been argued, as it has for Balzac, that Verga's very lack of sympathy for egalitarian ideas or movements saves him from facile humanitarianism or an idealized picture of the proletariat, and makes his 'the most convincing representation of the people produced in Italy during the nineteenth-century'.[33]

NOTES

1. Letter to Capuana, 25 Feb., 1881. See G. Verga: 'Storia de *I Malavoglia*: carteggio con l'Editore e con Luigi Capuana', with a note by L. and V. Perroni, in *Nuova Antologia*, 16 March, 1940, anno 75, fasc. 1632, pp. 130–1. The letter has also been republished in *Documenti e prefazioni del romanzo italiano dell'Ottocento*, ed. R. Bertacchini, Studium, Rome, 1969. Translations from Italian are mine, unless otherwise indicated. *Mastro-Don Gesualdo* itself is quoted from the Penguin translation by D. H. Lawrence (see n. 3.)
2. G. Verga, *I Malavoglia*, Treves, Milan, 1881, in *Opere*, ed. L. Russo, Ricciardi, Milan, 1955. Translated by E. Mosbacher, *The House by the Medlar Tree*, Weidenfeld and Nicolson, London, 1950. There is an annotated Italian text for English students, prepared by M. D. Woolf, Manchester University Press, 1972.
3. G. Verga, *Mastro-Don Gesualdo*, in *Nuova Antologia*, xiii–xxiv, 1 July–16 Dec. 1888, and republished in a much-revised book version by Treves in 1889. Present-day Italian editions are based on that brought out by Mondadori in 1940. Extracts from the first version are reprinted in G. Verga, *I grandi romanzi*, Mondadori, Milan, 1972. The translation by D. H. Lawrence was published by Thomas Seltzer, New York, 1923, and Penguin Books, 1970. The page-references in this chapter are to the Penguin edition. There is a critical monograph on Verga in English: T. Bergin, *Giovanni Verga*, Yale U.P., New Haven, 1931.
4. Jenkins, ch. I, p. 11.
5. See G. J. Becker, 'Introduction—Modern Realism as a Literary Movement', in *Documents of Modern Literary Realism*, Princeton U.P., 1963, pp. 3–38 (on Verga, p. 14).
6. The letter to Salvatore Farina first appeared as a preface to the story 'L'amante di Raja' in the Naples journal *Rivista nuova*, Feb. 1880. The story was republished, with the new title of 'L'amante di Gramigna', but with the same preface, as the opening story in the volume *Vita dei campi*, Milan, Treves, 1880. This original version of the prefatory letter differs slightly from that printed in the 1940 Mondadori edition of Verga's short stories, *Tutte le novelle*, Vol. I, on which subsequent editions of the preface are based, including that in D. Maxwell White's annotated Italian texts of '*Pane nero' and other stories* by Verga, Manchester U.P., 1962, and Giovanni Cecchetti's English translation, included in his Verga selection, *The She-Wolf and Other Stories*, University of California Press, 1958 (see pp. 86–8). Bertacchini's *Documenti e prefazioni*, op. cit., gives both texts of the letter (see pp. 226–9). All Verga's letters relating to his two great novels are reproduced in *I grandi romanzi*, op. cit.
7. See the last note.
8. See G. Verga, *The She-Wolf and Other Stories*, translation by Giovanni Cecchetti, op. cit., pp. 86–8.
9. One of the most important channels by which Zola's influence reached Italy was the 'Studio sopra Emilio Zola' by Francesco de Sanctis, which appeared in eleven parts in 1878 in the Neapolitan newspaper *Roma*. These, and other essays by De Sanctis on Zola and Realism, are published in De Sanctis' *Saggi critici* (ed. L. Russo,

and published by Laterza, Bari, 1952 and 1957). Capuana's view of Zola, Natural-
ism, and Realism can be studied in his collected essays, *Studii sulla letteratura
contemporanea*, Brigola, Milan, 1880, and Giannotta, Catania, 1882, and *Per l'arte*,
Giannotta, Catania, 1885. See also Carlo A. Madrignani, *Capuana e il naturalismo*,
Laterza, Bari, 1970.
General works on the influence of French Realism and Naturalism on Italian
verismo are: G. Marzot, *Battaglie veristiche dell'Ottocento*, Principato, Milan, 1941;
P. Arrighi, *Le vérisme dans la prose narrative italienne*, Paris, 1937; G. C. Menichelli,
Bibliographie de Zola en Italie, Institut français de Florence, 1960; R. Ternois, *Zola
et ses amis italiens. Documents inédits*, Les belles lettres, Paris, 1967, including an
essay on 'Zola et Verga'. See also Roberto Bigazzi, *I colori del vero : vent'anni di
narrativa, 1860–1880*, Nistri-Lischi, Pisa, 1969, and R. Bertacchini, *Documenti e
prefazioni*, op. cit.

10. Letter from Verga to Salvatore Paola Verdura of 21 April 1878, first published by
G. Villaroel in *Giornale dell'Isola*, Catania, 28 Jan. 1922. See Bertacchini, op. cit.,
pp. 230–1.

11. This preface appeared in the first edition of *I Malavoglia* and is always published
with the novel. Bertacchini's *Documenti e prefazioni* reproduces both this preface
and an alternative which Verga sent to his publisher at the same time. See Bertacchini, op. cit., pp. 242–6.

12. Edmond de Goncourt, *Les frères Zemganno*, 1879.

13. The first chapter of Verga's unfinished novel, *La duchessa di Leyra*, can be read in G.
Verga, *Opere* (ed. L. Russo), op. cit.

14. Federico De Roberto, *I vicerè*, 1894, translated by A. Colquhoun, *The Viceroys*,
1962, and Giuseppe Tomasi di Lampedusa, *Il gattopardo*, 1958, translated by A.
Colquhoun, *The Leopard*, 1960.

15. Italo Svevo (pseudonym of Ettore Schmitz), *Una vita*, 1892, translated by A. Colquhoun, *A Life*, 1963.

16. See Giovanni Cecchetti, 'L'elaborazione della fine del *Mastro-Don Gesualdo*', in his
book *Il Verga maggiore. Sette studi*, La Nuova Italia, Florence, 1968, and Romano
Luperini, 'I due *Mastro-Don Gesualdo*', in *Pessimismo e verismo in Giovanni Verga*,
Liviana, Padua, 1968, pp. 191–210 (see esp. p. 194 n. 1, and p. 201 n. 4).

17. A classic discussion of Verga's narrative style in *I Malavoglia* is Leo Spitzer,
'L'originalità della narrazione nei *Malavoglia*', in *Belfagor*, xi, n. 1, 1956, pp. 37–53.

18. It was Croce who first argued that the influence of Naturalism merely gave Verga a
'spinta liberatrice', a liberating shove. (See Benedetto Croce, 'Giovanni Verga', in
Letteratura dellaNuova Italia, iii, Laterza, Bari, 1922.) The argument on this point
can be followed in Luigi Russo, 'La lingua di Verga', added to the 1941 reprint of
his classic study, *Giovanni Verga*, Laterza, Bari, and in G. Raya, *La lingua del Verga*,
Le Monnier, Florence, 1962, esp. p. 17.

19. For Capuana's 'Comparatico', see A. Alexander, *Luigi Capuana's 'Comparatico,' a
story which made literary history*, Ciranna, Roma, 1970, and C. Di Blasi, 'Lu "cumpari" canto popolare . . . anonimo (ma del Capuana) e il "miracolo" verghiano', in
Luigi Capuana originale e segreto, Giannotta, Catania, 1968, pp. 81–95.

20. For De Sanctis' writings on Zola, see note 9 above.

21. See the already mentioned works on Verga by L. Russo and G. Raya.

22. See R. Luperini, op. cit., pp. 169–70.

23. The short story 'La roba' ('Wealth') is in *Novelle rusticane* (1883), now available in
G. Verga, *Tutte le novelle*, 2 vols, Gli Oscar, Mondadori, Milan, 1968 (see Vol. i,
pp. 282–7).

24. See Denis Mack Smith, *A History of Sicily* (2 vols): Vol. ii, *Modern Sicily: after
1713*, Chatto and Windus, London, 1968.

25. A. Manzoni, *I promessi sposi* (1st ed. 1825–7; revised ed. 1840–2), translated by A.

Colquhoun, *The Betrothed*, 1951, and B. Penman, *The Betrothed*, Penguin, 1973.

26. See Aurelio Navarria, 'Spunti storici nel *Mastro-Don Gesualdo*', in *Belfagor*, XI, 1956, pp. 528–41. Some of these points are taken up in R. Luperini, *Pessimismo e verismo*, op. cit., pp. 161–5.
27. See n. 26 above.
28. Verga was born in Catania, Sicily, in 1840, and died there in 1922. On Verga's life see, in Italian, G. Cattaneo, *Giovanni Verga*, U.T.E.T., Turin, 1963, and, in English, A. Alexander, *Giovanni Verga—A Great Writer and his World*, Grant & Cutler London, 1972.
29. See D. Mack Smith, *Modern Sicily*, op. cit., esp. pp. 439–40. A more detailed and very readable account of the same events in English can be followed in Raleigh Trevelyan's *Princes under the Volcano*, Macmillan, London, 1972, pp. 193–200.
30. See D. Mack Smith, *Modern Sicily*, op. cit., esp. ch. 49, 'Repression and Revolt', pp. 453–61. See p. 447 on Verga's avoidance of military service.
31. See note 30 above. Sicilian brigandage receives generous mention in two well-known books by E. J. Hobsbawm, *Primitive Rebels*, Manchester U.P., 1959, and *Bandits*, Weidenfeld and Nicolson, London, 1969, and Penguin Books, 1972.
32. Letter to Dina di Sordevolo of 22 Sept. 1904, in G. Verga, *Lettere d'amore* (ed. G. Raya), 3rd ed., Ciranna, Rome, 1971, p. 189. Verga's social attitudes are well known. See, for instance, G. Cattaneo, *Giovanni Verga*, op. cit., pp. 291–2, on Verga's approval of the bloody repression by the Italian Army of the agitation in Palermo in 1898.
33. Alberto Asor Rosa, *Scrittori e popolo*, Samonà e Savelli, Rome, 4th ed., 1972, p. 60. See also the same author's *Il caso Verga* (Palumbo, Palermo, 1972).

My cordial thanks to Professor B. Moloney, Elizabeth Mahler-Schächter and Wendy Joyce for their kind and useful comments on this chapter.

Theodor Fontane:
Effi Briest (1895)

DAVID TURNER

ON HIS last spool of tape Beckett's Krapp records a final attempt to recover the intensity of his dreams:

> Scalded the eyes out of me reading Effie again, a page a day, with tears again. Effie . . . (*Pause*). Could have been happy with her, up there on the Baltic, and the pines, and the dunes. (*Pause*). Could I? (*Pause*). And she?[1]

For a number of reasons the passage is something of a literary curiosity. After all, what business has the heroine of a Realist novel in the Theatre of the Absurd? More remarkable than that, however, is the fact that a non-German writer of our own day should have been acquainted with a German novel of the nineteenth century and should then have conceived the idea of introducing an allusion to it into his work, an allusion intelligible to only a tiny fraction of his audience. For although Fontane conforms least to the traditional conception of the German novelist—he wrote no *Bildungsromane*, he was not given to philosophical reflections—he has been no more successful than the rest in gaining an international reputation.[2]

In Germany the picture is different. Especially since World War II interest in Fontane has increased steadily, so that now, in both East and West, he has become the object of a major academic industry. Nevertheless, although it is customary for the critics to enlist the support of Thomas Mann, who regarded *Effi Briest* as one of the six best novels he knew and who earlier paid silent tribute to the work by taking the name of a minor character as the title of his own first novel, *Buddenbrooks*, one cannot suppress a lingering doubt whether Fontane has still met with genuine appreciation. And this doubt will remain as long as it is still possible for a German paperback version of the novel to display on its cover the title *Effie Briest* (Beckett as a foreigner may perhaps be forgiven the spelling mistake!) and for numerous scholars and critics to give the heroine a husband called I*n*stetten.

It is generally accepted that the German Realists were regional writers and that this fact alone reduces their exportability. Fontane too was a regional writer, but was more fortunate than most in that his region included the emergent metropolis, Berlin. Again, although largely self-taught and lacking a university education, he read widely in non-German literatures to the end of his life. Among the novelists he particularly liked were Scott, Dickens, and Thackeray; and among those for whom he had more of admiration or respect than real liking were Turgenev and Zola. Perhaps most important of all, Fontane had gained a perspective on life in Germany through his visits abroad, especially those to England, which had opened his eyes to the poten.ialities and dangers of a complex modern society.³ In his last completed novel, *Der Stechlin*, he takes as the central symbol a lake tucked away in the countryside of the Mark Brandenburg, yet possessing mysterious subterranean connnections, so that if there are volcanic eruptions elsewhere in the world, it joins in with its own rumblings. It is possible, I believe, to see in this lake a picture of Fontane himself: a writer who is in one sense regional in approach, but who is also very much aware of the big world outside and its social stirrings, and is able to relate the big and the small, the near and the far together.

If one stops to consider why Fontane's novels give a greater sense of the influences and tensions within a modern society than do the works of any of his fellow German Realists, a third factor must be added to his wider experience of the world and his intimate knowledge of a rapidly growing city: it is the simple point that he began his career as a novelist so late, at a time of great political activity, when Bismarck was at the height of his power, a time, too, of far-reaching social change, when Berlin was drawing vast numbers of workers from the land. Such events certainly coloured Fontane's thinking, as his many letters attest; and yet, compared with Balzac's portrayal of Paris, Galdós's portrayal of Madrid, or even Strindberg's panoramic view of contemporary Stockholm, it must be admitted that the picture his novels give of society in Berlin and its hinterland is considerably restricted in scope.

Fontane's late arrival also meant that he wrote most of his novels *after* encountering the works of Zola and the Goncourt brothers,

Theodor Fontane

and some time after the noisy eruption of German Naturalism in the late 1880s, which he observed with close attention as an unbiased yet acute theatre critic. The encounter with Naturalism, however, cannot be said to have changed the pattern of his writing to any marked degree; it proved rather to be a means of defining his own position more clearly.

Effi Briest comes last in this book, as is only right and proper in a chronological scheme of things. And yet it is worth emphasizing that Fontane is by no means the youngest author represented. He was born in 1819 and so belongs to the generation of Turgenev, Flaubert, and George Eliot rather than that of Howells, Verga, Galdós, or Strindberg. But it took nearly sixty years for him to find his métier as a novelist. Even his earlier *literary* activities were devoted to journalism, lyric poetry and ballads, and a group of travel books that combined elements of geography, history, local culture, and pure anecdote. After the publication of his first novel in 1878, however, there followed a steady stream of novels and stories until his death in 1898.

At various stages of his life, though more particularly during the later years, Fontane made numerous and important pronouncements which have a clear bearing on the problems of the Realist novel. In a double sense, however, these pronouncements were not dogmatic. Fontane was suspicious of 'absolute truths' and doctrinaire statements and so expressed his beliefs in terms that allowed for exceptions, that acknowledged both sides of the coin. Secondly, he was not by nature a theorist, who could develop abstract concepts and build them up into an internally consistent system, a dogma. His theories —if such they may be called—were derived from practical experience: from impressions gained by reading other authors, from the problems that arose in the writing of his own novels, or from public reaction to these works. Although he did publish literary reviews and essays, some of his most penetrating insights are to be found in his very readable correspondence, couched in simple, down-to-earth terms that the layman can readily understand. Since they are so undogmatic, it is more appropriate to introduce his literary ideas as they arise in conjunction with the particulars of the novel, rather than present, and to some extent misrepresent, them as a unified, systematized whole.

In *Effi Briest*, one of his last novels and published in 1895, Fontane followed a practice he had adopted before in basing his novel on an event from the 'chronique scandaleuse', as told him by the wife of the editor of the *Vossische Zeitung*. Remarkably enough, only a year later, in 1896, the same event was used as the basis of another novel, *Zum Zeitvertreib*, by Friedrich Spielhagen, a writer of society novels, known to Fontane, a man in fact with whom he corresponded about the writing of *Effi Briest*. Direct comparisons between the two novels are tempting, but must be treated with care, since it is unlikely that both writers had equal access to the same information. (We know, for example, that Spielhagen was well enough acquainted with the original 'Effi' to be in correspondence with her.)[4] Nevertheless a few simple points of contrast may be made here, which lead into the important question of treatment. While Fontane's interest is concentrated on the heroine, depicted as little more than a child who after only a few years of marriage drifts into an adulterous affair, Spielhagen makes his heroine a 'femme fatale' and then lays the greater stress on her unfortunate lover, a schoolmaster, who is ruined by the affair. Spielhagen also extracts the maximum of melodrama from his material: the lovers' embrace coincides with the sudden illness of one of the schoolmaster's children; the lovers are trailed by detectives and caught *in flagrante delicto*; and after the duel, in which desire for personal revenge is a strong motive in the wronged husband, the dead schoolmaster's widow physically assaults the heroine who has robbed her of her husband. Fontane, by contrast, with his customary distaste for sensationalism, keeps the emotional temperature cool throughout. Indeed, it is possible to argue that, in a similar way to George Eliot in aspects of *Middlemarch*,[5] Howells in *The Rise of Silas Lapham*, and Galdós in *Fortunata and Jacinta*, he has written his novel *against* the implied pattern of the popular romance or the cheap novel, just as he also did in his earlier masterpiece *A Suitable Match* (*Irrungen, Wirrungen*), where the unfortunate lovers, separated by insuperable class barriers, contemplate in turn the extremes of elopement and suicide, only in the end to reject both and opt for a modicum of happiness in basically loveless marriages with partners from their own class. Given the basic ingredients of Fontane's source, what may loosely be called the 'romantic' recipe for *Effi Briest* might read something like this:

A beautiful young heroine is forced by tyrannical parents into marriage with a much older man, who soon proves to be a monster. On the arrival of a handsome young officer she falls passionately in love and forms a liaison with him. The affair is discovered by the husband, who takes his revenge by shooting the lover in a duel and banishing his wife, whereupon she falls into deep remorse and spends her remaining years in a convent, while he leaves everything behind and goes off to Africa.

If that should appear an unnecessarily crude and meretricious invention, it is worth recalling that it is probably not so far removed from the sort of novel read by Flaubert's Emma before her marriage. And for that very reason it is a useful means of illustrating how Fontane circumvents the popular clichés, and in such a way as to underline some of the fundamental practices of the Realist novel.

In the first place, Effi's parents are not tyrannical and do not force her into marriage. There is much less blatant compulsion than, for example, Verga depicts in the marriage to which Isabella must submit in *Mastro-Don Gesualdo*. Instead the Briests apply more insidious, though still powerful *social* pressure to a daughter who is still only a child, appealing particularly to her ambition: she will be married before any of her schoolfriends and will therefore be one rung ahead on the climb up the social ladder. Although Effi herself has been sufficiently inculcated with the social attitudes of her parents to accept their view without protest, it is quite clear that there is no personal desire or fulfilment involved. When questioned by her friends about her feelings as a newly-betrothed young woman, she can answer only in the impersonal voice of one who reacts as society expects her to react:

'Is he really Mr. Right?'
'Of course he is. You don't understand, Herta. *Anyone* is Mr. Right. Of course, he's got to have a title and a situation in society and look presentable.'
'And so you're really happy already?'
'When *someone*'s been engaged for two hours, *they're* always really happy' [p. 26; my emphasis].[6]

Effi's marriage to Innstetten, especially its inauspicious start as they tour the cultural shrines of Italy, may remind us of Dorothea's marriage to Casaubon in *Middlemarch*. Yet the similarity is only superficial. For while Dorothea resists the social pressures, which are all against this particular union, and pursues her own ideal in the footsteps of St. Theresa, Effi, on the other hand, emerges as the consenting victim of a social ritual.

Second, Innstetten is no monster. And in his correspondence

Fontane had several times to defend him against what he saw as un-just or exaggerated attacks, especially from his female readers. True, like his Tolstoyan counterpart, Karenin, Innstetten is a man of ambition, character, and strict principle and has something of the punctilious schoolmaster about him. Yet Fontane is also careful to portray him as a good master of his servants, to distinguish him from the more reactionary and chauvinistic gentry who seem to dominate life in the neighbourhood of his Pomeranian home, to show him in acts of consideration for Effi, even moments of genuine longing for her return when she is away. The trouble is that he can-not express emotion without embarrassment, reserve, or the fear of somehow damaging his career. It is characteristic of him that he has to be prompted to kiss his wife. The fairest assessment of Innstetten is provided by Effi near the end of the novel in words which are spoken in a spirit of reconciliation, but which nevertheless imply an inescapable indictment: 'He had a great deal of good in his nature and was as fine a man as any one can be who doesn't really love' (p. 266).

Third, Effi does not fall desperately in love with Major Crampas, but drifts into the affair without real love, more out of dissatisfaction with her marriage, desire for adventure, and, perhaps also, the pro-vocative attraction of a man who is the very opposite of her husband. She knows nothing of that unique passion which so powerfully and repeatedly asserts itself in the adultery of Galdós's Fortunata. And Crampas himself, though something of a ladies' man, is nevertheless older than Innstetten, already married, and is physically deformed as a result of an earlier duel. Altogether it is difficult to visualize him as the dashing young hero.

Fourth and most notable of all, since it represents a significant adaptation of his source, Fontane has introduced a gap of some six years between the adultery and its discovery. A move from the Baltic resort of Kessin to Berlin has provided Effi with a means of breaking off the affair, to the relief of both Crampas and herself; she has put the affair behind her and begun a new life together with Innstetten in the more lively and interesting capital city. These six years of new life not only indicate that, given the appropriate cir-cumstances, her marriage might yet have succeeded tolerably well; they also mean that when Innstetten discovers the tell-tale letters, there can be absolutely no question of jealousy or revenge; indeed he openly admits that he still loves his wife. Instead the duel is fought

largely in deference to an abstract principle (honour) embodied in
the collective attitude of an abstract entity (society), which ultimately proves stronger than personal desire, stronger too than that
other important consideration in the novel, the healing effect of time.

Fifth, as to the question of penitence, the feelings that come
closest to this in the heroine are not activated by her banishment, but
pre-date the discovery by almost the full six years. They are not,
moreover, penitential and lack a truly religious dimension. In a rare,
extended passage of psychological analysis the heroine looks back
over her affair, but discovers no deep-seated sense of guilt, only the
fear of being found out and shame at the pretence she has been forced
to keep up. Indeed it is her very lack of a sense of guilt that causes her
greatest sorrow, for if all women are like that, it is bad for the world,
yet if others feel differently, then she alone is bad (pp. 200–1).
As far as Innstetten's final gesture is concerned, the mention
of an escape to Africa is not part of my invention. He does contemplate precisely that, late in the novel, when promotion has come
but he is no longer in a position to enjoy it. Yet the important and
characteristic point is that this essentially romantic notion is soon set
aside; he follows the advice of his friend and stays at his post, content to accept what little happiness comes his way (cf. pp. 260–2).

At every turn, therefore, Fontane disappoints any 'romantic'
expectations the reader might have and presents a more truthful picture of human behaviour. If it is argued that, compared with other
great novels, *Effi Briest* is a work lacking in passion, the point may
readily be conceded as long as it is not taken to imply a criticism.
Effi marries and commits adultery. Innstetten banishes his wife and
shoots her lover—all without passion. Yet this is precisely Fontane's
insight as a Realist: that in a society such as that of the late nineteenth
century in Germany it requires no overwhelming passion to cause
great suffering and wreck the lives of individuals—and that includes
Innstetten as well as Effi and Crampas. For it is one of the bitterest
ironies of the novel that the highest point of his career in social
terms—his decoration with the order of the Red Eagle—coincides
with his lowest moral and spiritual ebb, the time when he sees his
own life as a 'mess', his ambition as folly, society as 'fiddle-faddle',
that is to say, when he rejects all that has motivated his action and
behaviour hitherto.

In spite of the middle-class orientation of German Realism in general, in spite also of Fontane's own middle-class origins, he tended to draw the characters of his novels mainly from the lower ranks of the nobility, less frequently from the middle classes, and almost never from the working classes. From the social and political point of view he came to regard the Prussian *Junkers* as anachronistic, conceited, and unbearable, but his aesthetic judgement nevertheless pronounced them rewarding material for literary treatment.[7] The main characters of *Effi Briest* are also members of the gentry. Yet for all that they are quite unexceptional and remain completely within our intellectual and sympathetic grasp. Whatever the social background, Fontane's literary preferences lay always with the average man and woman in ordinary situations; and that meant a denial not only of Romantic excesses, but also of the Naturalist excesses he detected in the more degenerate characters of Zola and his German imitator, Max Kretzer,[8] the sort of excesses which, according to Georg Lukács, may be interesting clinically, but lack social typicality.[9]

Representativeness is easier to assert than to prove. And in the case of a novel like *Effi Briest* the sceptical scientific mind would probably require statistics showing the incidence of adultery, divorce, and duelling among the Prussian gentry in the last quarter of the nineteenth century before pronouncing judgement. The literary commentator may nevertheless be forgiven for presuming to argue, without statistics, that Fontane has here written much more than an individual history. In the first place, although the particulars of the novel have to do with adultery, divorce, and duelling, these in their turn raise much wider social issues: the power of convention and taboo, the possibility of individual freedom, the conflict between the natural self and the public persona, the relationship between the sexes and between parents and children. And in the second place, the reaction of Fontane's reading public is evidence that, especially in the depiction of his female characters, he frequently touched a raw nerve. After the publication of *Effi Briest* he had every reason to be alarmed, as he once confessed to being, at the prospect that the original of his heroine might one day pick up the novel and find her own story recorded there;[10] and yet he could also with equal justice describe the whole thing as 'a story of adultery no different from a hundred others'.[11] There is after all something symptomatic in an amusing yet touching little incident that occurred not long after the appearance of *A Suitable Match*. A woman came to see him and, in floods of tears, declared that *she* was the heroine, that he had written *her* story.[12] She was not of course the heroine. And yet, since Fontane had clearly captured the essence of her fate too, was she really so mistaken? The point of all this is well summed up in what he once had to say in countering the accusation that in publishing the earlier novel *L'Adultera* he had betrayed the secrets of a particular family: 'The explanation is probably that much in our social life is so typical that, if you are acquainted with the general state of affairs, you cannot fail to hit upon the particular case.'[13]

In considering how Fontane avoids popular clichés the importance of social factors has already begun to emerge. This aspect merits further discussion. Major social, political, and economic issues of the day (the rise of the proletariat, for example, or the problems of industrialization and capitalism) Fontane tends either to ignore in his novels or else to deal with only marginally. In *A Suitable Match* a group of workers are observed, but only at their lunch-break outside the factory; in *Der Stechlin* a modern glass factory appears, but quite literally on the horizon. In much the same way in *Effi Briest* the major political figures of the day, the Kaiser and Bismarck, are treated peripherally. Although Bismarck is the one who ultimately decides Innstetten's political and therefore social future, he, like the Kaiser, is kept just out of view all the time and appears most frequently as a topic of conversation. As to money, that obsession of the nineteenth century, which has been a crucial factor in so many of the novels discussed in this volume and is of considerable importance even in some of Fontane's other works—notably for the impoverished aristocracy in *A Suitable Match*, *Die Poggenpuhls* and *Der Stechlin*—it is practically ignored in *Effi Briest* and certainly never appears as a problem. The poor of Kessin, who live on the *edge* of the town, are mentioned only as their children *pass by* in their clogs. And towards the end favourable market conditions for Briest's crops constitute only one among a number of factors in his eventual decision to call his daughter home out of her banishment.

If one may describe this work as a social novel, it is in the double sense that it both portrays the day-to-day life of a given social class and casts a critical eye on some of its fundamental weaknesses. On the one hand, therefore, Fontane is content to operate within the conventions of the 'fashionable novel'[14] and reflect the social habits of his day—the pastimes of the gentry, their obligatory dinner-parties, amateur theatricals and musical evenings; the ladies' visits to the watering places and their shopping expeditions to the capital;

the treatment of servants, and so forth. His more critical scrutiny, on
the other hand, is directed towards the social problems associated
with love, sex, and marriage.

Notice particularly how important stages in Effi's fate as a woman
are marked and influenced by social attitudes and pressures. From
the conversation between the four schoolgirl friends in the opening
chapter it is clear that in their world marriage is regarded as the
highest aim in life; not to marry is a disgrace. That is why Effi's
sudden engagement is not really a surprise and why, incidentally, for
much of the rest of the novel her friend Hulda has to maintain the
(for the reader) comic pretence that she has a man in the offing,
while her mother can barely conceal her annoyance with Effi.
Marriage is the subject of a competition, and Effi has won.

After the heroine's marriage and move to Kessin her boredom and
dissatisfaction have their roots largely in social causes: the necessity
for people in their position to visit the local gentry in all their narrow-
minded provincialism, and the absences of Innstetten, who, with his
concern to make a successful career, cannot refuse invitations to go
and see Bismarck. Similarly, it is official duties which, although they
lead to promotion, also prevent him from accompanying his wife and
Crampas on their horse-rides and so help to throw them closer
together.

These causes of unrest Effi voices or at least is aware of. What she
does not complain about, presumably because it is accepted as a
matter of course in her society, is the way in which the wife is
regarded as an extension of, even appendage to the male: the way in
which Innstetten sees her as a means of gaining popular support for
his election victory (p. 68) or is concerned about the favourable
impression she will make at the Ministry in Berlin (p. 202). And one
may interpose that her very silence on this point, together with the
fact that she drifts into a liaison, makes it difficult to consider her
adultery as an expression of revolt against a patriarchal society in the
manner of other novels of adultery.[15]

After the end of the affair and the move to Berlin, why is Effi away
from home when Annie has her accident and the letters are discovered in the search for bandages? She is taking a cure to overcome
her temporary infertility so that she can provide Innstetten with a
male heir. And why does he not accompany her? He is too busy at
the office. Finally, after the divorce, why do her parents refuse for so
long to receive her back home? Because, writes Effi's mother, that

would cut them off from society and they must nail their colours to the mast, that is to say, show the condemnation of her act that society demands. In this unhappy state of ostracism the only ones to show genuine humanity and to give natural expression to their affection for Effi—and it is difficult to see this as anything but a judgement on the society of the day—are her clumsy, plebeian maid, Roswitha, and the dog Rollo.

In the long, important dialogue with his colleague Wüllersdorf that precedes the duel Innstetten says, 'There's no hatred or anything of that sort and I don't want to have blood on my hands merely for the sake of the happiness I've been deprived of, but the *something* which forms society—call it a tyrant if you like—is not concerned with charm or love, or even with how long ago a thing took place. I've no choice, I must do it' (p. 215). Innstetten's formulation smacks of the more extreme scientific determinism we normally associate with Naturalism, suggesting a conception of man as a creature deprived of free moral choices and subject instead to the influences of his environment. And the whole weight of these influences seems almost to operate like Fate—Atropos in nineteenth-century dress, so to speak. For the debate on the necessity of the duel, which takes in Crampas as well as Innstetten and Wüllersdorf, is framed by the two phrases 'Is it necessary?' (p. 212) and 'It's got to be done' (p. 219), which in the original German not only answer each other directly, but already possess fatalistic overtones from their use by Beethoven as a motto over the finale of his last string quartet: 'Muss es sein?—Es muss sein.' Taken as a whole, however, the novel speaks with a rather less deterministic, let alone fatalistic voice. The strength of social pressures is clearly exposed, but so also is the often active support they receive from the individual, including Effi herself, who is second only to Innstetten in her ambition. At one point or another most of the characters perceive the folly and fallibility of the social code, and yet they continue to live *as if* they still believed in it. As Wüllersdorf puts it, speaking what might almost be the motto of this society, 'All that high-falutin' talk about "God's judgement" is nonsense, of course, and we don't want any of that, yet our own cult of honour on the other hand is idolatry. But we must submit to it, as long as the idol stands' (p. 216). What is remarkable here is not only that traditional religious values have been replaced by social factors, but that these receive almost religious veneration even while their vanity is openly acknowledged.

Although the novel therefore acknowledges the importance of external pressures, it does not absolve the characters of blame, ignore their personal guilt: the homage paid by Innstetten to honour rather than affection, for example; his failure to tell Effi of the possibility of his promotion and move to Berlin (which might so easily have saved her from involvement with Crampas); or his excessive pedagogical impulse, revealed most tellingly in that scene where his young daughter is permitted to visit her divorced mother, but can only parrot the words 'Oh yes, if I *may*' (my emphasis); the ambition and lack of resolve in Effi herself; or her parents' promotion of what can scarcely fail to prove a misalliance; their inability to act at decisive moments; their emphasis on conformity and appearances rather than parental affection.

In this world of social reality, of ordinary people and unremarkable events, one thing in particular seems to stand apart from the rest. This is the Chinaman, the ghost that haunts the Innstettens' house at Kessin. J. P. Stern rather disparagingly calls it 'a piece of bric-a-brac left over by poetic Realism.'[16] Yet Fontane himself regarded it as crucial to the whole novel.[17] Certainly, it introduces an element of unresolved mystery, but it also acquires an important function on the level of the social, moral, and psychological lives of the characters. Innstetten uses it as a pedagogical weapon to keep his wife on the straight and narrow and also as a status symbol to enhance the interest and reputation of his house—without, however, committing himself as to the actual existence of the ghost. For Effi, on the other hand, it becomes an expression, sometimes even a projection, of her conscience and as such pursues her even after the move to Berlin.

In matters of narrative method Fontane always displayed a keen awareness of the need for accuracy of setting in the widest sense. 'I haven't the effrontery just to write things down without caring whether they are right or not', he wrote to his wife in 1885.[18] Consequently we find many topical references to important political events and personalities; to well-known cultural, religious, and scientific figures of the time; to the popular as well as the serious newspapers. Effi's mother pays a visit to a named eye-specialist of the day; when Effi herself goes on a cure, Fontane sends her to the right spa for her complaints; and of course, as a former dispensing chemist himself, he gives full and accurate details of the medicines prescribed for her by Dr. Rummschüttel.

The locations are of two kinds, the fictional and the real; and it is interesting to observe how the author's method differs accordingly. Effi's home, the manor-house at Hohen-Cremmen, is entirely fictional and so is created by the author in a lengthy and detailed description at the very beginning of the novel, a description whose solidity and homogeneity reflect something of the stable world from which his heroine is soon to be snatched away. Kessin, the Innstetten's home on the Baltic, is also fictional, although here Fontane has borrowed details from the town of Swinemünde, where he lived as a boy.[19] This setting too—town, house, and surrounding countryside—has to be created by description, although his method this time is to reveal the details piecemeal, as the heroine gets to know more of the place. When it comes to the third important location, Berlin, the author is of course faced with a different problem. To most of his readers it is a known quantity. Consequently, though in the sharpest contrast with Flaubert's treatment of the equivalent problem in his *Sentimental Education*, he virtually foregoes all description and contents himself with simply naming streets and districts, parks and public buildings, shops and restaurants, and leaves his readers to complete the mental picture.

In the matter of dialogue just as much as location Fontane was interested in accuracy. Indeed it is generally agreed that he was the first true master of natural dialogue in the German novel. Yet, much as one may admire his ability to use speech as a means of bringing his characters to life, of differentiating them as individuals or members of a particular social class, it must be stressed that this was achieved not by strict phonographic reproduction, but by a mixture of a keen ear and sheer artistry.

In all of these matters in fact—topicality, location, dialogue—Fontane held that accuracy of detail was subordinate to the total impression, a point made very clear in an illuminating letter of 1888, written in connection with the novel *A Suitable Match*. In it he speaks of his earlier practice where dialects were concerned, which was to have the speeches translated by an expert into the relevant dialect. The results, he comments, were disastrous; the effect was lifeless and clumsy. And so he reverted to his own approximations. Next he turns to the question of topographical accuracy, and lists a host of real or possible mistakes that might be spotted in his novel. And finally, he concludes with these words, the simple creed of an untheoretical Realist:

I'm convinced there is something wrong that could be found on every page. And yet I've made an honest attempt to describe real life. It just won't work. You have to be content if at least the overall impression is: 'Yes, that's what life is like.'[20]

One of the recurrent themes of the present volume has been the novelist's resolution of the conflict between the random nature of life itself and the demand for structure and organization in art, a conflict which in the eyes of one recent critic defines the history of the nineteenth-century novel as a whole.[21] In the early 1890s Fontane wrote a review of the German Naturalist play, *Die Familie Selicke*, a play which goes probably as far as is possible in practice in presenting an unstructured slice of life in a Berlin tenement block. While acknowledging that new ground had been broken, he sounded a note of caution: the experiment could hardly be repeated, since the public could not be expected to pay good money to see what was open to them every day on their own doorstep. Behind the comment lies a deep and consistent conviction: that however much art and life may impinge on each other, there is an important difference between them, and consequently that Realism consists in more than the mere copying of life.[22] To quote one of his own pronouncements, which in this case tackles the question from the opposite end: 'The only difference between real and fictional life is that of intensity, clarity, lucidity, and "rounding", and also therefore of that emotional intensity which is the transfiguring task of art.'[23] The notion of transfiguration, '*Verklärung*' in German, in fact occurs over and over again in the writings of the German Realists (Stifter, Storm, Keller, Raabe) when they are discussing the nature of poetic mimesis.[24] Sharing that important and widespread conviction of the need for transfiguration, a quality he found lacking in Zola, it is hardly surprising that Fontane did not hesitate to take liberties with his source: to lower the age of his heroine and increase the discrepancy between her age and that of her husband, so as to intensify the marital conflict; to introduce that gap of six years between the love-affair and its discovery, so as to throw greater weight on the social rather than personal causes of the duel and sharpen the implied criticism; to round off his novel with the heroine's death, when her prototype lived on and—though he could not have known it—reached the grand old age of ninety-nine!

Over and above that, *Effi Briest* is a highly organized work of art, which excludes extraneous matter and makes even the most trivial occurrences relate to the central issues. Consider, by way of example, such structural niceties as the way in which the opening chapter contains the germ of the whole novel, with its picture of the tomboy Effi and her love of danger, its anticipation of her fate in the solemn game with the gooseberry skins and the oriental tale of marital infidelity and its dire consequences; the way in which the novel returns to the opening scene at the very end, though with subtle, eloquent differences; the way in which the various settings are used to mark the different phases of Effi's life—the security of home and childhood at Hohen-Cremmen, the desert of married life at Kessin, the shattered hope of a new beginning in Berlin (even the locations seem fragmented in this phase), and the final return to home and a transfigured innocence back in Hohen-Cremmen;[25] the way in which leitmotifs—Effi's striped linen smock, her swing, the plane trees in the garden—are used to link important parts of the novel.[26] Two verbal leitmotifs, however, call for particular comment. The first is the catchphrase associated throughout with Effi's father, 'That is too big a subject' (*'Das ist ein zu weites Feld'*), which has since achieved proverbial status in the German language. It is more than a mere comic device; it is an expression, on the positive side, of his dislike of hasty, stereotyped, or absolute judgements and, on the negative side, of his inability to act as an individual and his unwillingness to take responsibility—the latter characteristics being important contributory factors in the fate that befalls his daughter. The catch-phrase is significantly absent during the conversation leading up to his decision to call his sick daughter home again, the one point where his supposed independence is put into practice, but it returns once more, a sad reflection on his basic incorrigibility, to round off the entire novel at the very end. The second verbal leitmotif will be completely hidden to readers of the present English version. It is contained in the words that Effi's exuberant friends call to her through the open window at the end of Chapter II, on the day of her engagement, the words which leave such a strong impression on Innstetten's somewhat superstitious mind, yet do not prevent him from going through with the marriage. In the original the identical words ('Effi, komm') are used as the simple message which Briest belatedly telegraphs to his daughter to call her home to Hohen-Cremmen before her death. A better translation to cover both occasions would, I believe, have been 'Come back, Effi'. For on both appearances the phrase is meant to convey the appeal (in the literal and figurative sense) of childhood and home. And we can be sure that the echo was important to Fontane, because he once reported that, as he listened to the story of the original 'Effi', it was the occurrence of this very phrase that first made him resolve to write the novel.[27]

The last twenty years of the nineteenth century witnessed an important critical debate in Germany on the subject of what was usually called 'objectivity'. What was in fact under discussion was the withdrawal of the narrator, or 'impersonality', as Jenkins calls it is his introductory chapter. And the paradoxes arising from the attempts to create an illusion of objectivity are nowhere more neatly summed up than in the fact that the main champion of the cause of 'objectivity', none other than the author of *Zum Zeitvertreib*, Friedrich Spielhagen, often managed in his novels to combine the withdrawal of the narrator with a considerable degree of, for example, political subjectivity by the simple expedient of using one of the characters as his mouthpiece. Spielhagen's aesthetic doctrine was expressed in an essay entitled '*Der Held im Roman*' ('The Hero in the Novel'), written in 1874 and published again in 1883 as part of a well-known collection, *Beiträge zur Theorie und Technik des Romans*. It was developed, interestingly enough, in direct opposition to the practice of George Eliot in *Middlemarch*, whom he accused (anticipating the criticism which Howells puts into the mouth of Penelope in *The Rise of Silas Lapham*) of interfering with her characters, forever divulging little secrets about them behind their backs. His formula for the modern novel, expressed in simple terms, was one whereby, instead of beginning, 'Once upon a time there were two boys, one called Paul and one called Peter, and Paul was good and Peter was bad', the author should introduce the two boys in the course of some human action, from which the reader would immediately be convinced of their existence; give *them* the opportunity to call each other by name; and finally provide sufficient material, by way of dialogue and action, for the reader to decide for himself who was good and who was bad.[27]

Now Fontane's first novel, *Vor dem Sturm*, was written under the general stylistic influence of novelists such as Thackeray, Dickens, Scott, and Scott's German follower, Willibald Alexis, writers who were not averse to letting their presence be felt or to making observations behind the backs of their characters. When therefore Fontane saw a review of his novel by a supporter of Spielhagen, who attacked 'the direct appeals to the reader, which jeopardize the poetic illusion',[28] he responded in a letter to his publisher with the words 'sheer nonsense' and enlisted the best English novelists in his defence.[29] None the less his subsequent practice did undergo a change, especially in his novels of modern society. In these works, which also of course include *Effi Briest*, he usually kept his presence as narrator very much in the background and let the story tell itself as much as possible. In later years too, in his correspondence with Spielhagen, he gave general approval to the latter's theory, always, however—in his characteristic manner—reserving the right to make exceptions, leaving a loop-hole open:

The intrusion of the narrator is nearly always a bad thing, or at least superfluous. And what is superfluous is wrong. At the same time it won't always be easy to determine where the intrusion begins; the writer in his capacity as writer must after all do and say a great deal, otherwise it won't work, or will be artificial. The only thing is he must avoid making judgements, delivering sermons, trying to be wise and clever.[30]

What we find in *Effi Briest* therefore is a fairly complete withdrawal of the narrator as a discernible personality. He describes locations and events, even summarizes occasionally. For the rest Fontane relies very much on dialogue as a means of narrating events or commenting on them and, more especially, as a means of characterization. He is also able very often to depend on his skill at distinguishing his characters by their manner of speech in order to avoid those editorial allocations 'he said', 'she replied', and so forth. Only very rarely is this pattern of non-intrusion broken, and the effect is inevitably one of surprise. In Chapter XXXII, for example, Fontane rather affectedly asks the rhetorical question, 'Was Roswitha with Effi, then?' in order to introduce a brief flashback of recent happenings. And, perhaps most remarkable of all, near the very end he permits himself a sympathetic sigh: 'Poor Effi, you spent too long looking up at the marvels of the heavens and thinking about them and in the end the night air and the mists rising from the pond stretched her once more on a bed of sickness' (p. 264).

Although Fontane has virtually renounced the possibility of commenting himself on the events of the novel and the problems facing the characters, *Effi Briest* is by no means without implied comment, even criticism. In the first place, he seems to anticipate some of those many questions which naturally arise from time to time in the reader's mind about the course of the heroine's life as a woman. Would she have done better to resist the general pattern of marriage and choose another role in society? If Innstetten had kept her informed about the move to Berlin and she had never become involved with Crampas, or if her letters had not accidentally been discovered, what would have been the future of her marriage? Would her fate have been worse, or even different, if she had belonged to a different social class? But the answers Fontane provides are not to be found in any overt statements; they are implied rather in those other female portraits of the novel, which together form a series of variations on the theme of woman's role in society.

Effi's own mother is present from the start as an example of the social norm, the woman who has married not for love, but for the security offered by an older man, and who now lives out her life in a prosaic, unremarkable, but tolerably happy marriage, which is essentially the sort of marriage that the heroine's might have become if those letters had not been discovered. In Sidonie von Grasenabb Fontane presents a picture of the unlovely and unloving spinster, who lives out her days in narrow-minded, malicious bigotry. This alternative to the customary marriage, which is perhaps also a warning of the fate that awaits Hulda Niemeyer, is clearly more disagreeable than the prose of marriage. Frau Zwicker, the widow who accompanies Effi on her visit to the spa, exemplifies the woman who is now freed from the constraints of marriage and so can afford to be liberal in her ideas, for example in sexual matters (she is the one who reads Zola's *Nana*); but she has little moral substance and is in any case an exceptional character. This last point also applies to the figure of Mme Tripelli (*alias* Trippel), the daughter of a free-thinking Lutheran clergyman, an emancipated woman and a singer, now associating with a Russian prince. She has a blunt, self-assured manner and brings a welcome breath of fresh air into the novel. But she is acceptable only because she is an exception. She does not represent a role in society that could work for more than a few women. Indeed it is one of the paradoxes of Mme Tripelli that, although she can afford to be a free-thinking individual, she supports strict religious orthodoxy in public matters (p. 92). In other words, it is permissible for the individual to follow this course by way of exception, but it will not work for society as a complex whole. Among the lower classes the most important variation is provided of course by the story of Roswitha, not only because of the interest it arouses in Effi herself, but because it presents another version of the rejection that follows adultery and its discovery. Here it takes the form of a physical assault with a red-hot iron by her blacksmith-father. But who is to say it is ultimately more cruel than the social ostracism, the spiritual and emotional isolation, imposed by Innstetten and Effi's parents?

In addition to this variation technique Fontane makes skilful use of leitmotifs and symbols, of structural elements altogether in fact, to make his point. Consequently it is never sufficient simply to make the structurally interesting point that he has introduced into Effi's life at Kessin three important male characters, her husband, Major Crampas, and the eccentric, deformed apothecary, Gieshübler. His purpose is to make us aware of his heroine's various needs, which fail to find satisfaction in her marriage. Innstetten answers to her ambition, but is too reserved and too busy; Crampas answers to her love of danger and adventure, but is untrustworthy; and Gieshübler answers to her need for affection and loving consideration, but would be ridiculous if considered as a lover and a social embarrassment if considered as a husband. Again, it is possible to show that Fontane has punctuated his narrative at important phases by reflective dialogues between Effi's parents—one on the day after her marriage, one after a visit of Effi, following the move to Berlin and the break with Crampas, one at the very end after her death. But in that repeated preposition 'after' lies the clue to Fontane's implied criticism. For it is characteristic of the Briests that they are wise *after* the event and fail to act at the right moment. Even the title of the novel is more than merely a reference to the central character. After all, Effi is married in only the fifth out of thirty-six chapters and so for the greater part of the novel is Frau von Innstetten. In the two other nineteenth-century novels that are sometimes compared with this, *Anna Karenina* and *Madame Bovary*, the authors have chosen either the heroine's married name or, with added detachment, her social appellation as a married woman. Fontane, on the other hand, wishes to remind us in his title—as he also does by the cyclical structure of the novel and the simple inscription on his heroine's gravestone— that she was little more than a child who ought not to have been transplanted so young from her native soil at Hohen-Cremmen.

By now it will perhaps be apparent that Fontane's characteristic mode of narration entails not only withdrawal, but also much oblique statement, the use of hints. Since it is a method which relies very much on the attentive, imaginative co-operation of the reader, things can go wrong—and on one notorious occasion did go wrong in a rather elementary matter. Not long after the publication of the novel Fontane received a letter from a puzzled lady reader, inquiring whether adultery had actually taken place. In his reply he could not of course point to a particular spot in the narrative; all he could do was to draw her attention to some of the subsequent details that *implied* the adultery.[31]

Clearly we have here a reflection of the prudery of the times—and the novel provides its own humorous gloss on this prudery in the little incident where Effi's maid, Roswitha, sent to the lending library to borrow books for her mistress, deletes one title from the list on her own initiative, because it includes the word 'trousers' (p. 182). At the same time it must be remembered that Fontane himself, though by no means a prude, preferred discretion in his novels, not only in sexual matters. Note, for example, the brevity, the understatement of his account of the duel (p. 221); contrast the elegiac quietness of Effi's death, not actually narrated but reported retrospectively, with the explicit and detailed horror of Emma Bovary's death. Fontane also refrained from prying too closely or too often into the minds of his characters, choosing much of the time to externalize their mental state or to reveal it by means of gesture and speech—the manner of their speech, the things they avoid saying as well as those they do say.

Outstanding instances of externalization are the way in which the heroine's moral and spiritual uncertainty, insidiously undermined by the advances of Crampas, is projected in the image of the Slough, the quicksand through which she must pass in Chapter XXII,[32] and the way in which her renunciation of all participation in life and society and her melancholy reflection on the fleeting association with Crampas are evoked by the picture of her near the end of the novel, as she sits watching the trains pass by and observes 'two plumes of smoke which merged with each other for a moment and then went off separately again to left and right' (p. 263). As far as the relation between psychology and dialogue is concerned, one must keep in mind one of the shrewdest comments that Frau von Briest makes about her daughter: 'She certainly feels the need to talk now and again but she doesn't feel the need to empty her heart out, and she keeps a lot to herself; she's informative and discreet at the same time, almost secretive' (p. 42). For an important consequence of this is that the reader must be acutely attentive to the nuances of her speech, to the many unwitting half-revelations: to that illogical but all too understandable request for a fur-coat, for example, which lights up like a flash her subconscious dread of marriage away from home (p. 33); to those confused expressions of uncertainty at the amateur theatricals directed by Crampas, which betray her fear of his insidious influence on her marital fidelity (p. 135); to her passionate concern at the plight of some shipwrecked sailors and her excessive relief at their rescue, which give us a brief glimpse of her own anguished sense of moral danger (pp. 155–6); to the rebuke she gives Roswitha for dallying with the coachman, which is in reality a warning to herself (p. 163); or to her almost morbid interest in the detailed life-story of her maid, Roswitha, precisely because it mirrors her own painful situation. All of this is part of Fontane's characteristic art of suggestion.

J. P. Stern sees the perennial mode of realism as one of balance, as a middle course between extremes;[33] and J. M. Ritchie describes German Realism in terms of ambivalence.[34] The Realism of *Effi Briest* possesses something of both these qualities. It pays due homage to the given facts of the world and strives for accuracy in their presentation, but it also imposes its own structure and order; its author does not intrude his own personality, yet he is able to make his attitudes felt by less overt means; its subject-matter verges on the sensational, but the treatment is entirely unsensational; it portrays individual fates and at the same time manages to suggest a wide social reality; it presents characters whose attitudes and behaviour are very much influenced by the collective ethos of their environment, but it also reveals their individual responsibility.

The total result of this for the reader, besides aesthetic pleasure, may be a more sympathetic understanding of the human condition, an intensity, even clarity of vision; yet it is also likely to entail some uncertainty of response. The society Fontane portrays is clearly unsatisfactory; its standards are hollow, its conventions are rigid and lifeless and help to cause considerable suffering. 'Would it therefore be better', the reader may well wonder, 'to escape altogether or to fly directly in the teeth of society?' The answer which the novel, through its characters, seems to give is a resigned 'No'. The advice, as we have seen, is rather to stay where you are and accept what little happiness life may afford you. What, then, is the reader to make of these characters? Are they the only conceivable heroes of such a world? Or are they perhaps just fools? That is *too* big a subject.

NOTES

1. Samuel Beckett, *Krapp's Last Tape* and *Embers*, Faber, London, 1965, p. 18.
2. Cf. Brian A. Rowley, 'Theodor Fontane: A German Novelist in the European Tradition?', *German Life and Letters*, xv (1961), 71–88.
3. Cf. Hans-Heinrich Reuter, 'Fontanes Realismus', in *Fontanes Realismus: Wissenschaftliche Konferenz zum 150. Geburtstag Theodor Fontanes in Potsdam*, ed. Hans-Erich Teitge and Joachim Schobess, Akademie-Verlag, Berlin, 1972, especially pp. 44–6.
4. Letter of Spielhagen to Fontane dated 23 February 1896, quoted in *Erläuterungen und Dokumente: Theodor Fontane: Effi Briest*, ed. Walter Schafarschik, Reclam, Stuttgart, 1972, p. 93.
5. Compare, for example, the way in which the author deliberately avoids writing the romance which would simply cast Casaubon as the dragon, Dorothea as the damsel in distress, and Will Ladislaw as the young knight who rescues her (Chapter XXI). See also the earlier chapter on *Middlemarch* in the present volume, p. 126 above.
6. All quotations from *Effi Briest* are taken from the translation by Douglas Parmée published in the series of 'Penguin Classics', Harmondsworth, 1967.
7. See Paul Böckmann, 'Der Zeitroman Fontanes', *Der Deutschunterricht*, xi (1959), especially 66–70.
8. Pierre Bange, 'Fontane et le Naturalisme: Une Critique Inédite des Rougon-Macquart', *Etudes Germaniques*, xix (1964), 142–64; and Theodor Fontane, 'Max Kretzer: Drei Weiber', *Aufzeichnungen zur Literatur: Ungedrucktes und Unbekanntes*, ed. Hans-Heinrich Reuter, Aufbau-Verlag, Berlin and Weimar, 1969, pp. 111–12.
9. Georg Lukács, 'Der alte Fontane', quoted from *Erläuterungen und Dokumente*, p. 136.
10. Letter to Marie Uhse dated 13 November 1895. Quoted from *Dichter über ihre Dichtungen: Theodor Fontane*, ed. Richard Brinkmann and Waltraud Wiethölter, Heimeran, Munich, 1973, ii. 453.
11. Letter to Friedrich Spielhagen dated 21 Feb. 1896, ibid. ii. 460.
12. Letter to Paul Schlenther dated 20 Sep. 1887, ibid. ii. 370.
13. Letter to Joseph Viktor Widmann dated 27 April 1894, ibid. ii. 273f.
14. See Peter Demetz, 'Über Fontanes Realismus', *Orbis Litterarum*, xvi (1961), 34–47.
15. Cf. Judith Armstrong, *The Novel of Adultery*, Macmillan, London, 1976.
16. J. P. M. Stern, '*Effi Briest, Madame Bovary, Anna Karenina*', *Modern Language Review*, lii (1957), 366.
17. Letter to Joseph Viktor Widmann dated 19 Nov. 1895, *Dichter über ihre Dichtungen*, ii, 454.
18. Letter to his wife dated 3 June 1885, ibid. ii. 394.
19. See Mary E. Gilbert, 'Fontanes *Effi Briest*', *Der Deutschunterricht*, xi (1959), 65.
20. Letter to Emil Schiff dated 15 Feb. 1888, *Dichter über ihre Dichtungen*, ii, 371f.
21. Walter Killy, *Wirklichkeit und Kunstcharakter*, Beck, Munich, 1963, p. 16.

256

Theodor Fontane

22. See Bange, 'Fontane et le Naturlisme', p. 156.
23. See Reuter, 'Fontanes Realismus', p. 43.
24. See Wolfgang Preisendanz, 'Voraussetzungen des poetischen Realismus in der deutschen Erzählkunst des 19. Jahrhunderts', in: *Formkräfte der deutschen Dichtung vom Barock bis zur Gegenwart*, ed Hans Steffen, Vandenhoeck & Ruprecht, Göttingen, pp. 199–202.
25. Cf. Richard Quabius, 'Die Gestaltung des Raumes in Theodor Fontanes Roman *Effi Briest*', *Acta Germanica*, v (1970), 133–52.
26. Cf. Gilbert, 'Fontanes *Effi Briest*', pp. 63–75.
27. Letter to Spielhagen dated 21 Feb. 1896, *Dichter über ihre Dichtungen*, ii, 460.
28. Friedrich Spielhagen, *Beiträge zur Theorie und Technik des Romans*, Stackmann, Leipzig, 1883, p. 92.
29. The review by Eugen Zabel appeared in the journal *Mehr Licht*, i (1878), no. 13, and is quoted here in translation. See also Emil Aegerter, *Theodor Fontane und der französische Naturalismus: Ein Beitrag zur Geschichte und Theorie des naturalistischen Romans in Deutschland und Frankreich* (Diss. Berne), Heidelberg, 1922, p. 35.
30. Letter to Wilhelm Hertz dated 14 Jan. 1879, *Dichter über ihre Dichtungen*, ii, 231.
31. Letter to Spielhagen dated 15 Feb. 1896, ibid. ii, 456f.
32. Letter to an unknown lady, quoted in *Erläuterungen und Dokumente*, pp. 109f.
33. Cf. Gilbert, 'Fontanes *Effi Briest*', pp. 72f.
34. J. P. M. Stern, *On Realism*, Routledge & Kegan Paul, London, 1973, pp. 103, 114, 122, 142, 173.
35. J. M. Ritchie, 'The Ambivalence of "Realism" in German Literature 1830–1880', *Orbis Litterarum*, xv (1961), 200–17.

The Practice of Realism

D. A. WILLIAMS

THE NOVELS examined in this book were written in different languages, from within different cultural traditions and with a different body of life on which to feed. They need not, however, be confined within the context—linguistic, literary or living—in which they were produced. In the first place, it is clear that the novelists themselves were responsive to the aims and achievements of Realists in other countries. Balzac provided the world with the prototype of Realism; all Realists—in particular, Strindberg and Howells—are indebted to him and all Realists—in particular, Flaubert—felt the need to modify the prototype. Turgenev was an international literary figure, known to Flaubert and Strindberg, greatly admired by Howells and Fontane and himself familiar with the work of the major French novelists. The development of French Realism was also closely followed by Howells, Strindberg, Galdós, and Verga. In some cases, of course, there were reservations; Howells was critical of George Eliot's direct intrusions in *Middlemarch* whilst she could hardly have approved the absence of subjective, or evaluative commentary in a novelist like Flaubert. But quite apart from the strong inter et that they show in each other's work, the Realists can be viewed collectively by virtue of the profound mimetic urge which underlies and determines much of their literary practice. The novelists discussed have much in common because they are all fired by the same naïve enthusiasm, the same quixotic passion for the real, a passion admirably captured by James when he described Balzac as 'charging with his heavy, his heroic lance in rest, at every object that [springs] up in his path'.[1] What the Realist comes across as he ventures forth on the high road varies considerably but his reaction to it is remarkably constant. Faced with 'that tempting range of relevancies called the universe' (G. Eliot), the Realist's attitude is one of repressed gluttony. Knowing the dream of total absorption of the real to be impossible, the Realist resigns himself to working with a scaled-down model of reality. The fictional world cannot possibly capture or cover the whole of reality but, skilfully designed and carefully structured, it can provide a paradigm of the conditions and circumstances, laws and relationships which are deemed to prevail in the 'real' world. In constructing his working model, the Realist aims at being as complete and comprehensive as possible, at totalizing as well as miniaturizing the real. George Eliot's Middlemarch and Galdós's Madrid are both marked by a striving for totality, by the desire to represent all sections of society, to depict the full range of human activity, to show reality in all its complexity and variety. In the past literary conventions governing what was appropriate subject-matter had allowed novelists to leave a good deal out, but the Realist, like the scientist, is committed to the view that no aspect of reality is 'beneath the dignity of his inquiry' (Howells). Consequently, he has to make room for a whole range of new material, for characters of low social status—though the coverage given to the life lived by the majority is, with the exception of Galdós, not as extensive as might be expected; for the dull routines of provincial life; for a good deal of experience which is humdrum or unpleasant; for the mundane conversation and banal texture of everyday life; for the unremarkable bulk of the physical world. A special place is generally reserved for all that makes life harsh and disagreeable for, as one critic puts it, 'the painful is . . . the very nerve of representation'.[2] In addition to the brutal facts of illness and death, the Realist picks out various forms of emotional anguish generated by the failure of reality to live up to expectations or human beings to love or understand one another. Tears flow in abundance, tears which may be 'hot and silent' like those of Bianca in *Mastro-Don Gesualdo* or effusive like those of the lovesick Louise Roque or the homesick Effi.

The Realist's urge to be comprehensive is restricted to a greater or lesser extent by the novelistic imperative to tell the story of an individual or group of individuals. In some cases (*Effi Briest, Mastro-Don Gesualdo*) the title itself is an indication that the novel will be mainly concerned with a single person. In other cases (*Middlemarch, Fathers and Sons*) the title gives notice of wider ambitions. But just as the 'panoramic' or 'multifocal' novels tend to be dominated by one character—Lucien, Bazarov, Dorothea, Fortunata—so the 'imaginary biographies'[3] do not focus consistently on the main character. The limitations inherent in the latter form can, in fact, be overcome in several ways; the hero can be made to circulate through a wide variety of social milieux so that the reader, like Falk, can have 'the opportunity to observe man as a social animal in every possible aspect' (*The Red Room*, p. 157). Where mobility is restricted—as is the case with most of the female characters—the predicament of the protagonist can be made to illustrate a general pattern. Fontane's study of the trials of the married woman allows him to explore the nature of the restrictions imposed upon the individual by society. Lastly, in dramatic or emotional confrontations, the other side's point of view can be presented. A sense of expansiveness is created when the feelings of Madame Arnoux, of Casaubon, or of Innstetten are described. Lucien, Frédéric, Falk all have friends whose point of view is intermittently adopted. Thus, whilst in every case one character is used as a unifying agent, this does not mean that the fictional world becomes too narrow to suggest the complexity and variety we attribute to 'reality'.

When constructing their working model of reality, the majority of the novelists considered employ the technique of impersonality which, Jenkins argues, allows the Realist to resolve the conflict between objectivity and subjectivity. The ideal of impersonality is consciously adopted in several cases. Howells is strongly opposed to any novelist who 'permits himself to come forward and comment on the action'; Fontane states that 'the intrusion of the narrator is nearly always a bad thing'; Verga and Flaubert share the belief that the author should be invisible, that he should disappear *into* rather than *from* his fictional world which, as a result, 'will seem to have made itself' (Verga) or to be 'a second nature' (Flaubert[4]). Absolute impersonality is, however, not easily attained. The problem, as Fontane saw, was that 'the writer in his capacity as writer must after all do and say a great deal, otherwise it won't work, or will be artificial'. Writing a novel is primarily a question of telling a story and the material which makes up the story of necessity must originate from and be presented by a narrator, avowed or implied. But although the need for a narrator can never be overcome, an impression of impersonality can be created if the narrator avoids 'making judgements, delivering sermons, trying to be wise and clever' (Fontane). The apparent objectivity of the Realist is the result not of dispensing completely with the narrator but of his withdrawal as a discernible personality. This withdrawal is never complete; few Realists succeed in bringing the narratorial presence down to zero

degree. Howells allows the narrator to condemn Lapham's behaviour; Flaubert's narrator embarks upon an impassioned critique
of early Socialism; Strindberg's narrator speaks *ex cathedra* about
the abuses of modern society; in *Effi Briest*, the narrator may be
heard to heave 'a sympathetic sigh' and even Verga—who comes
closest to being completely impassive—allows his hand to slip on one
occasion and tugs unashamedly at the reader's heartstrings. But it is
doubtful whether these occasional lapses into misplaced out-
spokenness seriously mar the overall impression of narratorial
impersonality.

Having definite opinions and being prepared to pronounce judgement is one thing, enjoying a certain amount of omniscience is
another. Although, generally, he does not emerge as a recognizable
human being, the narrator needs to be omniscient if the Realist is to
provide the insight into the way both society and individuals work
which his claim to be either annalist or analyst implies. Whether he is
giving a historical survey of the conditions of an earlier age or an
'archaeological' account of vanishing architecture, whether he is dissecting hidden motives with his scalpel or peering down his microscope at 'the play of minute causes', the Realist cannot but exercise
the prerogative of omniscience. Omniscience facilitates the novelist's
task in giving antecedents, defining character, portraying the inner
life, describing the physical setting or mapping out historical
developments. Of all the novelists, Verga makes least use of omniscience, dispensing with linking narrative and withholding information about the past and nature of the protagonist, with the result
that the story hardly seems to be told at all, but even in this extreme
case the postulate of a latent omniscient narrator is necessary if
there is going to be someone to assume responsibility for the 'barest
bones of narrative and description' or justify the access which the
reader has to the inner thoughts and impressions of Gesualdo.

Although no Realist dispenses with omniscience altogether, all
restrict their use of it. In some cases, the novelist makes the narrator
parade his uncertainty or his ignorance. Howells and Flaubert use
words like 'perhaps' in connection with motivation to disclaim absolute knowledge; in emotionally crucial scenes, the narrator will often
tread delicately or avoid 'prying too closely into the minds of his
characters' (Turner); even a novelist like George Eliot who does not
share the reservations of other Realists about omniscience, makes
effective use of the narrator's ignorance when she writes of the final

uniting of Dorothea and Will that 'it was never known which lips were the first to move towards the other lips' (p. 869). Discretion, clearly, on occasions is the better part of omniscience. As several contributors point out, the 'dramatic' or 'scenic' method of presentation is often used by the Realist as a result of his desire to be impersonal. James's comment on Turgenev—'Everything, with him, takes the dramatic form'—applies equally well to several other novelists, Verga, in particular. The extensive use of dialogue, which is associated with the dramatic mode, gives the work of several novelists immediacy; as Henry points out, it 'enhances the illusion that events occur entirely in the present', whilst also 'giving the illusion that [the characters] are acting independently' (Foster). The reader has the impression of being in closer contact with the real since the same substance (language) makes up what is being imitated and what is doing the imitating. Character, several contributors emphasize, rather than being clearly defined at the beginning, often emerges or is revealed gradually through words and actions and the same could be said of the main ideological differences. The Realist puts his trust in the ability of the reader to draw the appropriate inferences from what characters say or fail to say, or from the discrepancy between what they say on one occasion and what they do or say on another. In some cases—in *Fathers and Sons* and *Fortunata and Jacinta*, in particular—a 'stagey quality' can be detected when characters are made to overhear conversations or disguise their true meaning and there is also a danger that dialogue will become diluted if used too extensively. Dialogue seems, on the whole, to work best when there is a clear ideological confrontation (as in *Fathers and Sons*), a clear social confrontation (as when the Coreys invite the Laphams to dinner) or a violent dramatic conflict (as in *Mastro-Don Gesualdo*). For subtler effects, the novelist needs to have recourse to other devices, such as the controlled use of the physical setting to reflect mood.

Most Realists avoid too heavy a reliance on dialogue, feeling a periodic need to go inside character. It is arguable that the almost unbroken use of dialogue in *Mastro-Don Gesualdo*, when contrasted with its more intermittent use in the other novels, produces precisely the effect of artificiality which Verga wished to avoid; Gesualdo's fictional life depends so much on the words he utters that he seems curiously incomplete when compared with characters in other novels. Verga's preference for 'external' rather than 'internal' observation of character represents the most consistent and thorough-going attempt to restrict the narrative to what plausibly could be known to another human being and may therefore seem 'empirically true' but it violates the reader's knowledge that an individual's experience includes an internal flow of thoughts and impressions which is not open to empirical investigation. Omniscient analysis may in itself be epistemologically unsound but it does allow the novelist to present the full range of human experience. Verga's reticence about what goes on 'inside' character is, in fact, atypical; most Realists are ready to report on the inner life at appropriate moments, combining 'internal' and 'external' observation. On the whole the Realist prefers to render rather than summarize the contents of his character's mind. The most extensive rendering of the inner life is found in *Sentimental Education*, much of which consists of an account of Frédéric's perceptions. The effects of point of view are similar to those of dialogue; the *style indirect libre* which characterizes Flaubert's method of rendering Frédéric's experience has been described as 'a strategy through which the narrator appears to withdraw from the scene and thus present the illusion of a character's acting out his mental state in an immediate relation with the reader'.[5]

The technique of impersonality is not adopted by all the novelists examined in this work. The narrator of *Fortunata and Jacinta* claims to be personally acquainted with several of the characters and to have gained much of his information from minor characters like Villalonga or Estupiñá and he also freely expresses his views on a wide variety of topics. As Macklin points out, however, the narrator is not to be equated with the author; he is used, rather, to authenticate the account given and his 'complacent, almost bland, vision of society' is gradually eroded. Galdós sets up the same ironic perspective on the narrator's view of the *pueblo* as on Juanito's; the narrator is therefore closer to the characters than to the author at the beginning, though subsequently he will 'display great psychological omniscience with regard to a character's inner thoughts and feelings'. In contrast, the narrator in *Lost Illusions* and *Middlemarch* seems close, if not identical, to the author. Both George Eliot and Balzac break with the Realist canon of impersonal detachment by allowing themselves the same freedom as Fielding who, in George Eliot's words, 'seems to bring his armchair to the proscenium and chat with us in all the lusty ease of his fine English' (p. 170). Although frowned upon by the majority of Realists, such latitude does not necessarily destroy either the fictional illusion or the impression of objectivity. The author/ narrator may speak about his characters with such an air of conviction that their fictional reality is enhanced and once he has established a line of communication with the reader he can control his response and try to hoodwink him into believing that 'all is true' (Balzac). Stoneman makes the interesting claim that the central conflict of Realism can be resolved by setting up a balance between objectivity and subjectivity *within* the narrator. One kind of objectivity is achieved by the impartiality to which George Eliot's narrator lays claim (p. 411) and which is abundantly evident in the judicious commentary and sage reflections found throughout the work whilst 'it is through the emotional reactions of the narrator that we are invited to share the subjective experiences of the fictional characters'. The narrator of *Middlemarch* thus provides 'the paradigm' of balanced consciousness, illustrating an ideal blend of objectivity and subjectivity beyond the reach of the majority of the characters. But there is an element of duplicity in this solution. The narrator's beneficent and generous vision is made possible by an unreal immunity to the threadlike pressures which frustrate the characters. If they are akin to flies caught in the web of a reactionary provincial society, the narrator's dark side can be likened only to a spider whose predatory instinct has been miraculously transformed into a deep sympathy for its victims. The usefulness of a personalized narrator is, however, indisputable. It is no accident that the three novels which employ such a narrator are those with the widest scope. Without a personalized narrator, the novelist is under more pressure to keep the focus firmly on a single character in the interests of unity.

Impersonality is not just a question of narrative technique—it is also achieved through plot-structure. Complete impersonality runs counter to the ingrained ethical idealism of writers like Howells and George Eliot who have felt the effects of living in a Protestant country. The narrator in Howells may maintain the mandatory silence but there is a sense in which his treatment of the regeneration of an American businessman is moralistic whilst Balzac, despite his interventions, manages, Lukács claims, to avoid moralistic presentation by showing 'the objective dialectic of the rise and fall [of his characters]'.[6] Howells imposes a pattern of sin, guilt, retribution, and regeneration on the plot of *The Rise of Silas Lapham*; Lapham's final decision is meant to have absolute moral value and illustrate his 'rise' to a position of greater moral worth but it violates the Realist imperative that all changes of heart be socially and psychologically plausible. What mars the work is not the repentance itself but the fact that the ground for it is not adequately laid; the reader suspects that Howells, like Bromfield Corey, 'found a delicate, aesthetic pleasure in the heroism with which Lapham withstood Rogers and his temptations' (p. 331). Verga, on the other hand, does not engineer uncharacteristic changes of heart in his self-made man. Gesualdo may soften with time and become more generous to his relations and the poor but his basic philosophy remains unchanged ('I stick up for my own possessions', p. 292). George Eliot, in contrast to Howells, is able to reconcile a strong ethical concern with the Realist recognition of the laws and causality governing human behaviour. Like Howells, she is drawn to a scheme of moral improvement but the whole process by which egocentric individuals are weaned and come to recognize an 'equivalent centre of self' in others is fully illustrated and rests on rational or human considerations. Whilst Howells toys with the idea of a providential scheme when he makes Mrs. Lapham say: 'I don't know as *I* believe in his interference a great deal; but I believe he's interfered this time' (p. 122), George Eliot deals harshly and incredulously with Bulstrode's 'belief that he did everything for God's sake, being indifferent to it for his own' (p. 665).

One of the paradoxes of Realism is that the novelist's passion for the real results in a fuller exploitation of the expressive possibilities of the form and a more self-conscious craftsmanship. Once the novelist has bowed out of the novel, it is necessary for him to en-gineer 'an elaborate orchestral or suggestive structure whereby meaning *emerges*—as a function of the structure itself' (Jenkins). All Realists, however, have misgivings about imposing too rigid a structure on experience. There is a widespread feeling that too much aesthetic manipulation runs counter to the need for fidelity to what is taken to be the random nature of life. 'Life in the raw' is at a premium for the Realist; like Galdós, he cannot altogether endorse the view taken by the critic who is imagined discussing the way Fortunata's story should be exploited:

the artistic fabric would be of the finest if certain essential strands were woven in to transform the coarseness of life into aesthetical material. He did not tolerate life as it really is being elevated to art; rather it should be *sweetened* and *seasoned* with fragrant substances and then put on the stove to cook well [p. 1062].

Realists usually like to think of themselves as 'biophiles' (the term is used by Henry), warmly welcoming life in all its chaotic variety but, as most contributors show, they are in fact latent 'necrophiles' whose real instinct is to impose pattern and order on their 'raw' material. But if Verga's artlessness is shown by Gatt-Rutter to be extremely artful, Henry can claim that the conscious artistry of Turgenev does not result in artificiality. The 'slice of life' which the Realist offers the reader is never completely raw but neither has it been cooked to nothing.

Nearly all the novelists considered create a basic impression of unity by concentrating on the destiny of a single character, but the impression that the novelist is 'following' real life is created by the presentation of the experiences of this character in a 'natural', chronological sequence. No novelist attempts to give an exhaustive description of the protagonist's life; it is clearly necessary to select certain key experiences although these are usually 'set' in the context of the banalities of everyday life, the routine of social intercourse, the flow of mundane occurrence, the extraordinary and the significant being blended with the ordinary and insignificant. The extent to which the Realist is prepared to defer to the undramatic, uneventful nature of the lives lived by the greatest number varies. Flaubert goes furthest in this direction; Frédéric's life seems to drag on interminably, an anti-climactic succession of 'one damned thing after another'. In contrast, 'Lucien's career is compressed into an incredibly short period' (Mount) and the story of *Fathers and Sons* is not a 'steady flow of events but rather a skilfully linked series of episodic scenes' (Henry). Verga, too, differs from Flaubert: *Mastro-Don Gesualdo* seems to consist of one dramatic crisis after another. Novelists who rely heavily on the dramatic mode are not, on the whole, as successful at conveying the passing of time because of the rarity of 'panoramic' passages describing habitual action or the slow changes that are taking place within character.

The various 'discriminated occasions' which make up the main plot are usually bound together by a strict causality, as Gatt-Rutter shows clearly in Verga's case. But it is not only in *Mastro-Don Gesualdo* that 'the two principles, of aesthetic coherence and causation, are one and the same'. It is for this reason that the patterns established by the Realist are not felt to be an arbitrary imposition—

in real life, too, there is an underlying order, a 'play of minute causes' which the Realist, in his more analytic frame of mind, detects beneath the surface confusion of reality. The Realist's habitual determinism provides the philosophical sanction for the patient display of the hidden connections which bind disparate phenomena into an aesthetically satisfying whole.

Pattern of a different kind grows out of the conviction that the world is a hard place in which to live and reality on the whole recalcitrant to the needs of the individual. Balzac, Flaubert, and Strindberg organize their material in a similar way, imposing a series of humiliations and defeats upon their idealistic hero and leaving him finally chastened or completely demoralized. Equally strong is the conviction that life is not as it is represented in a good deal of literature, in particular the romantic novel. Turner shows how Fontane systematically 'writes against the implied pattern of romance and thereby disappoints romantic expectations'. A common pattern is for the romantic expectations of character to be shown conflicting with reality. Casaubon is 'a benefactor with collective society at his back' not the dragon or ogre imagined by Ladislaw. Jacinta's hope that she will find Juanito's lost child is frustrated and she has to cease 'living in a world of romantic novels' (p. 295). A romantic view of the opposite sex is undermined in several novels. Frédéric's vision of Madame Arnoux as a figure of saintly purity is at odds with her straitened circumstances and her real desires. The true nature of actresses is shown to be opposed to their admirer's idealized image of them. In *The Red Room*, when Agnes learns that Rehnhjelm has fallen in love with her, she exclaims, 'The idiot!' (p. 151) and Niní Rubiera's passionate admiration of Signora Aglae is rudely interrupted by a voice shouting, 'Hey! . . . Do you want them fried or with tomato sauce?' (p. 189). The more explicit the criticism of the pattern of romance, the closer, ironically, the novelist comes to following it. Foster argues that the main sub-plot of *The Rise of Silas Lapham* 'serves primarily to illustrate the substance of a literary argument' and that the criticism of *Tears, Idle Tears*, introduced into the novel, is part of 'an obvious and conscious protest'. The subsequent behaviour of Penelope, however, illustrates precisely that 'misplaced heroism' and 'gratuitous self-sacrifice' which had been censured by the Reverend Sewell. Likewise Galdós may state that 'only in bad novels do unexpected babies occur when the writer needs something to complicate the plot' (p. 194) but he does use a long delayed if not totally unexpected baby to bring about the final resolution of the conflict between Fortunata and Jacinta. The cited examples of romantic plotting, far from inhibiting, in fact adumbrate the specified development.

The plot of several novels possesses a cyclical structure which amounts to an eloquent denial of the possibility of purposeful progression. Effi returns at the end of the novel to the home from which she had been exiled at the beginning and regains the name (p. 266) she had rashly surrendered. Frédéric discovers that the best moment in his life was the one briefly alluded to at the beginning, the schoolboy visit to the local brothel. Holmes has commented on the way Falk goes round in a circle and on how, despite his trials, nothing has really changed. The richness and diversity of the material encompassed by the 'panoramic' novels precludes such obvious cyclical patterns. The urge to achieve aesthetically pleasing form is apparent, however, in the way Galdós seeks to 'multiply certain themes by working them out in a series of variations' and George Eliot manages to 'unite the one with the many'. In both cases, 'the most varied group of relations' is 'bound together in a wholeness'; the unity and symmetry which embrace sprawling complexity and interwoven relationships are evoked by images of organic totality—the labyrinthine tree or creeper and the web. Aesthetic manipulation is clearly apparent in the repeated use of controlled oppositions between characters—Lucien and David, Bazarov and the well-bred, self-regarding aristocrats, Frédéric and Deslauriers, the two Falk brothers, Silas and Bromfield Corey, Fortunata and Jacinta, Don Gesualdo, the self-made man, and the aristocratic but penurious Traos—and of analogies or parallels—Frédéric and Dussardier, Dorothea and Lydgate, for instance. A staple Realist procedure is to engineer telling contrasts between the reactions of characters to the same stimulus; Stoneman discusses the different attitudes to Rome in *Middlemarch*, Henry the variety of male responses to Fenichka. The 'meaning' of a given response is largely determined by its place within the internalized paradigm of possible responses. Lastly, the controlling hand of the artist can be discerned in the use of objects like Dorothea's widow's cap, the money-box in *Fortunata and Jacinta* or the silver casket in *Sentimental Education*, or places like the slough in *Effi Briest*, to produce carefully contrived symbolic effects.

The impact of the Realist's working model can be heightened by the technique of impersonality and restrained through insistent patterning but his main asset is what Marx attributed to Balzac—'a deep grasp of the real situation',[7] an understanding of the social and economic relationships which obtain at a particular juncture, together with an awareness of the main ideological differences separating generations and classes. The main component of the miniaturized model of society constructed by the Realist are representatives of the various classes, ranging in a novel like *Middlemarch* from Dagley (rural proletariat) to Sir James Chettam (landed gentry) or in *Sentimental Education* from Dussardier ('revolutionary' proletariat) to Dambreuse ('reactionary' aristocracy), from Fortunata (the *pueblo*) to the Baldomero upper middle-class dynasty in *Fortunata and Jacinta*. The Realist is particularly sensitive to the social gradations, the subtle differences between 'the habits of the different ranks' (*Middlemarch*, p. 470). Although the narrator in Galdós claims that the class-structure has broken down to form one amorphous middle class, there is a clear distinction drawn between the Baldomero family and the Rubín family when it comes (say) to whether the male children have to work to earn a living. In Verga the distinction between that section of the old baronial caste which has adapted to the need to engage in productive activity and that section which is obsessed with status is brought out by the contrast between the baroness Rubiera who is first seen with her skirt hitched up on her hips and her hair all dusty, supervising the winnowing of the corn (p. 21) and Don Ferdinando whose life of haughty inactivity leaves him 'in his dirty little bedroom, stretched out in a bed no better than a kennel' (p. 105). The typicality of Realist characters is repeatedly emphasized; Lucien is both the *arriviste* and the budding poet; Juanito is the idle *señorito* and 'embodies the values and attitudes of a whole class'. The Realist is particularly interested in new social types; Henry shows how, in Bazarov, Turgenev succeeds in illustrating the essential features of the *Raznochintzy* whilst Verga, in pinpointing Gesualdo's 'drive to monopoly' has seen 'the brand-new characteristic of the brand-new class'.

The model constructed by the Realist is not a static one—the main interest lies in observing how the various parts work, both individually and in relation to each other. The Realist's grasp of the real situation can be illustrated in his understanding of motive forces. Balzac's concern, Mount writes, is 'to show the essential self-interest and financial greed at the heart of the society in which he found himself'. Similarly Verga 'explores the working of the inescapable principle of self-interest as motive force of society'. Balzac and Strindberg both describe a literary world dominated by commercialism in which literature has become a commodity and the writer someone to be exploited. Property relations are in several novels shown to be all-important; in Verga they determine everything, 'dissolving all other considerations, even bonds of kinship and sex'; in Turgenev, the landed gentry are shown making the reforms necessary for their survival. Financial necessity may be extremely important, driving several young men to compromise their ideals, but money and work are shown making limited inroads into the vested interests of the propertied class.

The conflicts and tensions between the various classes and groups in society open up dramatic possibilities. The antagonism between different classes is captured in a number of memorable scenes; the auction of the communal lands where Gesualdo outwits the baronial caste; the dinner to which the Coreys invite the Laphams where Howells shows 'the awkwardness and misunderstanding which never completely disappears between young and old society'; Brooke's visit to Freeman's End during which Dagley gives the lie to his landlord's reformist zeal. The final outcome of the struggle between different groups and interests is carefully calculated. The end of *Fathers and Sons* shows that there is as yet no place for the likes of Bazarov. The old order will continue. The star of the landed gentry (represented by Arkady) has not yet set. Gesualdo's final defeat at the hands of the baronial caste captures the essence of a broad historical process. The reactionary swing at the end of *Sentimental Education* is an indication of the power and determination of the bourgeoisie to resist the call for equality. The final reconciliation between Fortunata and Jacinta is intended to illustrate the cross-fertilization of the natural and social forces associated with the *pueblo* and the middle class respectively but as the exchange is so one-sided, Fortunata giving her child to Jacinta, having given her body to Juanito, what is actually being shown is an exploitative middle class successfully quarrying the rocklike vitality of the *pueblo*. The outcome of the struggle between young and old varies; Arkady is finally converted to the values of the fathers whilst Dorothea successfully escapes the clutch of 'the dead hand of the past' and lives her life as she, rather than Casaubon, sees fit.

Although he rarely takes up a clear political stance, the Realist tends to convey an unfavourable view of society as a whole. Despite the commitment to impartiality, the analysis of how society works frequently becomes an attack upon the abuses and corruption of society. *Lost Illusions* denounces a social order in which human beings are forced to exploit or be exploited; Turgenev considered his novel to be 'directed against the gentry as the leading class'; Strindberg exposes the humbug, greed, and corruption of Stockholm society and directly attacks financial chicanery in the chapter on the Triton Finance Company; it is difficult, Turner argues, to see the ostracism of Effi as 'anything but a judgement on the society of the day'; Macklin shows how in various ways 'the narrator's idealized vision of society' In Part I is gradually eroded in *Fortunata and Jacinta*. A critical attitude is often implicit in the totalizing images of society proposed by the narrator. Despite its suggestions of pleasing symmetry and delicately interwoven destinies, George Eliot's web has predatory overtones and when a leaf falls from Galdós's great tree, we are told that 'the tree felt nothing in its vast mass of branches' (p. 902). Images of mud in Balzac point more directly to the corruption of society whilst the image of an idol in *Effi Briest* indicates the basic hollowness of the cult of honour at the centre of a despotic social system.

There is general agreement, too, about the prevailing ideological bankruptcy, the absence of any 'coherent social faith ... which would perform the function of knowledge for the ardently willing souls' (*Middlemarch*, p. 25). The new outlook represented by Bazarov ('I don't believe in anything', p. 33) is presented in negative terms as a rejection of all other ideologies but in itself is devoid of positive force. Its fundamental inadequacy is that it makes no allowance for the powerful emotions which sweep over Bazarov's parents or, love being seen as 'mouldy aesthetics', Bazarov himself. The Utopian Socialism of the equally doctrinaire Sénécal has an ominously authoritarian dimension and fails to take stock of the fatal play of economic forces. Although both Dorothea and Silas Lapham resolve their problems in a way which is personally satisfying, the general validity of their 'ethical' solution in a manifestly 'imperfect social state' is open to question. In *Mastro-Don Gesualdo*, despite Gesualdo's protestations that he is a Christian, no active religious faith or social vision tempers the blind self-interest of all members of society; as Gesualdo puts it, 'everybody leads the water to his own mill' (p. 335). Fontane, like several other novelists examined, shows 'the fallibility of the social code'. In *Fortunata and Jacinta* 'it is clear that much of middle-class morality is little more than a façade'. Astute or unscrupulous members of society recommend that one simply pay lip-service to standards which have become hollow and formalities which have become empty; Vautrin's 'tout est dans la forme' is echoed by Feijóo's 'Form is all important' (p. 693).

All Realists are profoundly aware that, whatever its shortcomings, 'we're not isolated persons, we belong to a whole society' (*Effi Briest*, p. 215). It is nonsensical therefore to try to separate the individual and society; the two are related in numerous ways and need to be considered together. Society can be viewed as the hero's natural opponent. Falk's raising of his clenched fist, 'challenging the poor city' at the beginning of *The Red Room* is the almost archetypal expression of this view of society as something which is likely to thwart the aspirations of the individual. But society is also a kind of arena in which the mettle of the hero is tested; it 'gives the parameters in which the individual can act' (Gatt-Rutter). The individual often finds that he is entangled in that against which he pits himself. Lydgate is a good example of someone who is caught up in the 'hampering threadlike pressures of small social conditions'. Middlemarch society is presented as an embroiled medium which proves too strong for him, a web in which youthful idealism falls prey to a reactionary provincialism. There is something labyrinthine about Middlemarch society, just as there is something labyrinthine about Madrid society; in both cases the individual risks losing his way.

It would be wrong to suggest that Realists set up a black-and-white opposition between society and the individual. A balance is frequently held between the resistance offered by a society hostile to new ideas and the lack of determination of those who fail to persevere in their struggle against it. If failure is a pervasive theme, it is the product as much of inner weakness, of 'spots of commonness' as of the blind decrees of a society viewed as 'Atropos in modern dress' (Turner). Gesualdo, Gatt-Rutter writes, 'is his own victim, as well as the victim of the society whose values he lives' and Effi, Turner stresses, is 'the *consenting* victim of a social ritual'. Several characters manifest a fatal softness. Falk is described as 'too soft to get on in this world' (p. 59); Lucien has a weak 'feminine side' to his nature; Frédéric emerges as a flabby, spineless being; Arkady is accused by Bazarov of being 'too soft' (p. 186) yet, ironically, he himself, as Henry points out, 'is endowed with weaknesses that were seriously to affect his capacity for decisive action and for fulfilment of his life's purpose'. George Eliot believed in 'the power of the individual will as a counterbalance to environmental determinism' and Galdós thought that the conflict between the individual and society was potentially creative; without such a belief, the optimistic vision of the future would collapse. But Strindberg in his portrayal of Sellén and Balzac in the picture he paints of the *cénacle* also lend support for the idea that 'if we had been greater, circumstances would have been less strong against us'. Clearly, the more the individual is at fault, the less society is, in any simple way, to blame.

The treatment of the theme of failure is varied. The Realist often makes a distinction between what happens materially and what happens morally or emotionally. Lapham's rise, which involves the vindication of his moral integrity, is made possible by his decline as a businessman. The destitute—particularly starving artists in Balzac and Strindberg—having miraculously survived the pangs of hunger, often achieve an artistic success which is denied those that seek material prosperity. The loss of inheritance and gentlewoman's status pave the way for a more fulfilling way of life for Dorothea. The battles Gesualdo wins in his struggle for economic dominance are accompanied by crushing emotional defeats. The failure of Lucien which is both material and moral is something of an exception. Generally failure is relative; Lydgate, as Stoneman points out, may not fulfil his grandiose ambitions, but in material terms, he suffers nothing worse than 'an excellent practice . . . alternating between London and a continental watering-place'. Juanito may have lost the respect of his wife at the end of *Fortunata and Jacinta* and failed to fulfil the promise he shows at the beginning but the Baldomero dynasty has been revitalized by the injection of proletarian blood. Neither resounding success nor resounding failure are admissible since they imply an exceptional destiny. As Foster points out, Realist heroes tend to 'endure' and even when they succeed, like Dorothea, they will be laid to rest in the necessary obscurity of an 'unvisited tomb'.

The treatment of the theme of illusions is equally complex. Illusions inspire young men like Lucien, Falk, or Lydgate to great things, but they stand in the way of material success. When shed in the process of the hero's adjustment to society, they tend to leave a moral and emotional vacuum. As Lucien's youthful, provincial illusions crumble in the face of the brutal realities of metropolitan life, he gradually becomes more and more hollow, an empty shell which Vautrin finally occupies. Frédéric's loss of sentimental illusions leads to a state of emotional desiccation. The characteristic imagery of withering and shrinkage associated with the process of disillusionment by several novelists suggests that illusions make up the 'organic' substance of the self. In contrast to the French novelists and to Strindberg, George Eliot does not assume that illusions will inevitably wither and die. Stoneman examines her more optimistic outlook which insists that, although they can be harmful when not integrated into the life of the individual, illusions may, if 'corrected by the processes of disenchantment, be seen as a "wider vision", a means of integrating the individual in the larger life of humanity'. Contrasting destinies suggest that illusions have a vital role to play. Dorothea may at first be led into error when 'the fine inflammable material of [her] youthful illusions' (p. 110) is set alight and then extinguished in the initial disillusionment of marriage but her ardent nature is shown constantly rekindling and finally having an 'incalculably diffusive' effect on those around her. Mary Garth, on the other hand, who 'neither tried to create illusions, nor indulged in them for her own behoof' (p. 140), though she does not fall into error, makes a smaller contribution to 'the growing good of the world'.

The theme of illusions prompts the Realist to construe the relationship between the individual and society in dialectical terms, for illusions are not simply generated from within but are also implanted or inculcated in the individual by society. Rather than see the individual exclusively in conflict with society or 'hemmed in by a social life which seemed nothing but a labyrinth of petty courses' (*Middlemarch*, p. 51), the Realist recognizes that the individual is a pearl-like product of the secretions of society. Lukács's concept of the type, to which several contributors refer, formalizes such a relationship between the individual and society. A type is constituted by the concrete manifestation or production within the individual of the 'totality of socially decisive forces', brought to their highest level of expression but not operating in a mechanical manner. Thus Lucien is a type by virtue of the conflict enacted within him, between, on the one hand the illusions generated by an earlier more heroic period of French bourgeois evolution and the finally more powerful financial considerations which necessarily prevail once 'the spirit of man is drawn into the orbit of capitalism'.[8] Lucien is a good example of a character whose inner being seems to be taken over by social forces. At one stage he is literally swamped: 'two sorts of corruption were advancing towards him in parallel motion like two sheets of water uniting to form a flood. They swirled over the poet' (p. 293). A similar phenomenon is observable in *Mastro-Don Gesualdo* in which the individual is no longer seen as an autonomous universe but is eaten into by an 'all-pervading', 'all-determining' social environment (Gatt-Rutter). Flaubert, too, shows how the same idealism in different forms traverses a wide range of individuals. The social ambition of the young man can be seen as the interiorization of the acquisitive ethos which dominated nineteenth-century society.

Despite their recognition of the importance of cultural conditioning, most Realists cling to a belief in a core identity—the grain of sand around which the pearl is formed—which allows the individual to offer various degrees of resistance to the social pressures which encircle and assail him. Women, who might easily be represented as ideologically permeable, are shown to possess a distinct being of their own, a kind of authenticity over which man-made social pressures ride rough-shod. The sufferings of the female characters in *Mastro-Don Gesualdo* 'are evidence to Verga both of the strength of social pressures, and of their inhumanity, of their antagonism to all that is authentic in ourselves' (Gatt-Rutter). Fontane repeatedly stresses that Effi's fate is marked and influenced by social pressures (as Turner argues) but her inability to feel real guilt, her sense that Innstetten was basically wrong to have fought the duel and that he could have allowed the past to 'die a natural death' (p. 244) show her reluctance to accept the validity of a value-system that has become fossilized. A similar point is made by Galdós. Various attempts are made to tame Fortunata, to make her accept the yoke of conventional 'civilized' morality but she reverts to her 'pre-civilized' view that Juanito really belongs to her and 'breaks out of the passive role others have created for her' (Macklin). Feijóo's view that sexual passion and natural instinct will always prevail over the 'artificialities of society' (p. 667) is largely borne out when Fortunata's desire for respectability gives way to her desire to have a child by Juanito in order to assert her natural superiority over Jacinta. Fortunata's final gesture in giving the child to Jacinta 'so that you may be comforted for the bitterness your husband has made you undergo' (p. 1049) and her final apotheosis ('I'm an angel too', p. 1054) are not convincing precisely because they do not seem compatible with the savage, uncompromising vitality at the core of her fictional being.

Several novelists show the conventional morality of society being transgressed by the clamorous demands of the heart and senses. The men to whom Dorothea, Fortunata, and Effi are married are slow or unable to respond to their wife's needs. What George Eliot describes as the 'pilulous smallness [of] the cobweb of pre-matrimonial acquaintanceship' (p. 45) and the huge age-differences make for the same 'sensual disparity' (Stoneman) between Effi and Innstetten as existed between Dorothea and Casaubon, and Maxi, as Doña Lupe puts it (p. 445), is 'only half a man' whilst Fortunata is 'a real woman'. The bonds of marriage, sanctioned by society, strain or snap under the pressure of Dorothea's rebellious nature, Effi's sensual needs, and Fortunata's conviction that Juanito belongs to her. The Realist, then, often takes a keen interest in individuals who collide with society and, even though the outcome of the collision is often tragic, he does not necessarily endorse the fatalistic attitude of Innstetten when he *chooses* to submit to 'that *something* which forms society—call it a tyrant if you like' (p. 215).

The Realist pays close attention to the physical and historical setting as well as to the social context. There are detailed descriptions of the face of several cities—Paris, Boston, Madrid, and Stockholm —and domestic interiors are carefully evoked by all novelists except Verga. Balzac may claim that the physical environment has a deter-minative influence on behaviour but, most typically the physical setting can be read as effect rather than cause, an indication of rather than an influence upon character. There is a widespread tendency—most marked in Verga and Fontane—to exploit the symbolic poten-tial of the physical setting, although this need not necessarily detract from its authenticity. Attentiveness to the physical setting grows, too, out of an 'archaeological' interest in the shape of things in the past. Although it is commonly assumed that the Realist deals with the present, most of the novelists discussed in this volume set the action on average between ten and twenty years in the past. Tur-genev, in setting the action only two years earlier and Eliot and Verga in making the action begin over forty years in the past, represent two extremes. The existence of a temporal gap allows the distinction between now and then, *hoc tempus* and *illud tempus* to be underlined, the past to be objectified and the understanding between narrator and reader who together look back on it to be strengthened.

The straw bonnet which Eliot says 'our contemporaries might look at with conjectural curiosity as at an obsolete form of basket' (p. 49) and the 'refinements' of Rosanette's apartment 'which would seem paltry to Rosanette's present-day counterparts' (p. 124) are presented as museum pieces which provoke a certain degree of mirth or scorn. 'Those days', Strindberg observes, very rapidly become mythologized as 'the good old days' (p. 112). The most obvious explanation of the Realist's preference for the recent past is that the retrospective view makes for a clearer understanding of how society works. Also, as Stoneman suggests, 'research and documentation could be more easily accomplished at a distance in time, when records were more easily available and judgement had the benefit of perspective'. In some cases setting the novel in the past allows the writer to 'pull his punches' (Holmes) or to avoid, like Verga, a critical period in the history of his country. On the other hand, moving back in time takes Flaubert into the thick of one of the most turbulent periods of French history out of which no group or class emerged unblemished. Setting the novel in the recent past does, however, simplify the novelist's task, since it allows him to leave out whatever might interfere with or complicate the working of his model of society, without causing the reader to object. And as well as allowing him to be selective it also allows him to be evasive. Eagleton has pointed that in some respects *Middlemarch* is lacking in historical substance: 'The Reform Bill, the railways, the cholera, machine-breaking; these "real" historical forces do no more than impinge on its margins.'[9] Turgenev's silence about Bazarov's past and his possible connections with other radicals might seem a more serious omission to the reader of the time, who would like some indication of the strength of the faction he represents.

It could be argued that the Realist, whilst appearing to be concerned with the past, is in fact mainly preoccupied with the present. A period of twenty years earlier is sufficiently distant to admit the simplification and stylization necessary for his purpose but at the same time is sufficiently close for more up-to-date issues not to seem anachronistic when projected back into it. The commercialization of literature was particularly acute in the thirties but its backdating to the twenties in *Lost Illusions* allows it to be isolated and visualized more clearly in the context of an age whose contours, since the Revolution of 1830, have become sharper and more schematized. Likewise the rise of Gesualdo may, Gatt-Rutter points out, have been put a decade or two too far back in history but this allows the 'drive to monopoly' to emerge more powerfully as the salient characteristic of a new class, since the contrast between old and new becomes accentuated.

In some cases the effort to bring out the specificity of an earlier phase of history is perfunctory. There are some surprising omissions from Balzac's account of the year 1821-2 and Verga, in fact, confuses the years 1820 and 1821. Balzac, Mount argues, is concerned only with the general features of the age, not with precise details. On the other hand a novelist like Flaubert feels the historian's compulsion to make sure the factual details are correct and in documenting himself for his novel proceeds very much like a historian. Too much historical material, however, can be an embarrassment and Flaubert was worried that his insipid hero would be eclipsed by colourful historical figures such as Lamartine. The common practice, adopted by Eliot, Strindberg, Galdós, and Fontane is to avoid the two extremes represented by Balzac and Flaubert, making passing reference to the major events and figures of the age in which the novel is set, whilst omitting references to more transient phenomena and figures of the kind that Flaubert inserted into the political discussions of *Sentimental Education*. The balance between the historical accuracy to which the Realist is ostensibly committed and the 'dehistoricizing' to which his interest in 'perennial' problems and 'basic' human nature conduces, is always a delicate one. It is not clear, Gatt-Rutter argues, whether Verga sees Gesualdo as a particular embodiment of a timeless, universal figure, 'homo economicus', or as the embodiment of a unique moment in the evolution of society. Flaubert's attitude to Frédéric is also ambiguous; on the one hand, he illustrates the deleterious effects of the Romantic legacy, on the other, his psychological state is viewed as a permanent possibility.

There is one way in which the Realist can avoid 'overloading' when integrating historical material into his model and that is to 'use history as a means of characterization' (Macklin) by setting up parallels between what happens in the public, historical sphere and what happens in the private, fictional sphere. It may simply be a question of making developments in the fictional microcosm conform with what is happening in society at large, as when George Eliot writes: 'While Lydgate . . . felt himself struggling for Medical Reform against Middlemarch, Middlemarch was becoming more and more conscious of the national struggle for another kind of Reform'

(p. 499). Subtler parallels may be engineered between political and emotional régimes. These are present in *Middlemarch* but more carefully orchestrated in *Fortunata and Jacinta* and *Sentimental Education*. In both cases changes of political régime are aligned with changes of heart in the hero. In *Fortunata and Jacinta* 'Juanito's oscillations between mistress and wife are an image of Spain's swing from order to revolution, from anarchy to peace.' In *Sentimental Education* each of Frédéric's affairs is closely associated with a distinct phase of French history. In both cases a jocular analogy is drawn by the character himself; Frédéric's 'I'm following the fashion. I've reformed' is akin to Juanito's 'Anyway, I can't stand any more and this improper relationship is going to end today. Down with the republic!' (p. 632). In *Fortunata and Jacinta* the country alternates between 'intermittent fevers of revolution and peace' just as Juanito switches backwards and forwards between Fortunata and Jacinta but in *Sentimental Education* the movement does not seem reversible. The drama of profanation in both spheres prevents the swing back to earlier hopes and aspirations and the reactionary movement, when it comes, is decisive. Whilst Galdós emphasizes the basic instability of both political régimes and marriage, Flaubert stresses the necessary deterioration and gradual impoverishment which overtake both high political hopes and high emotional enterprise.

Despite the rich diversity of contexts in which the various novels are produced, there is clearly much that they have in common—the technique of impersonality, the movement towards a more dramatic presentation, an elaborate though rarely obtrusive patterning, a profound understanding of the way society works and affects the individual, an interest in the forces and changes which characterize different phases of historical development. These various features will not necessarily all be found in any single novel nor, when they are present, need they be identical. There is, however, much to be gained from viewing Realism as a family likeness which, as this book shows, undoubtedly exists between novelists working at different times and in different places throughout the nineteenth century.

NOTES

1. *The Future of the Novel* (ed. Leon Edel), Vintage, New York, 1956, p. 107.
2. Quoted by G. J. Becker in the introduction to *Documents of Modern Literary Realism*, Princeton U.P., Princeton, 1963, p. 31.

3. For a discussion of the concept of 'imaginary biography' see F. W. J. Hemmings, *Stendhal, a Study of his Novels*, O.U.P., Oxford, 1964, p. vii.
4. *Correspondance*, ii. 61.
5. G. Dillon and F. Kirchhoff, 'Form and Function of Free Indirect Style', *PTL*, i (Oct, 1976), p. 438.
6. *Studies in European Realism*, Merlin Press, London, 1950, p. 53.
7. Quoted in T. Eagleton, *Marxism and Literary Criticism*, Methuen, London, 1976, p. 48.
8. *Studies in European Realism*, p. 49.
9. *Criticism and Ideology*, N. L. B., London, 1976, p. 120.

Select Bibliography

1. REALISM

THE CONCEPT of Realism has been examined in a number of essays: R. Wellek, 'The Concept of Realism in Literary Scholarship', in *Concepts of Criticism*, New Haven and London, 1963; D. Grant, *Realism*, Methuen, London, 1970; Alice R. Kaminsky, 'On Literary Realism' and George Levine, 'Realism Reconsidered', both in *The Theory of the Novel* (ed. John Halperin), O.U.P., New York, 1974. A more challenging view of Realism is taken by Roland Barthes, in particular in *S/Z*, Seuil, Paris, 1970. The first chapter of Stephen Heath's *The Nouveau Roman*, Elek, London, 1972, is a stimulating development of Barthes's view.

There are several good surveys of Realism considered as a European movement. G. J. Becker's 'Modern Realism as a Literary Movement' in *Documents of Modern Literary Realism*, Princeton U.P., Princeton, 1963, is a useful and wide-ranging introduction. F. W. J. Hemmings, *The Age of Realism*, Penguin, Harmondsworth, 1974, covers the nineteenth-century Realist novel in all the major European literatures with the exception of English.

There have been three notable attempts at allowing the concept of Realism to emerge from the close analysis of texts. Chapters 18 and 19 of E. Auerbach, *Mimesis*, Doubleday Anchor Book, New York, 1957, examine the Realist tradition in France and suggest criteria for modern literary Realism which have gained general currency; G. Lukács, *Studies in European Realism*, Merlin Press, London, 1972, elaborates the concept of the type in relation to the work of Balzac; J. P. Stern, *On Realism*, Routledge and Kegan Paul, London, 1973, attempts to illustrate the basic features of realism considered as a perennial tendency by drawing upon a wide range of authors not all of whom belong to the nineteenth century.

2. BALZAC: *LOST ILLUSIONS*

The reader of Balzac in English translation is fortunate in having at his disposal so much valuable criticism in the same language. A comprehensive review of Balzac's life and work is provided by H. J. Hunt, *Honoré de Balzac; a Biography*, Athlone Press, London, 1957, and H. J. Hunt, *Balzac's Comédie humaine*, Athlone Press, London, 1959.

Most useful for a general appreciation of Balzac as well as for their sections on *Lost Illusions* are F. W. J. Hemmings, *Balzac: an interpretation of 'La Comédie humaine'*, Random House, New York, 1967, and

S. Rogers, *Balzac and the Novel*, University of Wisconsin Press, 1943. Available in translation is an important French study, F. Marceau, *Balzac and his World*, Greenwood Press, Westport, 1976.

Also in translation is the valuable chapter on *Lost Illusions* seen from a Marxist viewpoint in G. Lukács, *Studies in European Realism*, Hillway, London, 1950.

There is an interesting introductory chapter on Balzac's general method and an analysis of his Realism in E. Preston Dargan, W. L. Crain and others, *Studies in Balzac's Realism*, Russell and Russell, New York, 1932.

Balzac is one of the five authors perspicaciously examined in H. Levin, *The Gates of Horn. A Study of five French Realists*, O.U.P., New York, 1963.

Studies of the social and psychological aspects of Balzac's work include C. Affron, *Patterns of Failure in 'La Comédie humaine'*, Yale U.P., 1966, G. R. Besser, *Balzac's Concept of Genius. The Theme of Superiority in the 'Comédie humaine'*, Droz, Geneva, 1969, and B. N. Schilling, *The Hero as Failure: Balzac and the Rubempré cycle*, University of Chicago Press, 1968.

A detailed examination of a complex subject is to be found in A. R. Pugh, *Balzac's Recurring Characters*, University of Toronto Press, 1974, in which the index and a system of code-numbers enable the reader to trace the references to *Lost Illusions* and to individual characters. Another specialized study is a re-assessment of Balzac's debt to Sir Walter Scott: D. R. Haggis, 'Scott, Balzac and the historical novel as social and political analysis: *Waverley* and *Les Chouans*', *Modern Language Review*, lxviii (1973), 51–68.

A thought-provoking article on the nature of Balzac's Realism is C. Prendergast, 'Chance and Realism in the *Comédie humaine*', *Forum for Modern Language Studies*, x (1974), 109–20.

The relationship between Balzac's characters and their real-life models is explored in H. J. Hunt, 'Balzac's Pressmen', *French Studies*, xi (1957), 230–45, B. R. Tolley, 'The "Cénacle" of Balzac's *Illusions perdues*', *French Studies*, xv (1961), 324–34, and B. R. Tolley, 'Balzac the Printer', *French Studies*, xiii (1959), 214–24.

Finally, the importance of Balzac's contribution to the development of Realism as a world-wide movement is explored in A. Carey Taylor, *Non-French Admirers and Imitators of Balzac*, J. W. Ruddock and Sons, London, 1950.

3. TURGENEV: *FATHERS AND SONS*

The most authoritative histories of Russian literature in English are D. S. Mirsky, *A History of Russian Literature*, edited and abridged by Francis J. Whitfield, Routledge, 1960, which, though now somewhat dated, is a valuable and well written work; and Marc Slonim, *The Epic of Russian Literature, From its Origins through Tolstoy*, O.U.P., 1964, which deals with a.o. The Critics and Nihilists, Literary Trends of the Sixties, and Turgenev, in separate chapters.

On Russian Realism, there are the works of the Marxist scholar G. Lukács, *Der russische Realismus in der Weltliteratur*, Berlin, 1949 and *Studies in European Realism*, Hillway, 1950; and Ernest J. Simmons, *Introduction to Russian Realism*, Indiana U.P., 1965, which consists of essays on major Russian prose writers, but perversely omits Turgenev. A thorough and rewarding work is Klaus Städtke, *Studien zum russischen Realismus des 19. Jahrhunderts, Literatur und Gesellschaft*, Berlin, 1973, which stresses the ideological and socio-political context of literature.

There are several very helpful studies on the Russian Novel. E.-M. de Vogüé's pioneering work *The Russian Novel*, translated by Col. A. H. Sawyer, London, 1913 is still valuable. Janko Lavrin, *An Introduction to the Russian Novel*, Methuen, 1942, is a compact overview of the subject. A short, selective, but very perceptive work is Henry Gifford, *The Novel in Russia*, Hutchinson, 1964, with a chapter on *Fathers and Sons*. F. D. Reeve, *The Russian Novel*, Frederick Muller, 1967, is an original and stimulating work, also containing a chapter on Turgenev's novel. Richard Freeborn, *The Rise of the Russian Novel, Studies in the Russian Novel from 'Eugene Onegin' to 'War and Peace'*, C.U.P., 1973, traces the evolution of the genre, but is scant on Turgenev (but see below). A good introductory work is Alexander T. Boyd, *Aspects of the Russian Novel*, Chatto and Windus, 1972.

Turgenev's complete works are contained in *Polnoye sobraniye sochinenii i pisem*, ed. M. P. Alekseev, vv. 1–28, AN SSSR, Moscow-Leningrad, 1960–8. The greater part of his fiction was first translated by Constance Garnett in seventeen volumes, Heinemann, 1894–9. There are also numerous more recent translations of his novels and stories (see Notes,* p. 72 above). A selection of his literary reminiscences was translated by D. Magarshack, Turgenev, *Literary Reminiscences, with an Essay by Edmund Wilson*, Faber, 1959.

The earliest full-scale biography of Turgenev in English is Edward Garnett, *Turgenev, A Study, with a Foreword by Joseph Conrad*, Collins, 1917. Both D. Magarshack, *Turgenev, A Life*, Faber, 1954, and A. Yarmolinsky, *Turgenev, The Man, His Art and His Age*, 1960, The Century Co., are full and well-documented works. A recent study is V. S. Pritchett's elegantly written *The Gentle Barbarian. The Life and Work of Turgenev*, Chatto and Windus, 1977, which probes into some of the complexities of Turgenev's private life.

Henri Granjard, *Ivan Tourguénev et les courants politiques et sociaux de son temps*, Paris, 1954, is still the most comprehensive and authoritative study of Turgenev to appear in the West. The outstanding study of Turgenev the writer is Richard Freeborn, *Turgenev, the Novelist's Novelist*, O.U.P., 1962. In his *Fathers and Children, the Romanes Lecture*, O.U.P., 1972, Isaiah Berlin achieved the impossible, this being a brilliant, compact survey of the interaction of Russian literature, thought, and politics; also printed in the second edition of *Fathers and Sons*, Penguin Classics, 1975. For translations and Turgenev scholarship in English, see R. Yachnin and D. H. Stam, *Turgenev in English, a Checklist of Works by and about him*, The New York Public Library, 1962.

T. G. Masaryk, *The Spirit of Russia, Studies in History, Literature and Philosophy*, Allen and Unwin, 1919, is still the standard work on Russian intellectual history and is specifically valuable on Nihilism. F. Venturi, *The Roots of Revolution, A History of the Populist and Socialist Movements in Nineteenth Century Russia*, Weidenfeld and Nicolson, 1960, is another full and authoritative study of the subject. E. Lampert, *Sons against Fathers, Studies in Russian Radicalism and Revolution*, O.U.P., 1965, focuses on Chernyshevsky, Dobrolyubov and Pisarev. For an introduction to the writings of the 'democratic' critics, see Belinsky, Chernyshevsky and Dobroliubov, *Selected Criticism*, ed. R. E. Matlaw, Second Edition, Indiana U.P., 1976, and D. I. Pisarev, *Selected Philosophical, Social and Political Essays*, Foreign Languages Publishing House, Moscow, 1958.

4. FLAUBERT: *SENTIMENTAL EDUCATION*

The development of Realism in France is well documented in P. Martino, *Le Roman réaliste sous le second empire*, Hachette, Paris, 1913, and E. Bouvier, *La Bataille réaliste*, Fontemoing, Paris, 1913. The critical reaction to Realism is examined in B. Weinberg, *French Realism: the Critical Reaction (1830–70)*, O.U.P., 1937. More recent historical accounts include R. Dumesnil, *Le Réalisme et le naturalisme*, del Duca, Paris, 1955, and J.-H. Bornecque and P. Cogny, *Réalisme et naturalisme*, Hachette, Paris, 1958.

Several critical biographies are available in English: P. Spencer, *Flaubert*, Faber and Faber, London, 1953; E. Starkie, *Flaubert, The Making of the Master* and *Flaubert, the Master*, Weidenfeld and Nicolson, London, 1967 and 1971; B. Bart, *Flaubert*, Syracuse U.P., 1967. It is well worth anyone familiar with French tackling J.-P. Sartre's monumental three-volume *L'Idiot de la famille*, Gallimard, Paris, 1971–2, which contains a penetrating analysis of Flaubert's 'passive constitution'.

Of the general studies of the work, V. Brombert, *The Novels of Flaubert*, Princeton University Press, 1966, is the most perceptive analysis of the major themes; A. Thorlby, *Gustave Flaubert and the Art of Realism*,

Bowes and Bowes, London, 1956, is brief and to the point, R. J. Sherrington, *Three Novels by Flaubert: A Study of Techniques*, O.U.P., 1970, contains a full analysis of narrative techniques, in particular point of view, in Flaubert; M. Tillett, *On Reading Flaubert*, O.U.P., 1961, makes some interesting comparisons with other novels; and J. Culler, *Flaubert: The Uses of Uncertainty*, Elek, London, 1974, adopts a refreshingly new and provocative approach. In French, the most elegant general study is A. Thibaudet, *Gustave Flaubert*, Gallimard, Paris, 1935; the most detailed R. Dumesnil, *Gustave Flaubert, l'homme et l'œuvre*, Desclée de Brouer, Paris, 1947; and the most succinct C. Digeon, *Flaubert*, Hatier, Paris, 1970.

The best and most concentrated study of *Sentimental Education* is the long article by A. Fairlie, 'Some Patterns of Suggestion in *L'Éducation sentimentale*', *Australian Journal for French Studies*, vi (1969), 266–93. This article encompasses the complex themes and characters of the novel more successfully than P. Cortland, *The Sentimental Adventure*, Mouton, The Hague, 1967. In French, R. Dumesnil, *L'Éducation sentimentale de Gustave Flaubert*, Société des belles lettres, Paris, 1943, concentrates on the autobiographical elements and P.-G. Castex, *Flaubert, L'Éducation sentimentale*, Centre de documentation universitaire, Paris, 1959, on the literary and historical sources. A more recent, if one-sided, interpretation can be found in J.-P. Duquette, *Flaubert ou l'architecture du vide*, Les Presses de l'université de Montréal, 1972, and P. Cogny, *L'Éducation sentimentale de Flaubert*, Larousse, Paris, 1975, is a useful synthesis of various critical approaches. A. Cento, *Il Realismo documentario nell' Éducation sentimentale*, Liguori, Naples, 1967, is an exhaustive investigation of Flaubert's documentation for the novel.

Some of the best detailed studies of various aspects of the novel have been collected in special numbers of *Europe*, (Sept.–Oct.–Nov. 1969) and *Littérature*, 15 (1974) and in two books, *La Production du sens chez Flaubert*, 10/18, Paris, 1975, and *Langages de Flaubert*, Minard, Paris, 1976.

A succinct account of the period in which the most important historical events take place can be found in R. Price, *The Second French Republic*, Batsford, London, 1972, and a spirited analysis of the underlying forces at work, which in some respects coincides with Flaubert's, is provided by Marx's 'The Class Struggles in France: 1848 to 1850' and 'The Eighteenth Brumaire of Louis Bonaparte' in *Surveys from Exile*, Penguin, Harmondsworth, 1973.

5. G. ELIOT: *MIDDLEMARCH*

Middlemarch first appeared in book form in 1871–2 (4 vols, Blackwood's, Edinburgh). A good modern edition is by Penguin, Harmondsworth,

1965. *Quarry for Middlemarch*, ed. Anna Theresa Kitchel, University of California Press, Berkeley and Los Angeles, 1950, is George Eliot's working notebook for the novel, while Jerome Beaty's *Middlemarch from Notebook to Novel*, University of Illinois Studies in Language and Literature No. 47, Urbana, 1960, documents the phases of the novel's construction. The most important of George Eliot's theoretical writing on Realism can be found in 'The Natural History of German Life', *Westminster Review*, N.S. x (July–Oct. 1856), 51–79. This is available with her other essays in *The Essays of George Eliot*, ed. Thomas Pinney, Routledge and Kegan Paul, London 1963. An essay by George Henry Lewes on 'Realism in Art: Recent German Fiction', *Westminster Review*, N.S. xiv (July–Oct. 1858), 488–518, probably represents joint opinions, and argues that 'Realism is . . . the basis of all art, and its antithesis is not Idealism, but *Falsism*'.

George Eliot's theoretical position on Realism has been thoroughly analysed in modern critical articles. Alice R. Kaminsky's 'George Eliot, George Henry Lewes, and the Novel', *PMLA*, lxx, (1955), 997–1013, is the most detailed, but other useful articles are James R. Rust's 'The Art of Fiction in George Eliot's Reviews', *Review of English Studies*, N.S. vii, (1956), 164–72, and G. S. Haight's 'George Eliot's Theory of Fiction', *Victorian Newsletter*, x (1956), 1–3. A. J. Sambrook gives the 'scientific' basis for George Eliot's Realism in the 'Natural Historian of our Social Classes', *English*, xiv (1963), 130–4, and Bernard Paris, in 'George Eliot's Religion of Humanity', *English Literary History*, xxix (1962), 418–43, gives the philosophical reasons for her bias towards moral idealism. Art as a 'moral mission' is stressed by Richard Stang in 'The Literary Criticism of George Eliot', *PMLA*, lxxii (1957), 952–61, and Ian Milner demonstrates the delicate balance between the contrary urges to document and to idealize in 'George Eliot and the Limits of Victorian Realism', *Philologia Pragensia*, vi (1963).

On the question of Realism and form, Darrell Mansell Jr. shows in 'George Eliot's Conception of Form', *Studies in English Literature*, v (1965), 651–62, how George Eliot's organic conception of form leads to her structural use of analogy, and David R. Carroll demonstrates this in 'Unity through Analogy in *Middlemarch*', *Victorian Studies*, ii (1959), 305–16. A particular instance can be seen in Suzanne C. Ferguson's article, 'Mme Laure and Operative Irony in Middlemarch: A Structural Analogy', *Studies in English Literature*, iii (1963), 509–16. Brian Swann extends this idea to include classical and folk-lore allusion in '*Middlemarch* and Myth', *Nineteenth Century Fiction*, xxviii (Sept. 1973), 210–14. Contemporary historical allusions are discussed by Jerome Beaty in 'History by Indirection: the Era of Reform in *Middlemarch*', *Victorian Studies*, i (1957), 173–9. He confirms the analogical structure and like Richard

Ellmann in 'Dorothea's Husbands: some biographical speculations', *TLS*, 16 Feb. 1973, 165–8, argues that George Eliot thoroughly absorbed her sources into the texture of her novel.

Among book-length studies of George Eliot, Barbara Hardy's *The Novels of George Eliot*, Athlone Press, London 1959, is undoubtedly the best overall treatment, though W. J. Harvey in *The Art of George Eliot*, Chatto and Windus, London, 1961, has detailed discussions of the omniscient technique and various kinds of structure in the novels. *Critical Essays on George Eliot*, ed. Barbara Hardy, Routledge and Kegan Paul, London, 1970, contains articles by Derek Oldfield on the language of *Middlemarch*, Isobel Armstrong on George Eliot's 'wisdom', and W. J. Harvey on 'Idea and Image in the Novels of George Eliot'. More specifically on Realism, Ian Milner in *The Structure of Values in George Eliot*, Prague, 1968, argues that George Eliot reconciles Realism and Idealism by concentrating on growth points in the *status quo*, while Terry Eagleton, in a brief section of *Criticism and Ideology*, *NLB*, London, 1976, argues that her omniscient narration is the formal concomitant of a characteristic Victorian displacement of social problems into personal terms.

6. A. STRINDBERG: *THE RED ROOM*

Alrik Gustafson gives an account of the advent of Realism in Sweden in a chapter, 'Strindberg and the Realistic Breakthrough' in his *A History of Swedish Literature*, University of Minnesota Press, Minneapolis, 1961. Gunnar Ahlström *Det moderna genombrottet i Nordens litteratur*, Rabén and Sjögren, Stockholm, 1974, is a sociological approach to Realism in Scandinavia as a whole which refers extensively to Strindberg.

Martin Lamm's classic biography *August Strindberg* is to be found in an English translation, published by Blom, New York, 1971. Other surveys are Walter Johnson, *August Strindberg*, Twayne, New York, 1977 and Brita M. E. Mortensen and Brian W. Downs, *Strindberg. An Introduction to his Life and Work*, C.U.P., 1965.

The only substantial study of *The Red Room* is Carl Reinhold Smed-mark's *Mäster Olof och Röda rummet*, Almqvist and Wiksell, Stockholm, 1952, which concentrates upon the relationship of the work to contemporary literature, Strindberg's characterization and social criticism. Erland Lagerroth includes a study of the novel's structure, imagery and pattern of ideas in his *Svensk berättarkonst*, C. W. K. Gleerup, Lund, 1968, and Eric O. Johannesson devotes a chapter to the work in *The Novels of August Strindberg*, University of California Press, Berkeley, 1968. In 'Krukan och bitarna. Strindberg och 1800-talets romantradition', *Bonniers Litterära Magasin*, xxx (1964), 740–55, Göran Printz-Påhlson attempts to place the novel in the major tradition of nineteenth-century Realism, and in particular examines its relationship to the 'novel of development'. In 'Krukan och bitarna II. Vad händer i Röda rummet?', *Bonnier Litterära Magasin*, xxxi (1965), 12–28, Printz-Påhlson investigates the themes and characters of the novel in greater detail. *Perspektiv på Röda rummet* edited by Erland and Ulla-Britta Lagerroth, Rabén and Sjögren, Stockholm, 1971, is a symposium of essays on the novel, which includes, as well as several essays listed above, an examination of the imagery of the work by Karl-Åke Kärnell.

7. W. D. HOWELLS: *THE RISE OF SILAS LAPHAM*

Several fairly recent works are useful for providing a general introduction to the ideas and practice of American Realism in the nineteenth century, putting Howells in a literary-historical context and viewing him alongside some of his contemporaries. Warner Berthoff, *The Ferment of Realism: American Literature 1884–1919*, Free Press, New York, 1965, gives a brief introductory discussion of American Realism, and looks at Howells's novels in the light of contemporary trends. Donald Pizer, *Realism and Naturalism in Nineteenth Century American Literature*, S. Illinois U.P., Carbondale, 1966, stresses the source and range of the critical systems within which Howells and his peers were working, while Robert Falk, *The Victorian Mode in American Fiction 1865–1885*, Michigan State University Press, East Lansing, 1965, examines Howells's first mature phase with reference to contemporary perspectives in fiction, suggesting a kind of realism in his writing different from the modern sense of it. Harold H. Kolb Jr., *The Illusion of Life: American Realism as a Literary Form*, University Press of Virginia, Charlottesville, 1969, is a particularly valuable work which discusses the definitions, nature, and problems of American Realism, and analyses Howells's novels against this background, referring in detail to *The Rise of Silas Lapham*, including its moral concerns and its deliberate lack of clear-cut lines. In his book of interconnected essays, *The Light of Common Day: Realism in American Fiction*, Indiana U.P., Bloomington, 1971, Edwin H. Cady aims 'to clarify a view of that portion of American literary history usually called the movement or period of realism'; though he gives no extensive attention to *The Rise of Silas Lapham*, he discusses Howells in a general context and examines him as a psychological novelist—'The Howells Nobody Knows'. The chapter on Howells by James W. Tuttleton in *The Novel of Manners in America*, University of N. Carolina Press, Chapel Hill, 1972, praises Howells's ability to bring vividly to life the social experience of nineteenth-century America and to dramatize the problems of the middle classes. Helpful for background consultation is *American Literary Realism 1870–1910*, a periodical started in 196? which provides thorough annotated bibliographies of individual authors, including lesser figures; a

Special Bibliography of writing about Howells was produced in 1969. Of the critical works specifically concerned with Howells, Everett Carter, *Howells and the Age of Realism*, J. B. Lippincott, Philadelphia, 1954, provides a sound analysis of the development of Howells's realism, examining his attacks on sentimentality and the growth and practical application of his theories of literary realism; detailed comments on *The Rise of Silas Lapham* include reference to its moral themes and concern with the relation between individual conduct and the wider problem of social ethics. Edwin H. Cady, *The Road to Realism: The Early Years, 1837–1885, of William Dean Howells*, Syracuse University Press, Syracuse, 1956, the first of his two-volume treatise on Howells as a Realist, offers a comprehensive account of Howells's life and literary career, describing his developing theories and practice, and discussing individual novels; *The Rise of Silas Lapham* is shown to be a critique of the moral confusion of the times, with wider relevance (Howells is called an agnostic moralist and literary realist). The subsequent work, *The Realist at War: The Mature Years, 1885–1920, of William Dean Howells*, 1958, traces Howells's later development as critic and novelist in the context of the continuing critical debate about Realism. Olov W. Fryckstedt, *In Quest of America: a Study of Howells's Early Development as a Novelist*, Harvard University Press, Cambridge, Massachusetts, 1958, carefully investigates Howells's literary ideas and innovations, and his conviction that American life, faithfully recorded, was essential material for the American novelist, though it confines itself chiefly to the pre-1885 fiction. George N. Bennett's *William Dean Howells: the Development of a Novelist*, University of Oklahoma Press, Norman, 1959, is a straightforward examination of Howells's fiction, which argues that in *The Rise of Silas Lapham* the social and moral concerns are fully integrated, while William McMurray, *The Literary Realism of William Dean Howells*, S. Illinois U.P., Carbondale, 1967, offers a reading of twelve of the major novels, including *The Rise of Silas Lapham*, to support the thesis that Howells's realism closely resembles William James's pragmatism.

Many articles have appeared since the growth of interest in Howells's work and only a few can be mentioned here. L. J. Budd's 'W. D. Howells's Defence of the Romance', *Publications of the Modern Language Association*, lxvii (March 1952), 32–42, usefully points out the distinctions which Howells made between good and bad examples of the genre, and shows that he ultimately defined realism in moral rather than technical terms. In 'The Ethical Unity of *The Rise of Silas Lapham*', *American Literature*, xxxii (Nov. 1960), Donald Pizer argues that the sub-plot and main plot of the novel have fundamentally similar themes, with the sub-plot thematically elucidating the ethical significance of the whole. J. E. Hart in 'The Commonplace as Heroic in *The Rise of Silas Lapham*', *Modern*

Fiction Studies, viii (Winter 1962–3), 384–392, continues the realism debate by arguing that Howells interprets ordinary material in the form and pattern of myth and romance—a middle-class morality of self-discovery, but focussed on real conditions—while E. R. Hedges in *César Birotteau* and '*The Rise of Silas Lapham*: a study in parallels', *Nineteenth Century Fiction*, xvii (Sept. 1962), 163–174, shows, by comparing the American novel with Balzac's, how Howells relies on a morality of romanticism, despite his Realist intentions. In 'The Architecture of *The Rise of Silas Lapham*', *American Literature*, xxxvii (Jan. 1966), 430–57, G. T. Tanselle takes up Pizer's thesis, and by weighing previous commentary and carefully probing the text decides that the interlocking and mutually supporting love and bankruptcy plots are one of the novel's triumphs. Eric Solomon's 'Howells, Houses, and Realism', *American Literary Realism*, iv (1968), 89–93, demonstrates how Howells puts man into a physical setting, by examining the descriptions of the houses Lapham builds. In 'Mimesis, Morality, and *The Rise of Silas Lapham*', *American Quarterly*, xxii (Summer 1970), 190–202, F. A. Berces explores the question of whether or not a realistic novel can be forcefully moral without injuring the quality of its realism, by measuring Howells's mimetic and moral principles against those of Plato and Aristotle. Giving a more specific slant to the realism/moralism issue, Paul A. Eschholz 'The Moral World of Silas Lapham: Howells's Romantic Vision of America in the 1880's', *Research Studies*, Washington State University, xl (1972), 115–21, interprets the novel as Howells's attempt to reassure himself that despite industrialism and economic progress the Jeffersonian morality remains intact in the New World.

8. B. PÉREZ GALDÓS: *FORTUNATA AND JACINTA*

The historical background to *Fortunata and Jacinta* can be found in R. Carr, *Spain 1808–1939*, O.U.P., 1966 and the literary background in D. L. Shaw, *A Literary History of Spain: The Nineteenth Century*, Benn, London, 1972.

The most comprehensive study yet attempted on Galdós has been J. F. Montesinos's *Galdós*, 3 vols., Castalia, Madrid, 1968, 1969, 1972, the result of a lifetime's work. *Fortunata and Jacinta* is dealt with in the second volume, pp. 201–73. M. Nimetz, *Humor in Galdós. A Study of the 'Novelas contemporáneas'*, Yale University Press, New Haven and London, 1968, contains chapters on satire, irony, metaphor, caricature, and type, and the final chapter on the 'humor of familiarity' is based largely on a study of *Fortunata and Jacinta*. Nimetz also examines Galdós's conception of Realism and his satire of Romanticism. G. Correa, *Realidad, ficción y símbolo en las novelas de Benito Pérez Galdós*, Instituto Caro y

Cuervo, Bogotá, 1967, traces the evolution of Galdós's treatment of reality from his concern with politico-religious problems in the early novels through the Realist-Naturalist phase with its emphasis on external reality to the later works where the main interest is the inner development of characters. R. Gullón, *Técnicas de Galdós*, Taurus, Madrid, 1970, examines aspects of narrative technique in four novels, including *Fortunata and Jacinta*, pp. 137–220.

Two important articles on Galdós's language are S. Bacarisse, 'The Realism of Galdós: Some Reflections on Language and the Perception of Reality', *Bulletin of Hispanic Studies*, xlii (1965), 239–50 and J. Whiston, 'Language and Situation in Part I of *Fortunata and Jacinta*,' *Anales galdosianos*, vii (1972), 79–91. K. Engler, 'Notes on the Narrative Structure of *Fortunata y Jacinta*,' *Symposium*, xxiv (1970), 111–27 sets out to demonstrate how Galdós creates a multiplicity of levels of reality in his novel. The character of Fortunata herself has, not surprisingly, attracted a fair amount of interest. S. Gilman, 'The Consciousness of Fortunata,' *Anales galdosianos*, v (1970), 55–65 follows the general assumption underlying his earlier article 'The Birth of Fortunata', *Anales galdosianos*, i (1966), 71–83, which is challenged by C. Blanco Aguinaga, 'On "the birth of Fortunata" ', *Anales galdosianos*, iii (1968), 13–24. Whereas Gilman stresses Fortunata's uniqueness, Blanco Aguinaga is concerned more with her typicality in a social sense. S. H. Eoff, 'The Treatment of Individual Personality in *Fortunata y Jacinta*,' *Hispanic Review*, xvii (1949), 269–89 shows how the personalities of Fortunata and Maxi develop through reaction to their environment, and this theme is taken further in 'The Deification of Conscious Process,' in *The Modern Spanish Novel*, Peter Owen, London, 1962, pp. 120–47. Eoff's highly persuasive study sees *Fortunata and Jacinta* as the high mark of 'Spiritual Naturalism' and by drawing on philosophical and scientific ideas current at the time offers a largely optimistic account of the novel whereby individual aspiration and social restraint purposefully interact in the evolution of the species. The individual and society theme is seen in terms of class conflict by J. Sinnigen, 'Individual, Class and Society in *Fortunata y Jacinta*,' *Galdós Studies II*, Támesis, London, 1974, pp. 49–68. For Sinnigen, Fortunata achieves self-fulfilment through the negation of bourgeois conventions, although the wider class conflict is unresolved. G. Ribbans, 'Contemporary History in the Structure and Characterization of *Fortunata y Jacinta*', *Galdós Studies*, Támesis, London, 1970, pp. 90–113 is a very interesting and detailed study of the way in which Galdós parallels private and public events in the novel.

9. G. VERGA: *MASTRO-DON GESUALDO*

The most useful books on Verga's life are, in English, A. Alexander, *Giovanni Verga—A Great Writer and his World*, Grant and Cutler, London, 1972, and, in Italian, G. Cattaneo, *Giovanni Verga*, U.T.E.T., Turin, 1963.

For the critical mediation of French Realism and Naturalism into Italian literature see the essays on Zola and on Realism in Francesco De Sanctis, *Saggi critici* (vol. 3), ed. by Luigi Russo, Laterza, Bari, 1952, and Luigi Capuana's three collections of essays: *Studii sulla letteratura contemporanea*, Brigola, Milan, 1880, and Giannotta, Catania, 1882; *Per l'arte*, Giannotta, Catania, 1885; *Gli Ismi contemporanei*, Giannotta, Catania, 1898. The ideas of Realism and *verismo* as they were understood and developed in Italy can be studied in R. Bertacchini (ed.), *Documenti e prefazioni del romanzo italiano dell'Ottocento*, Studium, Rome, 1969. These ideas, and some of the works in which they were put into practice, are surveyed and discussed in: P. Arrighi, *Le vérisme dans la prose narrative italienne*, Paris, 1937; G. Marzot, *Battaglie veristiche dell'Ottocento*, Principato, Milan, 1941; and G. Carsaniga, 'Realism in Italy', in *The Age of Realism*, ed. by F. W. J. Hemmings, Penguin Books, 1974, pp. 323–55.

The only full critical study of Verga in English is T. G. Bergin, *Giovanni Verga*, Yale University Press, New Haven, 1931. A shorter study of Verga's 'veristic' works is S. Pacifici, 'The Tragic World of Verga's Primitives', in *From 'Verismo' to Experimentalism: Essays on the Modern Italian Novel*, ed. by S. Pacifici, Indiana University Press, Bloomington and London, 1969. Of the many books and essays in Italian on Verga generally and *Mastro-Don Gesualdo* in particular, most useful are: L. Russo's classic study, *Giovanni Verga*, Laterza, Bari, of which the 1941 or any later edition should be read; A. Navarría, 'Spunti storici nel *Mastro-Don Gesualdo*', in *Belfagor*, xi (1956), 528–41; R. Luperini, *Pessimismo e verismo in Giovanni Verga*, Liviana, Padua, 1968; G. Cecchetti, *Il Verga maggiore. Sette studi*, La Nuova Italia, Florence, 1968; A. Asor Rosa, *Scrittori e popolo*, Samonà e Savelli, Rome, 1972 and (ed.), *Il caso Verga*, Palumbo, Palermo, 1972; G. Carsaniga, 'Verga, tra verismo e realismo', in *Italian Studies*, xxii (1967), 78–93. An article by Wendy Joyce and Elizabeth Mahler-Schächter, 'Verga and Zola: A Question of Influence', is in *Journal of European Studies*, vii (1977), 266–77.

D. Mack Smith, *A History of Sicily*, ii—*Modern Sicily: After 1713*, Chatto and Windus, London, 1968, is invaluable for the background to Verga's life and to the works he set in Sicily.

10. THEODOR FONTANE: *EFFI BRIEST*

For a comprehensive survey of German Realism one can do no better than turn to Fritz Martini, *Deutsche Literatur im bürgerlichen Realismus 1848–1898*, Metzler, Stuttgart, 1962. But there are also valuable short accounts of the main trends by Wolfgang Preisendanz, 'Voraussetzungen des poetischen Realismus in der deutschen Erzählkunst des 19. Jahrhunderts', in *Formkräfte der deutschen Dichtung vom Barock bis zur Gegenwart*, ed. Hans Steffen, Vandenhoeck and Ruprecht, Göttingen, pp. 199–202; J. M. Ritchie, 'The Ambivalence of "Realism" in German Literature 1830–1880', *Orbis Litterarum*, xv (1961), 200–17; and by the same author in a chapter on Realism in *Periods in German Literature*, ed. J. M. Ritchie, Wolff, London, 1966.

Of the many monographs on Fontane pride of place must go to Hans-Heinrich Reuter, *Theodor Fontane*, 2 vols., Nymphenburg-Verlag, Munich, 1968, which despite its sometimes controversial stance has an unsurpassed wealth of information and insight. A compact, critical survey of Fontane scholarship past and present is given by Charlotte Jolles in a slim volume, *Theodor Fontane*, Metzler, Stuttgart, 1972. A useful introduction for English readers is the essay by H. B. Garland in *German Men of Letters*, ed. Alex Natan, i, Wolff, London, 1961, 215–33, while the essay by Brian A. Rowley, 'Theodor Fontane: A German Novelist in the European Tradition?', *German Life and Letters*, xv (1961), 71–88, includes a stimulating discussion of some questions relevant to the present volume. Fontane's Realism is specifically discussed by Peter Demetz in an article entitled 'Über Fontanes Realismus' in *Orbis Litterarum*, xvi (1961), 34–47, and Hans-Heinrich Reuter in 'Fontanes Realismus', part of a collection of essays under the general title *Fontanes Realismus: Wissenschaftliche Konferenz zum 150. Geburtstag Theodor Fontanes in Potsdam*, ed. Hans-Erich Teitge and Joachim Schobess, Akademie-Verlag, Berlin, 1972, pp. 25–64. Roy Pascal in *The German Novel*, Manchester U.P., 1956, has a chapter on Fontane which not only discusses the nature of his Realism (pp. 207–14), but also contains a brief analysis of *Effi Briest* (pp. 198–206).

Other valuable contributions to the understanding of *Effi Briest* are J. P. M. Stern, '*Effi Briest, Madame Bovary, Anna Karenina*', *Modern Language Review*, lii (1957), 363–75, and Mary E. Gilbert, 'Fontanes *Effi Briest*', *Der Deutschunterricht*, xi (1959), 63–75. The volume of *Erläuterungen und Dokumente: Theodor Fontane: Effi Briest*, ed. Walter Schafarschik, Reclam, Stuttgart, 1972, includes detailed explanatory notes, documentary material illustrating how the novel came to be written and what contemporary attitudes were to some of the issues it raises (the role of women, duelling), and extracts from critical comments on the novel from the 1890s to the present day.

Index